LABORING

BELOW THE LINE

LABORING

BELOW THE LINE

The New Ethnography of Poverty,
Low-Wage Work, and Survival
in the Global Economy

Frank Munger
Editor

Russell Sage Foundation / New York

The Russell Sage Foundation

The Russell Sage Foundation, one of the oldest of America's general purpose foundations, was established in 1907 by Mrs. Margaret Olivia Sage for "the improvement of social and living conditions in the United States." The Foundation seeks to fulfill this mandate by fostering the development and dissemination of knowledge about the country's political, social, and economic problems. While the Foundation endeavors to assure the accuracy and objectivity of each book it publishes, the conclusions and interpretations in Russell Sage Foundation publications are those of the authors and not of the Foundation, its Trustees, or its staff. Publication by Russell Sage, therefore, does not imply Foundation endorsement.

Library of Congress Cataloging-in-Publication Data

Laboring below the line : the new ethnography of poverty, low-wage work, and survival in the global economy / Frank Munger, editor.
    p. cm.
    Includes bibliographical references and index.
    1. Working poor—United States. 2. Wages—United States. 3. Working poor—Government policy—United States. 4. United States—Economic policy—1993-2001. I. Munger, Frank.

HD8072.5 .L33 2002
362.85'0973—dc21

2001055713

Text design by Suzanne Nichols

RUSSELL SAGE FOUNDATION
112 East 64th Street, New York, New York 10021
10 9 8 7 6 5 4 3 2 1

Contents

Contributors   vii

Preface   ix

Introduction   IDENTITY AS A WEAPON IN THE MORAL
POLITICS OF WORK AND POVERTY

Frank Munger   1

PART I   WORKING TOWARD A FUTURE:
IDENTITY AND THE MEANING OF WORK

Chapter 1   IN EXILE ON MAIN STREET

Carol Stack   29

Chapter 2   LIVES ON THE LINE: LOW-WAGE WORK
IN THE TELESERVICE ECONOMY

Ruth Buchanan   45

Commentary   DECONSTRUCTING LABOR DEMAND IN TODAY'S
ADVANCED ECONOMIES: IMPLICATIONS FOR
LOW-WAGE EMPLOYMENT

Saskia Sassen   73

Commentary   UNDERSTANDING THE UNEMPLOYMENT
EXPERIENCE OF LOW-WAGE WORKERS:
IMPLICATIONS FOR ETHNOGRAPHIC RESEARCH

Philip Harvey   95

Commentary   LOOKING FOR STORIES OF INNER-CITY POLITICS:
FROM THE PERSONAL TO THE GLOBAL

Carl H. Nightingale   111

PART II	MAKING DECISIONS ABOUT WORK, FAMILY, AND WELFARE	
Chapter 3	TAKING CARE OF BUSINESS: THE ECONOMIC SURVIVAL STRATEGIES OF LOW-INCOME, NONCUSTODIAL FATHERS	
	Kathryn Edin, Laura Lein, and Timothy Nelson	125
Chapter 4	CUSTODIAL MOTHERS, WELFARE REFORM, AND THE NEW HOMELESS: A CASE STUDY OF HOMELESS FAMILIES IN THREE LOWELL SHELTERS	
	Aixa N. Cintrón-Vélez	148
Chapter 5	INFORMAL SUPPORT NETWORKS AND THE MAINTENANCE OF LOW-WAGE JOBS	
	Julia R. Henly	179
Commentary	THE LOW-WAGE LABOR MARKET AND WELFARE REFORM	
	Sanders Korenman	204
PART III	PATHS TOWARD CHANGE	
Chapter 6	CARE AT WORK	
	Lucie White	213
Chapter 7	WHO COUNTS? THE CASE FOR PARTICIPATORY RESEARCH	
	Frances Ansley	245
Commentary	QUIESCENCE: THE SCYLLA AND CHARYBDIS OF EMPOWERMENT	
	Joel F. Handler	271
Commentary	TAKING DIALOGUE SERIOUSLY	
	Michael Frisch	281
Conclusion	DEMOCRATIZING POVERTY	
	Frank Munger	290
Index		313

Contributors

FRANK MUNGER is professor of law and adjunct professor of sociology at the State University of New York at Buffalo. He is also visiting professor of law at New York Law School.

FRANCES ANSLEY is professor of law at the University of Tennessee College of Law.

RUTH BUCHANAN is associate professor of law at the University of British Columbia in Vancouver, British Columbia.

AIXA N. CINTRÓN-VÉLEZ is assistant professor of research and social policy, Graduate School of Social Service, and research associate, Center for Hispanic Mental Health Research, at Fordham University.

KATHRYN EDIN is associate professor of sociology and faculty fellow at the Institute for Policy Research at Northwestern University.

MICHAEL FRISCH is professor of history and American studies at the State University of New York at Buffalo.

JOEL F. HANDLER is the Richard C. Maxwell Professor of Law and professor of policy studies at the University of California, Los Angeles. He is also the director of the Foreign Graduate Law Program at the UCLA School of Law.

PHILIP HARVEY is associate professor of law and economics at Rutgers School of Law at Camden, New Jersey.

JULIA R. HENLY is assistant professor in the School of Social Service Administration at the University of Chicago and faculty affiliate with the Northwestern University–University of Chicago Joint Center for Poverty Research.

SANDERS KORENMAN is professor in the School of Public Affairs at Baruch College, City University of New York.

LAURA LEIN is professor of social work and anthropology at the University of Texas at Austin.

TIMOTHY NELSON is lecturer in sociology and assistant research professor at Northwestern University.

CARL H. NIGHTINGALE is associate professor of history at the University of Massachusetts, Amherst.

SASKIA SASSEN is the Ralph Lewis Professor of Sociology at the University of Chicago.

CAROL STACK is professor of social and cultural studies in education at the University of California, Berkeley.

LUCIE WHITE is the Louis A. Horvitz Professor of Law at Harvard Law School.

Preface

Since 1980, inequality of economic opportunity in the United States has grown catastrophically. We know that the wealthiest 20 percent of Americans own a greater proportion of the nation's wealth than ever before, and that the poorest 20 percent own less of that wealth. We know too that the labor market for the poor is organized differently from the higher-wage labor market: jobs are impermanent and inadequately compensated, and attachment to the workforce is marginal for those at the bottom of the income distribution scale. Yet even as they fall further and further behind, many of the poor *are working*. In New York State, for example, more than half of poor families include a wage earner, and more than one third have someone working full-time year round. Failure of the poor to find and keep jobs has fueled arguments that social welfare supports "unearned benefits"—according to those who advocate slashing them—constitute "moral hazards," and undermine "discipline" among low-wage earners and the unemployed. These arguments, along with counterarguments that point to institutional and historical causes of economic and social inequality, rage on within the academy and in national discourse about welfare and welfare reform, as politics makes examples (and stereotypes) of a few poor persons. Unfortunately, policy makers and the public never see more than a glimpse of life below the poverty line, and we hear very little from Americans who are fighting for survival there.

Over the past twenty years, however, scholars have amassed an extraordinary body of ethnographic research that gives voice to the poor and maps the contours of their daily lives. In September 1997, the Russell Sage Foundation funded a workshop at the State University of New York at Buffalo to explore the promise of this new literature on poverty. Together, researchers who pursue ethnography, oral history, qualitative sociology, and narrative analysis shared data about the experiences of poor persons as they struggle—out of the spotlight of public attention—to work in the new low-wage economy, raise families, carry on from one day to the next, and get ahead; and this core group discussed these data with other scholars who use noninterpretive or quantitative strategies for documenting and examining poverty. The energy of workshop participants comes from their belief that acquaintance with the life experiences of the poor enriches our understanding of poverty as personal plight and social phenomenon. At this moment of governmental retrenchment, ethnography's complex, nonstereotypical portraits of individual persons are especially important. Although these studies cannot always offer clear answers to questions about poverty programs or the effects of isolated economic and social factors on the income and behavior of poor persons, they reveal the ambiguities of real lives, the potential of individuals to change in unexpected ways, and the even greater intricacy of the collective life of a community.

Workshop participants talked at length about the challenges ethnographers face as they examine the implications of the experiences of their subjects and frame those experiences for an audience. Their discussions drew on many fields and disciplines to place ethnography in a larger context of scholarship on poverty and low-wage work. The cross-disciplinary investigation brought into focus the perennial criticism of interpretive or qualitative research by noninterpretive or quantitative researchers: that its objectivity and clarity are limited, and that it fails to illuminate *structural* inequality in the organization of institutions, communities, and the low-wage labor market. This book—which explores the role of interpretive research in understanding the causes and effects of poverty, examines global and local patterns of poverty, and evaluates recent policy making by the welfare state—continues the conversation and represents many of the disagreements among these scholars.

At the core of ethnographic research is an open-ended interpretive process. The interaction between researcher and subject does not proceed within fixed categories, but seeks to create and nurture a shared understanding of the meaning of thought and action. This book invites the reader to become a part of that dialogue between researchers and their subjects, consider the process by which such experiences are presented to others, learn more about poverty, and speculate about what comes next. By revealing a vast human potential, ethnography proves that it may educate us about poverty and serve as a catalyst for social change.

Drawing on the perspectives of the working poor, welfare recipients, and marginally employed men and women, the following chapters anatomize lifecourse circumstances and experiences that affect personal outlook, ability to work, and expectations for the future—the foundations on which survival and self-sufficiency are based. A picture of the unique social organization of the low-wage labor market emerges from points of contact between the characteristics of individuals and economic conditions and institutions: this helps us understand how and why many low-wage workers find themselves trapped in a low-wage ghetto. In counterpoint to the interpretive research presented herein, commentary by other workshop participants reflects on the role of ethnographic research and provides alternative viewpoints on the goals and methods of studies of poverty.

The authors offer their collective thanks to the Russell Sage Foundation, the Christopher Baldy Center for Law and Social Policy, and the Law School of the State University of New York at Buffalo for generous support of the 1997 Workshop on Poverty, Low-Wage Labor, and Social Retrenchment. The contributors also benefited greatly from engagement with colleagues who participated in the workshop, with special thanks to Harry Arthurs, Fadila Boughanemi, Megan

Cope, Bruce Jackson, Michael Katz, Peter Pitegoff, Alessandro Portelli, and Loic Wacquant, as well as faculty members of the Baldy Center's Program on Community and Difference who attended some of the workshop sessions. Our thanks also to the Baldy Center staff and students for their assistance in organizing the workshop: Associate Director Laura Mangan, Rebecca Roblee, David Johnstone, and Joane Wong. The manuscript could not have been prepared without the invaluable assistance of Joyce Farrell.

Frank Munger
Buffalo, New York

Introduction

Identity as a Weapon in the Moral Politics of Work and Poverty

Frank Munger

During an era of plenty, and despite intensive and often sympathetic reporting in the mainstream media about the persistence of poverty in the United States, public discourse continues to invoke negative stereotypes about the lives of the poor and the effects of dependence on welfare payments and other government-funded benefits on their families. Economists, sociologists, and ethnographers tell more complete and nuanced stories about poverty, Herbert Gans laments in his recent book, *The War Against the Poor*, but to no effect: despite research and scholarly argument, false stereotypes persist as journalists in all media tailor their accounts of poverty for an audience comfortable with hackneyed notions of what it means to be poor.

STORIES ABOUT POOR PEOPLE

Consider Jason De Parle's narrative of the life story of a welfare recipient, Opal Caples, in his report on welfare reform in Wisconsin in the *New York Times Magazine*.[1] De Parle uses the facts, dates, and circumstances of Opal's life to frame descriptions of the state's welfare-to-work programs from the perspectives of administrators, caseworkers, and public officials. Opal herself is an ambiguous figure. Bright and apparently capable, she doesn't seem to be fully committed to work. Problems with day care might explain her tenuous attachment to the labor force, but even when all her support systems are in place, De Parle remarks, "it wasn't a complete surprise to discover, earlier this month, that Caples was missing from work. . . . She and her boyfriend had had a fight, and he had moved out. She said she was too distraught the night of breakup to bother calling work." The consequences of her failure to let her employer know she won't be coming to work are uncertain. Opal might keep her job, she might lose this one and quickly get another, or she might find herself unemployed and unable to pay her rent. She might even be forced to give up her apartment and move in with her cousin. The audience doesn't know what comes next, and we're not going to find out; but De Parle does offer us a summary of Opal's situation: "She's striking off, on shaky legs, into an uncharted, post welfare world."

De Parle is a good reporter. He spends time getting details: Opal's marriage before childbearing and her subsequent single parenting, signs of job avoidance coupled with evidence of unreliable day care and inadequately compensated work. Though we learn much about what has *happened* to Opal Caples, we hear very few of her own words and almost nothing of her thoughts, how she judges her life and struggles for meaning. We don't know enough about Opal to form expectations about her behavior—until De Parle tells us, "it wasn't a complete surprise . . . to discover that Caples was missing from work."

Why not? Because Opal's is the story of the stereotypical welfare mother. The essential elements of her life appear to be those of thousands of her sisters. She moved from Chicago to Milwaukee to obtain higher benefits, her work history is erratic ("I knew I always had that welfare check!"), she looks for permanent employment—and it is relatively easy to find—only under the pressure of impending welfare reform. In this version of her life, Opal's problems are made to seem her own. We infer that she can surmount them if she wants to, if she tries to. The question is not whether she faces hardship or difficult moral dilemmas—we can agree that she does—but what kind of faith we place in her. Is Opal Caples one of us or not? De Parle doesn't answer the question.

In his thoughtful and exhaustively researched series of articles on welfare reform, De Parle presents the imperfect, sometimes perverse machinery of public assistance in precise and vivid terms. Yet the welfare recipients themselves are shadowy. We don't learn how they got into the system, what they make of the support they receive, whether it will help them change their lives. We don't learn much about Opal Caples as a person because she functions here as a type, a framing device. To see *her* steadily and to see her whole, we'd have to know much more about her background, her goals for herself and her children, how she values work and independence, how she has made choices in the past, how she makes them now, how she hopes to make them in the future. Certainly, Opal Caples inhabits the world we have created for poor African American women; but what strategies does she use to engage that world? Does she take the path of least resistance at every critical juncture in her life? Does "too distraught" always turn into absence from her job? What about "very happy"? Is she so marginally attached to work that any unusual event or emotion provides an excuse for staying home?

We see Caples through a narrow lens. This is how she looks now, when her children are small, at a point when she faces choices that are extraordinarily difficult for most women, whether poor or not. The particular material conditions that brought her to this moment are more or less hidden. Undefined as she is, though, we think we know her: she's a welfare mother who lives on handouts. This snapshot is reductive, one-dimensional. Truly to know Opal Caples and women like her, and thus to deepen our discussion of poverty in the United

States, scholars must focus our attention across their life courses. That is what the contributors to this book aim to do.

The issue that underlies welfare reform is moral identity, or in political terms, citizenship. Citizenship encompasses our understandings of mutual and universal obligations between all members of society; it is often said to be embodied in guarantees by the state of fundamental civil, political, or social rights. In the United States, civil and political rights are constitutionally based, but social rights of citizenship—that is, assurances of a minimum quality of life—are controversial and difficult to establish (see, for example, Bussiere 1997). Following hundreds of years of English legal precedents, American social thought distinguishes between the *deserving* poor, who merit social insurance and protection against the hardships of a free labor market, and the *undeserving* poor, who merit help only in times of severe hardship, and under conditions intended to reform their flawed moral character. More strictly than other industrialized societies, we measure the worthiness of all our citizens by the level of their commitment to the labor market, as the Social Security and Medicare systems demonstrate. Both establish contracts under which a lifetime commitment to compensated work is the precondition for benefits. Involuntary work and work for no exchange value, by the enslaved and by women, violates that precondition. In the aftermath of slavery, the tradition that one must work for a wage in order to prove worthiness still disables all American women, and women of color in particular.

Many European countries conceive social citizenship differently: based on the corporatist representation of workers in some places and the strength of the labor movement in others, entitlement to a minimum living allowance extends to all members of society. Against this background of American exceptionalism, De Parle and other journalists try to do the right thing when they explore the moral character of the poor, the foundation of their citizenship. Yet the medium makes symbolic politics and stereotypes hard to avoid. Editors and readers alike expect reporters to construct their stories within the parameters of the public debate. Thus welfare recipients acquire identities that test their deservingness directly: they become heroes, lazy bums, passive victims, able-bodied, self-indulgent, or dangerous clients of a too-generous social support system. Political leaders create these identities for the poor in order to serve their own political, policy making, and administrative ends,[2] strangling public discourse on poverty policy and on alternative identities for the poor.[3]

Poverty continues to marginalize millions of Americans. If we expect them to change their circumstances by changing their behavior, we must turn away from the distortions of negative stereotypes and work toward a more accurate *social* understanding of their lives, an effort that depends on a clearer understanding of the interdependence of poverty and wealth and the ways in which our institutions maintain that interdependence.

SYMBOLIC POLITICS IN POVERTY RESEARCH

In two insightful essays written more than thirty years ago, Lee Rainwater and Herbert Gans envision the kind of writing and research that might disrupt the stereotypes on which the public debate about poverty is centered. Rainwater (1970, 9–10) proposes a psychological explanation for these stereotypes: we are susceptible to them owing to the great social distance between mainstream and "disinherited" members of society.

> The central existential fact of life for the lower class, the poor, the deprived, and the discriminated-against ethnic groups, is that their members are not included in the collectivity that makes up the "real" society of "real" people. . . . Yet, at the same time, their activities are subject to surveillance and control by society in such a way that they are not truly autonomous, not free to make a way of life of their own.

As a consequence of our discomfort with our perceptions of the poor,

> [we] develop some understanding that "explains" the fact that there are people among us who are not part of us. . . . In order to cope with the presence of individuals who are not a regular part of a society, its members develop labels that signify the moral status of the deviant and carry within them a full etiology and diagnosis, and often a folk therapy. . . . The social scientist inevitably imports these folk understandings into his own work. They yield both understanding and misunderstanding for him.

According to Rainwater, recognition that others live their lives under conditions we regard as intolerable starts the engine of stereotyping. We choose to believe that the poor are different from us, either because they have chosen poverty for reasons we would reject (they prefer being poor to working or are happy being poor) or because they are incapable of making choices that would improve their lot. The first assumption romanticizes the poor and celebrates their resistance and creativity. The second assumption denies that the poor are like us and marks them as sick, infantile, irresponsible, or depraved, arguing that theirs is an inferior citizenship that ought to be managed by others.

So we must begin our research anew and "strive first for a phenomenologically valid account both of the inner reality of personal life and of the social exchanges that constitute the pattern of social life of the disinherited. We must learn to become much more precise about how this inner reality and way of life came into being historically, and about how they are sustained by the larger social system in which they are embedded" (Rainwater 1970, 27). As we seek this precision, we put ourselves at some risk.

> We will discover that a phenomenologically accurate account of the condition of the disinherited will make us and those who read us even more nervous

because the more accurate the account, the more it will heighten, at least initially, the deeply human perception that "they cannot live like that because I could not live like that." . . . Yet if we are to provide a satisfactory intellectual grounding for systematic policy making in this area, we must somehow achieve such a complex, accurate diagnosis rather than merely a satisfying and anxiety-reducing one. (Rainwater 1970, 27)

The more accurate the account of the condition of the disinherited, the more nervous it makes us, the more discomfort or cognitive strain it causes, and the more strongly we resist it. What kinds of phenomenologically accurate information about poverty will help us overcome such resistance, in ourselves and in others? How will that research address the principal barrier to public acceptance of greater support for the poor, namely, the perceived moral identity of the poor themselves?

In a contemporaneous essay, Herbert Gans (1969, 203) praises Rainwater's insight into the polar formulation (deserving–undeserving) of social support policies for middle-class and poor Americans.

Some feel that the poor share the values and aspirations of the affluent society, and if they can be provided with decent jobs and other resources, they will cease to suffer from the pathological and related deprivational consequences of poverty. . . . [M]any more social scientists share the feeling that the poor are deficient. Yet, others . . . suggest that poverty and the lowly position of the poor have resulted in the creation of a separate lower-class culture or a culture of poverty.

Gans concludes that all such judgments are based on oversimplifications of the kind Rainwater describes.[4]

The debate, however conceptualized, [is] irrelevant and undesirable. . . . Enough is now known about the economic and social determinants of pathology to reject explanations of pathology as a moral lapse . . . one cannot know whether the poor are as law-abiding or moral as the middle class until they have achieved the same opportunities—and then the issue will be irrelevant.

Gans understands that research also must address the critical moral issue that underlies welfare policy, namely, can the poor behave like the middle classes? Scholars who agree that they can, and who hope to influence the development of policies that will help the poor climb out of poverty must, he argues, convey their capacity to secure and hold jobs—passports to participation in mainstream life. To test this capacity, we must look not only at the sometimes maladaptive behavior of poor people, but also at their values and aspirations.

His reformulation of Rainwater's prescription is important because Gans acknowledges the interplay between research and the moral politics of welfare. Like Rainwater, he also recognizes the value of contextualized ethnographic research for exploring the relationship between aspirations and actions. To understand this relationship, Gans observes, scholars must examine the individual's own interpretations of the "existential situation" through which character, identity, and motivation are formed.

The call by Gans and Rainwater for more phenomenologically accurate research sets a different agenda but nevertheless leaves perplexing questions unresolved. Exploration of the aspirations and values of the poor—the stuff of their identity—ought to undermine the negative stereotypes that hobble effective policy making; but how to organize such research? What kinds of information should ethnographers gather? Are words enough? Can the voices of the poor, direct and unmediated, persuade scholars, journalists, politicians, policy makers, and middle-class Americans that they are enough like us to deserve generous social supports? Or must they muster deeds, jobs they have held, classes they have taken, sacrifices they have made for their children, to win approval and access to resources that many of us take for granted? Rainwater and Gans don't explain how we are to develop a fairer discourse about poverty without constructing simplified counterimages of the poor or making them accountable to idealized aspirations and values that are rarely realized even by those who are wealthier.

What does it mean to hold a single mother with small children to the standards of the middle class? How do we expect her to enact her values under conditions of deprivation, and how could our understanding of the interplay between her actions and her aspirations be enriched? An idealized middle-class standard for self-sufficiency includes a steady job, trust that work will lead to betterment, rational micromanagement of income and work opportunities, instrumental use of social support to achieve some degree of autonomy, and belief in the value of formal education. Standards shaped by middle-class experience and embedded in the language of microeconomics and policy studies structure our public discourse about poverty. Qualitative research must foreground these standards and question their provenance if it hopes to uncover the many layers of impulse and action that feed the apparent deviance of the poor.

Critical to the mobilization of qualitative research in the area of poverty studies is that we acknowledge the effects of the deep racial fault line in American society on the identity, self-concept, and behavior of those we stigmatize as poor. Race is nearly invisible in mainstream policy research on poverty, and this despite an incontrovertible reality: not only are the experiences of persons of color who are poor different, but different at least in part because persons of color are perceived and treated differently. Martin Gillens (1999) observes a fundamental premise—unexamined in most research on poverty—of the public perception of welfare in the United States: welfare (much like crime) is a province populated by African Americans. Although Gillens limits his focus to attitudes toward welfare recipients, Katherine Newman's (1999) study of low-wage workers in Harlem slips almost silently from framing poverty as a debate about the availability of work into one about the moral character of poor African Americans. Newman assumes without saying so that most middle-class Americans view African Americans as potentially shiftless nonworkers and welfare recipients. Without acknowledgment, Newman confirms what we have known since the mid-1960s—that our public discourse on poverty and welfare is almost exclusively a discussion about the African American poor.

Scholars who want to understand poverty and the public policy debates that surround it must grapple with race-coded discourse. Euphemisms such as the underclass, welfare poor, and cycle of poverty may sanitize language, but they cannot mask our racialized perceptions of poverty. Nor can they mask the continuing processes of cultural and institutional separation that isolate African Americans from the mainstream (Munger forthcoming). Our race-coded discourse about poverty divides the poor and working classes into two groups: whites who suffer the effects of declining wages, benefits, and job security and therefore are deserving; and blacks who a priori are stigmatized as potential welfare recipients and therefore are undeserving (Matsuda 1997). Until this divide is bridged, Gillens suggests, little will change in the symbolic politics of poverty.

Rainwater and Gans take for granted the need to demonstrate that the poor have the capacity to behave as we do, that they are like us. Although Gans suggests that the aspirations and values of the middle class set the standards by which we make moral judgments about the poor, neither he nor Rainwater names the characteristics poor people must demonstrate before we are willing to include them in the category *us*. Evidence shows that most Americans (along with the poor who share their values and aspirations) have complex, not simple or stereotypical, understandings of their own moral stature and dependency. Scholars must work to unravel these understandings and make transparent the process by which power holders, including voters and public officials, forge identities for the poor and judge their deservingness. The last chapter of this volume returns to these issues.

THE NEW ETHNOGRAPHY AS A POLICY DISCOURSE

Since Rainwater and Gans wrote their essays, and especially during the past decade, some journalists, biographers, oral historians, and ethnographers have shifted the ground of poverty research to mark out a larger terrain for their investigations of the lives of the poor. Poverty no longer looks static or monolithic. Now, as Michael Katz (1993) notes, we study it in many different contexts, in many different historical periods; and we begin to see the poor in new ways: not as passive victims of unfavorable circumstances and their own torpor, but as architects of survival strategies, social actors who are capable of political action.

Such shifts in perspective may heighten the ambiguity of the new ethnography as a corrective to familiar stereotypes of the symbolic politics of poverty. Counterhegemonic narratives of the lives of disadvantaged and oppressed persons show the poor as agents who are sometimes able to overcome economic and social constraints and do for themselves. The more fully we understand the power of agency in poor communities, though, the more self-aware and self-determining the poor appear to be, the greater the likelihood that their poverty may be seen as a choice, the more they may seem to resemble the "dangerous classes" of early modern England. The more varied their circumstances—as immigrants, as members of Hispanic, African American, Native American, or Asian minorities each with its own unique concerns, as ghetto residents, welfare recipients, or part-time service industry employees—the more the poor may resemble a tangle of special-interest groups determined to drain the resources of the dwindling, canonical working and middle classes. As poverty policies move to the top of the political agenda once again, the risk may be that ethnographic research turns into advocacy and the identity of the poor skews toward new stereotypes in a repetition of the very pattern that concerned Rainwater.

Long before the Great Society programs of the 1960s, studies of poverty in the United States focused on the condition of African Americans in the urban enclaves where they lived, separated by custom (and often by law) from their white neighbors (Du Bois 1903; Frazier 1939; Myrdal 1944; Drake and Cayton 1945). Often, though, they were able to leave those enclaves during the day to work in secure and adequately compensated jobs created by the industrial economy. Indeed, the availability of those jobs brought African Americans from the rural South to the urban North, and often they created in their neighborhoods thriving and colorful and self-sustaining communities. Yet economic and social policies after World War II altered conditions for the worse for African Americans in the urban centers, as the ethnographer Elliot Liebow (1967) was among the first to note.

Liebow links deepening poverty with deindustrialization of the inner city through his descriptions of the lives of poor black men who congregated on the street corners of Chicago's South Side. Ethnographic study of these men is important, he argues, because earlier research has targeted different groups—the "female centered" ghetto family, children at risk, and juvenile delinquents. Liebow's methodology is crucial because other approaches—interviews or questionnaires, for example—tend to produce caricature rather than "a clear firsthand picture" of the real lives of real people. Liebow isn't interested in testing hypotheses; he wants to understand the culture of the street corner and the "world of daily, face-to-face relationships with wives, children, friends, lovers, kinsmen and neighbors" of which the street corner is one small part. Above all, Liebow aims "to see the man as he sees himself, to compare what he says with what he does, and to explain his behavior as a direct response to the conditions of lower-class Negro life rather than as mute compliance with historical or cultural imperatives." Attachment to family, feelings of pride, the sense of honor, fears and frustrations—Liebow documents a full range of emotions and values the men share with most other Americans, along with conditions that frequently lead to self-destructive behavior and failure to realize aspirations.

Liebow's study signals a decisive break with prevailing theories about the lives of the poor. Rejecting the notion that they developed a unique "culture of poverty" that tolerates conduct anathematized by middle-class Americans— conduct that perpetuates the cycle of poverty (see O. Lewis 1966)—Liebow explains the actions of poor men as responses to the specific conditions of their lives, including their relative isolation from the mainstream (Liebow 1967, 209, quoting H. Lewis 1967). Liebow refuses to reduce these men to their most visible pathologies (crime, drugs, paternity without marriage) or interactions with officials (as participants in poverty programs and subjects of law enforcement). Instead, his portrait of poor men allows readers to appreciate the complexity of poverty, the redundant mechanisms that limit opportunities and shape expectations, and the survival strategies that preserve some degree of self-esteem and accomplishment.

Another pioneer researcher, Joyce Ladner, acknowledges the importance of her origins as an African American who grew up in Hattiesberg, Mississippi, steeped in the social ferment and rising promise of the civil rights movement. In 1964, as a twenty-year-old graduate student working with Rainwater, Ladner began interviewing women in the Pruitt-Igoe housing project in St. Louis. Interested in black women's coming of age, Ladner approaches her subject with a conceptual armament informed by the dominant theories of deviance and pathology—terms typically applied to the black family by social scientists. What Ladner (1971) finds, however, challenges the thinking of more established scholars. She does not find young women with values that deviate from those of the mainstream, nor are the women mired in pathological behavior. Instead, she finds that "each girl is conditioned by a diversity of factors depending primarily upon her opportunities, role models, psychological disposition and the influence of the values, customs and traditions of the Black community" (xxxx). These resources, Ladner argues, combined with the cultural heritage of their communities, have been crucial in determining the kind of women they have become. Furthermore, she perceives the women to be "resourceful, normal women who were simply trying to cope with some of the harsher conditions of life. What other scholars had traditionally viewed as weaknesses and pathology, I chose to view as strength and coping strategies in dealing with stress." Black womanhood gains its strength, Ladner argues, from "a 'Black cultural' framework which has its own autonomous system of values, behavior, attitudes, sentiments and beliefs" (xxxi).

In *All Our Kin* (1974), Carol Stack, an urban anthropologist, focuses on the patterns of daily life, the rules of friendship, parenting, love, and work in a poor black community in a midwestern city. Fascinated with the intricate kin ties that entangle people and resources across generations, and starting her research at a moment when African American communities had begun to embrace political activity to secure their civil and social rights, Stack disposes of mainstream assumptions that black poverty is born of dysfunction and passivity to strip away the layers of racism that render the lives of African Americans unintelligible to most white observers. Her methodology—initially, participant observation of the daily routines of women her own age—represents a conscious rejection of the ethnographical tradition of consulting community leaders (usually males) first. Stack's work marks the leading edge of the movement to study political change and the social history of institutions from the ground up.

Stack's exploration of the textured protocols of daily life in the community she calls The Flats demonstrates the importance of human capital (knowledge received from an older generation) and social capital (supportive relationships within the community) in the shaping of identity. Together, the women of The Flats and their families functioned as a repository of social capital, and they were willing to expend their resources to help individual children succeed. (Thus they demonstrate that they share middle-class aspirations.) Yet their interdependence was so profound that it threatened to interfere with their individual freedom. For women to move away from The Flats—to leave the sustaining community of friends and kin ties without imperiling their collective capacity to support their children's chances for success—was sometimes difficult.

Liebow, Ladner, and Stack revealed that the poor do live differently from the middle class, yet their survival mechanisms are adapted to institutions that serve the needs of the mainstream. Their research transformed our understanding of poverty and pioneered a tradition of studies of poor communities that tries to answer questions about how young men and women manage the interplay of experience, values, and social institutions to survive the street and the job market; how families form and flourish or die; and how the experiences of racial and ethnic communities differ (MacLeod 1987; Anderson 1990, 1999; Bourgois 1991; Wacquant 1998; Dodson 1998; Sheehan 1976; Finnegan 1998; Dash 1996).

Yet such interpretive research is relatively rare compared with the rush of policy studies that try, on the basis of statistical data alone, to identify the most important causes of poverty and test the effectiveness of welfare and income support programs. Although the War on Poverty legislated better funding, the framework for poverty relief continued to emphasize deservingness (Marmor, Mashaw, and Harvey 1990), and if, for a brief moment, the poor—and especially the African American poor—appeared more deserving than before or since (Schumann and Krysan 1999), retrenchment began almost immediately when new work requirements were added to welfare programs in 1967. Daniel Patrick Moynihan's report, *The Negro Family: The Case for National Action* (Office of Policy Planning and Research 1965) complicated the picture by appearing to blame the black family for its own dysfunctions (see Katz 1989).[5] The storm of protest against this report, along with the growing division between black and white civil rights advocates, made it difficult to continue ethnographic research on the conditions of African American poverty. Stack's insights into extended kinship networks among African Americans were lost to view as decades of contentious tinkering with welfare and poverty relief—and scholarship that assessed the results of that tinkering—displaced ethnography that explored the identities of the poor and the importance of class and race in the social organization of institutions and communities of color. The new poverty research was dominated by policy studies conducted by economists who hoped to improve programs by adjusting benefits to ever-evolving notions of what welfare recipients truly needed. Through microeconomic modeling and quasi-experimental research on the impact of undesirable behavior (out-of-wedlock births, educational failure, drug use, long-term welfare dependency, and refusal to work), such studies perpetuated the stereotypes that continue to distort our discourse about poverty.

Increasing pressure for welfare reform in the early 1980s fed on the identification of the poor (Murray 1984; Mead 1986) as a small, isolated, largely African American underclass. The term itself evokes a negative image: a substrate of unemployed persons who rank below the working class. The word stigmatizes those it describes, devalues their family structures and child-rearing practices, and attaches pathology to their neighborhoods and norms. The theory of the underclass assumes that significant numbers of the urban poor are inescapably enmeshed in multiple dysfunction and that their destructive behaviors are only reinforced by public assistance. The idea certainly reinforces prejudicial assumptions about the poor as an undifferentiated mass of flawed humanity, as Michael Katz (1993, 21) argues: "Areas of concentrated poverty emerge from much of the historical and contemporary underclass literature as monolithic islands of despair and degradation." The "rich array of people and associations within even the most impoverished neighborhoods" disappears when ethnography is silent, Katz says, and two of the most likely explanations of poverty—institutions and politics—are overlooked. In the last fifteen years a new ethnographic literature has developed, rich in detail and driven by the desire to address stigmatizing characterizations of the so-called underclass (see especially Wilson 1987, 1996; Edin and Lein 1997; Newman 1999).

The central figure in this research is William Julius Wilson, whose major accomplishment has been the restoration of poverty to the research agenda of American social scientists. Over the past two decades, Wilson has developed a theory of underclass formation that shifts responsibility for poverty from individuals to institutions. Although he accepts the hypothesis that a significant underclass marked with multiple dysfunctional behaviors exists in some urban ghettos, Wilson confronts the stigmatization of the poor by arguing that the formation of a ghetto underclass has been caused by a decline in the institutional environment—the loss of middle- and working-class families, the degradation of urban schools, the abandonment of inner cities by private organizations, the loss of businesses—and the replacement of these institutions of civil society by public supervisory and incarceral organizations—the welfare and prison systems and the police. Wilson suggests that behaviors associated with the ghetto—joblessness, parenting without marriage, and a street culture of crime and drugs—are related to lost opportunities for work and other forms of attachment to the values of mainstream Americans. Naturally, he observes, those behaviors and attitudes "often reinforce the economic marginality of the residents of jobless ghettos" (Wilson 1996, 52).

Because such behaviors and attitudes are found elsewhere in society, they cannot be regarded as ghetto-specific, and they cannot be counted as proof of the existence of a culture of poverty independent of material conditions. Nor is race the determining condition of the circumstances of African Americans who live in urban centers (Wilson 1980). Wilson has mounted a massive research project in support of the complex implications of his theory, which links urban ecology to poverty and rests on several important but contested ideas. Wilson assumes, for example, that joblessness reflects the collapse of the job market rather than choice, that access to good jobs would overturn joblessness, and that avoidance of marriage also is linked to joblessness. These hypotheses call for a comprehensive understanding of the lives of young men who "grow up in an environment that lacks the idea of work as a central experience" of adulthood and so acknowledge the likelihood that they will rely on illegitimate sources of income. Wilson's research focuses on male joblessness and male work ethic rather than on women and their reasons for choosing not to form two-parent families or on the development of perspectives, values, and behaviors in the children of those single women.

Wilson and his team use in-depth interviews and other ethnographic approaches in their research, but they do not explore the discursive consciousness of respondents who claim that they value work, nor do they examine how those asserted values play out in their respondents' lives. The interweaving of what poor persons say, what they do, and what they learn from the consequences of what they do—the materials of richly textured ethnographic research—has so far been beyond the scope of Wilson's investigations, most of which have been conducted in the city of Chicago. It has fallen to others to document a broad range of experience, as Liebow, Ladner, and Stack have done, and to examine the varied family and work histories of a cross-section of ghetto residents (see, for example, Newman 1999).

Wilson's theory has sparked controversy on all fronts: he has forced social scientists and advocates of the poor to reconsider the culture-of-poverty hypothesis that emphasizes individual responsibility and attributes poverty primarily to the bad behavior of the poor; and he has staked out new ground in his accounts of the complicated interactions that determine how individuals and families succeed or fail under conditions of poverty. The influence of specific institutions—schools, workplaces, governmental authorities, businesses and services targeted to the needs of the poor—will be part of the unfolding story, and subsequent studies now must account for the complex interplay between situation, identity, and choice.[6] Thus, by raising questions about the decision-making processes that create the intricate life patterns of poor persons, Wilson has set the stage again for qualitative research.

Still, the culture-of-poverty theory, however discredited, remains the chief argument for welfare reform. There was no significant national debate about the causes of poverty between President Clinton's 1992 election campaign and the ceremony at which he signed the bill in 1996 that dismantled federal entitlement to welfare and imposed strict time limits and work requirements on those who receive public assistance. Although Clinton attacked the low-wage job market that provided neither health insurance nor job security for poor white Americans, the president encouraged the public to associate welfare recipients with failure to work and culture-of-poverty values that blighted their own prospects and those of their children. The problem of "the economy" and the problem of welfare were distinct because different identities were involved: the deserving poor who held jobs were white, the undeserving poor who subsisted on welfare were black.

In 1997, Kathryn Edin and Laura Lein published a study of how poor women generate and manage income to sustain their families. Culture-of-poverty theory suggests that welfare encourages avoidance of work. The theory idealizes the "normal" or "rational" mother who responds to the incentives of a labor market that offers her family a better life, and uses her to measure the worthiness of welfare mothers, who, by ignoring such incentives, enact their ghetto culture, display their immaturity (or irrationality), and invite behavioral reform through sanctions that force them into the labor market. Yet Edin and Lein explode that model as they explore the importance of noneconomic factors in decision making about work and welfare. The need to safeguard her children, they argue, often outweighs the marginal gains a welfare mother can realize from employment, and the absence of opportunities for advancement also may dissuade a woman from looking for work in the low-wage labor market. Through in-depth interviews with welfare recipients, Edin and Lein reconstruct household income and expenditure patterns—budgets—for their families. The mothers with whom they spoke could not and in fact did not survive on welfare payments alone, but supplemented their income in a variety of ways—by working off the books, soliciting support from absent fathers, and bartering for services. Thus the welfare mother proves to be industrious, inventive, and capable of subverting the system on which she depends for sustenance. Edin and Lein find that poor women who work also struggle to supplement their wages.

Edin and Lein have greatly enriched the cost-benefit analysis of the policy makers by providing counterexamples to the culture-of-poverty stereotype of women who receive welfare payments or work in the low-wage labor market. Their research on decision making, however, does not take into account the ways in which identity and poverty might interact to *produce* the stereotypical behavior that middle-class Americans expect of the poor. What should we make of those who conform to that stereotype?

Lucie White (1994) studies one welfare mother who readily admits to "bad" behavior. "I am lazy," she says, accepting the mainstream moral position that interprets her failure in school, failure to work, and failure to form a two-parent family as matters of choice or preference. The commonplaces of public discourse about the poor powerfully affected her consciousness of herself. White, however, deconstructs her respondent's life course to disclose the true meaning of "I am lazy," which is that she made these "choices" because they were the only options left to her after every attempt to engage in traditional forms of self-help had been blocked by the dysfunctional organization of work and marriage that affects all women.

These focused ethnographies illustrate how qualitative research can illuminate moral identity by drawing attention to institutional and historical conditions that contribute to poverty. White and Edin and Lein decenter the discussion of underclass identity through detailed examinations of institutional realities that shape the decisions and ultimately even the self-concepts of poor women: a job market that offers low pay and no benefits; a welfare system that provides inadequate support for her family; oppressive conditions at work, in marriage, or in school. These constraints on the choices of poor women are subject to even larger social forces, the expansion of the low-wage service economy, inflation of housing prices, and exploitation of workers in the informal sector of the global economy. White and Edin and Lein move the discussion of identity from identity politics toward profound structural explanations for identity and action.

Owing to its success in expanding our understanding of institutional elements that constrain the behavior of the poor, White's description suggests that this welfare mother is not responsible for her condition. Her situation is not her fault, and she can't take responsibility for changing it. Her role is passive, her story is a classic victim narrative—a judgment that seems to confirm the stereotypical formulations of conservative critics of welfare policies, such as Lawrence Mead (1986). Edin and Lein rework the identity of the model welfare recipient so that we see her rational, self-sufficient activity and infer the instrumental values that make effective use of public assistance and other sources of income, formal and informal. She is a survivor, a classic heroine—a judgment that seems to confirm a different stereotypical identity outlined by other conservative critics of welfare policy, such as Charles Murray (1984).

In the longer run, the images of victim and heroine are too narrow to help us to a transparent understanding of identity and actions and circumstances that shape them. Where in Edin and Lein's account are the apparently blocked, counterproductive, and self-destructive lives created by the disastrous effects of poverty? Without them, how can we hope to acknowledge the needs of poor people for opportunities to rebuild their human capital, their self-confidence, their self-image? Where in White's account is her subject's potential work ethic, her sense of family responsibility, the capacity for strategic action that Edin and Lein discover in other poor women? Does White foresee a different future for her welfare mother? Might she mature into more responsible adulthood?[7] Most women—most people—do; poverty does not lock us into patterns of pathology. The poor display the same range of rational and irrational behavior, provident and improvident decision making, as other society members. Their failures and successes occur along a continuum of life stages and special circumstances, and with luck and social supports they can learn to change those circumstances over time.

As these two research efforts demonstrate, to characterize the agency of the poor without stirring up the negative identities we have constructed for them is difficult. If we show them actively adapting to their conditions, they may appear self-interested, manipulative, or dishonest. If we show them passively submitting to dependency, we condemn them to the disabling cycle of the culture of poverty. What kind of impact can such studies have on the play of public politics about welfare? They present powerful counterpoints to damaging stereotypes, show that decisions are contingent on circumstances created by the economy, the geography of the ghetto, and organization of low-wage work, and they invite further exploration of the processes that lie at the margins of conventional images of the poor. Still, these illuminating stories do not begin to examine the full effect of a life in poverty on both values and action.[8] Nor do these accounts examine how other stories might become instruments of liberation for the poor, increasing their individual self-awareness and collective political potential.

UNDERSTANDING THE IDENTITY OF THE POOR

Our primary goal is to render the identity of poor persons more transparent and intelligible to power holders and the general public. If we understand them not as sinners or saints but as constituents of the mainstream like ourselves, we will be willing to allow them the same latitude to fail or succeed that we grant insiders within our own communities.[9] The first challenge then is to identify the aspirations of the poor and explore the relationship between their aspirations, experiences, and activities such as work. Gans argues that an individual's behavioral culture—ways of behaving learned in specific situations—may change along with situations; yet a person's aspirational culture sets long-term goals that govern behavior when the situation permits. When Opal Caples fails to notify her employer that she does not intend to come to work, and because Jason De Parle does not offer what we regard as an adequate, responsible, grown-up situational explanation for that failure—"too distraught" isn't enough—we naturally infer that she lacks a work ethic. De Parle's story, however, does not and cannot weave the web of information against which we should judge Opal's reason for staying home, much less predict her behavior if she enjoyed greater job security, had safer day care, and expected that she would be able to provide for her children throughout their lives.

Public policy has been guided by particularly simplistic understandings of welfare recipients as rational maximizers (see the examples examined by

Williams 1992), and decades of microeconomic modeling of the effects of poverty programs have reinforced the idea that it is easy to move recipients from welfare to work by adjusting incentives and limiting moral hazards (the "natural" tendency to try to get an undeserved share of a "free" good such as welfare). Without actually demonstrating that such an approach will reduce poverty, reformers pay poor women the compliment of assuming that they will respond rationally to incentives or penalties that impact family finances.

This assumption reinforces a philosophy of welfare reform that is both morally deceptive and empirically invalid: morally deceptive because it embraces the notion that welfare recipients must be bribed or coerced to do the right thing, that they lack the moral character or will to act without such special prods;[10] and empirically invalid because it ignores the complexity of the circumstances within which poor women must choose to secure resources for themselves and their children. Edin and Lein document shortfalls in the budgets of most welfare recipients, who share competing goals with welfare policy planners: successful family rearing and long-term employment. Public assistance doesn't help poor women resolve conflicts between their children's immediate needs and their own career goals and, as Christopher Jencks (1997) adds in his introduction to the study by Edin and Lein, other essential values that make a life livable beyond bare survival are entirely overlooked by welfare planners.[11] Jencks observes that recent policy changes hold welfare recipients to standards of rationality and efficiency far higher than those we set for ourselves.[12]

The very shortcomings of poverty policies challenge ethnographers to deepen our understanding of the causes and effects of poverty. How should they proceed? What questions should they seek to answer, and what theory might guide their inquiry? As Herbert Gans has suggested, identity may be the most important key to change. The choices we make depend both on our experiences and understandings of our capacities and preferences. Such understandings of the self and desirability of particular decisions about education, work, marriage, and childbearing draw on cultural resources provided by interactions with others and our interpretations of those interactions over a lifetime. For all of us, poor and affluent, identity and self-esteem affect the goals we aspire to and the choices we make in particular settings or situations to move us toward those goals. Edin and Lein help us to appreciate the need to explore the relationship between identity, goals, and decision making in the lives of poor women.[13] Ethnography now must take another step.

Although Edin and Lein's interviews generally confirm their belief that women find neither welfare nor low-wage work adequate to meet the needs of their families nor their aspirations for long-term independence, these accounts provide no discussion of the formation and maintenance of such aspirations, which are by no means uniform even in their nonrandom samples. Nor do we know about the effects of poverty on the formation and interpretation of these goals, the effects of limited opportunities on persons raised in poverty, or the importance of the "irrational" goals suggested by Jencks—self-expression, happiness, self-esteem, and status—or the identity and value-shaping effects of the close networks of support that are an important form of social capital. Other than adding a little to resources provided by current welfare programs, we do not have a clear sense of the strategies for change that will work for these women.

Identity, as Herbert Gans argues, enables the poor to respond to opportunity, and thus is a key to change. Identity not only enables individuals to change, but also affects collective agency, the capacity of the poor to act as a group, binding social movement participants together through stories that create a shared sense of injustice (Cohen 1985). More fundamentally, identity incorporates a sense of efficacy, the element whose absence leads to working-class quiescence (Croteau 1995; Gaventa 1980). For brief periods in American history, the poor (and for still briefer periods, welfare recipients) have been able to assume identities as legitimate contenders for justice (for example, the National Welfare Rights Organization; see Piven and Cloward 1977). Of course, identities of competence and active participation are much more difficult to create and sustain when poverty is stigmatized and welfare is unpopular. Yet the poor have other potential identities: they comprise a larger constituency than welfare recipients; they share a class interest as well as a position of relative political powerlessness and economic insecurity; and they can learn to exploit their own numbers by agreeing on a few common stories of injustice and working together to achieve collective agency.

A final challenge awaits ethnographers dedicated to understanding poverty and our poverty policy. Research that presents in their own words the perspectives of those at the margins of the American economy by itself seldom has had the power to move our society to adopt more enlightened poverty policies. So we must explore how public perceptions of poor persons are created and how they grow. Beyond viewing the poor as citizens who share mainstream values and aspirations with the rest of us, scholars also must address the symbolic politics of poverty, examine the reasons for the prevalence of stereotypes, and liberate the political will by exploring the bases on which we evaluate the perceived moral identity of others.

The chapters that follow are not organized around familiar topics of poverty policy research. Instead, they problematize the concept of poverty as they examine particular life events spurred by, but not easily confined within, issues of employment or family formation or parenting or peer relations. The interpretive method intends to capture the multiple perspectives of social actors in those events, to bring into play all the sources of meaning that inform action. The more open-ended the observations and conversations between researcher and subject, the further they reach across time and space, the more they evoke the experiences of a sympathetic audience, the more complete the picture of individual identity and the more valid the interpretations of motivations and goals. The contributors are not of one mind about the significance of the subjects' perspectives. For some, the poor are able research assistants who provide data about circumstances that outsiders would find hard to describe and who depend on their interviewers to assess those data. For others, the poor seek help and knowledge as they speak for themselves, but they do *not* seek (or need) an interpreter or a tribune.

Participants in the workshop included scholars whose primary commitment is to qualitative research, those who pursue quantitative methods, and others who concentrate on economic or sociological theory building. Together, we considered the relationship of ethnography to hypothesis-driven forms of social science and to statistical research methods in particular. Some participants were concerned about connecting stories to the institutional and historical patterns that shape experience to theory and general findings. Others worried that full and accurate depictions of poverty would be complex, discouraging, and from the viewpoint of public policy making, counterproductive, exactly as Rainwater anticipates. Contributors address these issues both in the ethnographic chapters and commentaries—freestanding essays that may raise questions independent of the research or provide counterpoint to the ethnographies.

The book is divided into three parts, each of which reflects the variety of ways in which issues of identity function in poverty research. In the first part, the formation of identity, in particular the formation of identity as a low-wage worker, occupies center stage in different settings and through different activities. The second part continues this focus through studies of the dilemmas of family, shelter, and welfare faced by the most marginal workers. In the third part, identity becomes a moving picture as we consider how self-awareness and capacity for change are linked. The conclusion draws together the vision of life in poverty that emerges from the chapters and commentaries. In this emerging vision, the playing field for moral judgment about the deservingness of the poor is leveled both by better understanding of the way institutions, politics, and policies contribute to continuing inequality and poverty, and by our deeper and growing understanding of the poor as moral actors whose behavior sometimes has seemed unaccountable. The theme proposed for this vision—democratizing poverty—surfaced in resonances among the lives of those stigmatized as poor or welfare dependent and the lives of a much larger group who consider themselves part of the mainstream.

Each chapter explores identity and the capacity for economic survival from a different angle, and the commentary complements what the ethnographers have learned with perspectives from other fields of study and by suggesting further questions. Part I paints a complex picture of work aspirations by describing the lives of low-wage workers. Carol Stack views work aspirations through the eyes of a maturing teenager in Oakland for whom work is important but only one of many pressing interests that keep her out late, up early (when she can manage it), and teetering on the brink of disaster in school. Ruth Buchanan views aspirations through the stories of adult workers in a new global low-wage industry—telemarketing—who are attempting to move up the ladder through low-wage work while balancing family, education, and other important commitments. Comments by Saskia Sassen, Philip Harvey, and Carl Nightingale consider tensions between work and the shifting constraints on low-wage opportunities in a global economy. Ethnography confirms that work ethic is interwoven with aspirations for a better life. The commentaries force us to confront what will happen to these aspirations when there are not enough jobs (as Harvey demonstrates), when the informalization of low-wage labor truncates the ladder to better jobs (as Sassen shows us), and when the political and economic needs of global institutions isolate and exploit those at the margin (as Nightingale argues). Low-wage workers are not deadbeats but individuals who have fully embraced the work ethic and are attempting to give it meaning in an extremely inhospitable labor market.

Part II provides another window on work aspirations by exploring dilemmas in the lives of adults on the extreme margins of the low-wage labor market. Policy makers are particularly vocal about poor men, homeless mothers, and women on welfare, who seem to exemplify their concerns about lack of commitment to mainstream values. Kathryn Edin, Laura Lein, and Timothy Nelson explore poor men's family and work aspirations; Aixa Cintrón-Vélez describes homeless mothers in shelters; and Julia Henly compares women on welfare to other women in low-wage jobs. Their chapters illuminate the struggle to prioritize work, family, security, and daily survival when personal resources are insufficient. We learn that all of these individuals highly value work and family, though they often are perceived otherwise, and face daunting choices with few available resources. Sanders Korenman, a former member of the President's Council of Economic Advisers, affirms the policy-making value of in-depth descriptions of the complex choices and trade-offs facing marginal workers. His commentary on policy reminds us that policy makers have had little trust in the values and aspirations of marginal workers, and their policies are either punitive or address aspirations only indirectly by offering small improvements in resources as incentives for self-help. More trusting policy makers would be more generous and impose fewer restrictions to discipline recipients. Ethnographic research strives to create greater trust by providing more accurate portrayals of the poor, but policy makers often remain skeptical.

Part III considers the poor's capacity to change. The continuing skepticism of lawmakers encourages us to seek answers to poverty not only by creating a wider political consensus about the deservingness of the poor but also by increasing the poor's capacity for self-help. While policies for relief of poverty often presume the poor do not want to change, ethnography suggests that the poor are exactly like the mainstream—desiring a better life—but often are trapped by limited opportunity and a dominant culture that imposes negative images of them. Interventions that increase self-esteem, improve understanding of personal and institutional barriers to change, and convey practical forms of self-help build on the poor's aspirations for change. Lucie White describes remarkable personal encounters occurring in a government Head Start program that supply just the right mentoring and encouragement to help a woman break free of self-doubts and a destructive relationship. Frances Ansley describes how whole communities have learned about shared aspirations and possibilities for change through exploration and education guided by experts committed to participatory research—a form of inquiry that puts research skills at the disposal of the communities and groups to be benefited rather than politicians and policy makers. By such different and creative routes the poor and oppressed can attain greater self-understanding and take the initiative. Commentaries by Joel Handler and Michael Frisch that conclude this section explore hurdles faced by these aspiring agents of change—first, reaffirming their identity as individuals with capacity for change, and second, discovering what needs to be done.

Studies of poverty and low-wage employment that rely on understanding the perspectives of poor persons have an important role to play in creating a more effective policy debate. Interpretive research offers a direct response to the emphasis of some journalists, scholars, and politicians on the moral shortcomings of the poor. The voices of those who are struggling at the margins remind us that work and prospects for work shape perceptions and interpretations and, as a consequence, identities and choices for economic survival; they provide an eloquent response to the moral entrepreneurs of welfare reform whose characterizations of the poor often draw on stereotypes created by our reductive public discourse about poverty.

The value of firsthand interpretation of work and poverty lies not just in its capacity to reveal the otherwise hidden interplay between social circumstances, identity, and action but also in its power to make the experience of poverty—and thus the actions of those who live within it—intelligible to others. To interpret the causes and significance of life trajectories may be difficult, because the conclusions drawn from narratives often are ambiguous. The new ethnographic literature on poverty has been criticized for this ambiguity, especially for the moral ambiguity created by stories that show poverty as inextricably bound up with individual choice and seem to undermine their central implication: that a hierarchical, competitive socioeconomic structure makes poverty immensely more likely to occur in the lives of some individuals than in the lives of others. The *fact* and *effects* of poverty may be overlooked, while the very humanity of the poor—their ordinary virtue and fallible decisions—forecloses further discussion of the conditions that produce inequality and oppression. The contributors to this volume are particularly sensitive to the importance of integrating ethnography with research on the social structure and institutional contexts of poverty in order to provide a full understanding of these perspectives. Narrative, a powerful conveyor of identity, exerts a powerful influence on perceptions of the poor at all levels. Carefully crafted narratives such as those in this volume are therefore particularly timely correctives to the use of their identity as a cudgel with which to beat the poor.

NOTES

1. Jason De Parle is a Pulitzer Prize–winning journalist. De Parle's stories are as close as we may get to compassionate and objective reporting. He has provided a careful journalistic record of nearly every aspect of welfare reform, frequently based on in-depth interviews with recipients and administrators.

2. Images and arguments made in the political arena often are more extreme than perceptions of the public at large. The public's ambivalence about poverty relief is discussed further in the concluding chapter.

3. In a democracy, politicians attempt to invoke a sense of community, one that they can lead, and politics in the process creates membership—insiders and outsiders—by reinforcing the identity of ideal citizens. Politics and ascriptions of deservingness and undeservingness therefore are inseparable (Smith 1997).

4. Gans also took up Rainwater's point that stereotypes are institutionally reinforced by psychological strain and the material and psychological benefits derived from them. Information provided by scholars that contradicts these stereotypes may be resisted not only because it increases cognitive strain, but because there are considerable institutional benefits to maintaining them. Nevertheless, as Gans argues, the starting point for change always will be to challenge and problematize the stereotyped identities of the poor and the presumed differences between poor and nonpoor. Robert Wuthnow (1996) has rediscovered these arguments in *Poor Richard's Principle,* which decries the increasing materialism of society. Wuthnow argues that our discontent with materialism is manifested in middle-class life in many ways, one of which is our mistrust of the poor. Many believe that the poor have been corrupted by welfare, an attitude that projects our own loss of moral basis for our life goals (287–89).

5. As Katz notes, Moynihan placed great emphasis on unemployment as the ultimate source of social disorganization, but that emphasis was quickly lost in the public debate.

6. To date, the institutional implications of Wilson's theories—such as the experiences of ghetto residents in school, on the job, with public authorities, and the history of these institutions—have been left to other scholars (see, for example, Sampson and Groves 1989). Further, Wilson's own research downplays the role of race, but others have demonstrated that geographic entrapment of the African American poor and the disappearance of available jobs are due in part to race (Massey and Denton 1993; Neckerman and Kirschenman 1991).

7. Some of these questions have been answered in their own further research; see chapter 6, this volume, and Edin and Lein 1997.

8. Such stories create another, less benign possibility, namely, that they may provoke other, radically contrasting but equally "valid" stories based on instrumental framing that demonize welfare recipients, not only in the work of scholars with a more conservative social vision and the mainstream press, but in stories told in dining rooms and workplaces.

9. We have not yet given sufficient thought to Rainwater's parting concern, that the moral ambiguity and complexity of the lives of poor persons make for weak pol-

itics on behalf of egalitarian reforms. The more accurately we portray the poor as ordinary human beings under pressure of extraordinary circumstances, he argued, the less likely we are to persuade a public that employs stereotypes to reinforce values central to its beliefs about society. Rather, what we must do is to understand the foundations for the deservingness or undeservingness of the poor. With such an understanding of how the mainstream applies its citizenship rules to itself, we may be able to show that the moral identity of the poor is as complex and varied as the experience of the mainstream, yet shaped by the cultural and material conditions of poverty in intelligible ways. The central issue, therefore, both morally and politically, is whether the poor have and are perceived as having the will to better themselves given opportunities to improve their lives. The more they are revealed to hold values intelligible to the mainstream, the more generous will be the political responses of the mainstream.

10. Yet it is assumed the poor are rational enough to respond to such incentives. This is consistent with characterization of the poor as amoral but entrepreneurial members of the dangerous classes.

11. Amartya Sen (1999) has made a similar argument criticizing world development economics for reducing well-being to income, a concept he counters by noting that African American men in urban areas have many times the income of citizens of Bangladesh but a far shorter life span.

12. McCluskey (1998) has demonstrated that "efficient" reforms hide politically contestable choices by labeling decisions to reduce benefits to the poor as elimination of transaction costs, externalities, and moral hazards.

13. A number of different theoretical frameworks could be chosen to guide such an inquiry. In my research (Engel and Munger 1996) on the legal consciousness of individuals I have employed Jerome Bruner's cultural psychology to explore the formation of "distributed identities" through interaction with other individuals over the course of a life. We have found that identity plays an important role in decisions to bring rights to bear on opportunities for employment. Similarly, the sociology of Pierre Bourdieu emphasizes the importance of viewing action as a form of improvisation with a cultural field and habitus that provides elements of understanding and interpretation of events and their consequences, methods of acting, and expectations of the consequences of action (see, for example, Wacquant 1998).

REFERENCES

Anderson, Elijah. 1990. *Streetwise: Race, Class and Change in an Urban Community.* Chicago: University of Chicago Press.

———. 1999. *Code of the Street: Decency, Violence, and the Moral Life of the Inner City.* New York: W. W. Norton.

Bourgois, Philippe. 1991. *In Search of Respect: Selling Crack in El Barrio.* New York: Cambridge University Press.

Bruner, Jerome. 1990. *Acts of Meaning.* Cambridge, Mass.: Harvard University Press.

Bussiere, Elizabeth. 1997. *(Dis)Entitling the Poor: The Warren Court, Welfare Rights, and the American Political Tradition.* University Park: Pennsylvania State University Press.

Cohen, Jean. 1985. "Strategy or Identity: New Theoretical Paradigms and Contemporary Social Movements." *Social Research* 52: 663–716.

Croteau, David. 1995. *Politics and the Class Divide: Working People and the Middle Class Left*. Philadelphia: Temple University Press.

Dash, Leon. 1996. *Rosa Lee: A Mother and Her Family in Urban America*. New York: Basic Books.

De Parle, Jason. 1997. "Getting Opal Caples to Work." *New York Times Magazine*, August 24, 1997, F3.

Dodson, Lisa. 1998. *Don't Call Me Out of Name: The Untold Lives of Women and Girls in Poor America*. Boston: Beacon Press.

Drake, St. Clair, and Horace R. Cayton. 1945. *Black Metropolis: A Study of Negro Life in a Northern City*. New York: Harcourt, Brace.

Du Bois, William E. B. 1903. *The Souls of Black Folk*. Chicago: McClurg.

Edin, Kathryn, and Laura Lein. 1997. *Making Ends Meet: How Single Mothers Survive Welfare and Low Wage Work*. New York: Russell Sage Foundation.

Engel, David, and Frank Munger. 1996. "Rights, Remembrance, and the Reconciliation of Difference." *Law & Society Review* 30(1): 7–53.

Finnegan, William. 1998. *Cold New World: Growing Up in a Harder Country*. New York: Random House.

Fiscal Policy Institute. 1999. *Working but Poor in New York: Improving the Economic Situation of a Hard-Working but Ignored Population*. Latham, N.Y.: Fiscal Policy Institute.

Frazier, Franklin. 1939. *The Negro Family in the United States*. Chicago: University of Chicago Press.

Gans, Herbert. 1969. "Culture and Class in the Study of Poverty: An Approach to Anti-Poverty Research." In *On Understanding Poverty: Perspectives from the Social Sciences*, edited by D. P. Moynihan. New York: Basic Books.

———. 1995. *The War Against the Poor: The Underclass and Anti-Poverty Policy*. New York: Basic Books.

Gaventa, John. 1980. *Power and Powerlessness: Quiescence and Rebellion in an Appalachian Valley*. Urbana: University of Illinois Press.

Giddens, Anthony. 1990. *The Consequences of Modernity*. Stanford, Calif.: Stanford University Press.

Gillens, Martin. 1999. *Why Americans Hate Welfare: Race, Media, and the Politics of Antipoverty Policy*. Chicago: University of Chicago Press.

Handler, Joel, and Yeheskel Hasenfeld. 1997. *We the Poor People: Work, Poverty and Welfare*. New Haven: Yale University Press.

Jencks, Christopher. 1992. "Is the American Underclass Growing?" In *Rethinking Social Policy: Race, Poverty and the Underclass*, edited by C. Jencks. Cambridge, Mass.: Harvard University Press.

———. 1997. Foreword. In *Making Ends Meet: How Single Mothers Survive Welfare and Low Wage Work*, edited by K. Edin and L. Lein. New York: Russell Sage Foundation.

Jones, Jacqueline. 1985. *Labor of Love, Labor of Sorrow: Black Women, Work, and the Family from Slavery to the Present*. New York: Basic Books.

Katz, Michael. 1989. *The Undeserving Poor: From the War on Poverty to the War on Welfare*. New York: Pantheon Books.

———. 1993. *The "Underclass" Debate: Views from History*. Princeton, N.J.: Princeton University Press.

Ladner, Joyce. 1971. *Tomorrow's Tomorrow: The Black Woman*. Lincoln, Nebr.: University of Nebraska Press.

Lewis, Hylan. 1967. "Culture, Class and Family Life Among Low Income Urban Negroes." In *Employment, Race and Poverty,* edited by M. Ross and H. Hill. New York: Harcourt, Brace & World.

Lewis, Oscar. 1966. "The Culture of Poverty." *Scientific American* 215(4): 19–25.

Liebow, Elliot. 1967. *Tally's Corner: A Study of Negro Streetcorner Men.* Boston: Little, Brown.

MacLeod, Jay. 1987. *Ain't No Makin' It: Aspirations and Attainment in a Low-Income Neighborhood.* Boulder, Colo.: Westview Press.

Marmor, Theodore, Jerry Mashaw, and Philip Harvey. 1990. *America's Misunderstood Welfare State: Persistent Myths, Enduring Realities.* New York: Basic Books.

Massey, Douglas, and Nancy Denton. 1993. *American Apartheid: Segregation and the Making of the Underclass.* Cambridge, Mass.: Harvard University Press.

Matsuda, Mari. 1997. "Were You There: Witnessing Welfare Retreat." *University of San Francisco Law Review* 31: 779–88.

McCluskey, Martha. 1998. "The Illusion of Efficiency in Workers' Compensation 'Reform.'" *Rutgers Law Review* 50: 657–921.

Mead, Lawrence. 1986. *Beyond Entitlement: The Social Obligations of Citizenship.* New York: The Free Press.

Munger, Frank. 1998. "Immanence and Identity: Understanding Poverty Through Law and Society Research." *Law and Society Review* 32: 931–67.

———. Forthcoming. "Dependency by Law: Welfare and Identity in the Lives of Poor Women." In *Lives in the Law,* edited by A. Sarat and T. Kearns. Ann Arbor: University of Michigan Press.

Murray, Charles. 1984. *Losing Ground: American Social Policy, 1950–1980.* New York: Basic Books.

Myrdal, Gunnar. 1944. *An American Dilemma: The Negro Problem and Modern Democracy.* New York: Harper & Row.

Neckerman, Kathryn, and Joleen Kirschenman. 1991. "Hiring Strategies, Racial Bias, and Inner-City Workers." *Social Problems* 38 (November): 433–47.

Newman, Katherine. 1999. *No Shame in My Game: The Working Poor in the Inner City.* New York: Russell Sage Foundation.

Office of Policy Planning and Research. 1965. *The Negro Family: The Case for National Action.* Washington: U.S. Department of Labor.

Piven, Frances Fox, and Richard Cloward. 1977. *Poor People's Movements: Why They Succeed, How They Fail.* New York: Pantheon Books.

Pixley, Jocelyn. 1993. *Citizenship and Employment: Investigating Post-Industrial Options.* New York: Cambridge University Press.

Rainwater, Lee. 1970. "Neutralizing the Poor and Disinherited: Some Psychological Aspects of Understanding the Poor." In *Psychological Factors in Poverty,* edited by Vernon L. Allen. Chicago: Markham Press.

Sampson, Robert, and Walter Groves. 1989. "Community Structure and Crime: Testing Social Disorganization Theory." In *Crime and Inequality,* edited by J. Hagan and R. Peterson. Stanford: Stanford University Press.

Schumann, Howard, and Maria Krysan. 1999. "A Historical Note on Whites' Belief About Racial Inequality." *American Sociological Review* 64(6): 847–55.

Sen, Amartya. 1999. *Development as Freedom.* New York: Knopf.

Sheehan, Susan. 1976. *A Welfare Mother.* Boston: Houghton-Mifflin.

Smith, Rogers. 1997. *Civic Ideals: Conflicting Visions of Citizenship in U.S. History.* New Haven: Yale University Press.

Stack, Carol. 1974. *All Our Kin: Strategies for Survival in a Black Community.* New York: Basic Books.

Wacquant, Loic. 1998. "Inside the 'Zone': The Social Art of the Hustler in the American Ghetto." *Theory, Culture, and Society* 15: 1–36.

White, Lucie. 1994. "No Exit: Rethinking Welfare Dependency from a Different Ground." *Georgetown Law Journal* 81: 1961–2002.

Williams, Lucy. 1992. "The Ideology of Division: Behavior Modification Welfare Reform Proposals." *Yale Law Journal* 102: 719.

Wilson, William Julius. 1980. *The Declining Significance of Race: Blacks and Changing American Institutions.* 2d ed. Chicago: University of Chicago Press.

———. 1987. *The Truly Disadvantaged: The Inner City, The Underclass, and Public Policy.* Chicago: University of Chicago Press.

———. 1996. *When Work Disappears: The World of the New Urban Poor.* New York: Vintage Books.

Wright, Richard. 1945. *Black Boy: A Record of Childhood and Youth.* New York: World.

Wuthnow, Robert. 1996. *Poor Richard's Principle: Recovering the American Dream Through the Moral Dimension of Work, Business, and Money.* Princeton, N.J.: Princeton University Press.

Part I

WORKING TOWARD A FUTURE: IDENTITY AND THE MEANING OF WORK

Chapter 1

In Exile on Main Street

Carol Stack

We know very little about what life is like for teenagers today in America who start out at the bottom: their motivations for work, the way they find jobs, what motivates them to toil for low pay when many of their friends and neighbors have given up on paid work, the demands on their income, or where their work ethic comes from or might take them.

This chapter uses data from a large ethnographic study of fast-food workers in Oakland, California, to examine labor market dynamics for fast-food workers. These data include who gets hired and who doesn't, how scheduling and hourly rates fail to produce living wages for adults, and the resulting limitations of this work for young adults leaving the welfare system. By focusing on the actual experiences and interpretations of one young Latina worker, it will be shown that fast-food work, like other demanding jobs in which employers want readily available part-time workers, is a serious obstacle to the demands of schooling for poor teenagers. Attending school may actually impede a hard-working young person's chances for promotions at the workplace. Mobility ladders within fast food restaurants demand that workers be available all the time. Management benefits from, but pays little notice to, the invisible skills and competencies workers learn on the job, skills that could more easily be transferred if more widely recognized as job skills.

This research was jointly funded by five national foundations and also is a comparative study of fast-food workers and job seekers in Oakland and central and northern Harlem in New York City.[1] Over the course of three years, the Oakland team surveyed two hundred workers working in four inner-city fast-food restaurants in some of the poorest neighborhoods of Oakland: one third Asian, one third Latino, one third African American. My graduate students worked alongside these young workers at Flips—the name we have given the fast-food chain we studied.[2] The researchers worked at the counter and drive-through window; they mopped floors, witnessed holdups, and hung out with the fast-food workers and their friends. During the course of the study, they went along to school (high schools, community colleges, occupational nurses aide and beauty colleges), spent time with the families of workers, and joined in on the action at dance clubs, video arcades, and basketball courts, juggling busy schedules.

We then conducted extensive life histories with a representative sample of sixty workers, and from these, selected ten workers ages sixteen to twenty-one for an in-depth ethnographic study. About a dozen emerged as diarists—introspective young people who recorded the days of their lives, zeroing in on their own coming of age in Oakland. They wrote about parents who don't understand, bosses who get on their nerves, little sisters who can't keep a secret, good days, great parties, bad report cards, honor, dishonor, family poverty, and headaches that don't go away. Many of the young workers in the study were in a transitional moment in their lives (near the end of high school or considering dropping out), questioning how to navigate and negotiate the world of work, money, time management, and jobs. Some were young single parents, male and female. Many were children contributing income to their welfare-supported or low-income families. Two thirds were immigrants.

This study has many findings. The workers come from every imaginable configuration of family, between them they speak seventeen languages, they eat different food, listen to different music, wear different clothes, drive different cars. "That's Oakland," observes Santos Esposito, age seventeen, one of the workers. In the meantime, all of these young people share a particular kind of work experience. While they do not share a single perspective on this experience nor a single interpretation of its significance in their lives, their experiences are another index on the new urban poverty.

These teens want to work to put money in their pockets—and teenagers certainly need money. Poor teenagers' earnings furnish the only funds available for their personal needs; their families can spare very little. Some contribute generously to their families in moments of crisis, but generally our data show these young workers using all or most of their earnings to pay for their own basic needs (school expenses, food, transportation, gas, clothes) and luxuries (more clothes, entertainment, more food, cars, gas, CDs, nightclubs, and so on).

Many of these young people seek employment in fast-food restaurants because these are among the few legitimate places where they can get work. In pursuing these jobs, they also may be dodging or escaping from the underground economy, and like teens from more affluent communities, these young, low-wage workers struggle to manage the obligations of work, school, family, and friendship, and in the process learn valuable skills that should help them "make it" in the new "information" economy. Yet success is hard to come by. Despite their best efforts, most of these teens end up back where they started, as workers at the bottom of an increasingly polarized U.S. labor market.

The fast-food jobs that young workers hold after they graduate from high school and move on to community college (as do the majority of workers in our study) pay around minimum wage and do not provide full-time work. Among the 200 nonmanagerial workers surveyed, 43 percent earned less than $100 per week, 27 percent earned between $100 and $150 per week, 21 percent earned up to $200 per week, and 9 percent (managers in training) earned up to $300 per week. A young family could not survive on the income from one or more part-time jobs in a fast-food restaurant alone, and typically, part-time work does not provide health care benefits. Managers control work schedules and the number of hours crew are able to work. Week-to-week schedules are manipulated in seemingly arbitrary ways that make it difficult for these workers to hold down a second job—and for those in school to count on schedules that do not interfere with their classes.

Despite working conditions and wages in fast-food restaurants, that competition for jobs is fierce is no longer a surprise. A companion study of fast-food workers in Harlem took a look at job seekers applying to restaurants with hiring signs in the windows—establishments that were hiring to replace workers in an industry with astounding turnover. In this situation, in 1993, where a limited number of replacement workers would be hired, the ratio of applicants to hires was approximately 14 to 1 (Stack 1998).

In Oakland, we studied job seekers who applied to a new fast-food restaurant that had not yet opened. With the exception of a few managers who would be moved to this restaurant, all new workers were hired in 1994. There were 209 applicants for 46 jobs. The ratio of applicants to hires in this context, where the entire labor force would be hired (rather than replacement workers), was 4.5 to 1. In both Harlem and Oakland, these jobs are in demand, and a high proportion of individuals seeking these jobs are teens and young adults. At the new store in Oakland, 43 percent of the job seekers were between ages sixteen and eighteen, and 34 percent of those hired were under eighteen.

Our study also indicates that African Americans have a harder time gaining employment in fast-food restaurants than do Asians and Latinos of comparable age. In 1990, the population of Oakland was 42.8 percent African American, 13.9 percent Latino, 14.2 percent Asian, 28.3 percent white, and 0.5 percent Native American. The fast-food labor force we studied in the heart of Oakland is approximately 34 percent African American, 30 percent Latino, and 29 percent Asian (7 percent Other), and recent immigrants speak Cantonese, Vietnamese, Spanish, Tagalog, as well as English and several other languages and dialects. The percentage of foreign-born workers at the Oakland work sites we studied is more than three times higher than the percentage of foreign-born residents in the city.[3]

Blacks in our survey of workers in fast-food jobs in Oakland are rejected at a much higher rate than Latinos and Asians. Early on in the study we observed and documented a change in management and a mass firing of African Americans in a store located in a primarily black neighborhood. This drama, which took place under new owners of the restaurant, encouraged us to pay close attention to the location of the restaurants with respect to the labor force and hiring patterns. These hiring (and firing) patterns should hold true in store locations where African Americans make up between 50 percent to 98 percent of the residents in census tracks surrounding the restaurants. Similar to the

Harlem study, managers in Oakland appear to prefer immigrants to African Americans for these minimum-wage jobs.

Managers and owners interviewed indicated that they want the labor force in their stores to reflect the racial and ethnic makeup in their neighborhoods. In contrast to these stated objectives, our data show that the racial composition of the Oakland workforce does not typically reflect neighborhood composition. Indeed, in the four restaurants surveyed, African American workers generally lived less than one mile from the store where they are employed, while 71.2 percent of the Latino workers and 50 percent of the Asian workers lived three or more miles from the store where they are employed. These trends hold constant even in stores where African Americans make up between 50 percent and 98 percent of the residents in the census tracks surrounding the restaurants.

Additionally, our data show that Latino and Asian workers are generally given the daytime, weekday shifts at the restaurants. This presents a unique configuration of the workplace, including the organization of shifts, workstations, and job assignments by language groupings. This pattern creates troublesome workplace barriers with respect to opportunities for employment. Constructing shifts comprised of same-language coworkers (Spanish speaking) and Asians (many dialects that coworkers do not understand) creates barriers to African American employment that may account for the race–age structure of these workplaces, and for race and ethnic patterns of promotion to management.

As a result of the structure of work shifts, African American workers in Oakland were younger than other workers in these stores. One quarter of the workers in our survey were young African Americans age sixteen to eighteen, typically living with single mothers. These young workers, male and female, typically worked evening and weekend shifts while they were in school. Once they graduate or drop out of school, with few exceptions, they are effectively excluded from daytime or weekday work. Given that the youngest workers in these stores are primarily African Americans, typically work the night shift, and that when they graduate from high school or drop out they find it difficult to break into daytime work, relatively few African Americans have joined the management track. In Oakland, Latino and Asian managers, sometimes with very limited English skills, tend to hire and promote their own. The job gap problem in this study is not only a shortage of jobs, it also reveals racial, ethnic, and age-based patterns of employment.

In the proverbial global economy, a dreadful gap also has arisen between the work ethic of many of these young workers and the opportunities open to them. When these workers gain experience in fast-food jobs, does their experience lead to other, better jobs? Are the skills learned at Flips transferable? Our study found that experienced, reliable young workers in fast-food restaurants were continually searching for better jobs. As we followed these young people over the course of two years, few if any landed a job that paid above minimum wage or could be characterized as the next tier in the labor market. They expended energy while moving through a treadmill of equivalent jobs as security guards, cashiers in gas stations, and back again to the same fast-food store, the same chain down the street, or another chain where rumor had it that there was a good manager. Sometimes friends flocked together in these pursuits, moving to a "better" store; some had no expectation of a better job. One young person whose parents, older cousins, and siblings all worked in fast-food stores or equivalent jobs, when asked what she thought of her job at Flips, answered, "This is [what] work is, isn't it?" The young people in this study whose relatives appear to be stuck in the low-wage labor market are not able to see a better future for themselves.

Very few researchers, including those who study the low-wage labor market, have a vision of what constitutes the next tier of jobs for these workers (see, for example, Sassen-Koob and Appiah 1999; Sassen-Koob 1985). Likewise, the young people in this study find it difficult to make their way from regular fast-food employment into the "core" economy. Fast-food employers do not appear to place value on the skills their employees are acquiring. At best, employers argue that these jobs teach people to use an alarm clock, get to work on time, and arrive clean and well-groomed. The jobs are likened to boot camp; they are routinely seen as dead-end by employers in various sectors of the economy, including, ironically, fast-food franchise managers themselves.

Yet many of the young people interviewed considered the skills they were learning working in fast foods as indispensable to their own upward mobility. Indeed, they had much to say about these jobs, beyond the fact that life in the fast-food lane can be demanding, exhausting, and nonstop work. The following list of what workers perceived and valued as transferable skills included:

- learning about teamwork;
- how to do more than one thing at a time (multitasking);
- short-term and long-term planning on the job;
- time management;
- planning for and anticipating the ebb and flow of work;
- negotiating with workers from different ethnic groups;
- acquiring allies to help out during the busiest times.

In addition, workers also learn to recruit others and make recommendations that reflect on their judgment; develop new systems, short cuts, and improvements; learn the mechanics of fixing machines, computer skills, and dealing with often rude and bad-tempered customers; practice the notion that the customer is always right; and last but not least, learn to work with a diverse group of bosses who control both their schedules and hours they are able to work. While these skills should increase the attractiveness of experienced fast-food workers to the next tier of employers looking for workers in higher-skilled jobs, they are instead ignored and treated as unskilled workers with no real job experience.

Low-wage work satisfies a real need for money to cover daily necessities and an appetite for many of the same luxury items that middle-class teenagers have (and work for). Yet the time commitment required of work and school weighs in on these teenagers and takes its toll. Work steals from schooling, and being in school becomes an obstacle to the work ethic, so strong among these youth. The seemingly complementary practices of being employed and in school can work at cross-purposes, especially as youth confront the fact that they do not have enough time in any given day, a reality that hits many of us much later in life.

Much to our surprise, we discovered that many of the young people working at Flips have a fascination—indeed, even a fixation—with time. Jobs, school, and socializing consume many more hours than young people are able to manage. Given the time pressures they fuss about, these kids frequently negotiate with restaurant managers for better work schedules and more money—that is, raises, promotions, and additional work hours. As we have seen, all of these are hard to come by. The biggest sacrifice made by young workers, however, is sleep: the teens show up at school just hours after the early morning or late-night shift and an even later-night shift with their friends.

While these workers often talk with some resolve about the education and skills they will need, the future often appears vague and paradoxical, and today's schoolwork is not perceived by many as integral to long-term future goals. Here and now, school is obligatory, an agenda to work around and cram into an already cramped twenty-four-hour timetable. Time pressures that these hardworking, hard-socializing youth take on require diligent time management, a skill many are acquiring.

At some level, by the age of sixteen or eighteen the kids at Flips know that how they use their time today is related to the shape of their future. Many in our study insist rather vehemently that time is important. Sixteen-year-old Lidia Valesco, for example, is one of those vigorous, impatient, and unsinkable human beings on whom youth is not wasted. Yet she struggles to manage an amazingly crowded schedule of work, family obligations, school, and social activities. A detailed look at Lidia's experience shows just how hard it is for teens who gain employment in the low end of the service industry to keep up with all of the work, family, and leisure obligations that accompany life as a teen.

Lidia Valesco was sixteen when we first met her working at Flips. She was born in Michoacan, Mexico. At age five she came to California by walking for three days across the desert with her mother and baby brothers; the family was reunited with her father in Oakland and obtained legal resident status a few years later. Her father is a roofer and an alcoholic. Lidia left home at age fifteen and moved in with a boyfriend and his mother; she returned home a year later when the boyfriend began drinking heavily and refused to let her attend school. Working with Lidia at Flips are her mother, one of her brothers, and the mother of her ex-boyfriend. At her high school Lidia is involved in student government and numerous extracurricular activities. She also has worked as a model and organized a dance team that performs in Mexican-American nightclubs and at exhibitions throughout the Bay Area. She plans to go to college while waiting for her current boyfriend to finish his tour of overseas duty with the U.S. Navy.

Lidia keeps one eye on her watch as she writes in her diary. For the week of March 13, 1994, alone, she reports on what time it is twenty-six times. She discusses punctuality (or rather the lack of it) that she observes in herself and the people around her thirteen times. Lidia kept her diary throughout the spring and summer of 1994, when she was sixteen, and then again in the winter of 1995, when she was fully seventeen and, as we shall see, ever so much more mature.

From the diary of Lidia Valesco:[4]

Sunday, March 13, 1994

Today was my first day back at work because the computer took me off all the Schedules and wouldn't put me back on anymore until I take in my school work permit. I really did have my work permit, I just didn't feel like taking it in until yesterday, that way I didn't have to go to work.

Today I got up at 4:30 am and got dressed in 2 min. And then left to work with my mom. I decided that the car might not need any gas until after getting off from work that day. While going to work the car stopped and we were then stranded in the middle of the freeway with no money, food or a phone to make a call to someone that might of help us. Well anyways, we got some help at the last point and went to work. When I got home I went to sleep and then Gene called and invited me to go out with him. I asked my mom if I could go and she said no but I went anyways. I got back home at 1 o'clock am. Hopefully I don't have to explain why I'm so late. (To mom right now)

Monday, March 14, 1994

Today I was very tired and it was a very borring day. I got up at 10:30 am and cleaned the house before my mom got home. I took like five to six hours cleaning the dam house up.

After I finished I took a shower and got ready to go to Leticia's house, to the meeting. It was at 5:00 o'clock. I got there at 5:00 pm and I was the only one from the club there. Of course Leticia was there, you know she's the president of the club and I'm the vice president. All the guys got to Lety's house at 6:00 pm. I was so put off that I felt like going home and forgetting about the whole thing. But I couldn't do that so I just waited for everyone to get there. At the end it was a good meeting, because all together we were like 38 people, that's a lot. Well I got home until 10:30 pm (my mom got mad, too).

Tuesday, March 15, 1994

Right now I'm just starting to write because I'm waiting for the phone to ring. I'm waiting for Juan to call me back because I called him and asked him if he could pick me up for us to go to the club practice, at Lety's house. Its 5:50 pm now and I had to be at her house at 5:00 pm. Ain't that a shame. The vice-president being late.

Today at school I didn't go to first period because I was already late and any ways, I didn't feel like going to Mrs. Rees class.

It's 6:00 pm and I'm steal waiting for Juan to call me back. Dam, what the fuck is taking him so long.

It seems like if I were catching a cold or the flu.

Wednesday, March 16, 1994

Dear Diary, how are you today? I'm kind of tired right now, but I'll get over it.

Today when I got up and got ready to go to school, I felt kind of sick so I decided to take 2 Tylenol PM gel caplets. (Why PM I don't know). When I was walking to school I felt like just lying down on the sidewalk and going to sleep. It was the worst thing I had ever felt, trying to fight off the sleepyness.

Anyways I got to school but it was deserted. Find almost all of the school went on a field trip to a conference, even my stupid friends went. What in the hell are they going to be doing there if they don't even go to their regular classes. Well after being at school for half of third period and all of fourth period, I decided that I was too tired to be at school.

I don't know whats been happening to me. All of the sudden I don't go to school. I really think that its because of me being vice-president of club Banda La Bufa. I've been trying to go to school, work, and then the club, I think that it is to much for me in a way, but the kind of person I am, I like to be doing something every little second.

When I got home the first thing I did was to go straight to my room and into my bed. I slept from 12:30 to 4:30, enough to knock down those two caplets. After I woke up I took a shower and got ready to go to Leticia's house because we were going to meet there to go to Mexicali Rose with Banda La Bufa. It was a great night, we left at 6:00 pm and came back at 3:00 am the next day. I danced like never before in my life. Seriously, not that I don't dance a lot any other day, but this day was different. O, I almost forgot, Juan gave me two hikies. (That hoe)

Thursday, March 17, 1994

Today I decided not to go to school and stay home and just kick back. My mom told me to stay with her since she wasn't going to work that day. At 5:00 o'clock I had to go to work both me and my brother Jaime.

Friday, March 18, 1994

I didn't go to 1st period again but now I am in my second period, in Algebra Trig. It's really hard doing all this work. I really think about dropping out this class. I'll write in this journal again when I get home.

Now I didn't write until it is 10:05 pm. I got home at 3:19. I got out of school at 3:00 pm as always, and it takes me 15 minutes to walk home. Today in the afternoon I really didn't have anything worth wile to do. I went with my dad the disemployment office down at 5th street and E.12th st., then he gave me a ride to work.

I went to work at 4:30 and got out at 8:00 pm. When I got home I talked to Juan and went to sleep.

Saturday, March 19, 1994

Today I got up at 5:30 am because I had to be at work at 6:00 am. I got off work at 11:00 am and when I got home I called Juan and asked him if he was going to pick me up to go to Real Rock Club Latino to dance. He said that he would be here at 8:15, that way I wouldn't have to pay if we got there at or before nine o'clock. At 3:00 o'clock my brother Chequi went to sell fruit with Steven and Edie and I went to sleep. I woke up at 8:00 just as my sister Gris came into my room and asked me for a dollar that I had told her I was going to give her if she washed the dishes for me. That way my mom wouldn't say that I had to wash the dishes before leaving the house. My mom, dad, Jamie and Mario left to my aunty Alma Rosa's house.

Well of course Juan was late, as usual. I got back at 4:30 am; ain't that a shame. My mom didn't know at what time I came in my house, but if she ever finds out she'll KILL ME!

Sunday, March 20, 1994

Today I went to work as usual at 6:00 am.

When we first interviewed Lidia, a couple of months before these diary entries, she was one of the youngest kids working at Flips and still excited about her new driver's license; she insisted that one of the main reasons she'd gotten a job was "to have an excuse to get to drive my Dad's car on the freeway." In addition to driving, which was a new passion, dancing was (and had been, ever since she was little) Lidia's other passion. Yet incredibly, just six weeks after writing these tales of dancing till dawn and rehearsing till dark, she had resigned the vice presidency of her dance club and lost interest in the whole dance scene. Partly, she was growing up, trying to set priorities and tame her wild calendar; partly too she had a new boyfriend, who didn't dance.

For the moment, however, in the middle of March 1995, Lidia is living the life of the blessed. She can dance all night and show up for work at six the next morning. She can clean the whole house, top to bottom, to "try and suck up to my mother so she'll let me go out Saturday night." She can feel sick in the morning, "the worst feeling I ever had," drag herself to school anyway, nap on the couch in the afternoon, then shower and dress and go out to dance "like never before in my life."

Eight reports here concern people late for appointments or commitments or—worst of all—show so little respect for Lidia's own schedule that they make the vice president late herself. This is one vice president who does not waste time gladly, nor suffer fools who do; but the vice president is late a lot, actually. Sunday she runs out of gas on the freeway and presumably is late to work. Monday morning she's tired and sleeps late; Monday evening she can't begin her dance club practice until late because thirty-six of the club's thirty-eight members fail to show up on time. Tuesday she herself is late to the club meeting (Juan's fault). Wednesday she's late to school and very, very late for curfew. Friday she's late to school again, and she also takes herself to task for failing to complete her diary entry until later than she'd planned. And Saturday Juan is late again as usual, making Lidia run late for the ladies' discount hour at Real Rock Club Latino.

Lidia is constantly late, but she hates being late, and much of her diary is devoted to distributing blame for tardiness; Juan comes in for the lion's share of the blame, of course, but the vice president by no means escapes her own opprobrium. Running out of gas was her own fault; she was the one who decided the car might not need gas until after work. Being late to school is always her own fault: she decided to take Tylenol P.M. or decided to take it easy at home with her mother or decided she couldn't face her first-period teacher or decided to stay out all night the previous evening. Indeed, in these diary entries, "I decided" is Lidia's favorite sentence structure; she clearly likes to take responsibility for decision making and report on the consequences of her decisions, even when they are not the sort of consequences she was hoping for.

For Lidia, as for most of us, time management is a particularly problematic arena of decision making. Conventional wisdom would have it that adolescents in general—and poor, inner-city kids in particular and perhaps even most poor people—do not manage their time responsibly or efficiently: they run late, fail to plan ahead, lose track of time, neglect their commitments. The story of Lidia Valesco as a sixteen- and seventeen-year-old is in part the story of a young woman struggling to gain control of her time—floundering, but trying nevertheless to manage the hours of her days, not to mention the rest of her life.

While some might be inclined to interpret Lidia's diary as a testament to her irresponsibility, I believe that it shows quite the opposite. In particular, the entries demonstrate her overwhelming concern and conscientiousness about time, and an amazing capacity to juggle a variety of obligations and work tirelessly. Stereotypes about teenagers typically include that they have no sense of time, leave everything until the last minute, are always running late, ignore the consequences of their actions, do not defer gratification, and no matter how small the chore, say they'll do it later. They appear bored, with nothing to do, and at the same time stressed out, with too many demands on their time. Yet Lidia's diary shows that she, like other teenagers living in Oakland, was able to develop time-management skills very similar to the driven professional or corporate manager celebrated in U.S. popular culture. Because Lidia is poor, however, and therefore put under intensive scrutiny by individuals who want to blame her impoverishment on her own behaviors, she is held to standards of time management that more affluent individuals are not. To some degree Lidia understands this, which is why she tries to rationalize instances where she justifies to herself (and to us) the reasons why she is late.

Like other teens at Flips, Lidia will tell you that how well kids do in school determines their future prospects. School prefigures success and failure, and stands in for the future. Lidia and all the others insist vehemently that educated people have a chance to make it in America and uneducated people almost certainly do not. Lidia and most of the others are still enrolled in school, still trying, more or less, to educate themselves and hitch their wagons to that star. Yet many of them, like Lidia, hardly ever show up for class. Why? If they believe school is so all-fired important, why are they not fully engaged in it?

Readers may have noted that Lidia in her diary mentions only one of her high school courses, a math class she refers to as Algebra Trig. Advanced algebra with trigonometry is traditionally the fourth-year subject in the college-preparatory math sequence, for which students must already have completed two years of algebra and a year of geometry. In relatively wealthy, suburban-type school districts, some accelerated students begin this sequence in seventh or eighth grade, thereby enrolling in algebra-trig in about eleventh grade and becoming eligible to take college-level calculus in twelfth grade. The Hollywood movie *Stand and Deliver* looked at a group of poor Latino students in California who tried to follow this suburban success strategy—but most inner-city kids never even begin the college-prep math curriculum, much less make it through all the way to algebra-trig with a year to spare for calculus.

Lidia could have stolen the scene in *Stand and Deliver;* she enrolled in algebra-trig not in twelfth grade like traditional serious students, and not in eleventh grade like accelerated suburban students, but in tenth grade. In spite of a year of emotional and social turbulence, somehow she scraped by in math. As we learn more about her story and attempts to imagine a future for herself, one vital question emerges that readers may find helpful to keep in mind: When does Lidia do her homework?

Lidia's difficulty getting herself to school in the morning is something that has got her completely stumped. Any adult reading the diary would see the problem instantly: this child needs to get to bed on time. Yet Lidia is baffled that she keeps missing school, partly because sticking with school is a critical element of her self-image—and especially her self-respect—but partly too because she considers herself capable of getting up after just a few hours of sleep, even after one hour of sleep. She can simply will herself to wake up, no matter what, presumably by promising herself a nap later on. This is a time-management strategy she has practiced often, and one that she believes she may call on any time she wants.

Such an approach only works for a day or two, not for days on end—and school is the ultimate in day after day, semester after semester, year after year. Even Lidia, young and healthy as she is, blessed with high energy and fiery determination, cannot subdue the need for sleep.

Why don't her parents rein her in? On school nights, at the least, shouldn't parents see to it that teenagers keep reasonable hours? Lidia's parents make at least some effort in this direction—she does go through the motions of seeking her mother's permission before going out at night—but clearly no curfew is effective in the Valesco household. Several explanations seem likely.

The bottom line is that neither of Lidia's parents can stay up late enough to enforce a curfew. Her mother, Alma, is usually in bed by eight or nine o'clock at night, nine-thirty at the latest; she works the opening breakfast shift at Flips five mornings a week (with Lidia on weekends, and also with Lidia's brother and godmother and two of Alma's cousins). Alma has to get up by 4 A.M. to be ready when her ride honks for her at 4:30. Lidia's father also goes to bed early; he works pouring concrete for a curbing contractor and has to get up in time to drive an hour or more to construction sites in distant suburbs, where the workday usually starts around seven o'clock. When the contractor is between jobs or the winter rains are persistent—as was the case in March 1994—he gets laid off, but then he goes to sleep even earlier in the evening, according to Lidia. She says she hates it when he's out of work because he sits on the couch drinking all day and usually passes out soon after suppertime. So if Lidia's parents tell her not to go out on a school night or be sure to come home by a certain time, they have to rely on her to enforce her own curfew. Mom and Dad are no longer young enough to burn the candle at both ends.

Lidia can break curfew any time she wants and get away with it, as long as she doesn't make any noise fiddling with the three locks on the front door or creaking down the steps between the pantry and the stair landing near her parents' bedroom door. One night, she told us, she got back to the house at 3:30 A.M. and tiptoed so gingerly through the apartment that it was already four o'clock before she reached the back bedroom she shares with her two little sisters.

Clearly, Lidia's respect for parental authority is less than total. She does appear to respect her parents' expectations by assuming responsibility within the household: she spends many hours each week cleaning the house, and she is proud of paying some of the utility bills with her own earnings. But their rule is not her law, as she tells them repeatedly, loudly, combatively. When she is eighteen, she announces, she'll be moving out of the house; she'll get a place of her own, and nobody on earth will be able to stop her. Lidia's parents are inclined toward the traditional Mexican view that young women who live on their own are probably whores; when Lidia talks this way they cry and curse and issue frantic counterthreats and restrictions. They know she is not talking idly, because once before, a few weeks after her fifteenth birthday, she up and left.

After she left home and established and ended a romantic relationship with her godmother's son, Lidia first went to work. One thing she knew for certain about jobs was that she did not want to work at Flips with her mother. At first she didn't have to: within a week of her sixteenth birthday, she'd found part-time work in an earring store at the mall. Lidia liked the job but also settled down seriously into her schoolwork; she'd lost a lot of credits when she was romantically involved and hoped to catch up fast. The store owner begged her to work full time as manager of a new store he planned to open, but Lidia couldn't bring herself to leave school. Also, gang incidents at the store led Lidia eventually to inform the manager that she couldn't work there anymore.

She finally accepted her mother's offer to get her a job at Flips. Her former boyfriend's mother—her godmother, in whose household she briefly had resided—became her boss. Going to work felt too much like doing chores for her mother, especially when they worked side by side on weekends. Lidia was a good worker, though, and every time the managers offered more hours she agreed. Within a few months, she was working evening shifts on school nights and predawn breakfast shifts on weekends, virtually a full-time workload for a youngster who was unwilling to quit school and compromise a moment of her social life.

Like many youth working at Flips, Lidia works side by side with her mother or older brother, sometimes working the same hours. Some of the young people in the study work with as many as five or eight older relatives at the same workplace. Keep in mind these are not the old mom and pop stores, where the family owns the store, but fast-food franchises, where the store owns the family. They pay minimum wage, employ only part-time workers, and pay no benefits.

By March 1994, Lidia was desperate for a vacation. The Flips Corporation, of course, does not provide vacation time for hourly crew employees. When Lidia was told, however, that her name would be removed from the work schedule until she updated her school work permit, she saw the threat as an opportunity. "I really did have my work permit, I just didn't feel like taking it in." Lidia gave herself a vacation. For someone who insists on being up and about every single minute, hers was a long vacation: five days. During this respite she went to school and attended club practices and went out dancing most nights. Instead of going to work, she slept.

When Lidia has sleep to catch up on and no vacation at her disposal, she has to steal time to sleep. She can't steal it from work, and she won't steal much of it from play, so she—and many of her colleagues at Flips—sometimes wind up stealing it from school. Classes are missed, homework is neglected. "You don't have time to study," one community college student told us. "You don't have time to go over the chapters. You don't have time to go find the research, 'cause after you get off, you're tired. You should sleep."

"I put more effort into my job than school," said one high school student who claims to sleep only four hours a night. "I know it shouldn't be like that, but after I get off work, you know, I'm all tired, and then I'll go to school that way. Here I am, lazy, tired, 'cause I'm working all night at Flips. When I'm there I'm alive, since I'm used to working at night. Then I go to school drowsy."

Sleep is not a recognized policy issue. Politicians who propose youth work programs never talk about adolescent sleep patterns. Researchers investigating the school-to-work transition don't talk about sleep. But the kids at Flips talk about sleep—and especially about the lack of sleep. One of the lessons they learn from working concerns the importance of making sleep a priority.

Sometimes teens who deprive themselves of sleep are surprised when they can't get away with it. A sudden craving for sleep overtakes them outside on the basketball court or on the bench at the bus stop, or they suddenly realize that if they sit down on their work break their eyes are likely to shut. They sometimes fall asleep in class or over their schoolbooks. Many of them—certainly including Lidia—occasionally or often don't wake up when the alarm clock rings.

Monday, March 21, 1994

Today I got up at 8:00 am because the alarm clock was disconnected and didn't ring off. I guess the lights or electricity went off in the middle of the night, because the alarm clock was working pretty well before I went to sleep.

If you are supposed to be at school at eight o'clock and you don't even wake up until eight, then of course you will be late to class—perhaps by only a few minutes, if you can dress in a hurry and get over to the school quickly, but perhaps by an hour or even two hours, if the situation is particularly complicated. Lidia sized up her situation and decided the entire school day was already shot.

I didn't go to first second or third period, or fourth. After lunch time, me, Gena, Liz and Cirila came to my house and got my dad's car. I picked the girls up a block away from my house. I didn't want my brother to see that we were cutting. Then we left to go to Marina Park in San Leandro. When we past by 98th St., by McDonalds we saw Cuco and Felix, so we stopped to see waz up. When we left they decided to chase us down there. We ran too where there's this kind of steep hill and tryed to hide from them. Then me and Cirila decided to walk to this part where it looks like an island. Cuco then called me and told me if I wanted to jog around the island so I said ya. Liz got kind of mad with me. . . . After we came back I went home and got ready for Juan to pick me up to go to practice for the Club "Banda La Bufa."

To the politicians, employers, and researchers focused on young people's labor force participation, sleep is not the crux of the matter. Likewise, when we began this study, we didn't think that we would be talking about teenagers and sleep. Like Lidia, teenage workers think that sleep is the first thing to give up and the first to reclaim during a free moment or as time stolen from school, homework, and so on. Sleep is an account they feel they can borrow from at will. Moreover, when asked about time pressures between school and work, teenagers often will recast the issue in terms of conflicts between sleep and everything else: sleep and school, sleep and work, sleep and sports, sleep and social life, and sleep and diary keeping.

When teens are in positions of responsibility they are more judgmental than they might be otherwise. Attending school and trying to hold down a job, Lidia has little free time; she can claim more hours here and there by putting off sleep and by deciding that avoiding school or work is an option worth considering. Like so many adolescents, Lidia crashes for an hour at dawn, takes a shower and goes to work, naps on the couch in the afternoon, then takes a shower and goes out with friends. After a few days and nights at this full-throttle pace, she tends to collapse and sleep right through her alarm clock. Lidia always seems surprised when this happens, as if she expects perpetual motion to speed her through all the days of her life forever—but she's just a kid, after all, who has a lot to learn about time and mortality.

The young people in this study whose relatives appear to be stuck in the low-wage labor market are not able to see a better future for themselves. They are working in jobs that are critical to sustaining a teen lifestyle that commands some self-respect—a lifestyle beyond their parents' means. These jobs also provide a number of transferable skills related to planning, teamwork, and time management that should provide some entree into higher-wage work. Yet characteristics of the work—low wages, unpredictable, week-by-week scheduling, night shifts, the failure to recognize and reward learned skills—all conspire to produce sleep deprivation and a scarcity of time that is incompatible with full investment in schooling. For Lidia, extracurricular activities such as the dance club also serve as a training ground for organizing and leadership, an aspect of life valued for its relevance among middle-class suburban students (and for college admissions). Lidia has imagined a good future for herself, but she lives inside many personal and structural constraints.

In these times, to have a vision of what constitutes the next tier of jobs for these workers is difficult. Yet many of the young people interviewed showed pride in the skills they were acquiring and expected future employers to respect their job experience as well. That these young workers go on dizzying searches for better jobs comes as no surprise. Yet they move through a treadmill of equivalent jobs as gas station cashiers and back again to the same fast-food store or the same or a different chain down the street. Employers in fast-food chains do not acknowledge the skills these young people are gaining, and potential employers are blind to the skills they have acquired.

These hardworking young people, with their work ethic and faith in the importance of education (which they say they will get in the future), are blind to the fact that poor academic skills are major stumbling blocks to significantly better jobs. They graduated from high school, after all; they have that certificate! Painfully, I observed these young people on a treadmill, running in place. After high school, they become exiled on Main St.

NOTES

1. I am grateful for research support from the Russell Sage Foundation as well as from Ford, Rockefeller, W. T. Grant, and the Spencer Foundation. The Harlem study is reported in Newman 1999.

2. The following graduate research assistants participated in the study: Kamau Birago, Project Director, now Assistant Professor of Sociology, Connecticut College; Julio Cammarota, now Postdoctoral Research Fellow, Education, University of Califor-

nia, Santa Cruz; Ann Ferguson, Project Director, now Associate Professor of African American Studies and Sociology, Smith College; Regina Martinez, Social and Cultural Studies in Education; Christine Palmer, Anthropology; Pam Stello, Social and Cultural Studies in Education; Wendell Thomas, Sociology; Maria Yen, City and Regional Planning; and Daniel Jerome and Zappa Montag, undergraduates, all at University of California, Berkeley.

3. Only 36.5 percent of the Oakland workers we studied were U.S. born; the comparable figure for Harlem is 58 percent (Newman 1995).

4. Are the teens' diaries more or less "truthful" than other evidence about their lives? In any writing (including that of researchers), diary entries seem more carefully crafted than, say, oral responses to an interviewer's questions—but crafted, in the case of this study, to serve the teens' goals, not those of the researchers.

REFERENCES

Newman, Katherine. 1995. "Dead End Jobs—a Way Out." *Brookings Review* 13(4): 24–7.
———. 1999. *No Shame in My Game: The Working Poor in the Inner City.* New York: Alfred A. Knopf and Russell Sage Foundation.
Sassen-Koob, Saskia. 1985. "Changing Composition and Labor Market Location of Hispanic Immigrants in New York City." In *Hispanics in the U.S. Economy,* edited by George J. Borjas and Marta Tienda. London: Academic Press.
Sassen-Koob, Saskia, and Kwame Anthony Appiah. 1999. *Globalization and Its Discontents: Essays on the New Mobility of People and Money.* New York: New Press.
Stack, Carol. 1997. "Testimony." Presented at the Senate Committee on Industrial Relations on Working in California hearing: *Job Creation, Workers' Right and the Challenge of Welfare Reform,* February 5, Sacramento, Calif.

Chapter 2

Lives on the Line: Low-Wage Work in the Teleservice Economy

Ruth Buchanan

Cindy is twenty-three years old and works full time at a call center in New Brunswick, Canada, taking reservations for hotel chains in Canada and the United States.[1] She has worked there for two and a half years, at a wage of $7.50 an hour (Canadian). At the time of the interview, she earned almost $8 an hour. Cindy began working part time while she was going to school, but when she graduated from college with a degree in marine biology, she could find no jobs in her field. So she stayed on full time with the call center, describing the job as "just a way to make money." The center is open twenty-four hours a day and her shifts can begin as early as 7 A.M. and end as late as two o'clock the following morning. Every day she deals with several hundred telephone calls automatically relayed to her headset from a queue. She must handle each call quickly in order to meet her 150-second-per-call target, and to keep other callers waiting as briefly as possible. Yet she also must be sure not to deviate from a carefully written global script. In addition to working quickly and cleanly within her script, Cindy must be a convincing saleswoman for the hotels in her chain, as her "conversion" rate—the proportion of calls that result in reservations—is closely monitored. Indeed, the computer keeps track of every minute of her working day, including any time that she is not available to take calls (which is not allowed to exceed a half hour, in addition to scheduled breaks). Despite the low wage and highly regulated working conditions, Cindy has few complaints and no immediate plans to leave her job. Rather, her attitude is one of pragmatic acceptance. "It's not bad. I wish I had something degree-related. That's what I tell everyone. But it's not going to happen right now."

A constitutive tension between the privilege of being employed and the marginal nature of that employment underpins Cindy's call-center experience. This tension is not unique to call-center work, but is a central dynamic of the expanding market for low-wage labor in Canada in the 1990s. Labor markets in Canada and the United States have in recent decades become increasingly segmented, divided between a shrinking core of highly skilled, well-paid jobs and an expanding periphery of low-wage jobs. A growing gap in job creation between the few good jobs and a lot of bad jobs has become increasingly apparent in the fast-growing service sector of the economy (Economic Council of Canada 1990). In Canada, recent trends in labor markets also have led to an increase in non-standard employment (most of which also tends to be lower waged), which includes temporary, part-time, and casual jobs.[2]

In comparison to many low-wage workers, Cindy is seemingly fortunate to hold a full-time job that provides her with some benefits. Yet in other ways, her circumstances are similar to those of many other low-wage workers. Women and young people such as Cindy are overrepresented in low-wage jobs, particularly in the expanding service sector. Fast-food restaurant service, insurance sales, debt collection, and retail sales all are work that has become increasingly routinized, scripted, and monitored by firms anxious to maximize productivity and reduce labor costs (Leidner 1993). In many of these jobs, employees are not only expected to competently perform assigned tasks, but they also must look and sound as though they are enjoying themselves at the same time. Through the scripting of employees' interactions with the public, firms attempt to control unpredictability (and ensure consistency) in the interpersonal encounters at the heart of a service economy.

In addition to being positioned in the expanding periphery of polarized labor markets, low-wage service work is marginal in several other ways. Service employees exist at the furthest edges of a firm's organization, geographically remote from the head office and distanced from opportunities for internal advancement. Moreover, service employees often function as a buffer between the dictates of the firm and the demands of the customer; they must absorb the frictions and stresses of this position as intermediary. Their interpersonal skills are tested on a daily basis, yet this hidden emotional labor remains largely uncompensated and unacknowledged. When employees burn out owing to the stress and difficulty of the work, employers have no trouble refilling the positions, often with people just as apparently overqualified as Cindy. While most low-wage workers, such as Cindy, consider themselves fortunate just to have a job, as a society we need to examine more closely the personal and social costs associated with widespread low-wage employment. In terms of mounting everyday stresses, underutilized talent, and forgone opportunities, the low-wage labor market may be pricier than we imagine.

This chapter will use telephone work as a vehicle for assessing some of these costs and benefits. The following section explains the growth and significance of telephone work, with reference to the restructuring undertaken by firms and facilitated by governments, in response to the perceived demands of economic globalization. The closing section draws on interviews with call-center workers to explore the dynamics of low-wage work in the current economic order: who does it, what is required of them, and what it does or doesn't provide in return. As the economy has been restructured, so has the low-wage workforce. Call-center work, and those who perform it, form a significant part of the new periphery of the labor market. Along with the other studies in this volume, this qualitative examination of "lives on the line" hopefully will contribute to wider policy debates on the shifting terrain of low-wage work in the new economy.

WORKING THE PHONES: THE HIGH-TECH, LOW-WAGE GHETTO

Technological developments and corporate restructuring have transformed the ways in which services are provided, consumers are researched, and products marketed. The integration of communications and software technologies means that telephone and Internet interactions between producers and consumers frequently supplement and even replace the face-to-face service encounter in the bank, post office, courier company, airline, hotel chain, or department store. Increasingly, Canadians and Americans are called at home and asked (politely) whether they would like to switch long-distance carriers, purchase insurance, sign up for a new credit card, participate in a consumer information survey, or donate money to deserving children in a remote part of the world.

As companies turn to the telephone as a cheap and efficient means to service customers and market products, working the phones is an increasingly dominant feature of the low-wage labor market in Canada and the U.S. Although the vast networks of people, products, and services accessible via the Internet attract much media attention to the so-called information highway, much less public scrutiny is given to the most widespread applications of telecommunications and software technologies in call centers. Even less attention is devoted to the scores of faceless and placeless people who animate these scripts of the postindustrial economy.[3]

Nonetheless, attracting this type of work has become a preoccupation of local economic development agencies in a number of sites in Canada, including Winnipeg and New Brunswick, where interviews were conducted for this study. Local governments use the promise of available pools of well-educated, bilingual, unemployed individuals as bait to attract call-center investment (and tax dollars) to their localities. In areas where wage rates are generally low and unemployment is high, call centers might seem to be ideal vehicles for job creation. Yet policy makers know very little about the composition of this workforce and its longer-term implications for improving the skills and career opportunities of workers. In an effort to address some of these questions, this chapter investigates in detail the backgrounds and circumstances of people who do telephone work; it is drawn from a study of call centers in Canada that surveyed firms and interviewed workers in Winnipeg, Toronto, and three cities in New Brunswick.[4] The primary goal of the study was to better understand the impacts of globalization-driven restructuring within Canada on those who are positioned at its social and geographic margins. The study was designed to find out who performed this type of work, the economic, social, and educational circumstances that led them to it, and how it fit into their plans and aspirations. Was call-center work seen as a career in itself, a steppingstone to something better and more lasting, or simply a last-ditch way to pay the bills?

The people with whom I spoke often found themselves doing telephone work as a last resort. Many of them, such as Cindy, had some postsecondary education and aspired to more challenging work. Most occupied positions with little or no opportunity for advancement. Their experiences are reflective of the narrowing range of employment options in Canada as described in the Introduction, especially for women and youth, who make up the bulk of the call-center labor force. As a type of work that is easy to get but has little opportunity for advancement, and that draws on a labor force with few other employment options, call-center work can be described as a type of high-tech, low-wage ghetto.

Within the call-center industry, however, is a considerable amount of diversity. Not all workers are just marking time and eager to move on. Some are paid considerably more than $8 per hour, enjoy job security and benefits, and do not find the work overly stressful. A few felt they were able to learn and develop their skills on the job. For some, call-center work represents a step up from a previous job. Acknowledging these differences, the larger study aspires to provide some insights into the ways in which labor markets for telephone work are differently constituted in a range of locations and workplaces, and how these differences affect the opportunities of frontline telephone workers. While this diversity is evident in the following accounts, exploring fully geographic and sectoral variations within the call-center industry in Canada is beyond the scope of this chapter. Rather, this chapter presents a number of accounts of telephone work from the perspective of those performing it, in a range of locations and workplaces. The focus is on the substantial commonalities, rather than the differences, among these narratives.

Two interrelated processes—globalization and restructuring—provide the backdrop to the emergence of call-center work in Canada. Globalization here can be defined as the qualitative expansion of flows of money, goods, people, and ideas across international borders (Giddens 1990; Twining 2000). In recent years, these accelerated processes of integration and exchange have had a profound impact on the way in which corporations and governments do business. Increasing flows of international investment have led firms to reorganize their operations across provincial and national borders, seeking the most attractive environments in which to operate. Factors that influence firms' location decisions include the cost and quality of the local labor force and the regulatory environment. As firms have become more mobile, governments at a subnational level have become even more actively involved in courting those firms, and the jobs and investment they bring with them (Kassab and Luloff 1993; Milne 1995). Local economic development strategies include the active marketing of a locality, its workforce and regulatory environment, as well as the provision of financial incentives and the development of increasingly targeted training and job-creation policies.[5] Often, restructuring strategies adopted by firms and facilitated by local governments in response to globalization converge on an issue at the heart of this book and this chapter: the location and recruitment of a low-wage workforce.

GLOBALIZATION

The prairie city of Winnipeg or the even smaller urban centers of St. John, Fredericton, and Moncton in the tiny province of New Brunswick (home to only three quarters of a million people) might seem unlikely places to look for evidence of an increasingly globalized economic order. Yet the rapid emergence of call centers in these unlikely locations is an excellent illustration of the complex realignments of institutional, physical, and human geography taking place in the globalized economy. Call centers bring together a number of familiar globalization themes: the expanding significance of the service economy, diffusion of new technologies, restructuring of firms through downsizing and relocation, and heightened competition for investment and jobs among provincial and local governments. Call centers bridge the old divide between core and periphery in new ways, linking marginal workers and locations with global networks of capital while at the same time reinscribing hierarchies of place and identity. Field studies, such as the research reported in this chapter, attempt to locate this reorganized low-wage work within the context of these larger shifts.

Revealing the connection between the reorganization of work and broader shifts in both the structure and ideology of the market in the late twentieth century is a task that also calls for new approaches in policy-oriented research. The proliferation of rapidly moving circuits of capital, commodities, labor power, and ideas in the new economy have led some to emphasize these flows in their analyses (Lash and Urry 1994; Castells 1996; Appadurai 1996). Important to keep in mind, however, is that these transnational flows are themselves significantly determined by and mediated through a range of institutions including multinational corporations, trade alliances such as the World Trade Organization (WTO) and the North American Free Trade Agreement (NAFTA), nations, states or provinces, nongovernmental organizations, municipalities, industry associations, and other less formal local forms of social organization (Lash and Urry 1994). Indeed, as other types of institutional barriers collapse or are dismantled, the specificity of places, workforces, regulatory environments, and local social networks become more important (Harvey 1993). The empirical task of mapping the circuitry of global flows—an important element in understanding the architecture of the new global order—therefore must include the study of these types of social institutions and the local variations they produce.

This empirical study of call-center work is one such attempt. It examines the interrelationship between global flows of investment and technology and local governments and labor markets. Call centers are made possible by telematics—the combination of telecommunications and software technologies that can coordinate, through the predictive dialing of outbound or switching of inbound calls, the simultaneous connection of a telephone call and the display of account information to a service representative. Although this technology is not particularly new, its dissemination to such places as New Brunswick facilitates the corporate reorganizations that are bringing the call centers there as well. Back officing—the corporate restructuring strategy that brings jobs to places such as Moncton and Winnipeg—creates a particularly footloose type of investment. Most firms rent their premises and bring in computers and other equipment purchased elsewhere. Telephones ordinarily are supplied by the local phone company, and the provincial government provides significant "training" grants to offset whatever remaining costs might be associated with the relocation.

In studying the changes associated with globalization, including ideas and images in public circulation is also important. Dominant understandings, as articulated in print and visual media, can have a powerful effect on public perceptions about the appropriate range of possible solutions to particular issues. One might think of dominant understandings of globalization in terms of a script, in which the various actors must play their designated parts.[6] Policy makers can be constrained or enabled by this script. The globalization script, for example, makes neoliberal policies, such as privatization of public services, much easier to embrace than more social democratic policies, such as implementing increases in the minimum wage or the corporate tax rate.

The power of ideas and images in structuring what are considered the reasonable parameters of policy cannot be underemphasized. Building on and extending scholar Benedict Anderson's insight that print capitalism enabled a new form of "imagined community" in the emergence of the idea of the nation, Appadurai (1996) argues that technological innovations in our own time have given rise to a new social role for the imagination: "The image, the imagined, the imaginary—these are all terms that direct us to something critical and new in global cultural processes: the imagination as a social practice."[7]

Thus the circulation of discourse and images play a powerful role in shaping the terrain on which social and economic dramas of our era are enacted. Competition among provinces and municipalities for investment is one place where the circulation of ideas and images through marketing and public relations can directly impact economic realities. The New Bruswick government's strategic marketing of the province as a premier site for call-center operations, for example, involved the constructive work of the imagination along two intersecting dimensions. First, it was necessary to sell an image of New Brunswick to firms as a site that offers a business-friendly environment and a plentiful, productive, and cheap labor force. Yet it was equally necessary to market the jobs to New Brunswickers, in order to constitute a willing, committed, and docile labor force to work at those centers. To construct itself as a site for this type of investment, the province commissioned studies, placed advertisements, sent representatives to telemarketing conferences, and arranged private meetings between the premier and corporate heads, in addition to paying incentives to firms choosing to relocate. At the same time, the province represented the call centers to residents as their "on-ramp to the information highway," connecting poor and isolated New Brunswick to wealth and opportunity elsewhere. The information highway image can be particularly powerful for those in geographically and economically isolated areas, as it promises a high-speed route to a virtual place of economic opportunity. Similar marketing initiatives were launched by several other Canadian provinces, including Alberta, Manitoba, and Nova Scotia, although none has been as aggressive, or as evidently successful, as the New Brunswick strategy.[8]

RESTRUCTURING

While economic globalization both sets the stage for current transformations and provides the script, corporations and governments are the actors. This section examines two important themes suggested by the globalization script— the restructuring of firms and the reorganization of work—and argues that the call-center industry provides an exemplary context in which to study these interrelated processes.

The rapid emergence of the call-center industry is commonly attributed to developments in telematics over the last several decades. Had firms not perceived any advantages to reorganizing their operations to utilize these technologies, however, the transformation would not have taken place. Providing services or marketing products over the phone today presents a number of opportunities for firms to reorganize work. First, workers who perform these tasks are centralized in less costly work locations, away from the head office. Relocating these workers away from the rest of the firm also in some cases facilitates the segregation of internal labor markets—that is, limiting the opportunities of teleworkers to obtain more desirable positions within the firm.[9] Finally, the implementation of information systems that enable the tracking of a courier package by a teleworker for a customer, for example, also presents the opportunity for management to track the performance of the teleworker with similar precision.[10] With telematics, it becomes possible to monitor every minute of the employee's working day and implement productivity quotas so that poor performers are weeded out. Many companies base their evaluation of employees on these quantitative indicators, despite the possible distortions or subversions they might reproduce or encourage. In addition, most of the teleworkers with whom we spoke had their calls monitored randomly, so that, as in Bentham's Panopticon, the employee effectively internalized the experience of being under constant surveillance with only a limited amount of actual observation.[11]

Lower-skilled jobs such as telemarketing, teleservice, data entry, and rate or credit checking now can be segregated from the rest of a firm's operations and relocated to a suburban or offshore location where labor, rents, and other costs are generally lower.[12] Preferred locations for call centers therefore are usually in towns or areas where other opportunities are limited—places such as Moncton, Winnipeg, Halifax, or Hamilton. In addition to taking advantage of preexisting geographic divisions in the labor market to reap immediate productivity gains, call centers also take advantage of localized gender and racial labor market hierarchies. Indeed, the call center has become a prime example of the growing category of feminized labor on the periphery: a majority of women perform the work, and those men who do it are often young, gay, or otherwise marginalized.

The approach to back officing reflected in the call-center phenomenon has been described as the "dark side" of flexible production (Harrison 1994). Opportunities for advancement and skills acquisition in these positions usually are limited, so that one would expect employees to invest little in their jobs and continue to seek employment elsewhere. In labor markets where opportunities are plentiful, this job seeking leads to an unattractive (that is, for firms) combination of high turnover and low productivity. By relocating to labor markets where few other options exist, such as New Brunswick or Winnipeg, the returns for firms can be significant.[13] Yet the gains produced by relocating work are fixed; firms seeking further advantage are forced either to increase the productivity of their workforce by other means, or relocate production farther offshore in search of even cheaper labor (Appelbaum 1993). From the perspective of the employees, this can mean being presented with ongoing demands for more work with negligible wage increases (sweated labor) in a context where unsatisfactory performance can mean the loss of the company to another location.

The extent to which labor markets are locally constructed and the ways that companies are able to exploit these local differences became apparent during research for this project, which involved conducting interviews in Winnipeg, Toronto, and three smaller cities in New Brunswick (Fredericton, St. John, and Moncton). For example, interviewees in New Brunswick suggested that wages and working conditions in call centers there compared unfavorably with those in other parts of the country. An employee with one firm that had another call center in London, Ontario, said, "People sort of know that the rules are quite different in London—they don't know in a big way, but they don't work overnight shifts. They, you know, I think they've got more clout in London."[14] A similar observation was made by a service representative from Ontario, who recently transferred to a newly opened St. John call center.[15] Based on information he had gained from many years of experience with the company and his recent access to work logs at other locations, this worker concluded that the company had established higher productivity quotas at the New Brunswick location. He further speculated that the longer-term goal would be to phase out more costly centers in other locations, on the basis of the convenient argument that they were not performing as well.

The contrast between local labor markets also was reinforced by interviews conducted with call-center employees in Toronto, who generally represented their jobs as marginal, temporary stop-gaps until something better came along. Teleworkers in Toronto often had worked at many different call centers; if one place did not work out, finding work at another was easy enough. One eighteen-year-old interviewed had worked at nine telemarketing or survey research firms in the two years that she had been doing part-time phone work.[16]

In New Brunswick, while jobs tend to occupy the same marginalized place in firms' organizational structures, most employees interviewed did not intend for their call-center position to be temporary. For most, it was their first job, and no one had worked at more than two different call centers. Several of the younger employees interviewed in New Brunswick reported that they had picked teleservice as their chosen career. The seriousness with which New Brunswick call-center employees approach their jobs is bolstered by the fact that most of those who work at the centers have had at least some postsecondary education, including some with two-year degrees from newly minted community college courses in teleservice. Some had even paid $1,400 for a thirty-five-week course offered by a private firm that boasts of placing 90 percent of its graduates directly into local teleservice jobs. Yet when the idea of community college training programs for call-center work was raised in interviews with teleworkers in Winnipeg, several laughed spontaneously, and one described it as "a joke."[17] While some teleworkers interviewed in Winnipeg were attending a university, no one with a completed degree was still working the phones.[18]

Local governments were actively involved in assisting companies to recruit employees, particularly in smaller centers. In New Brunswick, in addition to the community college programs, local industry job fairs functioned as gathering points for those interested in getting involved in telework. Firms rarely advertised positions. Rather, openings were communicated by word of mouth, or additional employees were hired through temporary employment agencies. The temporary agencies drew on the lists of those "available for telework" generated at the job fairs, where people were invited to fill out a form listing their qualifications and contact information. The forms were entered into a database that was used as a means of hiring new employees, but also as a marketing tool for the business development association to use in its efforts to attract more call centers to the locality. The local job fair played an important role in the social construction of call-center work, as it was an opportunity for firms and economic development agencies to represent telework as steady, professional, and desirable employment.

LIVES ON THE LINE: TELEPHONE WORKERS IN CANADA

The globalization script thus is largely a structural account of current transformations; it requires that governments and firms alike heed the chorus of competitiveness, productivity, and restraint. The voices of workers are not being heard over this chorus. These workers are not even considered actors in the dominant understandings of this global drama. They are more like the "set"—pieces already out onstage, to be moved around during the action. The script limits spaces in which new actors might emerge and other stories might be told. It reduces the agency of both workers and governments. The remainder of this chapter is an attempt to revise the script to include workers' descriptions of themselves and their careers in relation to their understanding of this reorganized job market.

The differences between local labor markets in New Brunswick and Toronto suggest that one cannot evaluate current macro-level processes of corporate and government restructuring without also attending to the ways in which they intersect with specific local situations. The very meaning and function of telework in people's lives varied among study sites according to different social and cultural contexts, as well as in the ways firms and governments represented the work. As teleworkers' accounts will show, the shift to telework involves more than a structural account of the low road to labor flexibility. Rather, this research provides support for the view that the current process of economic transformation, of which telework is a small but significant piece, is as much the outcome of ongoing accommodations and conflicts among locally situated social actors as it is the product of structural forces. In Canada, individual teleworkers, in daily efforts to realize their aspirations of meaningful employment and utilize skills in marginalized and devalued jobs, are retelling, but also rewriting, the story of flexible labor.

The stories of the telephone workers with whom I spoke frequently revealed a tension between immediate needs and longer-term aspirations. People cope with the everyday stresses of this work in the short term because it helps to pay the bills, while hoping that someday they will get beyond it to something better. A feeling of ambivalence runs through these diverse accounts. As with Cindy, too often the benefit of having a job is counterbalanced by the everyday struggle to stick with work that can be monotonous, mind-numbing, emotionally draining and highly monitored. Although some telephone work may offer full-time hours and pay better than the minimum wage, it shares many characteristics with jobs that are lower on the economic ladder. Certainly, in the tenacity with which they cling to both their current opportunities and hopes for the future, many of the telephone workers interviewed revealed commonalities with other low-wage workers.[19] This section looks more closely at three aspects of these interviews that reveal the links between call-center employment and low-wage work more generally: the circumstances that push people into telephone work; the personal impact of such routinized and monitored work; and the potential for telephone workers to realize a life after telework.

Telephone Work as a "Last Resort"

Most telework requires little more than basic keyboarding skills and the ability to talk on the phone. Many interviewees explained that they had turned to the work after other avenues had failed because it was not difficult to get hired. As one woman in Winnipeg put it, "There's a lot of companies. . . . You can go through the newspaper any day and within an hour have a job phoning people, as a telemarketer, either selling furnace cleanings or carpet cleanings. . . . A lot of them are starting at $5.45—minimum wage, and people are taking the jobs because, you know, they need to work so they're taking the jobs." Jane started working in teleservice after her retail employer went bankrupt and she had been unemployed for several months. She described it as "a last resort." She had dropped off over a hundred resumes, but at that time in Winnipeg (just after Christmas), "It was next to impossible to get a job. . . . [I was out of work] I think four months, and then somebody suggested Survey Research because they'll hire anybody and everybody, so I thought, well, I've tried everywhere else, so I'll try that, and lo and behold, I became a Survey Research worker."

At first she was pleased with the work, because the wage was a bit above the minimum (though approximately what she had made at her previous retail sales job), but it soon "lost its appeal."[20] For others, telework offers a way out of a difficult situation, or a step up the employment ladder. Anthony, for example, now in his midtwenties, started doing telework part time for extra cash in a survey research firm when he was sixteen, while also working at McDonald's. When he graduated from high school, he took on full-time hours at the survey research firm so that he could get out of a difficult living situation at home. Looking back, Anthony understood that not going to the university limited his longer-term options, but he defended his choice as the right one.

> I just didn't think [going to the university] was viable considering that my home situation was a mess. If I'd gone to school and kept working at Survey Research part time, I wouldn't have been able to afford to move out on my own. The idea was that I was going to stay at my dad's place, despite these family problems, and go to school. To me, that was just absurd. Not that it would totally hinder me, but it would have an effect. . . . It made more sense to me to branch out on my own and get an apartment, work full time and just take it from there.[21]

Angela, who had been working night shifts as a baker at a donut shop for many years for minimum wage, had been fired from her last position without cause. Rather than attempting to bring a complaint against her employer, she shortly found a telemarketing position through a friend. Angela said she was happy about the change as telework paid more, she worked daytime shifts, and the work environment was an improvement over her baking jobs. She also enjoyed working with her mostly female coworkers at the call center better than the male cohort with whom she had worked previously.[22] In Winnipeg, a relatively large number of gay youth worked in a couple of large outbound centers. Telework offered some of these youth an opportunity both to live on their own and connect with the downtown gay community through their new coworkers.

Outbound call centers, particularly in Winnipeg, tended both to rely on a high proportion of part-time employees and on young people.[23] Many youth reported that telework was a way to pay some bills while going to the university. Many kinds of phone work—survey research and telemarketing in particular—have short flexible shifts that are easily worked around school or other obligations. That these jobs usually are part time is an advantage rather than a shortcoming for students who need extra cash. Some firms encourage hiring student employees, particularly when a firm's work fluctuations fit well with the academic calendar.[24]

Although the work can be very useful for those youth who want or need part-time shifts, others have found themselves trapped in call-center work at the beginning of their working lives, with few alternatives later on. Moreover, when one has no other economic assistance, to try to support oneself and go to school on call-center wages can be daunting. One twenty-year-old, Jane, told us that after several years of telework and living on her own, she thought she had "missed the boat" on getting an education.

> I know it's a job that I got because I couldn't get another job or because it's a real slack job, and it didn't encourage me to go any further as a young person, like I didn't go to school, which I should have done because I thought I could do this as a job.[25]

Later in the interview, Jane talked about how the part-time evening shifts fit in well with the "party" lifestyle that she and many of her teleworking friends found easy to slip into.

> You know, I had the whole day to sleep, and it was only five hours out of my life every day, and I made super good money, and I think I lost a lot of time doing that, and I can guarantee that this is the same way that a lot of the people at Survey Research think because I'm friends with a lot of those people, and I would go and party with a lot of those people. Like it's the same thing, and once you get in that cycle it's not helping anybody. I think it set me back a lot because I didn't have a goal, and what's my life? I could make money and I could do good and I could save and I could buy a house and I could do all these great things, but I wasn't becoming a better person. I wasn't getting any professional training in anything.

Jane's regrets about missed opportunities might be easy to dismiss as the product of individual lack of initiative. Yet others in very different circumstances frequently echoed the sense of ambivalence that is at the heart of Jane's comments. An older teleworker, also in Winnipeg, said,

> I've always felt exploited doing that kind of work, but yet, in another sense, it is work, and it's very flexible work, and it's there if you want it, and if you don't want it, then give it to somebody else. You don't have to be forced to take it.[26]

That most people choose telework with some awareness of its limits is true, but they often do so under circumstances of considerable social and financial constraint. The lack of real alternatives also can keep many in telephone work much longer than they had anticipated or would have hoped.

UNSKILLED LABOR?

Lisa is a twenty-two-year-old woman from Cape Breton Island, an economically depressed region in the province of Nova Scotia.[27] Unemployment levels there, since the decline of the coal mining industry two decades ago, have been steady at about 20 percent. Eighteen months prior to our interview, unemployed, Lisa made the eight-hour trip to Fredericton, New Brunswick, in a last-ditch effort to find work. Within a few weeks, someone at her church told her that a large corporation, which had recently consolidated its national call-center operations in the city, was hiring. She applied for the job, was hired immediately, and within a couple of weeks was working the phones as a customer service representative. She considers herself very fortunate, since her workplace is unionized and offers good wages (up to $15 per hour), benefits, and job security well beyond that found in most similar workplaces in the province.

Nonetheless, Lisa was close to quitting her job because of what she described as the "constant negative" that made up her working day. In a year and a half of taking dozens of calls a day, she said, only three people said something positive about the service. People were regularly abusive to her on the phone. Most of the time she did not have the authority to provide real assistance to customers. Handling irate callers often left her "pretty frustrated" and a "ball of tension." While difficult callers seemed to be the primary source of her work stress, the workplace itself did not seem set up to help. Lisa described the working environment as "very Big-Brotherish. You needed an identification card to get into the locked office. Once inside, the workday was highly regulated. One had to account for every minute."

At Lisa's workplace, once a person logged onto the computer, a record was made of the entire day. Like most other call centers, performance was evaluated in part through monitoring telephone calls. Lisa had received some negative reviews from her supervisors, and not much encouragement. While she made an effort to put a positive spin on her experience at the call center ("I'm tougher now; I don't get intimidated easily"), Lisa felt that it was only a matter of time before she would have to move on. "I don't think of myself as a quitter, but I want a future in my job."

When I returned six months later to speak with her again, Lisa was still working at the same teleservice position. She was also still trying to leave. For Lisa, "the money's a trap" that so far had kept her in a highly stressful, dead-end job. She was certain that her stress levels, after two years on the job, had begun to affect her life outside work. "I don't talk the same, I say things backwards, I can't think of words, I can't think clearly . . . that's not me." The company refused a request for unpaid leave, which she had hoped would give her some time to look for another job, without the insecurity of quitting. She now felt that her only alternative was to take stress leave, even though she thought it would reflect badly on her as a person. "I feel like a loser because I'm only twenty-two and I already have to take stress leave. . . . I feel less of a person, I feel like I can't handle life or something." Lisa said she was a person who believed in looking on the bright side. Yet despite the job security and comfortable pay she admittedly enjoyed at the call center, for her to be optimistic about the two years she had spent there was difficult. "I wish there was more positive to say about it, but it hasn't changed at all."

Lisa's narrative highlights the demanding nature of the emotional and interpersonal labor required by even inbound call-center work. The requirements go beyond the simple, unflaggable projection of a friendly telephone persona to the necessity of being able to "read" callers, anticipate their needs and expectations, and develop the ability to defuse (or at least "handle") difficult, angry, or unreasonable customers ("irates"). Some service representatives appear to be dramatically more effective at dealing with irates than others. People doing this work also appear to vary significantly in the extent to which negative calls affect them. Those workers who could establish a degree of emotional distance between themselves and callers appeared to be the least likely to experience overwhelming stress. Lisa, who describes herself as a "sensitive person," is an example of someone who, over time, found the work of dealing with irate callers to be increasingly draining, even as she reportedly improved at handling them.

While telephone jobs initially are attractive because they're flexible, easily obtained, and generally pay better than the minimum-wage alternatives, many workers such as Lisa quickly find that these jobs are far more demanding and stressful than they had anticipated. One of the reasons for this reaction is that telephone work, like much interactive service work that includes expectations about the performance of emotional labor, seems to have a much more direct impact on the employee's sense of self. Some (particularly young people) reported that they experience this aspect of the job as empowering, because they learned not to let anything get to them or can handle themselves better in difficult situations. Many others, however, such as Lisa, find the work to be full of dilemmas and confrontations that demean and undermine their sense of self.

Emotional Labor and the Gendering of Telephone Work

Dealing with difficult callers is one issue in which gendered differences in telephone service work experience seemed to emerge in individual interviews. Yet these personal differences must be seen in the context of how the work is socially constructed and understood. While the gender breakdown varies somewhat across work sites and sectors of the industry (men being much better represented in telemarketing, finance, and technology-related firms), this study revealed that women make up a substantial majority of the call-center workforce in each of the sites within Canada.[28] This is not surprising, given existing research on the feminization of low-wage labor markets in Canada and elsewhere (Armstrong and Armstrong 1994; Duffy and Pupo 1992; Jensen 1989, 1996). Although some suggest that transformations brought about by information technologies might serve to break down perceived boundaries between men and women's white-collar work, this has not happened in call-center work (Webster 1993; Belt, Richardson and Webster 1999). Rather, existing gendered hierarchies have become reinscribed in new positions and restructured work sites (McDowell 1991, 1997).

One of the mechanisms through which this process of reinscription has taken place in telephone sales, and service work in particular, is through the performative aspects of the job. Employees must enact scripts that reflect social expectations and assumptions, many of which have a significantly gendered nature. Studies of flight attendants and waitresses illustrate ways in which the social understandings about "good service" require workers to "do gender" by showing deference through accepting treatment as a subordinate, smiling, and flirting (Hall 1993; Hochschild 1983). Arlie Hochschild, in her influential study of flight attendants, described this performative, gendered, and largely invisible work as *emotional labor*. Emotional labor brings into focus one of the least visible ways in which women's social roles in their private lives are extrapolated into workplace expectations, so that they become required but not compensable. Just as women have been socialized into managing the emotional dimensions of their personal relationships, it is expected that they will voluntarily perform these functions in the workplace as well.

Work in the call centers, whether teleservice or telemarketing, is gendered in this way. The only difference is the narrow bandwidth of the method of communication. Call-center workers must have the ability to immediately communicate a friendly, helpful, and professional demeanor in a few spoken words. The work involved in projecting friendliness over the phone appears to be quite similar to that described in studies of waitresses and flight attendants, where a key component of the job is the ability to continue to smile regardless of how you feel or how others treat you. One call-center employee said that workers were told to smile while they were speaking to customers on the phone because it would make them sound friendlier. She said that she believed that it did work, and if she were having trouble with a particular caller, she would silently ask herself whether she was smiling. Not only must workers be able to sound friendly on the phone, they also must continue to be friendly when unhappy or upset customers complain and criticize, enacting the script of the deferential servant over the phone. Moreover, as in waitressing, call-center work apparently involves a component of scripted flirtation. Several young women, each of whom was a top performer in a telemarketing position, admitted that they were most successful in selling to men and that they used a different tone of voice for men and women. The pitch for men was higher, more singsong, and definitely more flirtatious; the pitch for women was lower, firm, and businesslike. One of these women had been told by her boss that she ought to pursue a career in "phone sex" because of the "seductive" quality of her voice. She quit telemarketing shortly thereafter.[29]

The gendered quality of telephone work is also reflective of wider trends in low-wage work. Not surprisingly, in Toronto, youth and recent immigrants also found themselves disproportionately represented in these feminized jobs. A significant amount of gender segregation appears within telephone work, with men concentrated in higher-paying technical or financial-oriented positions and women being disproportionately represented in frontline customer service and sales positions.[30] All of these divisions reveal the extent to which low-wage labor markets are socially produced: they are the effects of institutions and practices that divide, sort, and channel people's opportunities by race, gender, class, and age. The social processes by which labor is feminized—far from becoming less relevant in contemporary labor markets—are seamlessly woven into corporate decision making through the economic calculus of labor costs and productive benefits. Yet this calculus hardly conceals its underlying gendered assumptions: what it means to "give good service" and the difference between valuable *skills* and natural *attributes* that enables employers to describe these jobs as unskilled.

HIDDEN TALENTS: THE MISRECOGNIZED
SKILLS OF CALL-CENTER WORKERS

Despite the large number of call-center employees who reported that they found their jobs both stressful and monotonous, many of the younger employees responded positively to questioning about what they had learned from their call-center experience. One twenty-year-old woman reported that, after a year and a half of teleservice, the way she "deals with people" dramatically improved for the better (see note 27). In particular, she said that she could "no longer be intimidated, easily or at all," and that she was "tougher." After describing the pettiness of some of the customer complaints, she added that little things didn't bug her anymore. She had learned to expect to be treated with courtesy by customer service agents with whom she dealt. A twenty-one-year-old man reported that he enjoyed learning how to establish a professional, yet human, connection with the people with whom he spoke during the day.[31] He was a bilingual francophone from Moncton, and had learned to "tone down" his Acadian accent in a professional context. Irate calls were his favorites, he said, because he had become very effective at calming people down.

Call-center work thus calls for a number of interpersonal competencies that in other contexts (such as international diplomacy or business negotiation) indeed might be considered skills. Although firms and employees clearly are aware of a range of skills required for the delivery of high-quality customer service, the work continues to be referred to and understood by all as low-skilled labor. Since call-center work requires the development and use of interpersonal skills—including work I've described as emotional labor—both workers and employers understand it in terms of personal development rather than job skills. This assumption reveals another process by which work is gendered—the distinction between skill and talent (Jensen 1989). While work typically performed by men is identified as requiring certain kinds of skills, what women do is more often described as the utilization of their so-called natural talents. "Many of the skills which women demonstrate in their work—patience, consideration, friendliness, supportiveness, et cetera—are too often regarded as personal attributes" (Poynton 1993, 167). Moreover, the perception of women's competencies in the workplace is further eroded by equating certain functions they perform with female roles in the private sphere—the secretary as "office wife" being the prime example (Webster 1993, 1996).

This gendered misidentification of skill in call centers also means that firms are more inclined to undervalue quality service in favor of efficiency in the organization of call-center work. While some firms now attribute more value to quality customer service in terms of how they organize work and evaluate their employees, this has not translated directly into higher wages for workers, although it may have a significant effect on job satisfaction and working conditions. Other firms exacerbate job stress by binding employees between the competing demands of satisfying the customer and minimizing talk time, and penalizing employees who take extra time with a difficult customer or to help a colleague.

Another implication of failing to recognize skills developed in the call-center workplace is the failure to promote call-center employees to other positions within the firm. Anthony, introduced earlier as someone who had started telephone research part-time at age sixteen, found himself without further options for advancement at age twenty-five. Eight years later, he remains with the company, now a full-time supervisor, but still only making about a dollar per hour more than the frontline callers. Anthony had applied for a number of other positions within the firm without success.[32]

I got the impression that it was basically because I had long hair and didn't conform to any kind of appearance standards that are somewhat backhandedly enforced in the sense that they hire their own. Their own are the people who wear starched shirts and blue jeans. That's about as casual as they'll get. They'll wear their shirt and tie and they'll be wearing blue jeans too and sneakers. I've pretty much been told—not told directly—indirectly that because I don't have any university aspirations in terms of market research courses and because I don't have any university period because I decided to work full-time for the company that I'm not qualified for a variety of positions which they've given to other people who have less qualifications than me and some who haven't even gone to university.

The first step in having call-center employees' skills more effectively utilized and compensated is to name and recognize them as such. An example where work-related skills of call-center employees were made visible to an employer occurred in Toronto in a recent successful union drive at a telemarketing center. One key organizer explained how she and her colleagues were able to succeed in signing up the requisite number of employees in their workplace, despite serious opposition from their employer:

> We are telemarketers, right? We were using telemarketing techniques to sign people up! What better people. It got to the point where there were so many people we were signing up that we had almost like a script. . . . We used good selling techniques, so we would explain the situation to people, tell them how urgent it was, make them feel as if they were involved in something special, that's another technique. Tell them this is the first telemarketing center in Canada to have an organizing drive . . . you could just sort of figure out who you were dealing with and find their Achilles' Heel and use it.[33]

Unfortunately, the opportunities for most call-center employees to better utilize their capacities is limited by the structure of the industry and the dominant forms of workplace organization. Although most express a desire to move on to other, more rewarding work, their ability to realize these aspirations is likely to be similarly constrained.

EVERYDAY STRESSES AND SURVIVAL STRATEGIES

Individuals who did telephone work for any length of time developed myriad strategies for managing job stress or at least ameliorating its impact on their well-being and sense of self. These strategies were highly individual; for many, they simply amounted to certain ways of thinking about the work or representing it to others, while others manifested more concrete forms of subversion or resistance in how they performed the work and dealt with employers. While leaving was an option for some, most telephone workers opted for safer and more private techniques for everyday survival. Some developed a critical and evocative appreciation of the organization and mechanics of the workplace, describing the work in terms of "performance," or more vividly, as prostitution. Rosa, the call-center employee turned union organizer quoted earlier, described her relationship to workplace technology in terms of the *standing reserve*, that is, in Heidegger's (1977) words, "things that are not even regarded as objects, because their only important quality has become their readiness for use."[34] As Rosa put it, "you are standing waiting until that call comes in to use you to make money. And you are simply another part of that machine."

In addition to hidden expectations for the performance of emotional labor, firms often create more explicit conflicts for employees. For example, in outbound call-center work, supervisors commonly pressure employees to meet steep quotas. In telefundraising, this may include expectations about how much money to request from potential donors. Asking for large amounts from people whose income may be limited, such as senior citizens, did not sit well with many employees. Some simply set their own expectations and settled for fewer bonuses. Others found that their unwillingness to engage in high-pressure sales tactics jeopardized their jobs.[35]

When asked for comparisons between telemarketing and other types of work performed, employees often ranked phone work below waitering or retail sales. The difference seemed to lie in the greater scope for authenticity in the interpersonal relations of in-person service jobs. The scripted and monitored nature of telephone work led employees to feel that they were unable to "be themselves" at work. This usually was reinforced by the organization of work space and how call centers were managed. Employees generally had very little room for autonomy or individuality. Dress codes were common, despite the fact that employees were not seen by customers. While the extent and nature of supervisory discipline of behavior varied, several people commented that they were disciplined for laughing or talking between calls. Some workplaces allowed workers to read, knit, or draw if work was slow, while at other companies, only firm-related work was permitted. A very few were allowed to personalize their work spaces. One survey research worker commented, "It's almost like the army. It's very regimented. You punch in with a time clock. You come in and sit down, and the numbers are all computerized. As soon as you finish a call, the minute you hang up, another call comes up. It's just this constant, all day, repetitious, . . . constant sort of beating on a drum, but day after day."[36]

The effort to maintain a notion of one's self as a "good employee" or even as a "good person," however, often led people to persist in unsatisfactory workplace conditions. Lisa persisted in a job with which she was struggling because she knew she had no better options, but also because she "wasn't a quitter." Another woman, who was consistently the highest performer at her insurance sales center, put up with significantly lower pay than she knew she was entitled to as an insurance agent, because for her, "money wasn't the issue," it was doing the work well that mattered.[37] Although this perspective was most pronounced in New Brunswick, many call-center workers were anxious to be seen and to see themselves as good workers and reasonable people. The extent to which this impulse might work to the employer's benefit was observed by another woman working part-time shifts at a financial services firm that routinely sent workers home halfway through their shift if work was slow, even though many commute significant distances:

> But I guess I think companies owe—I think people are going more than halfway. The employees are good people, you know, they don't want the sun and the earth. There are just some things that would be fairer. They wouldn't say that, I don't think. So, I have been sitting on the fence watching, but people are pretty happy—I think the potential is there to abuse the situation.[38]

Among some workers, reluctance to complain may stem as much from fear of reprisal as from a general attitude of acceptance. Most call centers are not unionized and make no secret of their hostility toward the idea of unionization.

Although many might agree that unionization could improve conditions, one employee observed, "They're so afraid of that word because immediately they think they are going to lose their job if they talk union at all."[39] Fear and skepticism concerning the benefits of unionization appeared to be strongest in New Brunswick, where a recent history of polarized labor relations has left a negative impression on the province's young people.[40] Unfortunately, fears regarding job security and the Panopticon-like nature of the workplace leaves most call center workers isolated in both their critical analysis and symbolic acts of resistance.

Call-Center Careers?

Call centers tend to have a high rate of employee turnover. One of the driving forces behind locating centers in more remote areas is to obtain a more secure and stable workforce. This has been successful to some extent in the New Brunswick example, where new centers report lower rates of turnover than existing centers in other locations. Yet only one of the interview subjects had worked full-time at a call center for longer than three years, and that was in a supervisory capacity. Most people do not seem able to do telephone work indefinitely, even if they start out thinking they can. The story of Lois, a former telemarketer, is an extreme but illuminating case in point.

Lois is fifty years old and had worked at a number of other jobs, including restaurant manager and real estate agent.[41] For a little over a year, Lois worked thirty hours a week at an outbound center for $7.50 per hour with no benefits, but with the possibility of earning a few hundred extra dollars in bonuses for high performance. Her employer was an American-owned telemarketing company that obtained most of its contracts from large retail firms. For Lois, this meant two years of selling insurance to credit card customers of one of those firms. Although she had taken the initiative to become licensed as an insurance agent, the company refused to pay her at an agent's rate ($11 per hour) despite the fact that she would then be able to "verify" all of her own calls.[42]

Lois was one of her company's top performers and a loyal employee. The first time I spoke with her, she had been hand-picked by her manager for the interview. She was a model employee. Lois had few complaints about the management, wages, or working conditions. She claimed that working hard at a job she is good at is more important to her than the money. This is why she continued to work at the telemarketing firm, with no plans to quit or look elsewhere, even though she admitted she was not being adequately compensated for the insurance-agent work she was doing.

The second time I spoke with Lois, she was no longer working with the telemarketing firm. She had started a small home business selling candles and associated ornaments and was making approximately twice the income of her call-center job, with far less effort. Her doctor had advised against continuing at the call center after she collapsed at work from high blood pressure and was taken to the hospital on a stretcher.

> I had no lunch. They didn't allow us any lunch that day. It was too busy. See, they were just seeing dollar signs. Sales, sales, sales like crazy. . . . And the next thing I knew, I just went to Cathy and I said, "Cathy, I can't. . . . I gotta go outside, I gotta go outside." Oh, I didn't want to go, but I had to, I couldn't handle it. . . . So anyway I went out there and leaned against the next building—just to get some fresh air. I had to get some fresh air. So then I got that I could hardly stand up, so I came back inside and sat down on the stairs. And that was it. I just passed right out. And then I couldn't talk. . . . I was that close to a stroke . . . my doctor told me not to go back. He said, "You just can't." He said, "If you want to kill yourself, you go back."[43]

Lois's experience is uncommon, although many of the people who work in call centers report that they soon begin to find the work stressful. Even in "good" centers, with pleasant surroundings, well-designed work stations, and adequate rest breaks, the combination of monotony and the emotional strain of dealing with high numbers of irate callers can lead to burnout within a few years for many competent and willing workers.

Within the last decade in Canada, new approaches to labor market policy, emerging local economic development strategies, and the reorganization of firms have functioned to produce new markets for low-wage workers, particularly in sites such as New Brunswick and Manitoba. A market-oriented approach to labor policy would evaluate these developments as unequivocal successes; firms have found workers, and workers have found jobs. Yet this chapter has sought to establish another foundation on which to evaluate the social utility of these low-wage labor markets, using the accounts of workers themselves. Evaluating work from the perspective of those who do it reveals a number of troubling issues particular to low-wage service work at the end of the century.

Much of the frontline service work performed by low-wage workers, including teleworkers, is both highly routinized and monitored. Employees are given little or no autonomy, and yet firms hire them to act as a lubricant, smoothing out the rough spots between the corporate need for profitability and the public's demand for service. Telemarketing employees face even more friction as they invade people's homes for the purpose of selling their companies' products on commission. The emotional and interpersonal demands of these positions are large, yet the employees themselves are considered unskilled. They operate at the geographic and organizational margins of the corporate hierarchy and have only limited opportunities to gain transferable job skills or move to a better position within the firm. Job security is limited, benefits often are nonexistent, and the hours are either shifts, highly variable, part-time, or all three. The routinization of the work means predictability for employers but stress, monotony, and eventual burnout for employees. Further, wage and scheduling flexibility for employers translates into uncertainty and insecurity for low-wage employees, making it difficult for individuals to keep friends, find day care, pay their rent, or go to school.

A troubling backdrop to routinization and flexibility, which have become central features of the low-wage employment landscape, is the fact that policy makers seem not to have grasped its inherent contradictions. The highly demanding nature of "unskilled" work and severe personal and financial constraints imposed by "flexible" employment simply are not parts of the dominant policy discourse. Although call centers, for example, have become highly visible on the policy horizon as the targets of local economic development strategies, the only independent studies commissioned have been comparative cost estimates designed to encourage firms to make relocation decisions. When this project was undertaken, no information was publicly available on the gender and age composition of the call-center workforce. The difficult situations that lead many young people, most often women, into telework is not considered, nor are the workplace environments that lead so many to quit or lose their jobs within a year or two. Very few of those interviewed maintained they could imagine themselves doing such work full-time for more than a couple of years. Some suggested that the companies depend on the high turnover to keep their phones supplied with eager and productive newcomers. Strategies for dealing with the problem of high turnover (where policy makers acknowledge it) fail to identify the sources of the problems in the workplaces themselves. Rather, they focus on facilitating employers' recruitment among particular groups, notably high school students, or on developing community college training programs, which function more as recruitment avenues for firms than as training centers.

This chapter has argued that the problems of the low-wage worker have been exacerbated by the responses of both governments and firms to the perceived dictates of globalization. In response to dominant understandings of the globalization script, restructuring firms and retrenching governments have operated in concert to produce the flexible, yet predictable, frontline worker who is the mainstay of the new service economy. Although we have few tools at our disposal for appreciating the social costs of this convergence of purpose, the accounts herein at least have revealed some of the ways in which opportunities are lost, skills are misrecognized, and aspirations are crushed in these workplaces. In bringing together first-person accounts of low-wage work with dominant understandings of the globalization script, this chapter illuminates the inherent contradictions embedded within current approaches and challenges scholars and policy makers to continue the effort to produce alternative scripts in which both the perspectives and personhood of low-wage workers are recognized.

I would like to thank the call center workers who participated in the study for their insights and generosity, all those who commented on earlier versions of this chapter, and in particular, Frank Munger for his dedication to the project and careful review of several drafts. The fieldwork was supported by the Canadian Institute for Advanced Research, the Law Foundation of New Brunswick, and the Status of Women Canada Policy Research Fund. Sarah Koch-Schulte provided valuable assistance with both research and fieldwork.

NOTES

1. Cindy is a pseudonym for a call-center worker interviewed by the author in December 1997, St. John, New Brunswick (hereafter all names given for interviewees are pseudonyms).

2. Nonstandard jobs accounted for 33 percent of total employment in Canada in 1994, up from 28 percent in 1989 (Lowe 1999).

3. The term *teleworker* is used to identify collectively those whose work is performed primarily over the telephone, whether answering questions or providing services to callers who have requested them over a 1–800 number (inbound), or using the phone to make sales, perform surveys, or raise money for charities (outbound). Along with Heather Menzies, I make a distinction between *telework* and *telecommuting*, using the latter to refer to those who work outside a central office at their own discretion (see Menzies 1997).

4. This chapter draws on approximately sixty interviews with telephone workers in Moncton, St. John, Fredericton, Toronto, and Winnipeg conducted between June 1996 and July 1998. The interviews were conducted with Sarah Koch-Schulte as part of a larger study, funded in part by Status of Women Canada (see Buchanan and Koch-Schulte 2000b).

5. For more detail on local economic development policies in the New Brunswick context see Buchanan 2000.

6. See the excellent chapter by J. K. Gibson-Grahame (1996).

7. The passage (Appadurai 1996) continues,

   No longer mere fantasy (opium for the masses whose real work is elsewhere), no longer simple escape (from a world defined principally by more concrete purposes and structures), no longer elite pastime (thus not relevant to the lives of ordinary people), and no longer mere contemplation (irrelevant for new forms of desire and subjectivity), the imagination has become an organized field of social practices, a form of work (in the sense of both labor and culturally organized practice), and a form of negotiation between sites of agency (individuals) and globally defined fields of possibility.

8. One executive is quoted in an industry journal praising the province for its marketing prowess, "The province [of New Brunswick] and NB Tel probably have the finest marketing apparatus in North America. . . . They never quit" (Read 1997).

9. This was not always the case. A number of teleworkers employed by large multinationals described how positions were advertised within the firm and identified

the opportunities for advancement as one of the attractions of the position. How often teleworkers actually obtained better positions within their firms and how far those workers were able to advance is less clear from the interviews, which were generally confined to individuals who worked in call centers either in a frontline or supervisory capacity. One individual who had been with a survey research firm in Winnipeg for eight years advised us that despite his experience in training and supervising callers, he had reached the limits of his own advancement at a $10 per hour supervisory job. He identified his lack of postsecondary education and corporate "look" (he had shoulder-length hair that he wore in a small ponytail) as the reasons for his inability to advance further within the company.

10. For a more in-depth examination of the dual impact of information technologies on work see Zuboff 1988.

11. See Zuboff 1988, particularly ch. 9, "The Information Panopticon."

12. For another ethnographic account of feminized back-office work see Freeman 2000.

13. A recent half-page advertisement placed in the *Globe and Mail* by the government of New Brunswick cites a Deloitte and Touche Nacore 1995 Benchmarking Study, "It is not uncommon to achieve labor cost savings of more than 20 percent and real estate cost savings of more than 33 percent by back-officing."

14. Call-center employee, interview with author, July 1996, Fredericton, New Brunswick.

15. Tony, interview with author, 12 June 1997, St. John, New Brunswick.

16. Lisa, interview with author, 6 July 1998, Toronto.

17. Anthony, interview with author, 9 June 1998, Winnipeg.

18. In another article (Buchanan 2000), I elaborate on the intensive effort expended by both the government and the firms on conveying a public perception within New Brunswick of call-center work as "professional." The New Brunswick example reveals the extent to which local labor markets are actively constructed, and how the meaning of work can vary among locations.

19. See Stack, ch. 1, herein.

20. Jane, interview with author, 11 June 1998, Winnipeg.

21. Anthony, interview with author, 9 June 1998, Winnipeg.

22. Angela, interview with author, 12 June 1998, Winnipeg.

23. A survey mailed to personnel managers at all forty call centers in Winnipeg revealed that 45 percent of the employees worked under nonstandard (that is, temporary or part-time) employment contracts; across all study sites the average figure was 38 percent nonstandard employment. Across all study sites and all employment categories, the percentage of youth workers was significant, ranging from a low of 37 percent of full-time workers in Winnipeg to a high of 70 percent of temporary workers in Toronto (Buchanan and Koch-Schulte 2000).

24. One student worked at a hotel reservation call center, where the busy seasons are summer and Christmas, just the times that students are looking for work. Students were not uncommon there and also often were employed by survey research firms.

25. Jane, interview with author, 11 June 1998, Winnipeg.

26. Ellen, interview with author, 12 June 1998, Winnipeg.

27. Interviews with Lisa were conducted by the author in June and December 1997 in Fredericton.

28. Our survey data on the gender composition of call-center workforces was remarkably consistent. Across all categories of employment and locations, the proportions of female workers in call centers ranged from a low of 58 percent (permanent employment in Toronto) to a high of 81 percent (temporary employment in New Brunswick). The average percentage of women working at all sites in each job category was consistently between 70 and 72 percent (Buchanan and Koch-Schulte 2000, 9, and table, 10).

29. Maia, interview with author, 9 July 1998, Toronto.

30. Although the interview sample didn't include very many workers from the higher end of the call-center wage scale, several men with whom we spoke gave us insights into this phenomenon. One twenty-five-year-old man interviewed in New Brunswick worked in a small, all-male network applications "team" within a large call center. In contrast to the other service representatives, his team was permitted a weekly break from the phones to surf the net and download new applications. Another young man, working at a higher-paying mutual funds sales job for a bank in Toronto, also commented on the gender segregation within his workplace. "Its funny, though, because in our call center, it was overwhelmingly male, but that's because I think the supervisors themselves were kind of chauvinistic, admittedly.... They just thought that there were more men first of all, taking these courses, and they would be more experienced and more knowledgeable in investments and how to answer questions regarding money. There were only, when I started, two full-time female reps out of twenty-seven." Benoit, interview with author, 10 July 1998, Toronto.

31. Jacques, interview with author, 12 June 1997, St. John, N.B.

32. Anthony, interview with author, 9 June 1998, Winnipeg.

33. Rosa, interview with author, 18 November 1996, Toronto.

34. Heidegger 1977.

35. See article by Bill Gadsby, "Wrong End of the Line," which states that "asking for overly large donations just demoralizes workers" (Gadsby, Bill. 1996. "Wrong, End of the Line." Now Magazine [August 29]: 23). From clippings provided by Helen in Toronto, 6 July 1998, on file with author.

36. Ellen, interview with author, 18 December 1997, Moncton.

37. Lois, interview with author, November 1996, St. John, New Brunswick. Lois agreed to be interviewed again in December 1997. A more detailed account of Lois's story is provided in the following section.

38. Jill, interview with author, 14 July 1996, St. John, New Brunswick.

39. Moura, interview with author, 13 June 1996, St. John, New Brunswick.

40. For example, an eighteen-month strike by refinery workers against the powerful locally based Irving Corporation ended in the collapse of the union in 1996.

41. Lois, interview with author, 4 November 1996, St. John, New Brunswick.

42. Regulations ordinarily require that sales of insurance are performed by an accredited agent. Telemarketing firms usually hire one or two agents for each shift who will roam the floor and be available to "verify" the sale once the ordinary callers have concluded the deal.

43. Lois, follow-up interview with author, December 1997, St. John, New Brunswick.

REFERENCES

Appadurai, Arjun. 1996. *Modernity at Large: Cultural Dimensions of Globalization.* Minneapolis: University of Minnesota Press.

Appelbaum, Eileen. 1993. "New Technology and Work Organisation: The Role of Gender Relations." In *Pink Collar Blues: Work, Gender and Technology,* edited by Belinda Probert and Bruce Wilson. Melbourne: Melbourne University Press.

Armstrong, Pat, and Hugh Armstrong. 1994. *The Double Ghetto: Canadian Women and their Segregated Work.* 3d ed. Toronto: McLelland and Stewart.

Bakker, Isabella, ed. 1996. *Rethinking Restructuring: Gender and Change in Canada.* Toronto and Buffalo: University of Toronto Press.

———, ed. 1994. *The Strategic Silence: Gender and Economic Policy.* London, UK, and Atlantic Highlands, N.J.: Zed Books/North-South Institute.

Belt, Vicki, Ranald Richardson, and Juliet Webster. 1999. "Smiling Down the Phone: Women's Work in Telephone Call Centers." Presented at the RGS-IBG Annual Conference, University of Leicester. Unpublished paper (on file with author).

Bourdieu, Pierre, and Loic J. D. Wacquant. 1992. *An Invitation to Reflexive Sociology.* Chicago: University of Chicago Press.

Boyer, Robert, and Daniel Drache, eds. 1996. *States Against Markets: The Limits of Globalization.* London and New York: Routledge.

Buchanan, Ruth. 1995a. "Border Crossings: NAFTA, Regulatory Restructuring and the Politics of Place." *Indiana Journal of Global Legal Studies* 2: 371.

———. 1995b. "The Flexible Woman: Gendered Implications of Post-Fordist Narratives." University of Toronto Feminism and Law Working Paper Ser. 95–96(3).

———. 2000. "1–800 New Brunswick: Economic Development Strategies, Firm Restructuring and the Local Production of 'Global' Services." In *Globalizing Institutions: Case Studies in Regulation and Innovation,* edited by Jane Jenson and Boavenutra de Sousa Santos. Aldershot, U.K.: Ashgate.

Buchanan, Ruth, and Sarah Koch-Schulte. 2000. *Gender on the Line: Technology, Restructuring, and the Reorganization of Work in the Call Center Industry.* Ottawa: Status of Women Canada Policy Research.

Casey, Catherine. 1995. *Work, Self and Society: After Industrialism.* London and New York: Routledge.

Castells, Manuel. 1996. *The Rise of the Network Society.* Cambridge, Mass.: Blackwell.

Curtis, James E., Edward G. Grabb, and L. Neil Guppy, eds. 1998. *Social Inequality in Canada: Patterns, Problems, and Policies.* Scarborough, Ontario: Prentice Hall.

Day, Shelagh, and Gwen Brodsky. 1998. *Women and the Equality Deficit: The Impact of Restructuring Canada's Social Programs.* Status of Women Canada Policy Research.

Duffy, Ann, and Noreen Pupo. 1992. *Part-Time Paradox: Connecting Gender, Work and Family.* Toronto: McClelland and Stewart.

Economic Council of Canada. 1990. *Good Jobs, Bad Jobs: Employment in the Service Industry.* Ottawa: Ministry of Supply and Services.

Evans, Patricia. 1993. "From Workfare to the Social Contract: Implications for Canada of Recent U.S. Welfare Reforms." *Canadian Public Policy-Analyse de Politiques* 19(1): 54–67.

Evans, Patricia, and Gerda Wekerle. 1997. *Women and the Canadian Welfare State: Challenges and Change.* Toronto and Buffalo: University of Toronto Press.

Freeman, Carla. 2000. *High Tech and High Heels in the Global Economy: Women, Work and Pink-Collar Identities in the Caribbean.* Durham, N.C.: Duke University Press.

Gibson-Grahame, J. K. 1996. "Querying Globalization." In *The End of Capitalism (as We Knew It): A Feminist Critique of Political Economy,* edited by J. K. Gibson-Grahame. Cambridge, Mass., and Oxford: Blackwell.

Giddens, Anthony. 1990. *The Consequences of Modernity.* Stanford, Calif.: Stanford University Press.

Hall, Elaine. 1993. "Smiling, Deferring and Flirting: Doing Gender by Giving 'Good Service.'" *Work and Occupations* 20: 452–71.

Hanson, Susan, and Geraldine Pratt. 1995. *Gender, Work and Space.* London and New York: Routledge.

Harrison, Bennett. 1994. *Lean and Mean: The Changing Landscape of Corporate Power in the Age of Flexibility.* New York: Basic Books.

Harvey, David. 1993. "From Space to Place and Back Again: Reflections on the Condition of Postmodernity." In *Mapping the Futures: Local Culture, Global Change,* edited by Jon Bird, Barry Curtis, Tim Putnam, George Robertson, and Lisa Tickner. London/New York: Routledge.

Heidegger, Martin. 1977. *The Question Concerning Technology and Other Essays.* New York: Harper and Row.

Hirst, Paul, and John Zeitlin. 1992. "Flexible Specialization Versus Post-Fordism: Theory, Evidence and Policy Implications." In *Pathways to Industrialization and Regional Development,* edited by Michael Storper and Alan John Scott. London and New York: Routledge.

Hochschild, Arlie Russell. 1983. *The Managed Heart: Commercialization of Human Feeling,* Berkeley: University of California Press.

Jensen, Jane. 1989. "The Talents of Women, the Skills of Men: Flexible Specialization and Women." In *The Transformation of Work? Skill, Flexibility and the Labour Process,* edited by Stephen Wood. London and Boston: Unwin Hyman.

———. 1996. "Part-Time Employment and Women: Range of Strategies." In *Rethinking Restructuring: Gender and Change in Canada,* edited by Isabella Bakker. Toronto and Buffalo: University of Toronto Press.

Johnson, Andrew F., Stephen McBride, and Patrick J. Smith, eds. 1994. *Continuities and Discontinuities: The Political Economy of Social Welfare and Labor Market Policy in Canada.* Toronto and Buffalo: University of Toronto Press.

Kassab, Cathy, and A. E. Luloff. 1993. "The New Buffalo Hunt: Chasing the Service Sector." *Journal of the Community Development Society* 24: 175–95.

Lamphere, Louis, Helena Ragone, and Patricia Zavella, eds. 1997. *Situated Lives: Gender and Culture in Everyday Life.* New York: Routledge.

Lash, Scott, and John Urry. 1994. *Economies of Signs and Space.* London and Thousand Oaks, Calif.: Sage.

Leidner, Robin. 1993. *Fast Food, Fast Talk: Service Work and the Routinization of Everyday Life.* Berkeley: University of California Press.

Lowe, Grahame S. 1999. "Labor Markets, Inequality, and the Future of Work." In *Social Inequality in Canada: Patterns, Problems, and Policies,* edited by James E. Curtis, Edward G. Grabb, and L. Neil Guppy. Scarborough, Ontario: Prentice Hall.

Massey, Doreen. 1994. *Space, Place and Gender.* Minneapolis: University of Minnesota Press.

McDowell, Linda. 1991. "Life Without Father and Ford: The New Gender Order of Post-Fordism." *Transactions: Institute of British Geographers* 16: 400–19.

———. 1997. *Capital Culture: Gender at Work in the City.* Oxford and Malden, Mass: Blackwell.

Menzies, Heather. 1997. "Telework, Shadow Work: The Privatization of Work in the New Digital Economy." *Studies in Political Economy* 53: 103–23.

Milne, William. 1995. "Regional Development Policies: Time for New Solutions." *Policy Options* 16: 31–35.

Peck, Jamie. 1996. *Work-Place: The Social Regulation of Labor Markets.* New York: Guilford Press.

Piore, Michael, and Charles Sabel. 1984. *The Second Industrial Divide: Possibilities for Prosperity.* New York: Basic Books.

Pollert, Anna. 1988. "Dismantling Flexibility." *Capital and Class* 34: 42.

Poynton, Cate. 1993. "Naming Women's Workplace Skills: Linguistics and Power." In *Pink Collar Blues: Work, Gender and Technology,* edited by Belinda Probert and Bruce Wilson. Melbourne: Melbourne University Press.

Read, Brendan. 1997. "Good Location Buys in Boom Times." *Call Center Magazine,* August: 58.

Sabel, Charles. 1995. "Bootstrapping Reform: Rebuilding Firms, the Welfare State and Unions." *Politics and Society* 23: 5.

———. 1991. "Moebius Strip Organizations and Open Labor Markets: Some Consequences of the Reintegration of Conception and Execution in a Volatile Economy." In *Social Theory for a Changing Society,* edited by Pierre Bourdieu and James Coleman. Boulder, Colo.: Westview Press.

Sassen, Saskia. 1996. *Losing Control? Sovereignty in an Age of Globalization.* New York: Columbia University Press.

———. 1995. "When the State Encounters a New Space Economy: The Case of Information Industries." *American Journal of International Law and Policy* 10: 769.

Streeck, Wolfgang. 1996. "Public Power Beyond the Nation-State." In *States Against Markets: The Limits of Globalization,* edited by Robert Boyer and Daniel Drache. London and New York: Routledge.

Twining, William. 2000. *Globalization and Legal Theory.* London: Butterworths.

Webster, Juliet. 1993. "From the Word Processor to the Micro: Gender Issues in the Development of Information Technology in the Office." In *Gendered by Design? Information Technology and Office Systems,* edited by Eileen Green, Jenny Owen, and Den Pain. London and Washington, D.C.: Taylor and Francis.

———. 1996. *Shaping Women's Work: Gender, Employment and Information Technology.* London and New York: Longman.

Wharton, Amy. 1993. "The Affective Consequences of Service Work." *Work and Occupations* 20: 205–32.

Wilson, Patricia. 1996. "Future Directions in Local Economic Development." In *Local Economic Development in Europe and the Americas,* edited by Christopher Demaziere and Patricia Wilson. London: Mansell.

Zuboff, Shoshana. 1988. *In the Age of the Smart Machine: The Future of Work and Power.* New York: Basic Books.

Commentary

Deconstructing Labor Demand in Today's Advanced Economies: Implications for Low-Wage Employment

Saskia Sassen

T o what extent are employment-based economic insecurity and poverty features of advanced economies? This commentary examines major changes in the organization of economic activity over the last fifteen years that have emerged as a source of general economic insecurity, low-wage jobs, and new forms of employment-centered poverty. Several chapters in this ethnography emphasize the extent to which poverty and economic insecurity are not simply functions of an individual's failings (see Cintrón-Vélez, ch. 4; Edin, Lein, and Nelson, ch. 3; Henly, ch. 5 herein). This volume also examines the extent to which many low-wage workers in dead-end jobs take their jobs seriously, learn and deploy skills (see Stack, ch. 1; Buchanan, ch. 2 herein), and are ready to move up the work ladder, only to find that many such ladders have been eliminated by the new economy.

This is a broad subject. Confining it to the world of employment, we can identify at least three processes constitutive of or contributing to new (and possibly accentuating older) forms of inequality and distance between firms and workers at the bottom of the economic system and those who prosper. While not mutually exclusive, to distinguish them analytically is helpful. These processes are: growing inequality in profit-making capacities of different economic sectors and earnings capacities of different types of workers and households; socioeconomic polarization tendencies resulting from the organization of service industries and casualization of the employment relation; and urban marginality as a result of new structural processes of economic growth, rather than marginality produced through abandonment.

NEW EMPLOYMENT REGIMES

New employment regimes that have emerged in highly developed countries have reconfigured job supply and employment relations. Much analysis of postindustrial society and advanced economies generally posits a massive growth in the need for highly educated workers and little need for the types of jobs that a majority of people described herein are likely to hold. This suggests sharply reduced employment opportunities for these workers. Yet detailed empirical studies—especially of major cities in highly developed countries—show ongoing demand for low-wage workers and a significant supply of old and new jobs requiring little education and paying low wages. Wages in these jobs often are below subsistence standards, as several chapters in this book show (for example, Henly, ch. 5; Edin, Lein, and Nelson, ch. 3 herein).

One issue we need to understand better is whether this job supply is merely or largely a residual, partly inflated by a surfeit of low-wage workers with little if any human capital, or mostly part of the reconfiguration of employment relations that is a feature of advanced service economies. In the second case, the existence of a vast supply of jobs often paying below subsistence levels then would be a systemic development integral to advanced economies, rather than a function of the existence of a large supply of workers with inadequate human capital and an inadequate work ethic.

These conditions have no precise measures. Available evidence tends to consist of standardized measures of job characteristics (wage level and temporal features, such as full-time versus part-time) and workers (formal education, race, gender, age). Most likely the tendency to read more into these two kinds of evidence than is warranted has been unduly strong. One influential interpretation in general commentaries and among policy makers is to assume that workers' characteristics are a key variable explaining employment outcomes. Frequently this has been taken a step further and interpreted as a lack of ambition, the will to learn, or the proper work ethic among these workers. The policy implication is that better workers will reduce the supply of low-wage jobs.

What much of the evidence fails to provide is information about the interaction effects between workers and jobs, or workers and workplace, and how these shape employment outcomes. An important contribution by several chapters herein is the evidence they provide about one kind of interaction effect—specifically, what workers bring to these jobs. The evidence presented here shows that these workers bring skills, the will to learn, aspirations, and eagerness to advance, far more than is commonly understood or expected. Evidence also shows that this is not likely to be measured by employers or captured by the standard measures of job supply and workers' characteristics.

Skills, for example, often are not recognized by employers, nor are they typically captured in the job description, as is made clear in the chapter by Buchanan that focuses on teleworkers. Buchanan demonstrates how these workers must deploy enormous talents to be able to obtain responses from people who have been invaded by an unknown caller in their homes. Further, these teleworkers play a significant intermediary role between the firm's determination to sell and the consumers' notions about what they need or want. The chapter by Stack shows us to what extent the young workers she studied in fast-food restaurants in Oakland and Harlem want to learn and are determined to make the most out of their jobs. Further, Stack shows us that many of these jobs actually require skills and offer learning opportunities, yet that type of workplace leads nowhere, regardless of what individual workers bring to it. These findings also strengthen claims about the importance of participatory community-level research (see Ansley, ch. 7 herein).

To extract the full benefits that ethnographies can produce, we also need to understand some of the broader contextual variables. Several chapters focus on major policies that have affected the condition of low-wage workers, notably the new welfare legislation (Cintrón-Vélez, ch. 4; Henly, ch. 5 herein). Another type of contextual variable (focused on in the following sections) concerns growth dynamics in advanced service economies and, especially, its systemic outcomes in terms of labor demand.

GROWTH DYNAMICS IN ADVANCED SERVICE ECONOMIES

Central to the questions addressed here are the following three processes of economic and spatial organization. One is the expansion and consolidation of the producer services and corporate headquarters sector into the economic core of major cities in highly developed countries. While this sector may not account for the majority of jobs, it establishes a new regime of economic activity and associated spatial and social transformations particularly evident in major cities.

A second process is the downgrading of a broad range of manufacturing sectors, even as some are sharply upgraded, notably the high-tech sector. Downgrading is used here to describe a mode of political and technical reorganization of manufacturing that is distinguished from the decline and obsolescence of manufacturing activities. The downgraded manufacturing sector thus represents incorporation into the postindustrial economy rather than a form of obsolescence. When a growing number of manufacturing firms need to compete with cheap imports, and the profit-making capacities of manufacturing overall are modest compared with those of leading sectors (such as telecommunications or finance and related industries), downgrading is a form of adaptation.

The third process is the informalization of a growing array of economic activities that encompasses certain components of the downgraded manufacturing sector. Informalization too represents a mode of reorganizing production and distribution of goods and services: under conditions where a significant number of firms have an effective local demand for their goods and services, but cannot compete with cheap imports or for space and other business needs with the new high-profit firms engendered by the advanced corporate service economy. Escaping the regulatory apparatus of the formal economy enhances the economic opportunities of such firms.

Whether articulation and feedback effects exist among these different sectors is important. If articulation exists among the different economies and labor markets embedded in them, we may need to rethink some basic propositions about the postindustrial economy. Whether, for instance, the economy needs only highly educated workers, or whether informalization and downgrading are just a Third World import through immigration or an anachronistic remnant of an earlier era. The argument here is that we are seeing new employment regimes in services-dominated urban economies that create low-wage jobs and do not require particularly high levels of education. Politically and theoretically this points to an employment context wherein low-wage jobs are a systemic development in the advanced urban economy.

High-level business services, from accounting to decision-making expertise, are not usually analyzed as a production process or a work process. Such services are seen as a type of output that is high-level technical knowledge. Thus, insufficient attention has been given to the actual array of jobs, from high paying to low paying, involved in the production of these services. Focus on the work process in information industries brings to the fore the labor question. Information outputs need to be produced, and buildings that hold workers need to be built and cleaned. The rapid growth of the financial industry and of highly specialized services generates not only high-level technical and administrative jobs, but also low-wage, unskilled jobs. Table 2C.1 documents this for the case of New York City. (For a full development of these issues see Sassen 2001.)

The rapid growth of advanced corporate services—a fact in all highly developed economies—and the occupational and income distribution that characterizes these services have contributed to major changes in job supply. Consolidation of this economic core of top-level management and servicing activities needs to be viewed alongside the general move to a service economy and the decline of manufacturing. New economic sectors are reshaping job supply—yet so are new ways of organizing work in both new and old sectors of the economy. Components of the work process that even twenty years ago took place on the shop floor and were classified as production jobs today have been replaced by a combination of machine-service or worker-engineer. Activities that once were all consolidated in a single service retail establishment now have been divided between a service delivery outlet and central headquarters. Finally, a large array of activities that were being carried out under standardized forms of organizing work a decade ago today are increasingly characterized by informalization—that is, sweatshops and industrial homework. In brief, the changes in job supply, particularly evident in major cities, are a function both of new sectors and the reorganization of work in new and old sectors.[1]

The expansion of low-wage jobs as a function of growth trends implies a reorganization of the employment relation. To see this, we must distinguish the characteristics of jobs from their sectoral location—that is, highly dynamic, technologically advanced growth sectors may well contain low-wage, dead-end jobs. This is evident even in such high-tech, cutting-edge districts as Silicon Valley or the Princeton corridor. Furthermore, the distinction between sectoral characteristics and sectoral growth patterns is crucial: backward sectors such as downgraded manufacturing or low-wage service occupations can be part of

Table 2C.1 / New York City Median Hourly Wages by Occupation and Industry, 1996 to 1998 (USD)

Occupation	Occup. Code	Manufacturing (Selected Industries)					Services (Selected Industries)		
		SIC 23	SIC 25	SIC 27	SIC 35	SIC 37	SIC 72	SIC 73	SIC 87
Managerial and administrative	100003	36.69	32.64	40.49	41.17	38.93	18.09	38.77	45.27
Professional-paraprofessional and technical	200003	26.09	18.65	21.39	23.09	22.43	11.69	24.07	21.89
Sales and related	400003	27.86	18.86	19.06	22.53	21.35	8.29	17.76	14.78
Clerical and admin. support	500003	12.20	9.72	12.82	14.08	12.22	9.32	11.48	14.39
Service	600003	8.87	7.80	8.88	8.88	9.41	6.96	8.59	11.59
Product/construct/ operate-maintenance/ material handling	800003	7.29	10.35	11.94	12.01	12.79	7.14	9.42	13.73

Occupation	Occup. Code	Finance, Insurance, and Real Estate						
		SIC 60	SIC 61	SIC 62	SIC 63	SIC 64	SIC 65	SIC 67
Managerial and administrative	100003	44.03	50.14	55.99	40.99	45.80	30.88	40.42
Professional-paraprofessional and technical	200003	26.24	21.04	27.79	26.16	24.75	19.56	25.75
Sales and related	400003	20.64	15.94	25.92	15.59	19.57	21.53	26.22
Clerical and admin. support	500003	12.21	13.45	16.47	14.84	15.52	13.96	16.18
Service	600003	11.72	14.80	14.27	13.57	21.08	14.50	13.61
Product/construct/ operate-maintenance/ material handling	800003	13.03	14.98	16.54	14.18	15.79	15.22	15.66

Source: Sassen 2001, table 8.13. Author's calculations based on New York State Bureau of Labor Statistics; OES Survey 1996–1998.
Notes: SIC Codes and Descriptions listed: SIC 23 Apparel and Other Textile Products; SIC 25 Furniture and Fixtures; SIC 27 Printing and Publishing; SIC 35 Industrial Machinery and Equipment; SIC 37 Transportation Equipment; SIC 60 Depository Institutions; SIC 61 Nondepository Institutions; SIC 62 Security and Commodity Brokers; SIC 64 Insurance Agents, Brokers, & Service; SIC 65 Real Estate; SIC 67 Holding and Other Investment Services; SIC 72 Personal Services; SIC 73 Business Services; SIC 87 Engineering and Management Services.

major growth trends in a highly developed economy. Backward sectors often are assumed to express decline trends. Similarly, advanced industries, such as finance, are assumed to have mostly good white-collar jobs. In fact they contain a good number of low-paying jobs, from cleaners to stock clerks (see tables 2C.1 and 2C.2).[2]

The presence of a highly dynamic sector with a polarized income distribution has its own impact on the creation of low-wage jobs through the sphere of consumption (or, more generally, social reproduction). The rapid growth of industries with strong concentration of high- and low-income jobs has assumed distinct forms in the consumption structure that, in turn, has a feedback effect on the organization of work and the types of jobs being created. Expansion of the high-income workforce in conjunction with the emergence of new cultural forms has led to a process of high-income gentrification that ultimately rests on the availability of a vast supply of low-wage workers. High-price restaurants, luxury housing, luxury hotels, gourmet shops, boutiques, French hand laundries, and special cleaning services are all more labor-intensive than their lower-priced standardized equivalents. This has reintroduced—to an extent not seen in a very long time—the notion of the serving classes in contemporary high-income households (Sassen 2001, ch. 9). The immigrant woman serving the white middle-class professional woman has replaced the traditional image of the black female servant serving the white master. All these trends give these cities an increasingly sharp tendency toward contestation and social polarization.

INEQUALITY IN EARNINGS AND PROFIT-MAKING CAPACITIES

Inequality in the profit-making capacities of different sectors of the economy and in the earnings capacities of different types of workers has long been a feature of advanced economies. Yet what we see happening today takes place on an order of magnitude that distinguishes current developments from those of the post–World War II decades (Levy and Murane 1992; Nielsen and Alderson 1997; Gittleman and Howell 1995). The extent of inequality and the systems in which it is embedded and through which these outcomes are produced are engendering massive distortions in the operations of various markets, from investment to housing and labor.

Two major processes lying behind the possibility for increased inequality in profit-making and earnings capacities are an integral part of the advanced information economy: the ascendance and transformation of finance, particularly through securitization, globalization, and development of new telecommunications and computer network technologies; and the growing service intensity in the organization of the economy generally, which has vastly raised the demand for services by firms and households.[3] Insofar as a strong tendency exists toward polarization in technical levels and prices of services, as well as in wages and salaries of workers in the service sector, growth in demand for

Table 2C.2 / New York City Wage Ranges by Occupation and Selected Industry, 1996 to 1998 (USD, Numbers and Percentage)

Selected SIC	Mean Wage (Dollars)	Median Wage (Dollars)	Breakdown by Wage Ranges						Total Occ. Listed
			$50 above	$40 to $50	$30 to $40	$20 to $30	$10 to $20	$10 below	
SIC 23—Apparel and other textile products (total)	12.34	8.22	3	1	14	11	51	43	123
General managers and top exec. (highest hr. wage)	44.55	****	2.4%	0.8%	11.4%	8.9%	41.5%	35.0%	
Other textile and related (lowest hr. wage)	7.40	5.74							
SIC 62—Security and commodity brokers (total)	28.68	23.20	7	2	16	35	82	11	153
Managerial and admin. (highest hr. wage)	46.02	55.99	4.6%	1.3%	10.5%	22.9%	53.6%	7.2%	
Switchboard operators (lowest hr. wage)	10.18	8.29							
SIC 72—Personal services (total)	10.38	7.81	0	1	4	9	39	54	107
Other computer scientists and rel. (highest hr. wage)	38.71	42.08	0.0%	0.9%	3.7%	8.4%	36.4%	50.5%	
All other trans. and rel. workers (lowest hr. wage)	5.40	5.57							

(Table continued on p. 80.)

Table 2C.2 / Continued

Selected SIC	Mean Wage (Dollars)	Median Wage (Dollars)	Breakdown by Wage Ranges						Total Occ. Listed
			$50 above	$40 to $50	$30 to $40	$20 to $30	$10 to $20	$10 below	
SIC 73—Business services (total)	17.65	13.59							
General managers and top exec. (highest hr. wage)	44.96	55.04	2	3	17	43	88	61	214
Sewing machine operators, garment (lowest hr. wage)	6.75	5.95	0.9%	1.4%	7.9%	20.1%	41.1%	28.5%	
SIC 87—Eng. and management services (total)	24.40	20.06							
Financial managers (highest hr. wage)	47.96	*****	4	3	11	57	96	15	186
News, street vendors and phone solicitors (lowest hr. wage)	7.26	6.53	2.2%	1.6%	5.9%	30.6%	51.6%	8.1%	

Source: Sassen 2001, table 8.13. Author's calculations based on New York State Bureau of Labor Statistics, OES Survey 1996–1998.
Note: *****denotes value greater than $60. The first line of each SIC is the average wage within the sector among all occupations listed by the NY State Bureau of Labor Statistics. The second line is the occupation under the SIC with the highest mean wage; the third line is the occupation with the lowest mean wage. Wage ranges list the number and percentage of occupations within the SIC that fall above or on the listed range.

services contributes to polarization and, via cumulative causation, to repro-duce these inequalities.[4]

The growth of finance and specialized services, particularly concentrated in large cities, creates a critical mass of firms with extremely high profit-making capabilities. These firms contribute to bid up the prices of commercial space, industrial services, and other business needs, and thereby make survival for firms with moderate profit-making capabilities increasingly precarious. Among the latter, informalization of all or some of a firm's operations can emerge as one of the more extreme responses, further contributing to polarization in the urban economy. More generally, we see a segmentation between high profit-making firms and relatively modest profit-making firms.

One of the key dynamics feeding high profit-making capabilities has been the ascendance of expertise and specialization in the organization of the econ-omy. This ascendance of expertise in economic organization has contributed to the valorization of specialized services and professional workers—and has contributed to mark many other types of economic activities and workers as unnecessary or irrelevant to an advanced economy. As I have sought to show at length elsewhere, many of these other jobs are in fact an integral part of internationalized economic sectors, but neither represented nor valued (that is, waged) as such. (See tables 2C.1 and 2C.2 for an illustration of these trends in New York City.) This helps to create a vast number of both low-income and very high-income households.[5]

Key issues are the types of jobs being created and the systemic tendencies organizing the service sector that is setting the terms of employment for today and tomorrow. Jobs and organization clearly are overlapping and mutually shaping factors. Yet they do not overlap completely: labor markets associated with a given set of technologies (for example, teleworkers) or a given set of tasks (for example, paid household work) can, in principle, vary considerably and contain distinct mobility paths for workers. Yet sector organization, types of jobs, and labor market organization today are all strengthening the ten-dencies toward polarization.

Among the major systemic tendencies in the organization of the service sec-tor contributing to polarization is the disproportionate grouping of service industries at either end of the technology spectrum. Yet within industries at a given end of this spectrum, we can also find trends toward polarization, as is clearly evident in finance and high-tech manufacturing. The data for the United States are probably the most developed and also show the sharpest outcomes of these tendencies (see tables 2C.3 and 2C.4). Europe's generally more elabo-rate regulatory net for both firms and workers still prevents extreme outcomes.

THE CASUALIZATION OF THE EMPLOYMENT RELATION

Casualization assumes a range of specific forms, some of which have been doc-umented, and it raises a number of questions about the plausibility of others that still need to be studied. A growing body of research about the impact of

Table 2C.3 / U.S., New York City, Los Angeles, and Chicago: Employment in Business Services and Engineering-Management Services, 1993 to 1997 (Percentage)

	U.S.	New York City	Los Angeles	Chicago
Non-professionalized occupations (SIC: 7320, 7330, 7340, 7360, 7380)	25.2	23.1	11.3	26.0
Professionalized occupations (SIC: 7310, 7370, 8710–40)	25.7	11.7	14.2	24.6

Source: Sassen 2001.
Note: New York City includes five counties (New York, Bronx, Richmond, Queens, Kings); Chicago includes three counties (Cook, DuPage, Lake).

labor market characteristics on employment outcomes has established direct links between loose labor markets and the declining economic position of urban minority groups (see also Edin, Lein, and Nelson, ch. 3 herein). The fragmentary evidence available consists of both data on general trends that, at the least, support the plausibility of casualization, and data on particular, empirically established trends.

In the organization of labor markets new types of segmentation emerged in the 1980s and continue today (for example, Noyelle 1990; Appelbaum and Albin 1990; Sennett 1998; Armstrong 1996). Two characteristics stand out. One is a shift of some labor market functions and costs to households and communities (for example, Sassen 1995). The second is the weaker role of firms in structuring employment relations; more is now left to the market.

Table 2C.4 / New York and U.S. Percentage Growth in Earnings: Year-Round, Full-Time Workers (Percentage), 1979 to 1996, Selected Years

	Men			Women		
	1979 to 1996	1979 to 1989	1989 to 1996	1979 to 1996	1979 to 1989	1989 to 1996
United States						
Ninetieth percentile	10.1	9.4	0.6	27.7	17.8	8.4
Tenth percentile	−20.6	−13.9	−7.8	−13.6	−11.6	−2.3
New York–New Jersey region						
Ninetieth percentile	25.7	19.2	5.4	37.5	32.1	4.1
Tenth percentile	−21.0	−6.7	−15.3	−7.0	0.4	−7.4

Source: Federal Reserve Bank of New York, *Earnings and Inequality: New York–New Jersey Region,* "Current Issues in Economics and Finance," vol. 4, no. 9, July 1998.

The shift of labor market functions to the household or community is particularly evident in the immigrant community.[6] Possibly this is part of a more generalized pattern that deserves further research. Henly's chapter (herein) can be read as yet another instance of a shift of functions that ought to be located in the labor market or employment relation and is now moved to informal networks of friends and relatives. The displacement of labor market functions to the community or household raises the responsibility and costs of participating in the labor force for workers, even if these costs often are not monetized.[7] These subjects all require new research, given the current transitions.

As for the weaker role of the firm in organizing the employment relation, it takes on many different forms. One is the declining weight of internal labor markets in structuring employment. This corresponds both to the shrinking weight of vertically integrated firms and the restructuring of labor demand in many firms toward bipolarity—a demand for highly specialized and educated workers alongside a demand for unskilled workers, whether for clerical work, services, industrial services, or production jobs, as discussed in the preceding section. The shrinking demand for intermediate levels of skill and training, in turn, has reduced the need and advantages for firms of having internal labor markets with long promotion lines that function as on-the-job training mechanisms. The evidence discussed by Stack (ch. 1 herein) about dead-end jobs in fast-food restaurants, no matter how motivated the workers, illustrates this. Decentralization of large, vertically integrated manufacturing firms, including offshoring production, has contributed to decline in the share of unionized shops, deterioration of wages, and expansion of sweatshops and industrial homework. This process includes downgrading jobs within existing industries and the job supply patterns of some new industries, notably electronics assembly. Further, part-time and temporary employment are growing at a faster rate than full-time employment. In the United States, growing shares of service workers are in part-time jobs, and twice as often as average workers; involuntary part-time employment has grown significantly over the past decade (Tilly 1996).

Yet another empirical referent for casualization of employment relations is the rapid rise of employment agencies that take over the supply of a growing range of skills and occupations under highly flexible conditions. Terms of employment have been changing rapidly over the last fifteen years for a growing share of workers. The overall tendency is toward a casualization of the employment relation that incorporates not only types of jobs traditionally marked as casual, but also high-level professional jobs that in many regards are not casual (Sassen 2001, ch. 9). To differentiate a casualized employment relation from casual jobs is useful in that the latter connotes such added dimensions as the powerlessness of the workers—a condition that might not hold for some of the highly specialized professional part-time or temporary workers. This is a subject that requires more research.[8]

THE ANALYTIC IMPORTANCE OF LOCAL LABOR MARKETS

The local labor market is a far more concrete unit for analysis than the more macrolevel category of the labor market. (For a full treatment of the literature on this section see Sassen 1995). The local labor market also is a site where different dynamics come together, from employers' recruitment preferences to household survival strategies. Finally, the local labor market brings to the fore the importance of networks. In the case of immigrants, I have further argued (1995) that local labor markets can be transnational and hence, partly deterritorialized: the immigrant worker typically moves from one particular community in the country of origin to a particular community in the country of destination.

By now we have accumulated considerable information about various aspects of U.S. labor markets pertinent to an inquiry about low-wage workers. A key issue is the much talked about and often assumed replacement of native workers by immigrant workers. Immigration then easily may become the explanation for increased unemployment and insecurity among low-wage native workers, rather than systemic trends in the larger organization of the economy. Three important sets of findings frame this issue: those concerning little cross-industry mobility, the long-term nature of unemployment, and the fall in demand for low-skilled workers. These findings also raise questions about mechanisms through which immigrants gained access to a growing share of the low-wage job supply in several U.S. industries in the 1970s through the 1990s. At least some of these jobs probably represent a replacement of native workers; others represent job reorganization (that is, from union to nonunion); and yet others are new jobs. Although about 25 percent of workers with less than a high school education are immigrants, this still leaves natives in 75 percent of such jobs. In other words, an effective labor supply exists for these low-wage jobs among the native population, and an effective labor demand for native workers among firms with these kinds of jobs.

Thus we cannot take for granted the replacement of native workers by immigrants, especially if we consider the still rather large numbers of native workers with low education attainment (Card and Lemieux 1996; Blau and Kahn 1997). Further, high and increasingly long-term unemployment among such workers, limited unemployment benefits, and the fact that many of them are in jobs that pay less than in the past all suggest that their reservation wage has fallen and, hence, that they are more competitive with low-wage immigrants. Recent welfare reforms also contribute to lower reservation wages of low-wage workers. What is the process of competition that would lead to this replacement? How are the queues formed through which immigrants became an effective labor supply, and equivalent native workers—particularly blacks—did not, at least for 25 percent of these jobs?

Evidence shows that the most important determinant for immigrants' location is the existence of concentrations of the same nationality origin group. Most immigrants do not seem to choose to settle in high-wage locations per se, while natives of the same ethnicity do. These and other findings indicate that immigrants and natives do not respond to the same criteria for decisions affecting location. Gendering of location decisions also exists within each group (Hanson and Pratt 1995).

Moreover, evidence on employers' sensitivity to low-wage labor supplies in their location decisions is mixed. The presence of a low-wage immigrant workforce does not necessarily entail that it will be the labor supply of choice in firms with low-wage jobs, nor that it will replace other labor supplies. We therefore cannot assume that replacement will occur simply because immigrants are present and are cheaper than other workers.[9]

Employers' ties to a place is also a factor. In the New York region, for example, we found several employers who had started their own firms after their former employers (typically, large mass-production plants) had moved out of the region (Fernandez Kelly and Sassen 1992, 1995). The new employers wanted to stay in New York where they had ties of family, friendship, business partners, and so on. Employers' attachment to their workforce also matters.

A brief, partial answer to these questions is that due to the nature of the migration process, immigrants generally have far stronger networks than native workers who are similarly disadvantaged; and because of these networks, once a few immigrants enter a local labor market, they can more easily "colonize" it than their native counterparts (Waters 1999). Let me elaborate.

The general evidence about the importance of networks in patterning of job searches and outcomes is considerable. Much information about jobs flows through informal networks, and significant shares of workers obtain their jobs through this type of information (Fernandez Kelly and Sassen 1995). Considerable evidence for the case of immigrants also shows that kinship ties, residential networks, and association with coethnics facilitate job search and attainment among immigrants (Waters 1999; Mahler 1996; Smith 1997). One of the stark differences between low-wage immigrant and native workers is that immigrants can count on networks, households, and communities that are far tighter, more developed, and can be mobilized more easily and effectively. Since these immigrants come in with such a disadvantage, they need to rely on their networks and communities; in so doing, they strengthen these institutions and thereby accumulate social capital (Portes 1995).

Moreover, a central assumption in most models of labor mobility and location decision making is that all market behavior is voluntary. Constraining circumstances or agents are deliberately excluded from consideration, and likely to be cast aside as premarket differences. While this may be a reasonable proposition for large sectors of the population (particularly the middle strata), far less certain is that it holds for immigrants, especially if they reside in immigrant communities. Immigrant communities and households can be characterized by the weight of social ties that bind people into relations of trust and mutual obligation, the fact of *enforceable trust* (see Portes 1995), and the weight of collective rather than individual economic attainment strategies. All of these shape and influence the release and allocation of labor in the immigrant household.

Finally, that the immigrant household or community can allocate members to a labor market also works to the advantage of employers. Several studies have found that employers say they prefer hiring production workers via word-of-mouth. The figures in these same studies suggest that employers do not always get their way: a good proportion of all jobs were not filled via word-of-mouth. Thus we can infer that the immigrant community offers an advantage given the intensity of its networks and channeling of newly arrived immigrants into immigrant-dominated labor markets. A greater share of jobs most likely can be filled via word-of-mouth when immigrants and their communities are involved. Further, in the immigrant community, matters of control and enforceable trust give additional strength to these screening and coaching mechanisms.

Dependencies among employing establishments and communities or households are likely to emerge when networks used by workers to obtain information about jobs also become recruitment conduits for employers. Networks not only contain information circuits but also screening mechanisms. Employees are likely to know their employers' preferences and channel what they consider appropriate members of their networks when job openings arise at their workplace. In the case of the immigrant community, this knowledge about an employer's preferences and expectations may be crucial when it comes to language proficiency, legal status, and so-called cultural adjustment. We (Fernandez Kelly and Sassen 1992) found several cases where employers encouraged word-of-mouth recruitment *and* were very supportive of more senior workers coaching "their" recruitments on the job, helping them with the language (that is, translating instructions); employers often see additional benefits in this—that is, it strengthens worker cooperation.

In brief, by the time the immigrant is in the queue for a job, a multiplicity of processes have taken place that will tend to influence the labor market exchange moment—who gets offered what job and who accepts. Since the immigrant household is pursuing a collective economic attainment strategy, it can release one or more of its members, often women, to very low-wage and unstable jobs that may not cover the social reproduction costs of the individual worker. Furthermore, through the operation of enforceable trust, members of the household or community may be obliged to take jobs obtained by relatives or friends' ties even when they do not want these jobs. These household- and community-based decisions and capacities partly shape the immigrant labor supply.

Proximity to the workplace is assumed to be a key factor in the operation of local labor markets generally and in word-of-mouth recruitment and residential clustering of workers in particular. I would argue that the case of immigrant workers shows us that a *local* labor market can actually operate across borders, at a distance. Immigration offers perhaps some of the clearest examples of how two very different labor markets in geographic terms in fact can be two distinct segments of a single labor market system.

Elsewhere I argue that proximity should not be reified as a precondition for local labor markets or for the tightness of a local labor market (Sassen 1995); nor does proximity per se explain the formation of local labor markets. What is crucial is the existence and intensity of networks. These networks have spatial patterns, but they are not necessarily characterized by geographic proximity in the case of low-wage immigrant workers or, for that matter, the new transnational professional workforce (Sassen 2001, ch. 7). Networks may involve distances that go beyond the commuting norm in a metropolitan area; they may connect distant cities such as New York and Los Angeles, or they may connect communities in different countries.

THE INFORMALIZATION OF WORK

One of the most extreme forms of the casualization of the employment relation—and of changes in economic organization generally—is the informalization of a growing array of activities, a development evident in cities as different as New York, Paris, London, and Amsterdam.[10]

Theory about the informal economy until recently has been grounded in the incapacities of less developed economies: the inability to attain full modernization, stop excess migration to cities, and implement universal education and literacy programs. Correspondingly, the growth of an informal economy in highly developed countries has been seen as an import through Third World immigrants and their propensities to replicate survival strategies typical of their home countries. Related to this view is the notion that backward sectors of the economy are kept backward or even alive because a large supply of cheap immigrant workers are available. Both views posit or imply that, if an informal economy exists in highly developed countries, the sources are to be found in Third World immigration and in backward sectors of the economy.

Rather than assume that Third World immigration is causing informalization, what is needed is a critical examination of the role it might or might not play in this process. Immigrants, insofar as they tend to form communities, may be in a favorable position to seize opportunities represented by informalization; but the opportunities are not necessarily created by immigrants. Such opportunities are a structured outcome of current trends in advanced economies.[11]

If we are to go beyond a mere description of instances of informal work, we need to place informalization within a general context. Such is provided by the processes of economic restructuring that have contributed to the decline of the manufacturing-dominated industrial complex of the postwar era and the rise of the new, service-dominated economic complex. I find that the specific set of mediating processes that promote informalization of work are: increased earnings inequality and associated restructuring of consumption in high-income and very low-income strata; and the inability among providers of many goods and services that are part of the new consumption to compete for necessary resources in urban contexts where leading sectors have sharply bid up the prices of commercial space, labor, auxiliary services, and other basic business inputs (Sassen 1998, ch. 8).

One major trend is that the recomposition of the middle class, growth of a high-income professional class, and expansion of the low-income population all had a pronounced impact on the structure of consumption. This, in turn, has had an impact on the organization of work to meet new consumption demands. Part of the demand for goods and services feeding expansion of the informal economy comes from the mainstream economy and fragmentation of what once were mostly homogeneous middle-class markets (see also Mingione 1991; Tabak and Crichlow 2000). Another part of this demand comes from the internal needs of low-income communities increasingly incapable of buying goods and services in the mainstream economy.

Recomposition in household consumption patterns, particularly evident in large cities, contributes to a different organization of work from that prevalent in large, standardized establishments. This difference in the organization of work is evident in both the retail and production phase. High-income gentrification generates a demand for goods and services that frequently are not mass produced or sold through mass outlets. Customized production, small runs, specialty items, and fine-food dishes generally are produced through labor-intensive methods and sold through small, full-service outlets. Subcontracting part of this production to low-cost operations, and also sweatshops and households, is common. The overall outcome for job supply and range of firms involved in this production and delivery is rather different from that characterizing the large department stores and supermarkets, where standardized products and services are prevalent and therefore acquisition from large, standardized factories located outside the city or region are the norm. Proximity to stores is of far greater importance with customized producers. Further, unlike customized production and delivery, mass production and mass-distribution outlets facilitate unionizing.[12]

Expansion in the low-income population also contributes to the proliferation of small operations and the move away from large-scale standardized factories and chain stores for low-price goods. Consumption needs of the low-income population are met in good part by manufacturing and retail establishments that are small, rely on family labor, and often fall below minimum safety and health standards. Cheap, locally produced sweatshop garments, for example, compete with low-cost Asian imports, and the small, immigrant-owned grocery shop can replace the large, standardized, and typically unionized supermarket. A growing range of products and services, from low-cost furniture made in basements to gypsy cabs and family day care, is available to meet the demand for the growing low-income population.

In any large city, a proliferation of small, low-cost service operations is made possible by the massive concentration of people and daily inflow of commuters and tourists. This tendency creates intense inducements to open up such operations, as well as intense competition and marginal returns. Under such conditions the cost of labor is crucial and contributes to the likelihood of a high concentration of low-wage jobs.

This would suggest that a good share of the informal sector is not the result of immigrant survival strategies, but rather an outcome of structural patterns or transformations in the larger economy. Immigrants have known how to seize the so-called opportunities contained in this combination of conditions, but they cannot be said to cause the informal economy. Informalization emerges as a set of flexibility-maximizing strategies by individuals and firms, consumers and producers, in a context of growing inequality in earnings and profit-making capabilities (Sassen 1998, ch. 8).[13]

Thus the combination of growing inequality in earnings and in the profit-making capabilities of different sectors in the urban economy has promoted informalization of a growing array of economic activities. These conditions are integral in the current phase of advanced capitalism as it materializes in major cities dominated by the new advanced services complex typically geared to world markets and characterized by extremely high profit-making capabilities. These are not conditions imported from the Third World.

This commentary focused particularly on the growth of employment-centered insecurity and poverty. Insecurity and poverty per se have long been present in developed economies and often are seen as equivalent to unemployment. Of concern here is how new terms of employment also may contribute to insecurity and poverty. A key factor is the restructuring of labor markets that is part of deeply embedded features of advanced service economies.

We are seeing a series of new dynamics of inequality. New growth sectors—specialized services and finance—contain capabilities for profit making vastly superior to those of more traditional economic sectors. While many of the latter are essential to the operation of the economy and daily needs of households, their survival is made precarious in a situation where finance and specialized services can earn superprofits. Their profit-making capacities and the wages they pay fall relative to the high-profit sectors.

We see sharp increases in socioeconomic and spatial inequalities, particularly visible in major cities. Such increases may be interpreted as merely a quantitative increase in the degree of inequality. Yet they also may be interpreted as social and economic restructuring and the emergence of new social forms and class alignments in highly developed countries: the growth of an informal economy; high-income commercial and residential gentrification; and the sharp rise of homelessness.

Observed changes in the occupational and earnings distribution are outcomes not only of industrial shifts, but also of changes in the organization of firms and labor markets. Differences within major sectors, notably within services, have been strengthened. One set of service industries tends toward growing capital-labor ratios, growing productivity, and intensive use of the most advanced technologies, and the other toward continued labor intensity and low wages. Median earnings and education levels also are increasingly diverging for each of these subsectors. These characteristics in each set of industries contribute to a type of cumulative causation within each set. The first group of industries experiences pressures toward even higher capital-labor ratios and productivity levels given high wages. In the second group of industries, low wages are a deterrent toward greater use of capital intensive technologies, and low productivity leads to even more demand for very low-wage workers. These conditions, in turn, contribute to reproduce the difference in profit-making capacities embedded in each of these subsectors.

The combination of economic, political, and technical forces that contributed to the decline of mass production as the central driving element in the economy brought about a decline in a broader institutional framework that shaped the employment relation. The group of service industries that became the driving economic force in the 1980s and 1990s is characterized by greater earnings and occupational dispersion, weak unions, and mostly a growing share of unsheltered jobs in the lower-paying echelons along with a growing share of high-income jobs. The associated institutional framework shaping the employment relation is very different from the earlier one. This contributes to a reshaping of the sphere of social reproduction and consumption, which, in turn, has a feedback effect on economic organization and earnings. Whereas in the earlier period this feedback effect contributed to the reproduction and expansion of the middle class, currently it reproduces growing earnings disparity, informalization, and labor market casualization. The overall result is a tendency toward sharper economic polarization. Economic insecurity increasingly is built into these economies—and so is a growth of low-wage jobs.

NOTES

1. Metropolitan labor markets tend to reflect a variety of background factors beyond particular restructuring effects. The most important include their sheer size and density, the specific industrial and occupational mix of their employment base, the overall state of tightness or slack in labor demand, and in the case of some cities, the weight and characteristics of immigrant groups. Two key characteristics of labor markets in major cities—today as well as a century ago—are the fluidity and openness that influence the types of activity prospering there, as well as the labor market experiences of their residents.

2. The notion of circuits for the distribution and installation of economic operations is a useful analytic device to follow economic activities into terrains that escape the increasingly narrow borders of mainstream representations of the economy; the idea is also useful to negotiate the crossing of discontinuous spaces (Sassen 1998, chs. 1, 7, and 8). It allows me to capture the variety of economic activities, work cultures, and urban residential areas that are part of, for instance, the finan-

cial industry in New York City, but are not typically associated with that industry. For example, truckers who deliver the software and cleaners have work cultures, engage in activities, and reside in neighborhoods that diverge drastically from those of financial experts, yet they are part of the industry. These circuits also are mechanisms to resist the analytic confinement of the low-wage immigrant workforce to so-called backward industries just because the jobs appear as such.

3. This is a subject in itself, with a rapidly growing research literature; these issues are developed at length in Sassen 2001, chs. 5 and 6. In my reading, the growth in demand for service inputs—and especially bought service inputs—in all industries is perhaps the most fundamental cause of change in advanced economies. Using the value of bought intermediate service inputs as a measure, national accounts data were analyzed over different periods beginning with 1960 for several industries in manufacturing and services (Sassen and Orloff 1998). The results showed clearly that this value increased markedly since 1970 for firms in all industries, from mining and manufacturing to finance and consumer services. The increased value of bought service inputs has had pronounced impacts on the earnings distribution, industrial organization, and patterns along which economic growth has spatialized. This value has contributed to a massive growth in the demand for services. An added impact comes from services bought by households, both rich and poor.

4. The super-profit-making capacity of many leading service industries is embedded in a complex combination of new trends: technologies that make possible the hypermobility of capital on a global scale; market deregulation that maximizes the implementation of such hypermobility; financial inventions such as securitization that liquefy hitherto unliquid or relatively unliquid capital and allow it to circulate faster and hence make additional profits; the growing demand for services in all industries, along with the increasing complexity and specialization of many of these inputs, which has contributed to their valorization and often overvalorization, as illustrated in the unusually high salary increases beginning in the 1980s for top-level professionals. Globalization further adds to the complexity of these services, their strategic character, their glamor and therewith to their overvalorization.

5. A key development here is the rapid growth of a special type of household: the professional household without a "wife." This is a type of household that, regardless of its demographic composition (husband and wife, two men, two women, singles), cannot take care internally of essential household tasks that historically and culturally had fallen to the wife–mother–daughter "subject" and now is dependent on bought labor. Insofar as this household contains the types of professional workers, broadly understood, who are strategic to the new economy, that bought labor, which executes indispensable tasks for household maintenance, is also a significant input of sorts in the new economy (see Sassen 2001, ch. 9). But this bought labor is not recognized as such nor rewarded as such; nor does it allow workers themselves to recognize this. Here are important parallels with the analysis by Buchanan on teleworkers (ch. 2 herein).

6. A large body of evidence shows that once one or more immigrant workers are hired in a given workplace, they will tend to bring in other members from their communities as job openings arise (for example, Waters 1999; for an extensive review and discussion of the literature see Sassen 1995). Evidence also shows great willingness

on the part of immigrant workers to help those they bring in with on-the-job training, teaching the language, and generally socializing them into the job and workplace. This amounts to a displacement of traditional labor market functions such as recruitment, screening, and training from the labor market and firm to the community or household.

7. There is an interesting parallel here with earlier analysis in Gershuny and Miles (1983), showing that one of the components of the service economy is the shift of tasks traditionally performed by the firm onto the household: for example, furniture and even appliances sold unassembled, to be put together by the buyer.

8. These developments raise several questions. In my work these questions are raised particularly regarding the employment of immigrants. What is the impact of casualization in specific labor markets on employment outcomes for immigrants and, conversely, what is the impact of the availability of a casualized labor force on labor market characteristics? More specifically, does casualization of the labor market interact with, reflect, or respond to the availability of a large supply of immigrant workers, and if so, in what ways does this happen? To what extent are immigrant workers an effective supply for many of these casualized jobs? Finally, how does immigration policy affect the characteristics of immigrant labor supply, and in what ways does it contribute to casualize or decasualize this labor supply? Several chapters in this book (see, for example, Edin, Lein, and Nelson, ch. 3 herein) provide interesting information on some of these issues.

9. We found such a pattern in our comparison of the employment of Hispanics (following the census category) in the garment and electronics industries in southern California and the New York–New Jersey area (Fernandez Kelly and Sassen 1992; 1995). While both areas have large Hispanic populations, and both industries are known to seek low-wage labor (and Hispanics are among if not the lowest paid in both areas), the incidence of Hispanics is quite different. In southern California, approximately 72 percent of workers in the garment industry were Hispanic, compared to under 30 percent in the New York–New Jersey area. In the electronics industry, the figures were 64 percent and 16 percent, respectively. This pattern of differences contrasts to some extent with the greater similarity in the percentages for women employed, regardless of nationality. In both the southern California and New York–New Jersey regions, women are more than 50 percent of the garment labor force in our samples. In the electronics industry, 60 percent of workers in southern California and 34 percent in the New York–New Jersey regions were women. Each area had roughly a 50 percent Hispanic female workforce in garment production. While 35 percent of women workers were Hispanics in southern California, this figure was only 11 percent in the New York–New Jersey area. As is the case with findings in several other studies, gender frequently overrides nationality in labor market outcomes.

10. Although this subject is controversial owing to a lack of definitive data, a growing number of detailed field studies provide important insights into the scale and dynamics of the informal economy in major cities in highly developed countries. See Lazzarato et al. 1993, Perrin and Roussier 2000, Parnreiter et al. 1997, Rolleau-Berger 1999, and Tabak and Crichlow 2000 to name but a few reports on detailed field studies of the informal economy in advanced economies.

11. On this subject as it relates to immigration see, for example, Mingione 1991; Mitter, 1989; Pugliese 1983; Mahler 1996; Roulleau-Berger 1999.

12. Instances are numerous of how increased inequality in earnings reshapes the consumption structure in a city such as New York, and how this, in turn, has feedback effects on the organization of work, both in the formal and informal economy. For example, the creation of a special taxi line that only services the financial district, and the increase of gypsy cabs in low-income neighborhoods not serviced by regular cabs; the increase in highly customized wood work in gentrified areas and low-cost rehabilitation in poor neighborhoods; the increase of home workers and sweatshops making either expensive designer items for boutiques or cheap products sold by street vendors.

13. A broader fact is the growing tension in the relation between new economic trends that promote inequality in profit-making capacities and old regulatory frameworks that do not compensate for this new sharpening in inequality.

REFERENCES

Appelbaum, Eileen, and Peter Albin. 1990. "Shifts in Employment, Occupational Structure, and Educational Attainment." In *Skills, Wages, and Productivity in the Service Sector,* edited by T. Noyelle. Boulder, Colo.: Westview Press.

Armstrong, P. 1996. "The Feminization of the Labor Force: Harmonizing Down in a Global Economy." In *Rethinking Restructuring: Gender and Change in Canada,* edited by Isabella Bakker. Toronto and Buffalo: University of Toronto Press.

Blau, Francine, and Lawrence Kahn. 1994. "Rising Wage Inequality and the U.S. Gender Gap." *American Economic Review* 84(2): 23–28.

———. 1997. "Swimming Upstream: Trends in the Gender Wage Differential in the 1980's." *Journal of Labor Economics* 15(1): 1–42.

Body-Gendrot, Sophie, Emmanual Ma Mung, and Catherine Hodier, eds. 1992. "Entrepreneurs Entre Deux Mondes: Les Creations d'Entreprises par les Etrangers: France, Europe, Amerique du Nord." Special Issue, *Revue Européenne des Migrations Internationales* 8(1): 5–8.

Card, David, and Thomas Lemieux. 1996. "Wage Dispersion, Returns to Skills, and Black-White Wage Differentials." *Journal of Econometrics* 74: 319–61.

Fernandez Kelly, Maria Patricia, and Saskia Sassen. 1992. "Hispanic Women in Garment and Electronics Manufacturing in Southern California and the New York Metro Area." Research report presented to the Ford Foundation and the Tinker Foundation, New York.

———. 1995. "Recasting Gender in the Global Economy: Hispanic Women in Manufacturing and Electronics Manufacturing." In *Women in the Latin American Development Process,* edited by Christine Bose aned Edna Acosta–Belen. Philadelphia: Temple University Press.

Gershuny, Jonathan, and Ian Miles. 1983. *The New Service Economy: The Transformation of Employment in Industrial Societies.* New York: Praeger.

Gittleman, Marylin, and David Howell. 1995. "Changes in the Structure and Quality of Jobs in the United States: Effects by Race and Gender, 1973–1990." *Industrial Labor Relations Review* 48: 420–40.

Hanson, Susan, and Geraldine Pratt. 1995. *Gender, Work, and Space.* New York: Routledge.

Lazzarato, M., Y. Moulier-Boutang, A. Negri, and G. Santilli. 1993. *Des entreprises pas comme les autres: Benetton en Italie, Le Sentier a Paris.* Paris: Publisud.

Levy, Frank, and Richard Murane. 1992. "U.S. Earnings Levels and Earnings Inequality: A Review of Recent Trends and Proposed Explanations." *Journal of Economic Literature* 30: 1333–81.

Mahler, Sarah. 1996. *American Dreaming: Immigrant Life on the Margins*. Princeton, N.J.: Princeton University Press.

McCall, Leslie. 2000. "Gender and the New Inequality: Explaining the College/Non-College Wage Gap." *American Sociological Review* 65(April): 234–55.

Mingione, Enzo. 1991. *Fragmented Societies: A Sociology of Economic Life Beyond the Market Paradigm*. Oxford, Eng., and Cambridge, Mass.: Blackwell.

Mitter, Swazi, ed. 1989. *Information Technology and Women's Employment: The Case of the European Clothing Industry*. Berlin and New York: Springer Verlag.

Nielsen, François, and Arthur S. Alderson. 1997. "Income Inequality in U.S. Counties, 1970 to 1990." *American Sociological Review* 62: 12–33.

Noyelle, Terry, ed. 1990. *Skills, Wages, and Productivity in the Service Sector*. Boulder, Colo.: Westview Press.

Noyelle, Terry, and Ann B. Dutka. 1988. *International Trade in Business Services: Accounting, Advertising, Law and Management Consulting*. Cambridge, Mass.: Ballinger.

Parnreiter, Christof, Andrea Komlosy, Irene Stacher, and Susan Zimmermann, eds. 1997. *Ungeregelt und Unterbezahlt. Der Informelle Sektor in der Weltwirtschaft*. Frankfurt: Brandes & Apsel/Sudwind.

Peraldi, Michel, and Evelyne Perrin, eds. 1996. *Reseaux Productifs et Territoires Urbains*. Toulouse, France: Presses du Mirail.

Perrin, Evelyne, and Nicole Roussier. 2000. *Ville et Emploi: Le territoive au coeur des nouvelles forms de trevail*. La Tour d'Aigues, France: Editions de l'Aube.

Portes, Alejandro, ed. 1995. *The Economic Sociology of Immigration*. New York: Russell Sage Foundation.

Pugliese, Enrico. 1983. "Aspetti dell' Economia Informale a Napoli." *Inchiesta* 13(59–60): 89–97.

Roulleau-Berger 1999. *Le Trevail En Friche*. La Tour d'Aigues, France: Editiones de l'Aube.

Sassen, Saskia. 1995. "Immigration and Local Labor Markets." In *The Economic Sociology of Immigration*, edited by A. Portes. New York: Russell Sage Foundation.

———. 1998. *Globalization and Its Discontents. Essays on the Mobility of People and Money*. New York: New Press.

———. 2001. *The Global City*. Rev. ed. Princeton, N.J.: Princeton University Press.

Sassen, Saskia, and S. Orloff. 1998. "Measuring the Demand for Intermediate Services in Select Economic Sectors." Department of Sociology, University of Chicago.

Sennett, Richard. 1998. *The Corrosion of Character: The Personal Consequences of Work in the New Capitalism*. New York: Norton.

Smith, Robert C. 1997. "Transnational Migration, Assimilation and Political Community." In *The City and the World*, edited by Margaret Crahan and Alberto Vourvoulias-Bush. New York: Council of Foreign Relations.

Tabak, Faruk, and Michaeline A. Crichlow, eds. 2000. *Informalization: Process and Structure*. Baltimore: Johns Hopkins University Press.

Tilly, Chris. 1996. *Half a Job: Bad and Good Part-Time Jobs in a Changing Labor Market*. Philadelphia: Temple University Press.

Torres, Rodolfo D., Jonathan Xavier Inda, and Louis F. Miron, eds. 1999. *Race, Identity, and Citizenship*. Oxford: Blackwell.

Waters, Mary C. 1999. *Black Identities: West Indian Immigrant Dreams and American Realities*. New York and Cambridge, Mass.: Russell Sage Foundation/Harvard University Press.

Commentary

Understanding the Unemployment Experience of Low-Wage Workers: Implications for Ethnographic Research

Philip Harvey

One characteristic of low-wage work that is particularly important to the ethnographic research reported in this volume is its insecurity. As shown in figure 2C.1, average unemployment rates for persons with fewer than four years of high school are more than four times as high as corresponding rates for persons with four or more years of college. This means that even in periods of relative prosperity, low-wage workers experience levels of unemployment normally associated with recessions; during recessions, their unemployment rises to depression levels.

The negative personal effects of this joblessness on individual workers are likely to be significant. Unemployment is associated with increased poverty rates (Sawhill 1988; Hakim 1982; Marmor, Mashaw, and Harvey 1990), a wide range of adverse physical and mental health effects (Brenner and Mooney 1983; Liem and Rayman 1982; Burchell 1994), the corrosion of family life and personal relationships (Jahoda 1982; Kelvin and Jarrett 1985; O'Brien 1986), and increased criminal activity (Hakim 1982; Britt 1994; Smith, Devine, and Sheley 1992; Box 1987).

Ethnographic research is well suited for studying these adverse effects, and particularly for exploring how the experience of being unemployed (or being affected by the unemployment of others) is subjectively felt and understood. When unemployment is widespread, as it was in the United States during the 1930s, the experience can shape the identity of an entire generation. When particular population groups experience unemployment in concentrated doses, as racial minorities and the poor regularly do, it can have equally significant effects on the way members of the group view themselves and are viewed by others. Being unemployed can inspire self-pity, self-loathing, or rage at society, depending on how the experience is understood. Similarly, the unemployment of others may inspire the public's sympathy or contempt, depending on whether members of the affected group are perceived as victims of circumstance or of their own behavioral shortcomings. Ethnographic research provides an

Figure 2C.1 / Unemployment Rates of Persons Twenty-Five to Sixty-Four Years of Age by Educational Attainment

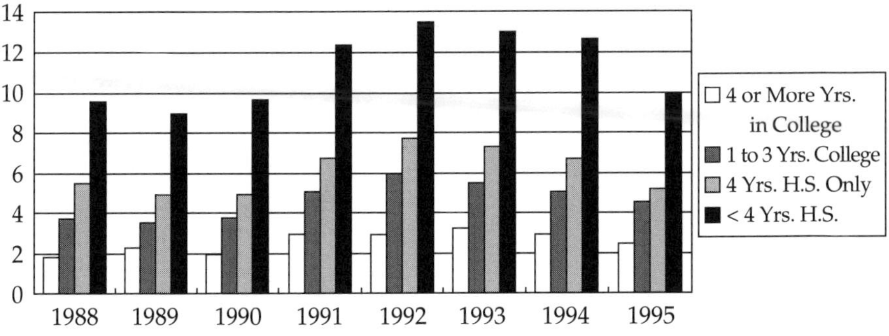

Source: Jacobs 1997, 110.

excellent window for observing how these varied responses emerge and interact with other factors shaping the life experience, attitudes, and behavior of different population groups.

Since unemployment and the social problems that attend it are an important public policy concern, insights drawn from this type of research can provide useful data for policy debate. To properly assess this data, however, we must understand how the experiences of individuals or discrete groups of individuals can mislead as well as enlighten us. The fallacy of composition—the mistake of assuming that what is true for individual members of a population is necessarily true for the whole population—is an ever-present danger when public policies are devised based on the teachings of individual experience. Just because each and every person attending a concert could see better if he or she were to stand up doesn't mean the entire audience would see better if everyone were encouraged to stand up. Does the unemployment experience of individuals—either our own or that of people we observe—provide a good vantage point for understanding the causes of the problem and its remedies? The answer to this question is surprisingly complex. The purpose of this commentary is to explore that complexity in order to better understand the policy implications of the research reported in this volume.

PERCEPTIONS OF JOB AVAILABILITY AND PUBLIC POLICY

Perceptions of job availability play an important role in shaping public attitudes and public policy toward jobless individuals. Both unemployment and low rates of labor force participation (that is, joblessness broadly defined) have been identified as primary sources of poverty in the United States, but when unemployment rates descended during the late 1990s to their lowest level in a generation, involuntary unemployment was not perceived as playing much of a role in giving rise to the poverty of low-wage workers. Instead, public debate about the economic circumstances of these workers tended to focus on the quality of jobs they held and whether those jobs allowed them to escape poverty.

I do not question the importance of this debate over job *quality* in assessing the effectiveness of work-based antipoverty strategies. A full-time, minimum-wage job pays substantially less than the census bureau's poverty line for a family of three (the average size of families receiving Temporary Assistance to Needy Families [TANF] benefits); and a more refined poverty measure proposed by a National Academy of Sciences panel would establish substantially higher poverty thresholds, especially for families with employed members (Citro and Michael 1995; Garner et al. 1998). In 1997, 2.3 million full-time, year-round workers had jobs in the United States with incomes below the federal government's official poverty line (Dalaker and Naifeh 1998, 17, table 3).

Nevertheless, the issue of job *availability*—the availability of *any* jobs, not just good jobs—also warrants attention in discussions of the causes and remedies for poverty among able-bodied adults. Does the American economy generate enough jobs of any description to employ everyone the American public expects to work? If a shortage of jobs exists relative to the number of people seeking work, as shall be argued is the case, what are the policy implications of the shortage? Finally, if a job shortage does exist, why are perceptions of ready job availability so widespread in the United States—possibly including perceptions by unemployed workers themselves—and what does the dissonance between these perceptions and actual labor market conditions mean for how the public views low-wage work and low-wage workers?

In other work (Harvey 1999, 2000) I have analyzed the development of public policy responses to joblessness in the United States and described the origins of these responses in three competing views of job availability. According to the first view, jobs are presumed to be plentiful, and joblessness is attributed to the failure of jobless individuals to seek and accept work on available terms. I call this view *behavioralist* because it attributes joblessness to the behavior of jobless individuals themselves. Policies based on the behavioralist view tend to put pressure on jobless individuals to seek and accept presumptively available jobs. Providing jobless individuals with income assistance is considered counterproductive because it encourages dependency rather than self-reliance. Humanitarian considerations may dictate that public assistance be provided to the able-bodied poor, but the aid offered should be both minimal and temporary so as not to discourage job-search activity. This approach dominated social welfare policy in the United States prior to the 1930s, and in recent years it has enjoyed a resurgence in popularity among conservative policy advocates. Welfare reform legislation enacted in recent years at both the federal and state level has been strongly influenced by this view.

According to the second view, joblessness is caused by a failure on the part of the economy to generate enough jobs to employ everyone who wants to work. This view, which I call the *job-shortage* approach, dominated the American public policy response to joblessness during the New Deal era in the 1930s, and it continues to influence public policy responses to jobless individuals during recessions. Policies based on the job-shortage approach seek to close the economy's perceived job gap either by increasing the total number of jobs available or by decreasing the total number of people seeking work. Examples of these policies include the New Deal's massive public employment programs and the establishment of publicly funded pension programs to make it easier for certain categories of workers to retire from the active labor force.

The third view of job availability, which I term *structuralist*, assumes that access to work is a problem only for certain population groups. According to this view, job shortages are not a problem in general, but barriers to equal employment opportunity limit the ability of certain groups to compete for available jobs. These barriers include employment discrimination, unequal access to job-training and education opportunities, and geographic mismatches between the location of available jobs and the communities where unemployed workers live. Structuralist analyses of joblessness may concede or even emphasize that the behavior of jobless individuals diminishes their employment prospects, but these behavioral tendencies are attributed to social conditions rather than to individual preferences or character defects.

The structuralist view of joblessness inspired major reforms in American employment and social welfare law during the 1960s and early 1970s, and it has dominated liberal policy positions since that time. Structuralist policies seek to eliminate perceived barriers to equal employment opportunity while providing compensating public assistance to individuals whose access to work has been limited. Reforms based on this approach include antidiscrimination legislation, education assistance programs for disadvantaged populations, and economic-development initiatives targeting low-income communities.

EMPIRICAL EVIDENCE CONCERNING JOB AVAILABILITY

Given the importance of differing views of job availability in shaping social welfare policy preferences, it is important to get the facts straight. Unfortunately, this is not an easy task, in part because the available evidence can be interpreted in more than one way, but mainly because job availability is not a well-defined concept in policy discourse. In particular, perceptions of whether "enough" jobs exist depend significantly on whether attention is focused on job vacancies or job turnovers.

Job Vacancy Data

A wealth of data concerning both employed and unemployed segments of the American labor force is regularly collected and reported. A similar abundance of data is available describing the number and characteristics of occupied jobs in the economy. Surprisingly little data is available, however, concerning the number and characteristics of vacant jobs. The result is that we know how many people are looking for work and a great deal about their personal characteristics, but we don't know very much about how many jobs employers are seeking to fill at any given point, nor the characteristics of those jobs. When job vacancy surveys are conducted, however, they tell a consistent story concerning job availability in the United States. Briefly stated, the American economy does not produce enough jobs to employ its entire labor force. The size of the economy's job gap varies across the business cycle, but in periods of relative prosperity as well as during recessions, more people are seeking work than there are jobs available for them to fill (Abraham 1983; Holzer 1989, 1996; Employment and Training Institute 1993–2000). Moreover, this data suggests that virtually all measured unemployment in the United States—above a frictional floor of 2 to 3 percent—is attributable to this aggregate job shortage (Harvey 2000).[1] In other words, neither structural nor behavioral factors appear to play much of a role in determining the amount of unemployment experienced in the United States economy at any given point. The job shortage explanation alone suffices to explain that level.

Job Turnover Data

A somewhat different picture is presented by job turnover data—that is, the proportion of all jobs that are newly created or become vacant over a period of time. The higher the job turnover rate, the greater the number of job vacancies employers are willing to fill over a given period.

The effect of job-turnover rates on job availability can be illustrated with a description of two different games of musical chairs. In both games there are ten players and only nine chairs. The first game is played in the normal way. Everyone is required to stand up when the music begins, and all ten players circle the nine empty chairs until the music stops. Then everyone scrambles to find a vacant chair. In the second game, however, only one player stands up when the music begins and circles the one empty chair along with the player who had no chair to begin with. When the music stops, these two players scramble to sit down in that one vacant chair.

In both games, one person is left without a chair at the end of each round of play. In other words, the rate of chairlessness measured at that point is 10 percent in both games, and that rate is wholly determined by the number of chairs in the game, compared with the total number of players. Yet seatless players have a better chance of finding a seat in the first game than they do in the second. In the first game, a seatless player has a 90 percent chance of finding a vacant seat, but that chance is reduced to 50 percent in the second game. A high job-turnover rate affects job availability in the same way: it increases the number of jobs available during a given period, relative to the number of people seeking work, even though the economy's aggregate job gap remains the same.

Job-turnover rates in the United States are quite high. In one recent survey of both public- and private-sector employers in four major metropolitan areas, the average job-vacancy rate (the proportion of all jobs vacant at any given time) was found to be only 2.7 percent, compared to unemployment rates in the 5 percent to 11 percent range. Yet the gross hiring rate (the proportion of all employees hired within the preceding twelve-month period) was found to be 25.7 percent (Holzer 1996, fig. 1.1 and table B.3). Moreover, the latter figure understates the total number of job vacancies filled during the course of a year, as it does not account for jobs that may have been vacated and filled more than once, or jobs that were filled and then eliminated.

Thus, despite the fact that the number of job seekers always exceeded the number of job vacancies, the number of openings for which job seekers theoretically could apply was quite large over time. The Depression-era refrain that "Nobody's hiring" does not apply to the American labor market, even though there are not enough jobs to go around.

Does this mean that jobs are plentiful despite the economy's job gap? That depends on how job availability is conceived and our choice of policy goals. If we think that adequate job availability means that enough jobs are available for everyone who wants to work, then clearly a job shortage exists in the American economy. If our standard of adequacy merely requires that the number of job vacancies be sufficient to ensure that job seekers do not have to wait too long to find a job when they are out of work, then job-turnover rates may be high enough, at least in theory, to provide the needed vacancies.

IS IT THE LEVEL OR THE DISTRIBUTION OF JOBLESSNESS THAT MATTERS?

Understanding the different ways in which job availability can be defined helps us to understand the lack of attention paid to issues of aggregate job availability in contemporary social welfare policy debates. Structuralist and behavioralist factors may play little role in determining the aggregate level of unemployment in the economy, but they play a very important role in determining who will suffer that unemployment.

To begin with, population growth and economic growth tend to be uneven across regions and communities, so the distribution of joblessness among population groups depends in part on where different groups of job seekers live as compared to where employers are creating jobs.[2] Second, given the strong association between an individual's level of education and the likelihood the individual will be unemployed (see figure 2C.1), differences in the quantity and quality of education opportunities available to different population groups also is likely to have a significant effect on the group's unemployment rate. Third, strong evidence shows that illegal employment discrimination still imposes significant handicaps on certain population groups, thereby increasing their exposure to unemployment (Fix and Struyk 1993; Holzer 1996). Finally, it is generally conceded that behavioral traits typical of certain population groups also influence their unemployment experience, although substantial disagreement exists as to whether these traits can be attributed to individual choice (as behavioralists argue) or are adaptive to social forces beyond individual control (as structuralists argue). (Compare Mead 1992; Wilson 1996.)

Accordingly, contemporary policy debates may ignore issues of aggregate job availability simply because those debates tend to focus on the *distribution* of joblessness among different population groups rather than on the total *amount* of joblessness experienced in the economy as a whole. The job-shortage explanation of joblessness tells us how many people are fated to suffer unemployment at any given point, but it does not tell us why some individuals and groups suffer more unemployment than others. If joblessness is a concern only because its burdens are unequally distributed, then policy debate understandably would focus on structuralist and behavioralist factors rather than on the economy's aggregate job shortage.

During recessions, the total amount of joblessness suffered in the economy is a matter of considerable public concern, and policy debate tends to focus on the economy's job shortage. At other times, however, joblessness is more likely to be perceived as a distributional problem, with policy debate focusing on how to eliminate differences in the amount of joblessness suffered by different population groups, rather than on how to reduce the total amount of joblessness suffered in the economy. If everyone lost just three weeks of work a year (an equal distribution of a 6 percent unemployment rate), joblessness would not cause very much poverty. Similarly, if minority groups suffered no more unemployment than whites, joblessness would not appear to perpetuate racial injustices.

If contemporary worries about joblessness during nonrecessionary periods are limited to concerns that its burdens are unequally shared, it may not be thought important whether enough jobs are available to provide work for all job seekers. All that matters is the quality of available jobs and whether enough of them are available to permit strategies for equalizing unemployment rates to work.

Understood in these terms, the neglect of the job-shortage view of joblessness in contemporary social welfare policy debates appears perfectly understandable. Even if the *amount* of joblessness suffered in the economy is almost wholly determined by the size of the economy's job gap, the *distribution* of that joblessness depends primarily on the structural and behavioral factors that are the focus of contemporary policy debate.

Nevertheless, to discount the importance of job-shortage concerns may be a mistake, even if our primary goal is to equalize unemployment rates among population groups. Consider the following parable (Harvey 2000, 683):

There once was an island with a population of 100 dogs. Every day a plane flew overhead and dropped 95 bones onto the island. It was a dog paradise, except for the fact that every day 5 dogs went hungry. Hearing about the problem, a group of social scientists was sent to assess the situation and recommend remedies. The social scientists ran a series of regressions and determined that bonelessness in the dog population was associated with lower levels of bone-seeking effort and that boneless dogs also lacked important skills in fighting for bones. As a remedy for the problem, some of the social scientists proposed that boneless dogs needed a good kick in the side to get them moving, while others proposed that boneless dogs be provided special training in bone-fighting skills. A bitter controversy ensued over which of these two strategies ought to be pursued. Over time, both strategies were tried, and both reported limited success in helping individual dogs overcome their bonelessness—but despite this success, the bonelessness problem on the island never lessened in the aggregate. Every day, there were still five dogs who went hungry.

The social scientists in this parable approached the bonelessness problem much as social scientists approach the problem of joblessness in contemporary social welfare policy debates. They focused their attention exclusively on the distributional aspect of the problem—why some dogs suffered more bonelessness than other dogs—and proposed measures designed to equalize the dog population's access to bones. In doing so, however, they missed something important. The reason a bonelessness problem existed in the first place is because a hundred dogs were on the island, but only ninety-five bones dropped from the sky each day. A more complete assessment of the problem would have noted this fact and concluded that the *amount* of bonelessness suffered by the dog population was wholly determined by the number of bones that dropped from the sky each day, while the *distribution* of that bonelessness was largely determined by the dogs' relative motivation and fighting skills.

This assessment of the problem suggests an additional policy option. The proposed training and motivation program for boneless dogs might have worked in achieving the intended goal, but the distribution problem also would have been solved if five additional bones were dropped from the sky each day. In fact, the latter policy would have been more certain to succeed, even if the only goal of the policy were to equalize the distribution of bones among the dogs; and if reducing the aggregate amount of bonelessness also were a policy goal, it is the only measure that would have worked. Ignoring cost considerations (which might cut either way), increasing the supply of bones would appear to be a plainly superior policy to trying to equalize the distribution of bonelessness. It would be more certain to achieve an equal distribution of bones, and it would reduce whatever suffering the dogs experienced from going without bones, if only for a day now and then.

The same may be true of policies based on the job-shortage approach to combating unemployment. If successful policies were implemented to eliminate the economy's job gap, inequalities in the distribution of joblessness would tend to disappear. Moreover, to the extent that structural and behavioral factors still prevented certain job seekers from finding work, or interfered with their access to the full range of employment opportunities available in the economy, the existence of full employment would be likely to increase the effectiveness of policies designed to address those problems. This latter point warrants special emphasis, as the existence of an aggregate job shortage diminishes the effectiveness of structuralist and behavioralist policies for combating joblessness in a number of ways.

REDUCING DIFFERENTIAL RATES OF UNEMPLOYMENT IN A JOB-SHORT ECONOMY

The existence of an aggregate job shortage is likely to reduce the effectiveness of structuralist and behavioralist strategies for combating joblessness among disadvantaged workers for several reasons.

First, labor markets tend to reward success with more success and punish failure with more failure. Analysts who acknowledge the existence of an aggregate job shortage sometimes describe unemployed workers as "queuing" for jobs (Holzer 1996, 29; Mead 1992, 86), but the workers are in a queue with peculiar features. The distinguishing characteristic of most queues is that people move from the back to the front as they wait. Among the unemployed, however, the hiring queue probably moves in the opposite direction. Among two otherwise identical candidates for employment, employers are likely to perceive the one who joined the unemployment queue more recently as a more desirable candidate for employment. In fact, job applicants who are still working in their old jobs are probably the most attractive to new employers, and there are large numbers of such job seekers.

A recent study found that during a three-month period in winter 1994 to 1995, a total of 5.6 percent of all wage and salary workers actively looked for a new job while still employed (U.S. Bureau of Labor Statistics 1997). During the same period, the national unemployment rate averaged about 5.5 percent with a mean duration of unemployment of about seventeen weeks. Owing to turnover within the population of unemployed persons, the total number of persons unemployed at some point in the three-month period would have exceeded the total number who sought work while still employed. Nevertheless, literally millions of currently employed job seekers competed with unemployed job seekers for vacant jobs during the period. In theory, at least, it is possible for an economy to have both a high job-vacancy rate and high job-turnover rate without any of persons unemployed job seeker ever finding work. All that is required is a high rate of job search among currently employed workers, and a hiring preference on the part of employers for employed applicants over unemployed applicants.

Jobless individuals can and do find work, of course, but the way in which hiring queues work makes it harder for them.[3] Efforts to move jobless individuals to the front of hiring queues work against a natural tendency for markets to discriminate against such persons. The larger the economy's aggregate job shortage, the longer the hiring queue will be, and the farther back in line unemployed job seekers—especially disadvantaged job seekers—are likely to find themselves.

Second, efforts to help disadvantaged job seekers find work, if they succeed, are likely to increase unemployment among workers who are only marginally better off and who probably have personal characteristics very similar to those of the assisted population. These are the workers most likely to lose job opportunities when previously less attractive job applicants are helped to the front of hiring queues. The increased economic stress and associated problems these workers are likely to experience may cancel and certainly will diminish the net social benefit achieved by helping disadvantaged job seekers find work. A redistribution of the burdens of joblessness among the lowest strata of the labor force may not reduce the harms caused by joblessness very much.[4] The severity of this problem also is linked to the size of the economy's job gap, because that is what determines the intensity of competition for jobs among employed and unemployed workers.

Third, efforts to increase the employment of disadvantaged individuals also may elicit a nullifying counterresponse from more privileged workers. This counterresponse may take socially beneficial or, at least, benign forms. Threatened workers may invest more in their own education and that of other family members, display an increased willingness to move where jobs are most plentiful, and intensify their own job search activities when unemployed. Yet their response may take less benign forms as well. Access-broadening initiatives may come under ideological, political, and legal attack as threatened workers seek to protect their advantages. Opposition by white male workers to affirmative action illustrates this kind of reaction. Whatever form it takes, however, the defensive behavior of more privileged workers threatened with a reduction in their own job security is likely to frustrate efforts to increase the job security of workers who are less advantaged.

Fourth, to the extent that the distribution of joblessness is a product of discriminatory hiring practices, the existence of a significant job gap makes it harder to alter employer practices. Surplus labor supply provides both a cover for discriminatory practices and an economic cushion that allows employers to indulge their biases. Proving discriminatory treatment is very difficult when large numbers of workers apply for a small number of jobs and are evaluated according to multiple, incommensurable, partially subjective hiring criteria. This may be one reason for the prevalence of discriminatory firing cases over discriminatory hiring cases in employment discrimination litigation (Donohue and Siegelman 1991). The existence of labor surpluses also permits employers greater latitude in deciding where to locate their businesses, avoiding minority populations if they want, without fear of being unable to recruit adequate numbers of workers (Holzer 1996, 131). As the economy's job gap shrinks, economic pressure on employers not to discriminate increases, and the deterrent effect of antidiscrimination law probably becomes more effective.

For these reasons, structuralist and behavioralist efforts to equalize the burdens of joblessness are likely to work better when the economy's job gap is small than when it is large. Ironically, this suggests that a precondition for the success of structuralist and behavioralist strategies for combating joblessness may be the implementation of an effective strategy based on the job-shortage approach. In other words, it may be more appropriate to think of structuralist and behavioralist strategies as useful complements to an effective job-shortage strategy than as alternatives to the job-shortage approach (Harvey 2000).

Properly understood, the goal of structuralist and behavioralist strategies for combating joblessness is not to reduce joblessness, but to reduce its social cost by redistributing its burdens more equally. In contrast, the goal of policies based on the job-shortage approach is to reduce the social cost of joblessness by reducing the total amount of joblessness suffered in the economy. To the extent the latter goal is achieved, inequalities in the distribution of joblessness among population groups will tend to be reduced, but the implementation of structuralist and behavioralist initiatives still would be needed to ensure that job opportunities are distributed more or less equally among all population groups.

LOW-WAGE WORKERS IN A JOB-SHORT ECONOMY

What are the implications of this analysis for how low-wage workers perceive their own experiences and are perceived by the general public? The key point is that how individual workers normally experience aggregate labor market conditions tends to reinforce behavioralist and structuralist views of the sources of and remedies for unemployment. The same is true of how the general public perceives low-wage workers. This tendency is illustrated by the changes that occur in public attitudes toward jobless individuals during recessions, the only times when aggregate job shortages are widely recognized.

In a nonrecessionary economy, high rates of labor turnover can create large numbers of job openings over time, even if job-vacancy rates are low at any given time. Job destruction may be occurring, but an equal or greater amount of job creation also is occurring. In this environment, a large proportion of the workforce has regular and successful experience seeking and finding work. To most workers finding a job does not seem that hard. Based on personal observation and experience, they see that individual behavior matters in the quest for work. They also may see that structural factors influence an individual's chances of finding employment. Everyone has stories to tell that illustrate and tend to confirm the behavioralist and structuralist roots of joblessness. In contrast, nothing in the personal experience of workers tells them whether enough jobs exist for all job seekers. A shortage of good jobs may be perceived, but jobs in general may appear to be plentiful.

Low-wage workers may have more doubts about the adequacy of job availability, but their perceptions of the labor market are likely to be dominated by the same experiences as other workers. If anything, these experiences are accentuated for low-wage workers, who change jobs more frequently, experience higher rates of unemployment, and are especially vulnerable to structural barriers to equal employment opportunity.

The lives of low-wage workers provide abundant evidence of the effects of behavioral and structural factors in causing joblessness, and of the efficacy of behavioralist and structuralist strategies for overcoming it. Low-wage workers can invest in their own education or seek specialized job training. They can move to communities where jobs are more plentiful. They can try to compensate for discriminatory hiring practices by trying to shed stigmatizing cultural traits, or they can join in legal or political action to challenge discrimination. They can increase their job search efforts, adjust their expectations, and try harder to conform their behavior to employer expectations. The nuanced insights of ethnographic studies have much to teach us about these strategies and the difficulties that low-wage workers face in implementing them.

What is not immediately apparent to labor market participants, including low-wage workers, is how their experience with unemployment and the process of seeking work is affected by the existence of aggregate job shortages in nonrecessionary periods. Job seekers are not just competing for better jobs, they are competing for scarce jobs. Successful job search strategies require job seekers not only to qualify themselves to do a certain kind of work, but also to leapfrog over other job seekers in hiring queues. In fact, successful job search strategies in this environment are all queue-jumping strategies, designed to give a job seeker a competitive advantage. That a variety of forces are at work that tend to undermine the effectiveness of these strategies merely raises the ante of effort required for job search success.

Individual competition for jobs is intense, and it undermines cooperative and solidaristic feelings among workers, except within narrow groupings. Family members and members of the same community or ethnic group may find it advantageous to support one another's job search efforts, but the success of one group of job seekers ultimately depends on the failure of some other group, and antipathy and resentment among different groups is likely to flourish.

Unsuccessful job seekers do not elicit much sympathy in this environment. As noted previously, high job-turnover rates mean that a large proportion of the workforce is accustomed to success in their job search efforts. This widespread success encourages workers to believe that other job seekers should be able to enjoy similar success. Indeed, this perception may be accurate when applied to individual job seekers; individuals who pursue reasonable job search strategies are likely to find jobs. The assumption, however, that everyone would find work if they pursued the same strategies is a classic example of the fallacy of composition. If all job seekers were to enhance their skills, lower their expectations, and increase their job search efforts to the same degree, the relative attractiveness of each applicant would remain unchanged. Nothing would change for the population of job seekers as a whole, even though employers would be pleased, as they would have larger numbers of better-qualified applicants from whom to choose. For the number of people finding work to increase, the total number of available jobs must grow.[5]

Given the seductiveness of the fallacy of composition in this context, the public is not likely to recognize a distinction between opportunities for self-help available to individual job seekers and opportunities available to the population of unemployed job seekers as a whole. This failure to distinguish individual opportunities from group opportunities probably diminishes public sympathy for jobless workers in general; and as low-wage workers suffer more unemployment than others, they are especially vulnerable to unfavorable attitudes on the part of the public. Jobless low-wage workers may be perceived as losers, and low-wage workers themselves may share this view, blaming each other (and themselves) for their lack of work.

People who believe that there are significant structural barriers to equal employment opportunity are less likely to blame jobless workers for being jobless, but the apparent failure of structuralist policies to reduce joblessness probably has undermined public support for this perspective. Widespread perceptions that structuralist policies associated with the 1960s have failed may even harden public attitudes toward jobless low-wage workers, as these workers are perceived as unable or unwilling to take advantage of special help when offered.

As noted earlier, the importance of public perceptions of job availability in shaping attitudes toward jobless workers is demonstrated by the way these attitudes change during recessions. When unemployment rises sharply, the existence of an aggregate job shortage is taken for granted. Large numbers of normally employed workers lose their jobs, and it is readily apparent that not enough new jobs are being created to provide compensating employment opportunities. In these circumstances, the public is more likely to blame joblessness on the economy's failure to provide adequate numbers of jobs rather than on individual behavioral or structural barriers to equal employment opportunity. Relief from the problem of joblessness is likely to be sought in additional job creation, and jobless workers are likely to be viewed with more sympathy than is typical in nonrecessionary periods. Job losers will get the most sympathy, but hardened attitudes toward the long-term jobless are likely to soften as well. Jobless individuals in general are more likely to be viewed as victims of circumstance than as authors of their own fate.

Changes in the public image of jobless workers therefore depend largely on what the public perceives to be the root cause of the problem, and these perceptions tend to shift with phases of the business cycle. While the reasons for such perceptions are not difficult to comprehend, we must understand that the experiences that shape these perceptions can be misleading. Only during recessions is the role of job shortages in causing joblessness widely recognized. Ethnographers can help us to understand how labor-market experiences of low-wage workers shape both their self-image and their public image, but we should be careful not to assume that perceptions of the causes of joblessness that flow from these workers' experiences are properly balanced.

NOTES

1. *Frictional unemployment* is used to describe unemployment that results from the job search and job-screening activities undertaken by job seekers and employers prefatory to an actual hiring. Because these activities take time, a certain amount of frictional unemployment would exist even if a surplus of jobs existed relative to the number of people seeking work, and even if job search activities by job applicants were both vigorous and unhindered by structural barriers to employment.

2. In September 1999, for example, when the national unemployment rate averaged 4.2 percent, the estimated unemployment rate in the nation's metropolitan areas ranged from a low of 1.1 percent in Columbia, Missouri, to a high of 33.4 percent in Yuma, Arizona (U.S. Bureau of Labor Statistics 1999, table C-3).

3. The likelihood that a job seeker will have received a job offer necessarily increases with the length of time the individual has been unemployed. This is because the number of job applications increases with time, not because the job seeker's "turn" has arrived. Even if your chances of winning a lottery declined each time you played (as an unemployed worker's chances of being hired as a result of any particular job application probably decline over time), your chances of winning still would increase the longer you played.

4. Increased cycling on and off public assistance rolls may be one result of such a policy. This kind of cycling was common in the Aid for Families with Dependent Children (AFDC) program (Spalter-Roth et al. 1995).

5. Actually, frictional unemployment would be reduced somewhat if the existence of a larger, better-qualified applicant pool caused employers to make more rapid hiring decisions. The size of this effect is uncertain, however, and it might not be felt at all, since employers would have larger numbers of qualified applicants to screen, and it might take them longer to identify the best candidates. Better candidates also could expect to receive a larger number of job offers (they would be applying to more employers), which could delay final hiring decisions. Widespread changes in the qualifications and job search behavior of workers also might affect macroeconomic trends, but more highly qualified and motivated labor forces do not necessarily experience lower aggregate rates of unemployment, even though more highly qualified and motivated workers in a population will tend to experience lower rates of unemployment as compared to other workers in the population (as figure 2C.1 shows). (For a more extended discussion of these issues see Harvey 2000.)

REFERENCES

Abraham, Katharine G. 1983. "Structural/Frictional vs. Deficient Demand Unemployment: Some New Evidence." *American Economic Review* 73: 708–24.

Box, Steven. 1987. *Recession, Crime and Punishment.* Totowa, N.J.: Barnes and Noble Books.

Brenner, Harvey M., and Anne Mooney. 1983. "Unemployment and Health in the Context of Economic Change." *Social Science and Medicine* 17: 1125–38.

Britt, Chester L. 1994. "Crime and Unemployment Among Youths in the United States, 1958–1990: A Time Series Analysis." *American Journal of Economics and Sociology* 53: 99–109.

Burchell, Brenden. 1994. "The Effects of Labour Market Position, Job Insecurity, and Unemployment on Psychological Health." In *Social Change and the Experience of Unemployment,* edited by Duncan Gallie et al. New York: Oxford University Press.

Citro, Connie F., and Robert T. Michael. 1995. *Measuring Poverty: A New Approach.* Washington, D.C.: National Academy Press.

Dalaker, Joseph, and Mary Naifeh. 1998. "Poverty in the United States: 1997." *Current Population Reports,* series P60, no. 201. Washington: U.S. Government Printing Office.

Donohue, John J., and Peter Siegelman. 1991. "The Changing Nature of Employment Discrimination Litigation." *Stanford Law Review* 43: 983–1033.

Employment and Training Institute. 1993–2000. *Survey of Job Openings in the Milwaukee Metropolitan Area.* Milwaukee: Employment and Training Institute, University of Wisconsin, Milwaukee.

Fix, Michael, and Raymond J. Struyk. 1993. *Clear and Convincing Evidence: Measurement of Discrimination in America.* Washington, D.C.: Urban Institute.

Garner, Thesia I., et al. 1998. "Experimental Poverty Measurement for the 1990s." *Monthly Labor Review* 121(3): 39–61.

Hakim, Catherine. 1982. "The Social Consequences of High Unemployment." *Journal of Social Policy* 2: 433–67.

Harvey, Philip. 1999. "Joblessness and the Law Before the New Deal." *Georgetown Journal on Poverty Law and Policy* 6: 1–41.

———. 2000. "Combating Joblessness: An Analysis of the Principal Strategies That Have Influenced the Development of American Employment and Social Welfare Law During the 20th Century." *Berkeley Journal of Employment and Labor Law* 21: 675–757.

Holzer, Harry J. 1989. *Unemployment Vacancies and Local Labor Markets.* Kalamazoo, Mich.: W. E. Upjohn Institute for Employment Research.

———. 1996. *What Employers Want: Job Prospects for Less-Educated Workers.* New York: Russell Sage Foundation.

Jacobs, Eva E. 1997. *Handbook of U.S. Labor Statistics.* Lanham, Md.: Bernan Press.

Jahoda, Marie. 1982. *Employment and Unemployment: A Social-Psychological Analysis.* New York: Cambridge University Press.

Kelvin, Peter, and Joanna E. Jarrett. 1985. *Unemployment: Its Social Psychological Effects.* New York: Cambridge University Press.

Liem, Ramsay, and Paula Rayman. 1982. "Health and Social Costs of Unemployment: Research and Policy Considerations." *American Psychologist* 37: 1116–23.

Marmor, Theodore R., Jerry L. Mashaw, and Philip L. Harvey. 1990. *America's Misunderstood Welfare State.* New York: Basic Books.

Mead, Lawrence. 1992. *The New Politics of Poverty: The Nonworking Poor in America.* New York: Basic Books.

O'Brien, Gordon E. 1986. *Psychology of Work and Unemployment.* New York: John Wiley and Sons.

Sawhill, Isabel V. 1988. "Poverty in the U.S.: Why Is It So Persistent?" *Journal of Economic Literature* 26: 1073–1119.

Smith, M. Dwayne, Joel A. Devine, and Joseph F. Sheley. 1992. "Crime and Unemployment: Effects Across Age and Race Categories." *Sociological Perspectives* 35: 551–72.

Spalter-Roth, Roberta, et al. 1995. *Welfare That Works: The Working Lives of AFDC Recipients.* Washington, D.C.: Institute for Women's Policy Research.

U.S. Bureau of Labor Statistics. 1997. *Issues in Labor Statistics: Looking for a Job While Employed.* BLS Summary 97–14. Washington: U.S. Government Printing Office.

———. 1999. *Employment and Earnings* 46(12).

Wilson, William J. 1996. *When Work Disappears: The World of the New Urban Poor.* New York: Knopf.

Commentary

Looking for Stories of Inner-City Politics: From the Personal to the Global

Carl H. Nightingale

Ethnography is suffused with politics. Ethnographers cannot divorce themselves from the complex consequences of their power to shape the stories of others. At the same time, the very concept of culture—ethnography's Holy Grail—is a deeply contested one, forever in political play. Indeed, ethnographers who specialize in the culture of the urban poor inevitably enter into some of the most critical debates in contemporary American politics. The idea that inner-city residents' culture causes their poverty is a central article of faith for the contemporary advocates of restrictive welfare reforms that emphasize driving recipients into low-wage job markets. The concept of a culture of poverty also has implications for racial politics. As Stephen Steinberg (1997) reminds us, the argument that inner-city residents suffer from a culture of "pathology" or "dependency" can often be used to evoke racist images of people of color as immutably degraded. Such innuendos regularly have been employed to justify the relaxation of civil rights enforcement, the abolition of entitlements to public assistance, and discriminatory forms of social control and incarceration.

Ethnographers have drained barrels of ink coming to terms with the power relations and political conflicts implicit in their work. At their best, they have explored ways to make their work more accountable to the communities that provide them with basic empirical material. Ethnographic essays such as those on inner-city work and poverty in this volume reveal inner-city lives that are complex, constantly changing, and responsive to a variety of value systems that come from both inside and outside the inner city. These essays tell stories of people engaged in striving for a better life—contrary to the images promoted by critics of the poor and opponents of generous welfare programs. The ethnographers who have contributed to this volume begin with the idea that culture itself cannot cause poverty, and they recognize that both culture and poverty respond to and interact with forces largely outside the control of inner-city residents.

Even the best stories, however, could dig more deeply into two aspects of inner-city politics. For one, inner-city culture, including the values that people espouse and act on and the emotions they feel, is a site of conflict with its own politics. Second, the dynamics of this culture and its relationship to institutions beyond the control of inner-city residents are inextricably bound up in the broader political currents of world historical change. Despite their relative powerlessness, inner-city residents *contribute* to currents of global change. Ethnographers collecting stories in such communities should keep an eye out for both political dimensions of inner-city life and work. As a result, their stories will not only be richer and more revealing, but new avenues may open up for contending with the dilemma of attempting to speak for inner-city residents through ethnography.

I come to these ideas from two different projects in my research agenda, one an ethnography informed by my training as a historian, the other a history informed by my experiences as an ethnographer. The first project focuses on inner-city youth politics and seeks to understand the connections between the personal dimensions of inner-city politics, the public struggles for power that define urban young people's lives, and the emergence of activist youth concerned with inner-city movement building. The second is a project in the field of global history, which offers an interpretive framework for understanding the roots of current inner-city poverty, segregation, and disempowerment in the context of world historical change.

THE POLITICS OF INNER-CITY LIFE

Behavior, beliefs, and emotions float in a sea of politics. The interconnections between actions, values, and feelings make most sense when they are related to people's ongoing negotiations for power—within their own consciences, with each other, and with institutions over which they have relatively little control. In turn, the negotiation of power by poor people is intertwined with evolving inner-city aesthetic traditions. Though the verbal, sonic, graphic, performative, sartorial, and stylistic expressions of inner-city residents are recognized worldwide, our stories about inner cities often overlook the ways their residents produce such cultural forms and aesthetic creations in their daily lives.

These reflections arise out of both admiration for and concerns about efforts to apply concepts such as *resistance, infrapolitics,* and *hidden transcripts* to the study of inner-city life. These concepts owe their roots to the work of the anthropologist James C. Scott (1990), who argued that the Malaysian peasants he studied employed both a "public transcript" that made them seem, on the surface, politically quiescent or complicit with structures of oppression, and a "hidden transcript" that contained more critical or even insurgent beliefs and practices occurring outside public view. Scott hypothesized that such hidden transcripts, or "infrapolitics," could be found among other groups of oppressed people and cited historians of the slave-holding South, who found daily patterns of resistance in such practices as field songs that contained veiled jabs at masters, slowdown tactics, petty theft, and sabotage of plantation equipment (Scott 1990).

The historian Robin D. G. Kelley has been at the forefront of efforts to apply these concepts to inner-city life. In a number of essays, Kelley has interpreted everything from the bus-riding behavior of African Americans in the wartime urban South to Malcolm X's early life in the streets, dance halls, and hustling scene of Boston's Roxbury—and from the subversion of work rules Kelley himself witnessed and took part in as a teenage worker at a Los Angeles McDonald's in the 1970s to the lyrics of Los Angeles gangsta rap groups in the 1990s—as evidence of ignored political activity (Kelley 1994, 1997). He argues that though this activity may not be organized, and though participants may not deem it either political or resistant, it nevertheless often serves as a foundation for more formal and deliberate acts of opposition to various forms of dominance. Tricia Rose (1994) has used the same concepts in her interpretation of rap in New York; and the self-described anarchist criminologist Jeff Ferrell (1993) has adapted them in his analysis of graffiti writing in inner-city Denver as an "anarchist act." For all three scholars, the imaginative and artful production of pleasure and play is also a central component of inner-city politics.

Over the past few years I have begun a long-term project on the politics of young people in inner cities, based on both print material and my experiences as a volunteer in both informal and formal projects of youth-led political activism. One goal is to illuminate the variety of arenas, strategies, expressive styles, emotional struggles, and moral and ideological debates involved in inner-city negotiations over power and accountability. The youth politics I am looking for operates within families, peer groups, romantic relationships, schools, workplaces, social welfare offices, public transport, stores, churches, neighborhoods, hospital emergency rooms, social movements, nonprofit agencies, police stations, prisons, cross-race or cross-class encounters, consumer culture, all sorts of governmental institutions, and the global economy—in addition to joking games, concert arenas, recording studios, and the "walls of fame" of graffiti writers. Within (and between) such varied avenues to power and accountability, young people themselves make critical distinctions about belief, feeling, style, rhetoric, strategy, organizing, and action. Each avenue of political activity can be perceived by young people as a more or less likely pathway toward the acquisition of personal power, or the site of one's own or a community's sense of accountability. Thus each can be chosen or rejected as a preferred place for social performance or action, whether such action involves strategies of concealment and hidden transcripts or not. Each of these arenas might be associated with a different set of beliefs and ideologies, emotional memories, or styles of personal expression. Alternatively, politics in one realm may color politics in another.

On what might be its most *micro*level, though, inner-city youth politics occurs within the realm of internal personal struggles for power and accountability. These consist of the negotiations young people carry on within the realm of their own moral consciousness and subconscious emotional memories when they make important decisions about their lives. Calling such internal struggles political may take some getting used to, but note that like all political struggles, individuals' efforts to resolve complicated moral conflicts or contend with painful emotional memories involve the mobilization of beliefs or ideologies, rhetoric, style, and personal resources in an often hostile world—a world that they may have partly internalized and that thus can operate from powerful positions inside their own consciences and emotions. Such personal struggles for power encompass what Bourgois (1996) calls "searches for respect," what Kelley (1994) refers to as experiences of fun, pleasure, and rebelliousness, and what inner-city residents often refer to as their effort to gain "props" (for "proper respect"), "power," or "to be my own person."

For example, young people writing for a newsletter called *The Beat Within* for incarcerated youth in the San Francisco Bay Area often refer to their personal struggles in terms of power, self-control, and accountability. They often find themselves, for instance, debating within their own moral consciences about whether they will resume gangbanging when they get out. They also speak of inner emotional turmoil. A short article by a young man named Rens One begins by recalling the day when his father left the family. "With abandonment comes loneliness," he writes, "and when there is loneliness, there is no love. And without love, my heart is filled with anger." Yet anger arising from loss is only one side of Rens One's inner struggle:

> As I stare into the mirror, as I stare into my eyes, as my reflection stares into me, I realize life without love is a life not worth holding onto. . . . But when I find this love it overwhelms me with joy . . . a joy that goes beyond the moon and the stars, a joy that replaces the anger and hatred in my heart with love. A reason to live, something to hold onto, the strength I need to pursue my struggle in life. (Rens One, n.d.)

The article by Rens One also suggests many ways in which his hidden internal politics can play out in public arenas, too, recasting his conflict to fit different circumstances and constituencies. Not only does Rens One negotiate with his own reflection in a hidden, private realm using love as his strategy for "strength," he wrote the article as a public expression, using vivid language as a strategy (the article also includes his elaborate graffiti-style drawing of the words *The Beat Within*). His feelings arose from the politics of family relationships. The act of creating the article, in turn, reflected the politics of a writing workshop run by a nonprofit organization that publishes *The Beat* under contract with the San Francisco Youth Guidance Center (YGC) where Rens One is incarcerated. We can only guess at the politics of Rens One's strategies within each of these realms. His article won the Piece of the Week award from the newsletter staff, an honor that may have benefited Rens One as an inmate as well as in other ways. Finally, Rens One titled his article "The Soundless Cries from the Inner City." In this way he may have been commenting on politics in two other realms. He could be referring to peer and gang life, or to the importance young men place on their ability to conceal their pain from one another in order to establish masculine heart and respect (a theme referred to often in the newsletter). He also may have been demanding that such "cries" be more a part of representations of inner-city and American life in mainstream media.

If political strategies can spill across the boundaries of different social realms, the informal politics of day-to-day life, as Kelley has argued, possibly may give us clues to the nature of more organized movement building in inner cities and to residents' activity within formal political institutions. We should not be surprised if the politics and motives of one realm evolves as it fuels contention beyond its original venue. Consider the case of the North End branch of the Almighty Latin King and Queen Nation (ALKQN) in Springfield, Massachusetts, which decided under the influence of one of its incarcerated leaders to abandon the politics of gangbanging and become a community organization. In 1996, ALKQN joined forces with Arise for Social Justice, a long-standing welfare rights organization in inner-city Mason Square. As police cars nervously swarmed on all sides, the two groups marched from Mason Square to the state government building downtown to present Governor William Weld with a Community Destruction Award in protest of his advocacy of a draconian welfare "reform" program. Here the strategy was quite public—though authorities strongly suspected that ALKQN's actions involved effort to hide a still-ongoing transcript of gang war politics. Indeed, at least one element from gang politics did persist, though again very publicly, in the beliefs underlying ALKQN's participation in the protest. To the consternation of some allied welfare rights advocates from Arise for Social Justice who weren't prepared to laugh at the irony, the spokesman from ALKQN repeatedly insisted to TV reporters that the new move was inspired by a desire to do good by their "Queens." (That and other more substantial political disagreements led to the decline and fall of the alliance some months later.)

These stories suggest a world that is both messier and less centrally driven by the pursuit of pleasure than Kelley's, Rose's, or Ferrell's portraits of the politics of inner-city expressive culture. Sometimes such political endeavors are more ambiguous than suggested by the term *resistance*. At other times (as suggested by my experiences with numerous dedicated youth activists in Boston and Springfield), inner-city politics is more thoughtfully radicalized and engaged in organizing for social change than either infrapolitics or conventional views of apathetic and apolitical inner-city residents would suggest. Moreover, inner-city residents have no monopoly on hiding their political transcripts; dominant institutions can falsely impute sinister and hidden agendas to poor people as well. Furthermore, residents' own hidden transcripts make up only one segment of a vast and creative variety of strategic options for responding to conditions of poverty and powerlessness in the inner city.

Analyzing the politics of inner-city life allows ethnographers to endow a living social context with complex decision making underlying the moral life, emotional memories, behavioral habits, and expressive styles of inner-city residents. Such analysis also allows ethnographers to think more completely about the possibilities for organized collective action emerging from inner cities to change economic and social conditions.[1]

ETHNOGRAPHERS AND THE GLOBAL INNER CITY

At the turn of the twenty-first century, when *globalization* is one of our hottest buzzwords, we have yet to find compelling ways to link our discussions of the contemporary global political economy with those of inner-city life (Nightingale 1998). Further, neither the contemporary discussion of globalization nor that of inner-city life seems to appreciate the close connection between these topics and understanding the influence of race and racial politics. Can ethnographers help with a project for telling world history? "By convention," Michael Burawoy et al. (2000, 1) notes, "global ethnography is an oxymoron"; and yet, he points out, no local time or place—or ethnographer—is untouched by "the fateful processes of our age" (4). Understanding how the local and momentary fits into the global and historical is a first step, Burawoy maintains, toward "deploying new cognitive maps" in the search for stories that will help us understand these significant broader contexts and meanings. Burawoy concludes that ethnographers not only can open their studies to the world but also make the world itself the subject of their investigations.

As a historian, I believe that ethnographers can improve our understanding of the connections between inner cities and broader global changes if they pay more attention to the cultural and political dynamics underlying global change. Doing so would distinguish such ethnography from the approaches taken by William Julius Wilson and Saskia Sassen—perhaps the two scholars of urban job markets and globalization most familiar to urban ethnographers. In *When Work Disappears* (1996), Wilson acknowledges the importance of "the new global economy" for inner-city residents. Though he does not attempt to build a systematic theory of the nature of that new economy, Wilson argues that deindustrialization and loss of jobs for the growing unskilled labor force has been driven, in part, by the globalization of production, importation of cheap-labor goods, and technological change favoring higher-skill jobs, as well as by rising inequality and increasing "strains on the welfare state" in all advanced economies, including the United States (1996, 236). The second approach to understanding the implications of globalization is the research undertaken by Saskia Sassen on the role of large cities in the emerging world economy. In *The Global City*, Sassen argues that the dispersion of economic activities characteristic of globalization has resulted in the centralization, within relatively few large cities, of certain highly specialized and highly remunerated tasks involved in the management of global financial and corporate institutions. When this happens, especially acute inequalities arise in those cities between a highly paid, globe-trotting managerial elite and a throng of low-paid workers—most of whom are immigrants, often in informal work situations—who provide services to the elite (Sassen 1991, 2000).

Ethnographers of the inner city and the lives of the poor, such as those who have contributed to this volume, have learned much from the work of Wilson and Sassen. They have focused on one of the principal causes of poverty identified in their work: the changes in the low-wage job market that have been caused by global economic change. This connection between low-wage job markets and inner-city life suggests another key point: ethnography of inner-city communities should not restrict itself solely to the lives of residents but rather should devote equal attention to institutions that work within inner-city communities, but that are run by people outside.

Although Wilson, Sassen, and other theorists of globalization open up avenues, they also obscure possibilities open to global ethnography in inner cities. From a world historian's point of view, concepts such as globalization, deindustrialization, automation, centralization, dispersion, informalization, and even migration depersonalize change and endow it with a certain inevitability—even teleology. Such "objectification," Burawoy notes, "can be a powerful source of mystification," and he suggests that we look at global "forces, connections, and imaginations" in terms of their essentially contested nature (Burawoy et al. 2000, 27–28). Indeed, from an ethnographer's point of view, the depersonalization of world historical change deemphasizes precisely those cultural and political characteristics of change that can be most deeply explored through participant observation and storytelling.

The current episode of global transformation is not simply a story of increasingly dense connections across the world, such as the globalization of production lines or the technologies that have enabled their creation. Perhaps even more important, it is a story about the people who seek to control those new webs of connection and technologies, the strategies they have employed, and the beliefs they use to justify their efforts. The history of contemporary global transformation is about how rival efforts to shape the world economy and world culture have come into conflict. Global change is contingent on the ways localities experience the very complex outcomes of such cultural and political conflicts.

Two of these global cultural and political conflicts have had the greatest importance for inner-city culture and its job markets. The first conflict concerned the political architecture of the increasingly internationalized world economy. Reformist liberals gained the upper hand between about 1944 and 1973 by successfully promoting a vision in which relatively extensive welfare and regulatory states governed nation-states and their economies; accords between labor and capital governed job markets; and the system of international capital regulations created at Bretton Woods governed transoceanic flows of money and investment. That vision lost ground after 1973 to a resurgent neoliberal vision of the world that used free market rhetoric to increase the power of multinational corporations within deregulated international and domestic financial systems, the affairs of national governments, the mass media, workplaces, and local communities. Neoliberals have whittled away at the institutions of welfare states: social provision, regulation states, and labor-capital accords.

A second global conflict concerned the politics of race. Unprecedented worldwide uprisings of people of color, united less by transnational institutions than by a common belief in ideas of racial equality, overthrew the system of formal Western colonization, disassembled legalized systems of racial segregation such as southern Jim Crow, and dealt a major blow to the scientific and ethical legitimacy of white supremacy. Since then, many of the victories won by those movements have been rolled back by opposing, self-styled New Right movements that have arisen in most of the world's multiracial societies dominated by people of European descent. These racially conservative movements take numerous forms, but all quietly defend institutions of white privilege by publicly avowing race-neutral beliefs in individualism, equality of opportunity, and the integrity of national traditions. At the same time, all employ racially charged code words to keep many white supremacist images alive, including suggestions that communities of color suffer from immutable "cultural" deficiencies. Such conservatives have undercut efforts to redress the world's racial inequalities and have imposed systems of draconian social control that disproportionately affect people of color.

When we go in search of stories about inner-city work culture, we should be aware that we are essentially looking for traces of the ways in which these global conflicts play themselves out—within individuals' consciences, in homes, on the streets, between residents and mainstream institutions, and within mainstream institutions themselves. The phrase *global inner city* means something broader and a bit different from Sassen's concept of the global city. *All* American inner cities—not just those located in large and more important places such as New York—are global phenomena, because like all local places, much of their essence is tied up in global change, and particularly, global political change. Inner cities deserve to be called *global* in at least four ways. First, they are the *creation* of global political conflict and change. Second, their residents help *to create* global political conflict and change. Third, they are an *important site*—a battle site, if you will—of that conflict and change. Finally, they are a *symbol,* one with multiple interpretations that are used by opposing interests in global economic and racial politics.

All of these aspects of the global inner city are accessible through ethnography. In some cases, indeed, ethnography may be the best way to derive a deeper understanding of global connections. To dig deeper into inner-city life as a creation of global conflict and change, ethnographers need to expand their study of the institutions that operate in inner cities, run by people from outside. What Burawoy (2000) calls a "welding of ethnohistory to ethnography" will be necessary here. On the ethnohistorical level, the foundations of globally connected institutions will need some excavation, as will the relationship of those foundations to global politics. Changes over time in the founding visions of such institutions will be an important aspect of the story. Historical understanding will help to establish the living nature of so-called mainstream values as they operate in the particular institution. On the ethnographic level, research will reveal that the ordinary lives of inner-city residents are influenced by both remote and proximate political processes that create and guide institutions that dominate their lives.

Many questions about low-wage job markets should be addressed, including the missions and operations of individual workplaces. How does the institutional structure of the workplace reflect global conflicts among different political interests and their ideologies—promarket neoliberal ideals, reformist or union-led campaigns, racial egalitarianism, and ideologies supporting racial exclusion? How do these ideals interact with regulatory agencies overseeing the operation of the workplace? How do these interacting ideals play out in the actions of personnel managers, immediate supervisors, and other people who have direct connections with inner-city residents? How do officials working in regulatory agencies, nongovernmental watchdogs, police departments, or immigration control agencies affect the diffusion of globally linked institutional cultures onto the work floor? What political values do customers bring to the cultural mix? How does mass marketing to the inner city—such as the McDonald's Is a Happy Place campaign described in Newman's study of low-wage employees (1999)—import global political struggles into the workplace?

Ethnography of job sites also may reveal how inner-city residents themselves *create* world history. By undertaking this research we will illuminate the relationship between inner-city culture and the mainstream, the extent and origins of inner-city resistance and other political behavior, and reception, appropriation, and recreation of messages from mass media and mainstream culture by the public at large. For example, how does the meaning of work for individual inner-city residents reflect, contrast with, or transform the values proclaimed by the contemporary political and policy decision makers, with their emphasis on the importance of market labor, reduction of welfare, and deregulation of the workplace? How do inner-city racial ideologies come into play? To what extent do inner-city residents know about and employ regulatory agencies or unionization campaigns? To what extent is their resistance more complex, perhaps drawing on several different, even conflicting, ideals or values to make it possible to preserve personal or a group of workers' dignity in a confusing or hostile environment?

Finally, the inner city is itself a symbol in global conflicts. All of the world's conflicting visions of society find the word *ghetto* useful to underscore their points. As a result, *ghetto* has become a familiar yet multivalent keyword across the world: some use it as a synonym for the dangers attendant on withdrawing from beliefs about the sanctity of wage work; others employ it to invoke unalterable cultural attributes of people of color and the need for restrictive immigration; and still others use it to inspire outrage at economic inequality and racial segregation. Residents of inner cities themselves use "ghetto" too. Some use it to denigrate their circumstances, and in so doing play on broader meanings of the word. As Kelley (1997) has argued, inner-city residents also may use *ghetto* to express local pride, or, like many hip-hop artists, as a powerful symbol of unity and resistance conveyed to communities of color worldwide. All such meanings have implications for inner-city residents' experiences of low-wage workplaces, for example, by affecting the marketing and location decisions of businesses, by shaping the meaning of a good or responsible employee, or by inspiring critiques of today's labor markets.

In addition to building on theoretical insights and involving themselves in historical research, it may be also necessary, as Burawoy and his colleagues (2000) have suggested, for ethnographers to engage in research that has been "unbound" from its single-site focus. Multisite ethnography may be especially critical for ethnographers interested in such topics as how employers view different communities of color, transnational migration systems, international reception of symbols and ideas linked to similar global political efforts, and in comparative studies, say, of reasons for differing levels of resistance among the world's urban poor.

All of the additional questions for reflection and fieldwork suggested here should be worth the effort. If our stories of low-wage work, economic survival, and other daily realities of the poor accurately reflect the complex, historical, and global influence of inner-city institutions, they will lead to deeper understanding of what is at stake for us all. If we are properly attentive to these stories, we may arrive at perspectives and answers that will enable those seemingly trapped by poverty to bring about change even in confrontations with powerful global institutions. As Burawoy (2000, 32) put it nicely, "global imaginations reconfigure what is possible, turning globalization from an inexorable force into a resource that opens up new vistas." In view of the worldwide forces in play and our need to face them, the final test of our endeavors may be whether our storytelling projects are able to support, strengthen, and answer to movements among inner-city residents themselves—movements that seek their connections worldwide and that promote their global visions.

NOTE

1. Another possible benefit to an expansive analysis of inner-city political life is that it may help us better frame researchers' problematic relationships to the community they are studying—though the following must be taken as an exploration of possibilities, not any clear prescriptions. At critical issue here is the extent to which any of these arenas of inner-city politics might be called legitimate *sites of accountability*— that is, places where community members deliberate matters of personal or collective concern in reasonably good faith and in which, to one degree or another, members have been entrusted to speak for the community at large, or at least a segment of it. The relationship between researchers and such sites of accountability could consist of an individual's decision about whether or not to bring a researcher into his or her life, or that decision could take place within the deliberations of families—perhaps within the "webs of mutual obligation" Carol Stack has spoken

of in her work on urban African American extended kin networks. Or, perhaps, such a decision could take place in a streetcorner hangout group, a crack operation, a more or less democratically run nonprofit agency, a local cell of a social movement, or a segment of the hip-hop nation.

REFERENCES

Appadurai, Arjun. 1991. "Global Ethnoscapes: Notes and Queries for a Transnational Anthropology." In *Recapturing Anthropology: Working in the Present*, edited by Richard J. Fox. Sante Fe, N.M.: School of American Research Press.

Bourgois, Philippe. 1996. *In Search of Respect: Selling Crack in El Barrio*. Cambridge: Cambridge University Press.

Burawoy, Michael, Joseph A. Blum, Sheba George, Zsuzsa Gille, Teresa Gowan, Lynne Haney, Maren Klawiter, Steven H. Lopez, Seán Ó Riain, and Milli Thayer. 2000. *Global Ethnography: Forces, Connections, and Imaginations in a Postmodern World*. Berkeley: University of California Press.

Ferrell, Jeff. 1993. *Crimes of Style: Urban Graffiti and the Politics of Criminality*. Boston: Northeastern University Press.

Kelley, Robin D. G. 1994. *Race Rebels: Culture, Politics, and the Black Working Class*. New York: Free Press.

———. 1997. *Yo Mama's DisFUNKtional! Fighting the Culture Wars in Urban America*. Boston: Beacon.

Lipsitz, George. 1994. *Dangerous Crossroads: Popular Music, Postmodernism, and the Poetics of Place*. London: Verso.

Newman, Katherine S. 1999. *No Shame in My Game: The Working Poor in the Inner City*. New York: Russell Sage Foundation.

Nightingale, Carl H. 1993. *On the Edge: A History of Poor Black Children and Their American Dreams*. New York: Basic Books.

———. 1998. "The Global Inner City: Toward a Historical Analysis." In *W.E.B. Du Bois, Race, and the City: The Philadelphia Negro and Its Legacy*, edited by Michael B. Katz and Thomas J. Sugrue. Philadelphia: University of Pennsylvania Press.

Rens One. N.d. "The Soundless Cries from the Inner City." *The Beat Within* 4(1): 1.

Rose, Tricia. 1994. *Black Noise: Rap Music and Black Culture in Contemporary America*. Hanover, N.H.: Wesleyan University Press.

Sassen, Saskia. 1991. *The Global City: New York, London, Tokyo*. Princeton, N.J.: Princeton University Press.

Scott, James C. 1990. *Domination and the Arts of Resistance: Hidden Transcripts*. New Haven: Yale University Press.

Steinberg, Stephen. 1997. "The Liberal Retreat from Race During the Post–Civil Rights Era." In *The House That Race Built: Black Americans, U.S. Terrain*, edited by Wahneema Lubiano. New York: Pantheon.

Wilson, William Julius. 1996. *When Work Disappears: The World of the New Urban Poor*. New York: Alfred A. Knopf.

Part II

MAKING DECISIONS ABOUT WORK, FAMILY, AND WELFARE

Chapter 3

Taking Care of Business: The Economic Survival Strategies of Low-Income, Noncustodial Fathers

Kathryn Edin, Laura Lein, and Timothy Nelson

They are young, poor and hard beyond their years, with resumes that often list jails, not jobs. Their earnings have spent decades in decline, and so has their likelihood to marry. Yet there is a growing sense that the nation's ambitious welfare overhaul cannot succeed without them.

—Jason De Parle, New York Times,
September 3, 1998

As states try to figure out how to implement time-limited welfare without disadvantaging millions of poor single women and children, their focus increasingly turns to noncustodial fathers. Many federal lawmakers and private foundations seem convinced that fathers must be economically reconnected with their families for welfare reform to work. In 1998, Clay Shaw, one of the authors of the welfare reform law, sponsored legislation to increase federal spending on education and training programs for noncustodial fathers. Dozens of private foundations also are funding work and training programs for men in this group. Several states are planning to spend millions of their "welfare-to-work" dollars (the $3 billion in federal funds set aside to help the most "hard to serve" families) on programs aimed at reconnecting fathers with families.

This chapter explores the economic lives of 125 low-income, noncustodial fathers whom we interviewed in-depth just as the new welfare law was being implemented (between 1996 and 1998). The media often portrays such men as irresponsible deadbeats who ignore their responsibilities to the children they father. These portrayals remain largely unchallenged, perhaps partly because surveys tend to underrepresent such men. Garfinkel, McLanahan, and Hanson (1998) have estimated that as many as 40 percent of all noncustodial fathers are missing from some surveys. Furthermore, they claim that no survey is free of large underrepresentation problems. They argue that roughly one half of the underrepresentation is due to the fact that some noncustodial fathers are missing from the survey, and the other half is due to the fact that some men surveyed do not admit that they are noncustodial fathers (whether from avarice or ignorance). Underrepresentation is particularly acute for noncustodial fathers at the low end of the income distribution, the group on which our study focuses. The undercount is more severe for black noncustodial fathers than for their white counterparts (43 percent versus 70 percent) and for men without a high school diploma than for men with a high school degree (48 percent versus 84 percent). The problem also is greater for fathers of nonmarital children than for those who married their child's mother (48 percent versus 78 percent). Low-income fathers are more likely to be minorities, less likely to have a high school diploma, and more likely to have children outside of marriage. Thus low-income, noncustodial fathers are much more likely to be missing from surveys than more affluent fathers (McLanahan et al. 2001).

Based on our research, this is not surprising. Many of the low-income, noncustodial fathers in the cities and neighborhoods we studied often shift residence, experience bouts of homelessness, or do not reside permanently in any one household. Since many surveys are household based, these fathers are easily missed because of their residential instability. Our research revealed other potential problems for survey researchers as well. Some fathers we spoke to are evading child support orders or are on the run from the law for other reasons. Others are engaged in crime for a living. Fathers in any of these situations would be less likely to participate in a survey than fathers in more conventional situations because they probably fear talking to anyone who is a stranger or looks "official." Thus the portrait we present in this chapter is one of a group of fathers that social science has not been able to describe reliably.

By employing ethnographic fieldwork techniques that promote trust between researcher and subject, we were able to identify a large and heterogeneous group of low-income noncustodial fathers across two large metropolitan areas (Austin, Texas, and Philadelphia, Pennsylvania). Through in-depth semistructured interviews with these fathers, we elicited detailed portraits of the day-to-day economic realities they face, gathered accounts of their own assessment of their ability to participate economically and emotionally in their children's lives, and descriptions of their actual fathering behavior. The men spoke of their feelings about themselves as fathers as well as the importance that being a father played in their larger life experiences.

Our research with low-income noncustodial fathers of African American, Latin, and European descent parallels earlier work two of us conducted with 379 low-income single mothers in four U.S. cities in the early 1990s (Edin and Lein 1997a, 1997b). In-depth, repeated interviews with these mothers showed that welfare recipients and low-wage working mothers both faced large budget shortfalls each month and routinely exposed their children to material hardship. From mothers, we learned that noncustodial fathers often made significant (although often covert) cash contributions to mothers' households. Though most mothers generated side income through a number of different channels, men provided the largest share of mothers' supplemental income.

Mothers' reports suggest that mothers recognize the difficulties their children's fathers face: how to eke out a subsistence living at the low end of the labor market; how to maintain a relationship with children for whom one does not assume either day-to-day emotional or financial responsibility; how to maintain self-respect through periods of incarceration, incapacitation, and unemployment; how to resist the lure of the drug economy when other work opportunities are scarce; how to resist the lure of drugs and alcohol; and how to avoid street violence. Though mothers said they understood fathers' circumstances, most still insisted that consistent financial support was a prerequisite for an ongoing relationship between a father and his children. These data, however, were drawn solely from mothers' reports of fathers' behavior, not fathers' descriptions of their own behavior. In this research, our goal was to understand the story from the father's point of view.

RESEARCH ON NONCUSTODIAL FATHERS

Prior to the 1980s, social scientists and policy makers paid little attention to the economic situations and parenting behaviors of noncustodial fathers. This is partly because prior to 1970, most children lived with their fathers, and most fathers were married to their children's mothers. In 1960, only 2.3 percent of white children and 22 percent of African American children were born to unmarried parents, and divorce among parents was relatively rare (U.S. Bureau of the Census 1986, 62). By 1989, the rate of white nonmarital births was 19 percent, and the rate of black nonmarital births had climbed to 64 percent (U.S. Bureau of the Census 1992, 69). In those three decades, divorce rates among parents also rose dramatically. By the late 1980s, demographers estimated that 60 percent of children born in the 1980s would spend at least part of their childhood living apart from one of their biological parents (Bumpass and Sweet 1989; Sweet and Bumpass 1987).

Another reason that academic interest in noncustodial fathers probably grew is due to the powerful correlation between single parenthood and child poverty. Nearly half of single-parent households live in poverty and nearly three quarters live below 200 percent of the poverty line (U.S. House of Representatives 1998). Furthermore, most poor children's poverty status is chronic rather than transitory. One analysis predicts that between 47 and 90 percent of poor children currently living in female-headed households will remain below the poverty line for six or more of the next ten years, depending on the race and education levels of their parents (Stevens 1995). Not only are children of single parents more likely to be poor than other children, they face other disadvantages as they mature into adulthood. Among the negative outcomes associated with growing up with a single parent are an increased probability of high school dropout, youth delinquency, teenage parenthood, adult unemployment, and decreased education and economic attainment overall (McLanahan and Sandefur 1994; see also Korenman, Miller, and Sjaastad 1995).

Changes in eligibility and use of social welfare programs probably increased interest in this population as well. As welfare rolls more than tripled during the 1960s and 1970s, legislators began looking for a way to make noncustodial fathers—whether divorced, separated, or unmarried—take financial responsibility for their children. In the early 1970s, only a tiny portion of nonmarital children had legal fathers (even in the mid-1980s, the paternity rate was only 31 percent for nonmarital births [Ooms and Herendeen 1988]), and only 37 percent of young men who admitted to the National Longitudinal Survey of Youth (NLSY) that they were unwed fathers said that they paid any child support in 1985. Furthermore, strong evidence indicates that men who admit to being unwed fathers overreport their child support contributions. A much smaller proportion of never-married mothers (13 percent) reported in 1985 that they were receiving child support provided as a part of a court order or voluntary agreement in 1985 (Lerman 1993, 46, 49). The problem of nonsupport was (and is) not limited to never-married fathers. Separated and divorced fathers also sometimes escape a formal child support order and often fail to pay even when they have a legal obligation to do so (Furstenburg, Morgan, and Allison 1987).

In 1975, the federal government amended the Social Security Act and mandated that child support be established and enforced through thousands of new state child support enforcement offices (Howe 1993). Welfare recipients were forced to cooperate with child support officials in identifying the fathers of their children, establishing legal paternity, obtaining a child support award, and collecting the money. Those recipients who refused without good cause could lose benefit eligibility. The federal government also required welfare recipients to sign their rights to child support over to the state. Though the services of the child support enforcement offices were available to everyone at little or no cost, most of their caseload was welfare-reliant. Though these offices' efforts proved somewhat effective, the collection rates for welfare-reliant children were abysmally low throughout the 1970s and 1980s (Ellman, Kurtz, and Stanton 1986).

In crafting the Family Support Act of 1988 (FSA), federal legislators tried to address the ineffectiveness of child support enforcement among the welfare poor by mandating that states increase the percentage of nonmarital births for whom legal paternity is established. The act also required all states to withhold child support payments from the father's paycheck automatically rather than rely on their voluntary payment (Howe 1993, 158). These and other FSA mandates have been phased in gradually over the last decade, and child support collections have improved somewhat, but not as much as federal lawmakers had hoped. An analysis of the Current Population Survey (CPS) shows that the percentage of single mothers receiving at least some child support increased from 27.6 percent in 1980 to 34.5 percent in 1996 (Huang, Garfinkel, and Waldfogel 1999). The welfare reform bill of 1996 contained additional legislation designed to further enable states to meet these mandates, yet past experience suggests that states continue to face formidable challenges.

Since it has proven so difficult to obligate noncustodial fathers to provide economic support for their children, researchers have focused increased attention on the economic circumstances of noncustodial fathers. The employment prospects of such men have declined dramatically since the 1970s. The percentage of year-round, full-time workers with low annual earnings (those who earn less than the poverty line for a family of four) increased from 7 percent in 1974 to 14 percent in 1990. For whites, the rate increased from 7 percent to 13 percent. For blacks, the rate increased from 14 percent to 22 percent, and for those of Hispanic origin, from 12 percent to 28 percent (U.S. House of Representatives 1993).

Thus unskilled and semiskilled fathers' ability to provide economic support for their children has declined. Academics focused not only on fathers' ability to pay, but also on their willingness and sense of obligation. The journalist Leon Dash's *When Children Want Children* (1989) develops a portrait of six young mothers who are victims of careless and irresponsible young men who encourage them to get pregnant yet feel no obligation to take on the responsibilities of parenting. Bill Moyers's well-known 1986 CBS special report *The Vanishing Family* features a young unwed father of four named Timothy who quips, "what I don't do, the government does" and "you know what they say; 'mama baby, papa maybe.'"

Ethnographic accounts suggest that structural and cultural factors intersect in ways that discourage noncustodial fathers' sense of obligation to provide financial and emotional support to their children. Mercer Sullivan's (1989) ethnographic work among young low-income black, white, and Latino teenage fathers in Brooklyn shows that although community norms strongly support father involvement, the paucity of labor market and training opportunities for very young minority fathers make successful performance of the fathering role difficult. Elijah Anderson's (1993) interviews with black teenage boys in Philadelphia shows the powerful role that bleak economic prospects and deviant peer group norms play in lessening these adolescents' sense of their obligations as fathers.

Both Sullivan and Anderson emphasize the experiences of teenagers, many of whom were not yet fathers when they were studied. Indeed, the majority of social science literature on nonresidential fathers concentrates on this age group (see Lerman and Ooms 1993). Yet two thirds of nonmarital births occur to adult women whose partners are two years older than they are, on average (Lerman 1993). In sum, the focus on very young fathers has meant that we understand very little about the experiences of older fathers. This deficit is serious, since longitudinal studies demonstrate that teenage fathers' involvement with their children falls off rapidly over time. Thus we know little about the process by which fathers disengage from their children over time.[1] Elliot Liebow's (1967) ethnography of street corner black men in Washington, D.C., does lend some insight in this regard; he suggests that over time, fathers find it more rewarding to support other men's children rather than their own. Liebow's study is several decades old, however, and provides little detailed information on the actual amounts these fathers contributed or the full range of financial resources that were available to them.

Data drawn from repeated in-depth interviews with nearly 400 low-income single mothers in four U.S. cities suggests that adult men make substantial, although irregular, cash contributions to the households containing their children (Edin and Lein 1997b; Edin 1993). Since the welfare system keeps most of the child support payments to reimburse itself for welfare benefits the child and mother receive, many mothers on welfare collude with fathers to hide their identity (thereby forestalling a child support order) while accepting cash payments on the side (Edin 1995). Even wage-reliant mothers may do this, because they are worried about losing food stamps or other means-tested benefits should the men's contributions come through the formal child support system. In addition, Edin and Lein (1997b) find evidence for a strong belief among African American mothers that fathers should not be "forced" to pay by "putting the law on them." Rather, a good father is one who "chooses" to pay to the best of his ability, even in the absence of a formal child support order.

A DESCRIPTION OF THE STUDY

Each of the fathers we interviewed between 1996 and 1998 lived in the Austin, Texas, or Philadelphia, Pennsylvania, metropolitan areas. About half of these fathers resided in Austin, where welfare benefits for poor single parents with children historically have been very low, and cash assistance to adults who are not custodial parents of children does not exist. Austin is among the fastest-growing cities in the United States, and had one of the lowest unemployment rates of any U.S. city in the mid- to late-1990s. Even though the Austin fathers live in a labor market flooded with jobs, precious few good jobs exist for men with limited skills and education. Indeed, a large Texas military base that had served as a route to upward mobility for the region's working-class and minority men closed in the early 1990s. Since neither manufacturing concerns nor unions have ever had a strong presence in the city, those who do not work in the public sector or high-tech industry often are relegated to jobs at the bottom end of the construction trade or service sector and do not command high wages. Thus most noncustodial fathers of poor children in Austin find steady work if they want it, but earn very little. Most do not bear a large share of the economic burden for their children's support.

The other half of our sample live in the large northeastern metropolitan area of Philadelphia. The city and its inner suburbs span two states, Pennsylvania and New Jersey. In both states, welfare benefits for single parents with children are moderately high, and the state has made limited cash assistance available to impoverished adults who do not have custody of children. The Philadelphia and Camden County (N.J.) neighborhoods we studied suffered dramatic population losses in the past few decades, and have long been plagued with very high unemployment rates (8.7 percent in Philadelphia City in 1998 and nearly

20 percent in Camden, New Jersey). Once home to hundreds of major manufacturing concerns, the Philadelphia-Camden area suffered from wholesale deindustrialization in the 1970s, but the trend actually began much earlier. Philadelphia was a manufacturing giant at the turn of the century, and its manufacturing base began to decline as early as the late 1940s. Minority men systematically were shut out of manufacturing jobs and union membership, but were able to find work in personal service. This occupation all but disappeared in the 1960s and 1970s. The Italian, Irish, Polish, and other European-origin men who formerly relied on low-skilled, moderate-wage union jobs in manufacturing, shipping, and textiles produced sons for whom these jobs were no longer available. These economic realities mean that men with little education and few skills—particularly if they are nonwhite—can easily remain unemployed for long periods, even if they are actively looking for work.

Although we chose not to try to sample low-income noncustodial fathers randomly, we spent the first year of the study conducting extensive fieldwork to ensure that we sampled across the range of low-income noncustodial fathers in the Austin and Philadelphia metropolitan areas. For each racial and ethnic group selected, we began by targeting neighborhoods that 1990 census data identified as containing large numbers of poor persons (30 percent or more), unemployed men (15 percent or more), and single mothers (30 percent or more). In Philadelphia, a city several times larger than Austin, we were able to further narrow our neighborhoods by accessing birth record data for 1990 to 1995. From this data, we identified neighborhoods with high rates of recent nonmarital births for each ethnic group in the study (30 percent or more).

In each of these target neighborhoods, we interviewed personnel from a wide range of social service agencies and community groups, talked with local employers and owners and managers of corner stores, restaurants, bars, dance clubs, and other businesses, and hung around on street corners engaging men in casual conversations. These individuals were asked about fathers in their communities and to help find and recruit them for the study. Thus many not only were informants but referral sources, acting as intermediaries between the fathers and our interviewers and vouching for our trustworthiness. This process allowed us to gain the trust needed to get fathers to cooperate and provide more accurate information. Fathers were recruited using the following sources:

- low-wage employers and small-business owners, including formal and informal day labor agencies;

- low-income single mothers with children who participated in Head Start, used local day care centers, or other social service agencies in their neighborhood;

- recreational settings such as pool halls, basketball courts, recreation centers, clubs, restaurants, and bars;

- education and training programs where low-income men received language instruction and job-training and placement services;

- nonprofit social service organizations that offered fathers health, legal, and other services, or through fathers' support groups;
- street contacts—casual conversations with fathers hanging out on street corners, in bars, hoagie shops, and corners where they were recruited for informal-sector day labor or peddled drugs (at these locations, we also disseminated "help wanted" flyers);
- referrals from respondents to others whom they feel we would not contact using the aforementioned methods.

Overall, fathers were recruited using more than three dozen sources of referral in each city.

Since so few of the fathers recruited had stable housing, men generally were interviewed in neighborhood parks and fast-food restaurants. Interviews lasted approximately one to two hours, and most fathers were interviewed more than once. One of us (Nelson) conducted roughly half of the interviews. The remainder were conducted by a team of well-trained graduate students with fieldwork experience. Though interviewers covered predetermined topics, ordering and wording of questions followed the flow of each conversation between respondent and interviewer. Each interview was transcribed, coded, and stored by topic in a database. Intact transcripts also were retained electronically for subsequent analysis using other coding schemes. Data were analyzed using standard inductive qualitative analysis techniques (see Corbin and Strauss 1990).

AN EMERGING PERSPECTIVE ON POOR MEN

We divide our findings into three broad sections: employment, housing, and relationships with children. We begin with employment because according to respondents, the economic situations of low-income noncustodial fathers often is the fundamental factor that shapes other aspects of their lives.

Employment

Men's employment is divided into three main categories: formal, informal, and underground (see table 3.1). Within the formal sector, *regular* jobs (jobs that offer steady employment) are distinguished from *day labor* jobs (short-term temporary jobs men find through a formally registered day labor agency). Fathers generally say they value formal-sector work above work in the informal and underground sectors if it offers consistent hours and pays above the minimum wage. As we will show, formal-sector day labor falls much lower in fathers' hierarchy of preferred jobs. Theoretically, some low-income noncustodial fathers might work at a formal-sector entrepreneurial trade, such as selling food or tourist trinkets from a pushcart, but no such men are in our sample.

Table 3.1 / **Types of Jobs for Low-Income Noncustodial Fathers in the Austin and Philadelphia Metropolitan Areas, by Employment Sector**

	Formal Sector	Informal Sector	Underground Sector
Steady employer	Regular Jobs	Off the books and under the table	
Temporary employer	Day labor	Off the books and casual labor	
Entrepreneur		Side businesses	Hustles

Source: Authors' compilation.
Note: Sample size = 92.

We divide informal-sector jobs into *off-the-books* jobs and *entrepreneurial* jobs, depending on whether the father is an employee or self-employed. Off-the-books jobs are those in which men work for an employer but get paid in cash and do not report their income to the IRS. Such jobs come in two varieties: relatively steady informal-sector jobs for a single employer (*under-the-table* jobs); and informal-sector temporary day labor jobs where the prospective employer uses a day labor agency to secure a temporary employee, but who then pays the employee directly (*casual labor*). These employers almost always pay workers in cash (without exception, in our sample), and workers do not report their earnings to the IRS.

Informal-sector *entrepreneurs* are self-employed men who work at side businesses for cash and take initiative in finding their own customers. These jobs range widely in terms of type of work, regularity, and amount of pay, and fall along a continuum rather than into types of employment that could easily be categorized as either steady or temporary.

Jobs in the underground economy in our sample are limited to entrepreneurial criminal "hustles" that are felonies and carry with them the threat of criminal prosecution: drug sales, robbery, fencing stolen goods, and prostitution. In our sites, none of these trades are controlled by gangs, and thus are entrepreneurial. If we had studied other cities such as Chicago, where gangs do control the drug trade, we would have considered these trades employer-based. Criminal hustles could have been subdivided into steady and temporary, since such variation exists in our sample, but in reality the regularity of men's employment in these underground trades fall along a continuum, making it difficult to determine which category to place some of these jobs in.

Formal Employment Some men work in the low-wage sector of the formal economy, nearly always without medical benefits, a regular wage increase, or any long-range security. They generally work as dishwashers, busboys, and prep cooks in hotels or restaurants, as low-end construction workers, as store clerks, as factory workers, in warehouse loading docks, as stock boys, or as janitors and maintenance men. Other occupations include teacher's aide, dietary aide, sales, shipping clerk, security guard, file clerk, horse groom, bicycle messenger, and truck driver. Although regular jobs in the formal economy provide some stability and a regular paycheck (earnings ranged from the legal minimum to $8 an hour), men often are laid off or have their hours reduced on short notice.

REGULAR JOBS Fathers value what they called "regular jobs" over many types of work, including some of the lower-level off-the-books jobs, many of the lower-end informal businesses, and especially over any strictly illegal form of employment, for several reasons. First, fathers recognize the secondary advantages associated with work in the formal economy. Several fathers spoke of how they prefer formal-sector work to other types of employment because their legal children could claim Social Security Survivors Insurance benefits in the event of their early deaths (the term *legal children* is used because not all fathers have established legal paternity for all of their children). Fathers also appreciate the fact that work in formal-sector jobs might provide access to other government benefits, such as worker compensation and unemployment insurance. They also dream of landing formal-sector jobs with employer-provided benefits such as health and life insurance. Interestingly, no father mentioned the availability of government-provided Social Security benefits or employer-provided pensions as an advantage of formal-sector employment—possibly because many doubt they will live to retirement age. Also possible is that retirement worries seem far off when their current economic situations are so unstable.

Second, fathers almost universally feel that landing a steady, full-time job will make them more desirable fathers—both in the eyes of their children and their children's mothers—and might lead to more access to these children. Full-time employment is seldom available in the unregulated sectors. In addition, fathers said that mothers often are very concerned about the source of their earnings—a theme to which we will return.

Third, fathers value formal work because they think it might bring them some level of respectability among family members, friends, and neighbors. In addition, many fathers said they want to feel that they are full participants in society, and want to achieve the status of "a taxpaying citizen." Interestingly, these marginally employed men frequently would equate citizenship with paying taxes. More than one man told us, "I want to be able to say 'I pay taxes' like everyone else."

Fourth, fathers almost universally see the formal sector as the only road to substantial social mobility. Most feel that if they can find civil service or union work, they might advance to the respectable working class. This working-class respectability not only would bring them physical comforts, but might well mean that they could reunite with their children and their children's mother, or enter into a long-term relationship with a woman who had not yet borne them a child. Why fathers felt that drug proceeds could not buy them this respectability will be explained later in this chapter.

Not all men view formal-sector work in these positive terms, however, and not all types of formal-sector work are viewed positively. Fathers nearly always made distinctions between types of formal-sector employment. Hourly wages are crucial, of course, but the steadiness of the work and the ability to claim full-time hours are as important to men as the amount they earn hourly. When added to considerations of whether the jobs had government or employer benefits attached to them, most men have a complex set of criteria by which they rate formal-sector work. In reality, however, many of the jobs in this imaginary hierarchy are not available to these fathers.

While it is true that most fathers had had at least one fairly good (that is, well-paying and stable) formal-sector job in the past, fathers also had had considerable difficulty moving laterally from one good job to another when they were laid off, fired, or quit. Thus most fathers also had had several very unstable and poorly paid formal-sector jobs, many of them contracted through day labor agencies.

DAY LABOR   Though also in the formal sector, a day labor job is much less desirable than a regular job. Men generally view this kind of work as a last resort because it is so unstable and pays so poorly. Furthermore, because so many day labor positions are within the construction or landscaping trades, often little or no work is available at all, particularly during the cold and rainy seasons.

Like cities everywhere, Philadelphia's diminished economy offers scores of opportunities for employers to make minimal commitments to their less skilled employees. Day labor operators in Philadelphia contract with businesses who need strong arms, legs, and backs but little skill to fill out their factory shop floors, move equipment before and after trade shows, clean up construction sites, and so on. Though traditional day labor operators pay their workers at or slightly above minimum wage, they charge employers considerably more. Employers like the arrangement because they don't have to recruit, screen, and hire laborers. They also are freed from regulations regarding employee benefits. To preserve their "take" from their operation, day labor operators also have rules prohibiting these employers from hiring any of their day labor employees directly for a substantial period of time after the contract ends (generally four months). Thus short day labor stints do not generally lead to long-term employment.

Nine day labor operators are in the city of Camden, New Jersey, where about one third of the interviews were conducted. Camden unemployment rates are five times higher than the national average, so competition for day labor work is heavy. Several of the fathers interviewed are loyal to one day labor operation or another, and say that their loyalty and reputation for working hard are rewarded during the winter months, when cold weather means that outdoor construction work dries up and day labor jobs become scarce. Other men team up with several partners, with each member assigned to a particular agency. When a given member learns of work to be had at his agency, he pages the others, who then will make their way over if prospects for work at their own agency appear less promising. Since most of Camden's agencies are within walking distance of one another, even men with no transportation can get from one agency to another in no more than ten to fifteen minutes. Being part of a team enhances their prospects of finding work on any given day. In the long term, however, men who move from agency to agency are perceived as less loyal by any given operator, and thus move down the queue in the winter months when work is scarce.

Day labor operators in the Philadelphia neighborhoods studied are less concentrated, and men cannot go from one to another quickly. Thus day labor is a less viable source of employment in most of these neighborhoods than in Camden. Interestingly, none of the fathers surveyed works out of formally registered day labor agencies in Philadelphia.

Informal Employment

CASUAL LABOR   Unlike Philadelphia and Camden, Austin has virtually no formal day labor agencies. As a result, the fathers interviewed in this site work as *casual laborers.* Casual labor is virtually the same as day labor, except that it is not taxed or regulated by formal agencies.[2] Typically, men find work simply by standing on well-known day labor corners. In Philadelphia, informal day labor is popular in the construction trade. Here men go to day labor corners or directly to construction sites to find work. The chances of employment depend on the relative need for such labor versus the available labor supply.

In addition to the obvious disadvantages of low and irregular hours and pay, casual labor presents significant risks to men. Workers claim that they are easily victimized by employers who are previously unknown to them before being picked up from gathering locations and transported to unfamiliar parts of town. Sometimes workers are abandoned at the site with neither money nor transportation back to the pickup location. More frequently they are dropped off with none or only part of the expected pay. As a result, many fathers insist on cash payment at the end of each day.

> You know, I don't take no checks. I want my cash money [or] I'm not getting out of the truck. You take me home with you, you ain't gonna pay me. . . . I never let nobody owe me. You know, like a guy say, "Well, we gonna work these three days, and I'll pay you on Friday." . . . You know it's no guarantee he's coming back.

Eventually, the men age out of some of these jobs. Some of the older men (the oldest in our sample was fifty-four) reported difficulty in handling some of the heavy physical work required for casual and seasonal labor jobs.

> Out on the street, there'll be trucks that come around wanting some help, digging a ditch or cement or something that you're going to take because nobody else wants and for cheap labor. There'll be guys out here that are willing to work hard labor for four bucks an hour. I mean hard-ass work. But if that's what you got [that's what you'll take].

According to one man, age affects his ability not only to do this type of work but his chances of being hired. The competition for casual labor can be intense, and his age proves a disadvantage when a contractor pulls up to the day labor lot looking for workers. "They [younger men] see a truck parked right there and whoooo! Right there, just like ants. By the time I see everybody over there, I just stand there and say 'whew.' Unless he knows me [I don't have a chance]."

OFF-THE-BOOKS JOBS   This type of employment is the informal equivalent of a regular job in that employees work for one employer who hires them for an indefinite period to fill a particular position. The difference between this and a regular job is that payment is in cash, or "under the table." Off-the-books jobs are among the best-paying positions that these fathers have held, and hourly pay ranges from $5 to $15 per hour. Yet none of these jobs offers full-time, year-round employment. The most common off-the-books jobs we observed are roofing and other low-skilled construction-related work, which offers few jobs in winter months. The most steady among them typically pays the most poorly (for example, part-time jobs as sandwich maker at a Korean convenience store and deli, apartment building superintendent, and janitor). Most of the higher-paying jobs, though, are not only seasonal (roofing, painting, landscaping), but also subject to weather-related interruptions during the working season. The exception is for men who drive trucks locally, earn a high wage, and work part-time throughout the year.

Note that many of these jobs would be unionized if they were in the formal sector. Presumably, this is part of the reason why employers like to hire their least-skilled employees under the table. Since unions have lost much of their influence to ensure high wages, and because they impose high dues on members, most of the men who work at these high-wage jobs said they would rather work off the books.

ENTREPRENEURIAL JOBS   The main feature that distinguishes these jobs from off-the-books employment is that the men who work them are not employees. This type of unregulated entrepreneurship can be highly profitable, but several factors limited the ability of many fathers to become successful in their efforts, or even to participate at all in this type of work activity.

First, many entrepreneurs work within the construction trades (such as roofing, painting, and plumbing), and either must own their own tools or be able to borrow them from friends or employers on a consistent basis. They must have ready capital to purchase materials needed for specific jobs. Finally, and not least importantly, entrepreneurs must have reliable transportation for themselves and their equipment (which generally means a truck and a valid driver's license).[3]

One of the fathers works full-time in the formal sector for a beer distributor. With his wages he was able to purchase his own exterminating equipment and started an unregulated weekend exterminating business, advertising through flyers posted throughout his neighborhood. Another common activity, *junking,* involves driving a truck around Philadelphia's wealthier neighborhoods and suburbs the night before trash pickup, taking salvageable items from the curb and selling them to scrap yards and thrift stores. This activity sometimes can be quite lucrative, but on many evenings fathers make nothing at all. Junking requires a truck and driver's license, and some fathers told us they were saving money in order to capitalize a junking operation.

Not all of these informal businesses are even this lucrative, however. This category also includes some very low-level jobs that men engage in only when they cannot get any other type of work. For example, some fathers wipe down cars at car washes for tips, often making as little as $1 an hour. Others collect aluminum cans and sell them to a recycling plant, again making only $1 or $2 an hour. Selling newspapers on the street is another common activity, though we have not yet interviewed anyone in this category. These are generally fathers who are drug addicted or who have other serious problems that inhibit regular employment. What is fascinating is that men work these jobs rather than participate in the drug economy, which can be far more lucrative. This point will be discussed further. Oftentimes, these very low-level jobs provided men with only enough cash to get high on a couple of "40s" of malt liquor or a six-pack of beer.

SEASONAL OR MIGRATORY LABOR This final type of informal employment is a subtype of casual labor, except that it requires extensive travel away from home. Seasonal or migratory labor is also very prone to sudden layoffs and reductions in hours. This type of work is plentiful in Austin but not in Philadelphia or Camden.[4] Virtually all of the work is off the books, and men travel from as far away as El Paso to take advantage of Austin's tight labor market—often living in shelters, on the street, or tripled or quadrupled up in fleabag hotels.

Underground Employment The underground economy includes activities relating to the sale of sex, drugs, and stolen goods. Sex for money was extremely rare in our sample. In fact, only one man reported income from this kind of activity, a heroin addict whose customers pay him $10 for oral sex. Theft also was quite unusual among men in our sample. Our sole thief sometimes steals ladders, rakes, and other tools from yards and garages, and resells them door to door or at informal flea markets. Other illegal hustles are more complex; one father discovered he can make extra cash when he needs it by purchasing liquor in New Jersey, illegally bringing it over the state line, and reselling it to thrifty restaurateurs in Pennsylvania. Finally, some men scavenge copper pipes, wire, and other metals from boarded up and vacant buildings. They sell these items to a local recycling plant, which pays them well for the material when the men can get it.

Though such jobs are illegal, most fathers do not view them as "serious" crimes. Drug dealing is another matter, however, and most fathers put it into a category of its own. Though half of the fathers in the sample say they had sold drugs at some point in their lives, most feel that dealing is a morally reprehensible activity for fathers to engage in, especially as they get older. Perhaps because of the low regard for this occupation, the vast majority of fathers who deal only use it as a side activity combined with other more acceptable forms of employment. For example, one father was laid off of a regular job and could only find part-time formal-sector work to replace it. To make up the difference between his part-time earnings and bills, he would buy an "eight-ball" of crack cocaine and sell it to old high school friends in the neighborhood. Another father began dealing when his day labor agency could not provide him with sufficient hours.

> When I seen that they really wasn't keeping me busy, that's when I started doing the drug thing. That kept me busy, [it] gave me more money and everything than just the temp service. So it was just whenever [the temp service] called me or whenever I felt as though the cops was trying to lock people up that I worked with the temp services.

For some of the fathers, participation in the underground economy began as a form of youth employment. The others generally began selling drugs in their late teens and early twenties, after losing a formal-sector job, getting laid off in the winter, or not getting enough hours. As fathers matured into early adulthood, many continued to use underground work as a way of smoothing income flows when other more "legitimate" forms of work were unavailable. By the time they reached age twenty-five, most fathers reported that they had aged out of the drug trade.

When young inner-city boys enter their teenage years, their taste for expensive clothing, tennis shoes, and other "luxuries" grows. Generally, their mothers are either on welfare or working at a low-wage job. If their fathers are involved, their employment is generally low paying and unstable. In many cases, no father is involved. Thus parents cannot provide the kinds of things teenagers feel they need to earn respect among their peers. Not surprisingly, these teenagers become obsessed with ways of making money. Since their communities offer few legitimate avenues for earning money, the drug trade becomes a major form of youth employment. In addition, the school-to-work transition often presents unskilled young men with few full-time or steady work opportunities, so low-level drug dealing often helps young adult men smooth income flows.

When boys and young men are still living at home and have few financial or relational responsibilities, working in the drug trade provides enough cash to buy an expensive sweat suit, pair of tennis shoes, a fast-food meal after school, and gifts for girlfriends. As men age, though, the trade begins to take a toll. Dealers work late into the night in all kinds of weather to ply their wares. While it is true that these older boys and young men might have a week or two with fantastically high earnings, in fact such weeks are rare. Far more common are weeks when men net only $7, $8, or $9 an hour for their efforts, or even less.

Meanwhile, these older boys and young men are in constant fear of police detection, arrest, and incarceration. Dealers perceive the risk of arrest as extremely high, and even if arrest doesn't lead to incarceration, such men become known to the police, thus lessening their ability to ply their trade openly on the street. Arrest and incarceration mean less to a juvenile than to an adult, and as boys move beyond their eighteenth birthday their altercations with the police become part of their permanent record. From there on out, the stakes increase dramatically with each arrest and conviction, and the prospect of spending years in jail become frighteningly real. The mounting penalties serve as a strong disincentive to working in the drug economy, and as men approach their middle twenties, most no longer think it's worth the risk.

Along with the risk of incarceration, drug dealing carries with it two other potential risks. First, men fear the street violence that often accompanies work in the drug trade. Most young men know of someone in their communities who has been killed as a result of drug-related activity, and as their involvement grows, so does their belief that they are potential victims of street violence. Second, drugs themselves pose a substantial risk. Fathers who sell seldom use at first (though some begin using, then try to sell to support their habit), but many succumb eventually. As fathers begin using, they are more likely to smoke or shoot up all of their profits, meaning that they get nothing but high for their labors. They also are more likely to get in trouble on the street or with the police. If men become addicts, their criminal employers often deem them unreliable, and thus their addiction eventually locks them out of the trade.

Finally, men who work in the underground economy often find that the money they earn can't get them ahead in the long run. Respondent after respondent described how he "blew" the money he earned selling drugs on his habit, on alcohol, on fast food, on clothing for himself, and on extravagant gifts for his girlfriend. No father saved any of the money he earned, no father bought a house (row houses could sometimes be had for $20,000 or less in these neighborhoods) or paid for a college education. Only one father bought a car for cash (which he abandoned while fleeing from the police), and fathers seldom used any of the money they earned to contribute to the income needs of their children or other kin. Indeed, men told us that such contributions likely would be refused by relatives if offered. Working in the drug trade is viewed in such strongly negative terms by the community at large that fathers who worked in it often found themselves completely cut off from family and friends. This exile was both self-imposed (fathers felt ashamed of their activities) and imposed from the outside (their children's mothers and their own mothers and other kin generally reviled them for their activities). Thus proceeds from the underground economy could not buy fathers what they most desperately wanted— ongoing contact with their children and a stable "common law" or marital relationship. In other words, their desire for a moderately respectable life in the eyes of their kin, friends, and neighbors is not attainable through drug dealing.

For all these reasons, most men had taken one of three paths out of the drug trade by their middle twenties: incarceration, addiction, or a move to other types of employment. The first two routes out of the drug trade often hurt fathers' chances at finding or keeping work in the formal sector. Men with criminal records told us of repeated failed efforts at trying to find legitimate employment (except through day labor and specialized niches such as food prep, where employers knew that prisons trained convicts for the job). Men with drug addictions seldom are steady enough workers to keep their formal-sector jobs even if they manage to get them, and only traditional day labor agencies are able or willing to employ them. Men with erratic work habits quickly become known around the day labor circuit, however, and soon become locked out of even this lowest level of formal-sector employment.

Housing

Men's difficulties with employment are closely related to their problems with housing. Men who face irregular employment, deal with substance abuse, and are in the hands of the criminal justice system can maintain a fixed residence only sporadically. Such men often are considered undesirable tenants. They cannot pay their rent regularly and reliably. They don't have the means to keep up their housing. The more stable men in our sample shared relatively permanent housing with a new partner or a roommate, or they were on good terms with a relative who helped with housing. A few of the men could maintain their own homes. Some men's housing changed so frequently, though, that to code their current housing status was difficult: it changed during the period of our interviews.

While only a minority of the men interviewed were out on the street, many more of them experienced virtual homelessness: they almost always could find a place to sleep, but their homes changed frequently and unexpectedly. The men often alternated among types of housing, moving among shelters, rooms rented by the day or week, and temporarily shared housing provided by more or less willing relatives or friends. As the men explained repeatedly in describing their search for employment, the lack of a residence made finding a job much harder. Often without a telephone to call prospective employers or a bathroom or laundry facilities necessary for presenting a good appearance, men's lack of housing contributed to their difficulties in finding and keeping work.

Lack of a home also affected how fathers could interact with their children. Fathers with a place to bring their children and a relatively stable location where children and their mothers could reach them had an important asset in maintaining these relationships. Fathers with only transient housing had a harder time. Fathers living rough often avoided their children even while they missed them, because they did not wish their children to see and remember them as destitute.

Relationship with Children

Children play a powerful role in the lives of these fathers, although contact with and support for their children vary considerably among the men in our sample. Some are heavily involved with the economic and emotional support of their children, while some have never or rarely seen their children. Nevertheless, most men told us that being a father is one of the most important things in their lives. When we asked fathers what their lives would be like without their children, we had expected them to tell us they would have more money for themselves, have less hassle from child support enforcement authorities, be able to finish high school and enroll in a training program, and so on. Instead, a significant number of fathers told us, "I'd be dead or in jail." One father said, "If I didn't have [children], then I guess I would be out trying to get some." Another said, "I just want to know that when I die, there will be something out there to show that I was on the planet, something that looks like me. That way, people will remember that I existed." Others said,

> Having a son is very important to me, because I know that even if I don't make nothin' out of my life, he might go beyond me and make something of his life. Something I can be proud if. He might go beyond me, you know.
>
> The best week I ever had was when my daughter was born . . . I mean that's one of the few happiest times in my life I could ever think of really having. . . . When I had her and, you know, held her, you know it was a good week. My first child. My only child. Something I really wanted.

Several described their lives before fatherhood as "falling apart" or "spinning out of control." These men told us that children helped them to "settle down" or "leave the fast life" and now give them "something to live for, something to strive for," or "a reason to get myself together and make something of my life, so he can be proud of me." While these views are not fully analyzed here, they illustrate the powerful symbolic importance children have for the men who fathered them, even if the fathers do not actively parent or support the child in any way.

Fathers view some jobs as compatible with being a father and some as incompatible. In general, fathers agree that activities that are both informal and illegal, and involve a felony offense (underground jobs), are not compatible with fathering. Off-the-books work and informal businesses do not always carry such a stigma, particularly if they pay well and are stable. Jobs that pay quite well and are only illegal in some respects also carry little stigma (hustles). The most incompatible jobs are the most dangerous for the fathers and, according to fathers, would be dangerous for the children should they follow their fathers' example and take them up as adults. Such jobs involve a significant risk of incarceration or even death, and could bring danger into the household.

Interestingly, some formal-sector jobs also are generally viewed as incompatible with fathering. These are minimum-wage jobs in the service sector, such as working at McDonald's, and formal-sector day labor jobs. Low-level service sector jobs are seldom full time, offer no benefits, and generally pay poorly. Fathers say these jobs are "good enough for me, but won't do anything for my kids." The same can be said for formal-sector day labor work, which also pays badly and is extremely unstable. Fathers use such jobs for their own subsistence when necessary, but constantly are looking for something better in terms of pay and stability.[5]

Men need to do things for their children to feel good about being fathers.

> My best week would be when I probably go and visit my kids. You know it feels good to go to work, go home, and buy dinner or something, because they only see me like maybe twice out of a week you know. That's not a lot. A lot would be seeing them every day. A lot of times, you know, I'm choosing to be this alcoholic, I just don't want them to see me like that. But that's a good week, to go see them. And have money. And take them somewhere. That feels good.

Men often go to great lengths in order to provide, even if this provision is minimal. Even great efforts, however, often produce only a slight increase in what the father can provide for his children. One father who had been in prison describes trying to stay in contact with his daughter during this period.

> I didn't have the money and stuff [to write to my daughter] so I would sell my food. Like when it was pizza day or sub day or whatever. 'Cause when you're there and you're indigent, you only get two envelopes per week. That means that I can only write her once. One envelope to mail to her, and the other self-addressed. There's always a way to do something, man. You have to think, you have to be enterprising. She saved all those things that I sent her. I sent her little cartoons, you know. I had guys that would draw stuff, little cartoons, letters, and everything. And when I got out, she had this big old bag. A big old bag with everything inside it.

Yet men's experience of fatherhood often is permeated by a sense of their own failures. The less a father can provide, the less likely he is to maintain contact with his children—a pattern that emerges in virtually all studies of non-residential fathering. When fathers cannot provide, they experience failure, and they usually simultaneously experience diminished relationships with their children.

Only a handful of fathers mention positive aspects of leaving responsibility for children behind. By and large, fathers respond to the questions about life without children much as this man did.

> [It is] almost unbearable (*sobbing*). For Thanksgiving, this past year, I just packed up and went up, because I wanted to be [with my kids] . . . and I wound up going back to jail . . . [the children's mother] found out I was there, and before I even had a chance to see the kids she had me thrown in jail.

While women's lives usually are organized around the need to support their children, men's lives often reflect, even to themselves, their failures as providers to their children. Over and over, men talk of themselves as fathers who are failing, who should be doing better, but are not.

> I wish I could be a better father.
> To me fatherhood is about being there . . . contributing something. . . . The first effort I guess is to get there and physically be there so she could see what I'm trying to do or at least that I'm trying to do something. Right now, like I say, I've been falling very short.
> Right now I'm not being a really good father. Not doing the things I should be doing. I'm not talking to my daughter because of the blocks I've put between me and my wife.

Fatherhood is inextricably bound up in work and financial provision for children. When fathers cannot provide this, mothers often are less supportive of the fathers' contact with the children. Fathers, however, often are separated from their children, not just by the legal system or by the mothers, but by their own shame and sense of degradation when they cannot support their children or even be economically self-sufficient.

> The only reason I don't see [my children] more is because I want them to be able to look up to me, and I don't think my appearance or status is good enough to be around. That's the only reasons I won't be around them. You know, because I don't want them to see me as a low figure . . . I don't like to be round them because I can't do that much for them, you know—take them out, give them money, buy them clothes.

Since 1992, more than a million unskilled and semiskilled single mothers have exited welfare and entered the formal labor market. As states seek to comply with quotas and impose time limits, even more single mothers with low skills will move from welfare to work. In *Making Ends Meet,* Edin and Lein (1997b) argued that when these mothers seek work in the low-wage sector, they will have less money and be more reliant on their personal networks for the financial help they need to pay their bills. (The additional costs of transportation, child care, medical care, clothing, and housing cost them an additional $300 per month as they exit welfare.) Chief among mothers' economic supporters are men: absent fathers, brothers, and boyfriends.

Our analysis here has explored the link between low-income noncustodial fathers' employment experiences in the formal, informal, and underground economies and fathering. Here the issues salient to these fathers' employment and fathering histories are highlighted, and the research shows that many fathers' economic situations have remained marginal despite years of effort to find and maintain stable employment. Without the anchor that custodial children provide, marginal employment often is coupled with a lifestyle that resembles an extended male adolescence. Such lifestyles can further impinge on men's subsequent efforts to find and keep stable jobs. Thus fathers' ability and willingness to provide regular financial and emotional support to their children is limited both by forces from without and within. Their children's mothers have learned that a father's support is not to be counted on, though they acknowledge such support is desperately needed. The men themselves sometimes conclude that if they cannot play the fathering role to their satisfaction (much of which is predicated on their ability to fulfill the breadwinner role), they would rather not "play" at all. Thus men's family lives often are as unstable as their working lives.

Yet many of these fathers want desperately to be a part of their children's lives, both economically and emotionally. These men generally describe becoming a father as the most significant and meaningful event in their lives. Men draw important aspects of their identity from their roles as fathers regardless of whether they remain involved with their children over time. Almost universally, though, the men feel that without regular employment, to maintain regular contact with their children is virtually impossible. In their view, steady work and fathering go hand in hand. Fathers told us they draw respect from both kin and peers when they fulfill the behavioral and financial obligations of a good "family man." Yet these men view fathers who "step off" or "run away from their responsibilities" with contempt.

Steady, respectable employment does not just enhance fathers' ability to participate economically and emotionally in their children's lives; fathers also credit their children with helping them to "go straight" and find the motivation to "work steady." In other words, the desire to fulfill the fathering role adds to men's sense of obligation to find steady, "respectable" (that is, noncriminal) work. The fathers with whom we spoke nearly always credited their children for keeping them employed, even marginally, rather than "running the streets."

Research reported in this chapter was supported by the Administration of Health and Human Services and the Russell Sage Foundation. A team of extremely talented and creative graduate students assisted in this work, including Mirella Landriscina, Martha Maria-Louisa, Fred McGhee, and Darrick Williams.

NOTES

1. In a study of fifteen white teenage mothers, Cervera (1991) found that fathers became more distanced over time. Comer (1989) and Conner (1986) studied young African American fathers and reported similar findings. None of these studies explore the process of father disengagement.

2. The day-labor agencies that did exist charged the employer a small fee for connecting them up with an employee for the day, but the employer paid the employee directly and in cash.

3. Although a vehicle was not strictly necessary. In one of the neighborhoods we interviewed in, we observed a man walking down the street with a grocery cart containing drop cloths, paint cans, brushes, rollers, and a twenty-foot ladder precariously balanced on top.

4. New Jersey's truck farmers do employ "day haul" farmworkers, but they no longer rely on migrant laborers. Nor do they tend to employ white, black, or Latino men, preferring instead to hire Southeast Asian immigrants (see Pfeffer 1994).

5. Age also might be a factor in explaining whether jobs are viewed as legitimate. Drug sales, for example, are more acceptable for teenage and young adult fathers then for "grown men" who should "know better."

REFERENCES

Anderson, Elijah. 1993. "Sex Codes and Family Life among Poor Inner-City Youth." In *Young Unwed Fathers*, edited by Robert Lerman and Theodora Ooms. Philadelphia: Temple University Press.

Bumpass, Larry L., and James A. Sweet. 1989. "Children's Experience in Single-Parent Families: Implications of Cohabitation and Marital Transitions." *Family Planning Perspectives* 61(6): 256–60.

Cervera, Neil. 1991. "Unwed Teenage Pregnancy: Family Relationships with the Father of the Baby." *Families in Society* 72: 29–37.

Comer, J. P. 1989. "Black Fathers." In *Fathers and the Family*, edited by Stanley H. Cath, Alan R. Gurwitt, and Linda Gunsberg. Hillsdale, N.J.: Analytic Press.

Conner, M. E. 1986. "Some Parenting Attitudes of Young Black Fathers." In *Men in Families*, edited by Robert A. Lewis and Robert E. Salt. Beverly Hills, Calif.: Sage.

Corbin, Juliet, and Anselm Strauss. 1990. *Basics of Qualitative Research*. Newbury Park, Calif.: Sage.

Dash, Leon. 1989. *When Children Want Children: The Urban Crisis of Teenage Childbearing*. New York: William Morrow.

Edin, Kathryn. 1993. *There's a Lot of Month Left at the End of the Money: How AFDC Recipients Make Ends Meet in Chicago*. New York: Garland Press.

———. 1995. "Single Mothers and Child Support: The Possibilities and Limits of Child Support Policy." *Children and Youth Services Review* 17: 203–30.

Edin, Kathryn, and Laura Lein. 1997a. "Work, Welfare, and Single Mothers' Economic Survival Strategies." *American Sociological Review* 61: 253–66.

———. 1997b. *Making Ends Meet: How Single Mothers Survive Welfare and Low-Wage Work*. New York: Russell Sage Foundation.

Ellman, Ira Mark, Paul M. Kurtz, and Ann M. Stanton. 1986. *Family Law: Cases, Text, Problems*. Charlottesville, Va.: Michie.

Furstenburg, Frank, Phillip Morgan, and Paul Allison. 1987. "Paternal Participation and Children's Well-Being After Marital Dissolution." *American Sociological Review* 52: 695–701.

Garfinkel, Irwin, Sara McLanahan, and Thomas Hanson. 1998. "A Patchwork Portrait of Nonresident Fathers." In *Fathers Under Fire: Revolution in Child Support Enforcement*, edited by Irwin Garfinkel, Sara McLanahan, Daniel Mayer, and Judith Seltzer. New York: Russell Sage Foundation.

Howe, Ruth-Arlene. 1993. "Legal Rights and Obligations: An Uneven Evolution." In *Young Unwed Fathers: Changing Roles and Emerging Policies,* edited by Robert Lerman and Theodora Ooms. Philadelphia: Temple University Press.

Huang, Chein, Irwin Garfinkel, and Jane Waldfogel. 1999. "Child Support and Welfare Caseloads." Unpublished manuscript.

Korenman, Sanders, Jane E. Miller, and John E. Sjaastad. 1995. "Long-Term Poverty and Child Development in the United States: Results from the NLSY." *Children and Youth Services Review* 17: 127–51.

Lerman, Robert. 1993. "A National Profile of Young Unwed Fathers." In *Young Unwed Fathers: Changing Roles and Emerging Policies,* edited by Robert Lerman and Theodora Ooms. Philadelphia: Temple University Press.

Lerman, Robert, and Theodora Ooms, eds. 1993. *Young Unwed Fathers: Changing Roles and Emerging Policies.* Philadelphia: Temple University Press.

Liebow, Elliot. 1967. *Tally's Corner.* Boston: Little, Brown.

McLanahan, Sarah, Irwin Garfinkel, Nancy Reichman, Julian Teitler, Marcia Carlson, Christina Norland Audigier. 2001. "The Fragile Families and Child Wellbeing Study, Baseline Report." Center for Research on Child Wellbeing, Princeton University, Princeton, N.J.

McLanahan, Sara, and Gary Sandefur. 1994. *Growing Up with a Single Parent: What Helps, What Hurts.* Cambridge, Mass.: Harvard University Press.

Ooms, Theodora, and L. Herendeen. 1988. "Young Unwed Fathers and Welfare Reform." Meeting highlights and background briefing report. American Association for Marriage and Family Therapy Foundation. Washington, D.C. (November 18, 1988).

Pfeffer, Max J. 1994. "Low-Wage Employment and Ghetto Poverty: A Comparison of African American and Cambodian Day Haul Farmworkers in Philadelphia." *Social Problems* 41: 401–21.

Stevens, Ann H. 1995. "Climbing Out of Poverty, Falling Back In: Measuring the Persistence of Poverty over Multiple Spells." Working paper series. Cambridge, Mass.: National Bureau of Economic Research.

Sullivan, Mercer L. 1989. *Getting Paid: Youth Crime and Work in the Inner City.* Ithaca, N.Y.: Cornell University Press.

Sweet, James A., and Larry L. Bumpass. 1987. *American Families and Households.* New York: Russell Sage Foundation.

U.S. Bureau of the Census. 1986. *Statistical Abstract of the United States.* Washington: U.S. Government Printing Office.

———. 1992. *Statistical Abstract of the United States.* Washington: U.S. Government Printing Office.

U.S. House of Representatives, Committee on Ways and Means. 1993. *Greenbook.* Washington: U.S. Government Printing Office.

———. 1998. *Greenbook.* Washington: U.S. Government Printing Office.

Chapter 4

Custodial Mothers, Welfare Reform, and the New Homeless: A Case Study of Homeless Families in Three Lowell Shelters

Aixa N. Cintrón-Vélez

Findings from a 1997 survey of households conducted by the Urban Institute show that, compared to the nation as a whole, families in Massachusetts are doing relatively well: they are less likely to be poor, more likely to include two parents, and have greater access to health care. In the wake of welfare reform and the shift of important social programs from the federal government to the states, however, the news is not uniformly good. Massachusetts had a relatively smaller percentage of low-income families, but low-income families in the state had a harder time coping than their counterparts nationally (Wong 1999). For instance, Massachusetts families with incomes at or below 200 percent of the federal poverty level for a family of four in 1996 had significantly higher rates of unemployment (41 percent, compared to 35 percent nationally), reported more difficulty paying rent, mortgage, or utilities (38.6 percent, compared to 28.4 percent nationally), and greater levels of poor mental health (31.9 percent versus 23.4 percent) and parental stress (30.8 percent versus 13.7 percent).

The Personal Responsibility and Work Opportunity Reconciliation Act of 1996 (PRWORA), among other administrative reforms, significantly changed the ways in which public programs help low-income families. The predominant social norm endorsed by PRWORA is that families ought to be economically independent, but income-poor families have fewer venues to do so (for example, earnings from low-skilled jobs rarely amount to a living wage). This chapter explores how routes to family stability and well-being, if not self-sufficiency, are complicated by one unexpected outcome of a robust economy: family homelessness. In particular, it examines the sex-selective impact of policy responses to this problem. I argue that housing instability precludes "self-reliance" by heightening stress, jeopardizing health status, and preventing families from staying together and taking care of their own. Yet housing as an issue has remained conspicuously absent from the discussions about reform.

I approach these themes through a case study of low-income families in homeless family shelters in Lowell, Massachusetts.

BACKGROUND TO THE STORY

Most of what we know about the dynamics of welfare participation and welfare-to-work transitions is of limited help in predicting the effects of the new welfare reform because the rules of the game have significantly changed. The Personal Responsibility and Work Opportunity Reconciliation Act of 1996 eliminated the sixty-one-year-old federal guarantee of assistance to poor families.[1] As a result, poor women with dependent children receiving public assistance are restricted to two years of benefits in any five-year period, with a total lifetime limit of five years. In addition, childless, unemployed adults between the ages of eighteen and fifty are limited to only three months of food stamps out of every three-year period. States are under no obligation to guarantee child care for working mothers, and legal immigrants may not be eligible for aid. The real impact of the new law will be felt when recipients start reaching their time limits or when the next recession hits, whichever comes first.[2]

In Massachusetts, the new welfare law translated into expanded work requirements, stricter sanctions for noncompliance with work requirements, increased income disregards, and reduced benefits for the able bodied:

- able-bodied recipients whose youngest child is school aged are required to work twenty hours per week at a job or community service;
- teenage parents who are recipients must live with a responsible adult relative or in a supervised group home, and stay in school or a GED program;
- a family cap denies additional benefits for children born to recipients;
- all able-bodied recipients will have their benefits cut by 2.75 percent.[3]

The state's overall welfare caseload fell from 114,000 in May 1993 to about 83,000 in September 1996.[4] At the time, the Weld administration was quick to attribute the drop in numbers to the new rules for teenagers and stricter work requirements for adult women. Yet the new law only became effective November 1, 1995 (time limits were implemented December 1, 1996), and teenagers represent less than 8 percent of the total caseload at any given point.[5] Moreover, state offices have no systematic way of determining the relative contribution of such factors as panic due to misinformation about the new law, changes in local labor market conditions, or differences in mode of implementation (that is, casework practices) across state offices.

Using Panel Study of Income Dynamics (PSID) data on the monthly pattern of AFDC receipt during the 1980s and early 1990s, Boisjoly, Harris, and Duncan (1997) estimated the number and characteristics of recipient families likely to reach the sixty-month limit on total receipt as 40 percent of the current caseload, or some 2 million families and 3.8 million children. In the Massachusetts context, this would mean slightly over 25,000 families. Recipients who lose benefits due to time limits have a limited number of options: they can combine households, work at very low wages, become visibly destitute and risk losing their children, or a combination thereof. Losing benefits will be one of the factors that will lead some families to become homeless. Boisjoly, Harris, and Duncan (1997) predict that those most likely to reach the time limits are young, never-married women with less than a high school education, who have preschool children at the time of welfare entry. These are the same traits describing the population most likely to become homeless.

In the last twenty years, both the incidence and visibility of family homelessness have increased. A recent study of welfare mothers in Worcester, Massachusetts, suggests that many poor, single-parent families headed by women are "only a crisis away from homelessness" (Bassuk, Browne, and Buckner 1996, 60). The study by Bassuk and colleagues shows that many had to repeatedly escape from abusive situations and lacked social supports in the form of family and friends. Both women in public housing and women in a homeless shelter in their sample had few relationships they could count on. "Because of the demands of single parenting, histories of family disruption and loss, and the ever-present threat of violence in their neighborhoods, many remained socially isolated" (63). This raises questions about the ability of already strained families and neighborhoods to provide material and other support.

Welfare reform is predicated on the assumption that jobs are available locally for women making the transition from welfare to work, that they can access these jobs, and that affordable day care and health insurance are available to them. Welfare reform supporters do not talk much about the role of affordable housing in routes to independence or self-sufficiency, yet for low-income single mothers to get off and stay off welfare, they cannot afford to spend more than a third of their income on housing.

Will all former welfare recipients be able to work and secure housing with their income from earnings? Most likely not. The robust economy of the 1990s generated a tight housing market and skyrocketing rents. Nationally, some 5.3 million households were considered worst-case needs in 1995, because they paid more than half of their incomes for rent. Further, 3 million were estimated to live in substandard housing—that is, dangerous, dilapidated structures (Center on Budget and Policy Priorities, cited in Brelis 1999). The lucrative private rental housing market also means that a significant number of subsidized Section 8 housing could be transformed into market-rate apartments if developers prepay their mortgages or choose not to extend their contracts with the Department of Housing and Urban Development (HUD), or landlords convert the units to condos and sell off the property. This has serious implications for low-income tenants, their families' stability, and the health and development of their children—and it complicates welfare-to-work transitions.

Issues of local availability of employment, job competition, and accessibility only begin to address the constraints low-skill single mothers face in the workforce, for these mothers' primary responsibility for the care of dependent children places them at an additional disadvantage vis-à-vis other workers (Bassuk, Browne and Buckner 1996). The role of the single provider and caregiver often means that poor single mothers with young children carefully must weigh the income gains from a paid job versus child-care expenses that can be 25 percent or more of their earnings (Kimmel 1992). These women also must secure adequate housing for their families. To do this, they must not earn too much to disqualify them for subsidies, but enough not to have housing expenses eat up 50 percent or more of their incomes.

Notwithstanding these barriers, those who can leave welfare often do. In fact, research in welfare dynamics consistently shows considerable movement into and out of welfare, with most periods of receipt lasting a short time (Bane and Ellwood 1994; Blank 1989; Harris 1993). Moreover, welfare recipients often leave welfare for work, combine welfare with work, or cycle between the two (Bane and Ellwood 1994; Edin and Jencks 1993; Harris 1993). We also know that welfare exits through work are no insurance against poverty, and that many who left welfare for work often return to welfare (Harris 1993).

If the prospects for escaping poverty through work seemed bleak before, they look no better now. With time limits, Edelman (1997, 53) reminds us, people will no longer have a choice "between the 'poor support' of welfare . . . and the even worse situation of a low-wage job, with its take-home pay reduced by the out-of-pocket costs of commuting and daycare, and the potentially incalculable effects of losing health coverage."

The dramatic changes in the structure of income support prescribed by PRWORA have important consequences for the poor's ability to secure permanent and affordable housing. Losing benefits jeopardizes poor families' ability to maintain their housing. A single mother in her twenties with very young children and an extremely low personal income is particularly at risk (Bassuk 1991; Jencks 1995; Rossi 1994); but this point is missing in much of the welfare reform debate.

The Local Housing Market

Needy families outnumber the low-rent apartments they can afford. An affordable unit is one that does not cost more than 30 percent of a family's income. For low-income families paying market rates for their housing, little money is left after rent. In Massachusetts, about a quarter of Boston renters spend more than half their incomes for rent, while earning less than 50 percent of the area's median income; and in Essex, Middlesex, and Worcester counties, for example, the number of such renters goes up to 35 percent (HUD, cited in *Boston Globe,* 1998). For welfare-to-work transitions to succeed, however, an adequate supply of stable housing and opportunities that enable poor families to rent in the private market are required.

Not all poor families actually become homeless, but an increasing number of them have begun to surface in the nation's homeless shelters. Families account for almost one third of the overall homeless population today and are considered the fastest-growing segment (Bassuk 1991). Rossi (1994) has outlined the reasons for the rise of family homelessness in the 1980s.[6] Some of the most important factors have to do with economics. Economic restructuring is deemed responsible for a decline in the demand for unskilled workers and the decreased value of the minimum wage, which, paired with the erosion of the purchasing power of cash benefits and contraction of the supply of cheap, privately owned rental housing, makes it difficult for poor families to afford housing. The economic factors are compounded by demographic ones: declining marriage rates, an increase in unwed parenthood among the very poor, and more poor single mothers living on their own (Jencks 1995).

A recent study of the state of housing in Massachusetts by the Donahue Institute at the University of Massachusetts concludes that 25 percent of households in the Commonwealth face a severe housing affordability problem and are at risk of homelessness, eviction, or foreclosure (Donahue Institute, cited in Babson 1998). The economic and real estate boom of the 1990s, which coincided with the end of rent control in three major cities, put many lower- and middle-income residents at risk. The most vulnerable in Massachusetts's tight rental market include single mothers living on their own, but also the elderly, immigrants, and the working poor. Homelessness is said to have increased by 100 percent since 1990 and evictions by 64 percent since 1993.

The Scope and Consequences of Homelessness Among Families with Young Children

What we know about homeless families in particular is largely influenced by eligibility criteria set by the shelters and their funders, and by the number of people they can serve (Rossi 1994). Shelter administrators and staff, along with advocates for the homeless, often state that homeless families are not much different from single parents among themselves—the guests are just down on their luck compared to the staffers. The fact is, though, that not all poor unwed mothers become homeless. A selection process makes some single mothers more vulnerable to homelessness, suggests Rossi (1994). For example, some waiting lists for public housing are years long, if they haven't been closed. Technically, this excludes very young families and recent arrivals from securing housing where the rent is adjusted to their income as long as they meet state or federal income eligibility requirements. Nationally, the average wait to get Section 8 housing vouchers is twenty-six months. Certificates, which are good for only 120 days, may expire before a prospective tenant finds housing. Oftentimes the demands of first- and last-month's rent and a security deposit make barriers to housing insurmountable. Only those with a safety net that includes accommodating family and friends can wait the wait.

The empirical literature suggests that young single mothers and their minor children are more at risk of reaching welfare time limits and experiencing residential instability. In the restructuring of housing and income-assistance programs, how will they fare? This chapter analyzes paths into homelessness and ways of coping with economic hardship and inadequate housing: it asks how ideology shapes the stories that women are able to tell about their own lives;[7] and it explores poor women's perceptions of opportunities after life at a homeless shelter, in the wake of welfare reform.

THE STUDY

This chapter reports on the methods and preliminary findings of a study of low-income families in a northeastern city. Families were interviewed in homeless shelters to provide a better understanding of how neighborhoods and families mediate housing and employment outcomes for low-income, women-maintained families and how the restructuring of welfare housing assistance programs affects poor families' life chances. In particular, the following questions are explored: Why do such families become homeless, and what does the world look like from their vantage point?

I rely on women's life stories as vehicles for exploring the choices they make, their awareness of policy changes, and perceptions of social and economic opportunity. The subjective interpretation of their experience—what it means to those who undergo dislocation—is determined by culture or ideology. In other words, whether moving into a shelter is perceived as a dead end or an opportunity depends on lived experiences and what we make of these experiences. Complexity is generated by our different positions within groups, linked to, for example, race or ethnicity, but also age, sex, and generation. A homelessness story can be a very personal account and at the same time a communal story. This study seeks to place personal narratives in the context of rapid social and economic change in postindustrial Lowell, Massachusetts.

Data and Methodology

Data are comprised of oral histories of fourteen women who are shelter "guests" or former guests. Shelter staff and volunteers also were interviewed, as well as some of the guests' partners or boyfriends and their school-age resident children. The interviews reconstruct the family relationships and the work, welfare, and homelessness experiences of the women living in shelters.

Prior studies of poverty, homelessness, and welfare participation typically have employed quantitative methods to investigate changes in the occurrence and duration of poverty, homelessness, or welfare receipt, and the patterning or correlates of these events. The life stories of women in shelters provide a complementary account of the important features of poverty and low-wage work from the women's points of view. By providing a personal window on motives and actions, the life stories of these women help us understand the complexities of homelessness and barriers to change, as well as opportunities for achieving better circumstances created by public policies.

The Site

Lowell is the fourth largest city in the Commonwealth of Massachusetts. From its golden era as the first planned industrial community in the United States in the nineteenth century to the present, Lowell has attracted a significant population of immigrants, female-headed households, and low-skilled labor. Through periods of technical innovation and obsolescence, the economic fortunes of the city have been tied to the fortunes of manufacturing and its working-class people.

Today, this urban center also is home to some of the state's most disadvantaged households (Witherbee 1998).[8] According to the 1990 census, 18 percent of Lowell's general population live in poverty, compared to 8.3 percent at the state level. Thirty percent of its children are poor. The Lowell unemployment rate in June 1998 was 5.9 percent, compared to 3.5 percent for the state.

Female-headed families represent 17 percent of all households in Lowell, and the majority of them are poor. In April 1997, 2,944 households (or 8 percent of all households) received Temporary Assistance for Families with Dependent Children (TAFDC). Some 1,478 of the families with children receiving income assistance from the state were expected to lose their benefits as of December 1, 1998. Only 38 percent of the heads of these families graduated from high school or obtained a GED; 60 percent have less than a high school education.

Much of the housing in Lowell is old and in need of renovation and upgrading. Almost 50 percent of the housing stock was built in 1940 or earlier. Affordable housing is in short supply and usually is located in economically depressed areas of the city, where absentee landlords and poorly maintained and unsafe housing are the norm. The market rate for a two-bedroom apartment in Lowell is between $580 and $650 a month. This is more than the average monthly TAFDC benefit for a single parent with two children and no income ($565) and more than half the average monthly income of a single mother working full-time, full-year, at minimum wage. Since more eligible families exist than subsidies or affordable units available, many poor families in Lowell are in the ranks of what Rossi (1994) aptly calls the "precariously housed." The picture is complicated by the city's plan to tear down Julian Steele Homes, the state's 284-unit public housing development, where 700 low-income residents and their 453 minor children now live. The proposal calls for construction of 90 single-family homes and 45 duplexes for a total of 180 units, with 58 units to be set aside for low-income family owners or tenants.

One of the things that sets Lowell apart from other Commonwealth cities is its demographic composition. In 1990, 77 percent of city residents were white, 11 percent Asian or Pacific Islander,[9] 10 percent Hispanic, and 2 percent black, but Hispanics and Asians are overrepresented among the poorest and most disadvantaged populations. The 1990 census showed 46 percent of Latinos and 36 percent of Asians living in poverty. Sixty-one percent of the Latinos and 51 percent of Asians had less than a high school education. Not surprisingly, the rate of welfare participation among these groups also is very high; as of January 1995, Latinos represented 27 percent and Asians 23 percent of the caseload. In Lowell's poorest neighborhoods the situation is even more troubling, with their large concentration of households with very low incomes, high welfare participation rates, and low education attainment levels.

The Sample

Lowell has three homeless family shelters. Participants were recruited from all three. The sample included all willing individuals who resided in any of the shelters from February through May 1998, both recent arrivals and not. Respondents were asked about their willingness to be contacted again and appropriate information was secured. Thus this is a nonprobability sample from among families awarded emergency housing at Lowell's three family shelters. Since the sample is not random, and because it includes only families in shelters during one four-month-long period who volunteered to be respondents, it is not necessarily representative of the homeless or at-risk (for homelessness) population in Lowell.

The Shelters

Of Lowell's three family shelters, two are run by a local nonprofit agency, Community Teamwork Incorporated (CTI), and one is independently run. The shelters are fairly small, accommodating an average of eight families with children (including pregnant women, but not always including men) and providing one or two community (that is, non-DTA) beds. The largest source of funding for all three is the Massachusetts Department of Transitional Assistance (DTA), which pays a fee-per-bed set aside for families whom they refer to the shelter. The demand has always been high. Both CTI and the private shelter turn down on average between seventeen and nineteen families (applying for their non-DTA spaces) each month. What has significantly changed in recent years is the average length of stay at the shelters. Even though federally prescribed preferences, used by local authorities, allow for families in shelters to be placed ahead in publicly assisted housing lists, they face a considerably long wait. Shelter administrators and staff remember a time when they did not get to know the families because the turnover was so fast. Lin-Wen, Family Life Advocate and Relief Coordinator, recalls, "When I first started work here, two years ago, it used to be a three- to six-month wait for a two-bedroom apartment; now it is six to eight months. And for a three bedroom, it is over a year, from nine months to a year." For a fortunate few who enter the shelter after they have already been on Public Housing, Project-Specific, or Section 8 waiting lists, the wait might not be as long. The long-term prospects, however, are not very encouraging. According to Diana, Shelter Housing Search Coordinator,

> Supply is an issue in Lowell. The state list [for Public Housing] has been closed to the public since 1994. The federal list just opened for families applying for five- and two-BR units. And there have been dramatic cutbacks in Section 8. With expiring contracts, landlords can go back to running at market prices. On top of that, a new regulation states that a landlord can decide, after a year, not to renew a contract with a tenant, no reason offered.

About 13,500 families are on the waiting lists for subsidized housing in Lowell—7,000 for public housing and 6,500 for Massachusetts Rental Program vouchers and Section 8 certificates.

Shelter "Guests"

Like welfare recipients, the homeless represent a heterogeneous population. They seek and gain emergency assistance for their homelessness for a variety of reasons. Administrative data fail to capture how varied the reasons can be. For example, although the intake interview asks about the "cause" for home- lessness, only the reason that made a family eligible for emergency housing assistance gets recorded. Thus most families currently in a Lowell shelter are there because of eviction or overcrowded living conditions (see table 4.1). Yet, as interview data show, a tenant may settle for an eviction notice from a land- lord who refuses to keep up with the maintenance of a unit or bring it up to code rather than taking him or her to court. Or, a young mother will bounce from one inadequate dwelling to another after a falling out in the relationship with the other or others with whom she was sharing a place initially.

Because DTA is the major gateway for entry into Lowell family shelters, they no longer house teen mothers or pregnant teen guests—the new law stipulates that these women must live with an adult relative or in a supervised group home. Since one of the shelters will not admit male spouses or male live-in part- ners of guests, and owing to implicit rules that discourage men's presence in congregate living quarters, single female-headed families predominate (twelve out of the fourteen families in the sample).

Houseguests, on average, were young. The median age of the respondents was 23.5 years. The majority had never been married. Three out of the fourteen in the sample were divorced or separated. All but one had children under the age of six. Most (more than two thirds) had had a first child in their teens. Only three of the women were relatively recent arrivals, having been in Lowell for two years or less. Most (64 percent) had had some work experience, and most (93 percent) had received welfare at some point. Most grew up in a one-parent household, but only half of the parental households ever received cash public assistance. Interestingly, more than two thirds of the mothers of the women in

Table 4.1 / Demographic and Background Characteristics of Homeless Family Shelter Sample

	N (Percentage)		N (Percentage)
Personal characteristics		Reason homeless or shelter admit	
Age (years)		Overcrowding	4 (29)
Median	22.5	Condemned or code violations	2 (14)
Race-ethnicity			
Non-Hispanic white	7 (50)[a]	Eviction by primary tenant	1 (7)
Hispanic	7 (50)	Eviction for nonpayment of rent, where rent > 50 percent of income	6 (43)
Education			
LTHS	7 (50)		
HS-GED	7 (50)		
Marital status		Abuse	1 (7)
Single, never married	9 (64)		
Unmarried couple	2 (14)	Ever victim of domestic violence	
Divorced or separated	3 (21)		
Health status[b]		Yes	8 (57)
Fair-good	9 (64)	No	6 (43)
Poor	5 (36)		
Age of youngest child (years)		Early Family History	
		Household type	
< Six	13 (96)	One-parent	9 (64)
Six to twelve	0	Two-parent	3 (21)
Thirteen to eighteen	1 (7)	Other (foster care, other)	2 (14)
Age at first birth (years)			
Thirteen to sixteen	5 (36)	Mother's education	
Seventeen to nineteen	5 (36)	LTHS	4 (29)
Twenty +	4 (29)	HS-GED	10 (71)
Tenure in the community[c]		Mother ever on welfare	
Long-term resident	10 (79)	Yes	7 (50)
Recent arrival	4 (21)	No	7 (50)
Work history		Grew up in urban area	
Some work history	10 (71)	Yes	14
No work experience	4 (29)	No	0
Public assistance history			
Some time on welfare*	13 (93)		
Never on welfare	1 (7)		

Source: Author's compilation.
Note: Percentages may not add up to 100 due to rounding.
*Includes child-only AFDC-TAFDC.
[a]Number and percentage, unless otherwise indicated.
[b]Self-report. Includes having a child with a serious health condition that requires specialized care.
[c]Recent arrival defined as having been a Lowell resident for two years or less.

the sample had at least a high school education, whereas only half of the women in the sample had either completed high school or obtained a GED.[10] All of the interviewed women had been born and raised in urban areas. More than half reported experiencing domestic violence. Exactly half of the respondents were non-Hispanic white and half were Hispanic.

These demographics are in agreement with what we know about the homeless families population in general (see, for example, Jencks 1995; Rossi 1994; Schlay and Rossi 1992), with one exception: ethnic composition. The two largest minority groups in Lowell are not non-Hispanic blacks, but Asians (Vietnamese, Cambodian, and Laotian) and Hispanics, who represented 11 and 10 percent of the city's population in the 1990 census, respectively. Both Hispanics and Asians are overrepresented among the poor and among those living in the economically depressed enterprise community area neighborhoods, but mostly whites and Hispanics show up at family shelters. Ethnic selectivity occurs because the shelter system gives preference to single-parent families (and such families are more prevalent among poor whites and poor second-generation Hispanics in Lowell), and because of cultural differences in prescribed family roles and what is considered an acceptable dwelling. Interestingly, in-group sanctions among Asians against seeking outside help do not apply to cash public assistance (for example, over 23 percent of Asians were in the AFDC caseload in January 1995).[11]

ON BECOMING HOMELESS:
THE STORIES AND THE STORYTELLERS

The protagonists of these stories share a history of economic hardship, dislocation, and social prejudice. The women are poor and have primary responsibility for their children, but they differ in terms of the resources and stability of their support networks. Non-Hispanic white families in the shelter are more likely to be at the receiving end of their extended families' help networks, while Hispanic families appear more often to be "a link in a chain of exchange" between more disadvantaged households (see Bassuk and Buckner 1994, Bassak et al. 1996; Roschelle 1997). This is reflected in both the style and content of their life stories.

Homeless Families: Individual Vulnerability or Institutional Failure?

Both the literature and demographic profile of this sample of homeless families in a northeastern postindustrial city raise a number of questions about how parental status, age, and personal and community resources determine who becomes homeless. I will argue that we can think of homelessness, as of welfare dependence, as an economic and political problem. Both result not just from personal deficiencies but also from structural inequalities in the economy and the family. For example, women get paid less (than men) in the labor market, yet they are primarily responsible for the care and welfare of children (Pearce 1990).

Perhaps because we have good, consistent measures of critical events in the life course (for example, years of education, fertility, union formation), we typically have approached both welfare participation and family homelessness from a behavioral perspective. As a result, we have developed reasonably strong and parsimonious models of welfare receipt, welfare-to-work transitions, and the onset of homelessness. Yet even the best social science models are simplifications of reality. Results must be interpreted, and interpretation depends, in part, on our point of view (that is, what we know and do not know, and what we think matters).

The following section examines the ways in which young single women heads of families at a homeless family shelter explain their "choices" and present life circumstances. With this is offered a glimpse into a more complicated story—one that goes beyond the more general differences in human capital and family structure proposed by models based on quantitative data alone. Complicating the story is important if we want to find more effective policies to redress poverty and family homelessness.

Paths into Homelessness

You call having a roof over your head jumping from house to house in the wintertime?
—Joannie, houseguest

About half of the study participants who had been primary tenants immediately before applying for emergency housing had been evicted, mostly because of nonpayment of rent, where rent was 50 percent or more of their incomes. The next most common reason was overcrowding; but there are many routes to overcrowded conditions. Joannie's case is an example. The twenty-three-year-old mother of one had left an abusive relationship in Lowell and moved to New York with her sister-in-law. When her sister-in-law, who was in the Air Force reserves, got called to serve in Kuwait, Joannie was left with few alternatives.

> I couldn't afford the apartment by myself. I had no other choice but to move back to Massachusetts. That was the worst. But I wasn't going to go into a shelter in New York, because they are so bad. [In Lowell] I stayed at [a] girlfriend's, but she was abusing her son, someone called DSS, and she asked me to leave. I then went to my uncle's—his sister and daughter were there, and us, all in a one-bedroom apartment.
>
> I applied for shelter. It took me the longest time to get it because "I had a roof over my head." I'm like, "You call having a roof over your head jumping from house to house in the wintertime?"

More households are eligible for housing subsidies than are units available, so it wouldn't be unreasonable to expect that needy families would do "anything" to move up the list. In reality, though, homeless families in Lowell shelters have doubled up and tripled up, jumped from one relative to another, and even accumulated considerable debt before moving into a shelter. Some have been homeless before. Maddy, age twenty-eight, gave the following account of her move to a shelter.

> I moved out of my parents' house when I was thirteen. My mother was very controlling and I did no right, no matter what. So, it was easier for me to get out and live on the street than it was to stay home and take it.
>
> I stayed with friends; bounced. Until their parents got sick of me and then I moved on to the next friend. My parents tried to "fix" me by sending me to Florida, my boyfriend followed, I was fifteen. When I came back (my aunt threw us out), I was sixteen and pregnant.
>
> I've slept in cars in the middle of the winter for days and just gone into a friend's house to take a shower and eat one peanut butter sandwich a day. I was a size three and I was almost five feet ten, you know? I could hide behind a telephone pole.

Lowell family shelters will not take in a victim of domestic violence because they cannot guarantee her safety. Victims of domestic violence are referred to a battered women's shelter and often placed out of town. Yet the line between ongoing and past abuse is a fine one. When Carla, age nineteen, left the Job Corps, she had $2,000 saved. She got an apartment and took a job at Dunkin Donuts and another temporary job with UPS, but the semblance of stability was short lived.

> The guy I was deciding to be serious with started getting possessive. I wanted to settle down but, goddamned, I had just started. He was married. He started trouble. And then I left. I just disappeared and started doing drugs. I got pregnant from the one who was selling.
>
> I had to get away, you see? I left something good, when I could have put a stop to it [the abuse] and called the cops for a restraining order. Instead of completely stopping my life for nobody, I disappeared. Just ran away, like I've been doing since I was a little kid. As soon as I found out I was pregnant, I called my social worker from DSS, my old social worker because they dismissed the case when I turned eighteen. I called her and she got me in here. I changed my name, so he couldn't find me.

We know that information matters in take-up rates among those who qualify for assistance. A homeless shelter is charity, housing of last resort. Stigma thresholds are lowered, however, when someone knows at least one other person who has gone through the shelter system. Applying for emergency housing and complying with DTA's myriad regulations is worth it if doing so allows a family head to keep her family together. No one's character is discredited for trying to be a good mother. In fact, the process of applying for shelter, at least on the surface, resembles applying for cash public assistance. A family member, close acquaintance, or service provider suggests that the individual apply. Thus to find sisters in Lowell's three family shelters is not uncommon. Three out of the fourteen women in the sample had had a sister in the shelter system, which confirms that relatives might be less able to take care of each other when their own resources are strained. Twenty-four-year-old Melannie's story is an example.

> I was sharing an apartment with my sister and her boyfriend. We were both paying rent. She worked too. We just worked different hours. We had to call the Code Inspector because there was mice, like, all over the place. My sister had her baby and they were eating the baby's cereal out of the boxes. After we called the Code Inspectors, we held back rent, so he [the landlord] took us to court and they gave us a little while to stay there and then we left. So, then, I came here. My sister first went with my mother but then I told my sister that there were places [here].

The decision to follow through is not without conflict. The young mothers interviewed often pointed out that others soon forget that they are "inside" and stop calling or stopping by. Some of the guests talked about feeling "abandoned," the sense that others might have wanted to get rid of them. When a boyfriend suggests the shelter solution but chooses not to join the woman and her kids at the shelter, gender differences in freedom and responsibilities soon become apparent. Only the prospect of getting their "own place," on terms they could afford, kept them from jumping ship. As the wait for housing prolonged itself, however, the women questioned their decision.

Social Ties and Networks

Obviously, you're on welfare for a reason: because we don't have family support, for whatever reason, like we don't get along. But they are thinking that we have all these hidden resources.

—Maddy, former houseguest

They are homeless because they are poor, and they are on welfare because they lack the family and community resources that would enable them to both work and take care of their families. Indeed, free child care from a relative, child support from an absent father, or free housing from parents can make a difference between a single parent who can make a living from earned income at a low-wage job and one who cannot (Jencks 1995). Holding two jobs or going to school and work at the same time are not options for most single female heads of households in the absence of a reliable structure of support.

On a typical day at the shelter, around that time when houseguests are supposed to take care of house chores or are expecting their kids back from school or day care, someone is on the pay phone in the middle of the hallway. These are calls from relatives; boyfriends call in the evening. A young woman reassures her retired, recently widowed father that he can have her food stamps this month; she's got food covered for at the shelter. At another shelter, a houseguest offers (for the time being) to take care of her cousin's young children, so that the cousin can go to work. And a young mother receives a "new" offer from her mother: the older woman, who gets disability payments for herself and public assistance for her kids, will take care of the younger one's kids *if* the young woman agrees to come back to live at home. These exchanges, that span physically distinct households, resonate with those described by the anthropologist Carol Stack some twenty-five years ago.

Certain segments of the general public and their representatives in government believe that if income support is denied to poor families, the families simply will rely on an extensive network of family and kin for survival. This perspective fails to take into account that families have become smaller, that both the real value of the minimum wage and of wages in general have significantly eroded, and that as a result, there are fewer resources to circulate. An extended household may not be an option at very low levels of income, because including another adult in the household may jeopardize receipt of transfer payments or housing subsidies (Tienda and Angel 1982), and also because familial safety nets are more likely activated as the socioeconomic status of the giver increases (Roschelle 1997). Thus Lowell's shelter families may not be socially isolated, but their social networks have little to spare.

Moving into a Shelter

I told you it was an emergency, that I had nowhere to sleep. And they're like, "We need a home assessment. Have you made an appointment yet?"

—Anette, houseguest

For a significant segment of the poor, moving is a fairly common and accepted part of life. Poor families move to escape violence, unsafe and unsanitary conditions, and exploitative landlords. This physical uprooting limits the claims that some poor families have on community and kin networks. At times, moving into a shelter is a stabilizing step. Maddy is a twenty-eight-year-old white single mother of three. Lowell born and raised, she was a shelter guest in 1993 for five months, before moving into public housing. She got her GED in 1996 and is a semester short of an associate's degree in mental health from Middlesex Community College. She has custody of her two sons, ages five and seven, but not of her eleven-year-old daughter, whom her parents took away eight years earlier when Maddy was twenty. She is now an intern at the shelter. When asked how she would begin her life story, Maddy replied,

I was thinking about it and I would begin with my life here [at the shelter]. Because when I came here was the only time I actually got my own independence to begin to grow. Because [before that] it was like I was stuck at thirteen, even though I was almost twenty-two. I was stuck at thirteen because I never had the stability and the constant structure. I never had anything that was really my own that I could afford, that I knew wasn't going to be taken away from me if I lost my job or if they cut my benefits or whatever.

Not that it wasn't hard. It was. Because at times the only thing you have left is your right to make your own choices and to set your own rules. And you have to give that up in the shelter.

For others, such as Anette, coming to a shelter means being able to stop running. On a typical day, weather permitting, the unofficial parade of strollers up and down Merrimack Avenue begins early in the morning—young mothers heading to doctors' appointments or social service agencies, the neat and clean homeless (to use Jencks's term, 1995), along with those who have a place to go back to at the end of their errands. Anette was one of the homeless.

Anette is twenty-one, Lowell born and raised, and Puerto Rican; she is also a single mother. She is a high school graduate with some work experience. Anette receives unemployment and child support. She was abused by her mother and by her former boyfriend, yet she depended on them for temporary shelter. Her son, Jamie, who is three years old, has some chronic medical problems. They are staying in a family shelter now, but in October 1997, they didn't have a stable place to go to at night.

> I was staying at my ex-boyfriend's house on the weekends, staying at my sister's house one day, on another day going to my mother's house and then going back and forth. It was terrible.
>
> I would wake up in the morning, you know, get him ready and everything, and then I would leave, and I would be gone all day. I would make sure all my appointments were like at least two in the same day so I would have something to keep me busy, so that I didn't have to go back.
>
> Then, my ex-boyfriend, one day he decided to lock us out. The next day he did it to me again and I had to go out walking around downtown all day with [Jamie]. You know? And we were still in our pajamas.
>
> I called the welfare department and I told them it was an emergency, that I had nowhere to sleep. And they're like, well, we need a home assessment, have you made an appointment yet? And I'm like, well, I am trying to tell you I don't live anywhere. I don't have a home. But no, they wanted a home assessment; so I had to have them do it at my sister's house.

Anette was denied assistance by the Emergency Housing coordinator at DTA. She went back to her mother's. Her mother started verbally and physically abusing Anette—a recurrent problem and one that led to a loss of a job earlier. One day, seven months after Anette first applied for emergency housing, after being kicked out of her mother's house once again, she went to a police station. The police escorted Anette back to get her things. That day she walked into a family shelter; they had an open community bed; she got in. She could stop running.

Revealing but not entirely surprising is that many of the young respondents described the times when they did not have to worry about shelter as their happiest: a year in a home for pregnant and parenting teens for Vivian (introduced later); Job Corps for Carla; a family shelter for Maddy; and a transitional home for young unwed mothers for Melannie. The hierarchical and authoritarian social order of the shelter is experienced as a stable and predictable—and therefore desirable—environment. The shelter has both symbolic and instrumental meanings; it is a place where one can potentially regain control or autonomy over one's life, or a step toward securing affordable housing. For those who have never had a place of their own, the first seems to matter most.

Homelessness Is Also About Violence in the Home

I made two transcendental decisions: I left and I took my children with me.
—Nilda, houseguest

Domestic violence has received renewed attention in the literature as a potential barrier to the employment and self-sufficiency goals of reform (Bassuk, Browne, and Buckner 1996; Kalil et al. 1998; Raphael, 1995). Traditionally, violence in the home has been considered a family and public health problem (Lystad 1986). Yet seemingly noneconomic factors that have sex-selective (or age-selective, in the case of child abuse) and economic consequences are closely related to economic opportunity and the resulting differences in power at home. Fraser (1989) calls wife battering an example of a structural political problem that has been inappropriately defined as a personal domestic problem. Thus to be free from their dependence on the abusers, Fraser argues, battered women need not just temporary shelter but also jobs paying a living wage, day care, and affordable and permanent housing. Domestic violence is an affordable housing issue because poor families who move a lot often sever ties with kin and neighbors, and family isolation is fertile ground for abuse.

When Nilda, a thirty-eight-year-old Puerto Rico–born mother of three, decided to break an eighteen-year relationship with an abusive husband, she was the one who had to leave the home and assume full responsibility for the kids. Nilda migrated to the United States. With immigration, the place-based survival strategies of the past were no longer available to this head of household, who then had to negotiate language, work, and housing in a different cultural setting, away from community and kinship networks. Homelessness thus means different things to Nilda than to her much younger counterparts at the shelter. Her recent arrival status and limited English language skills, despite some college education, place her at a disadvantage in Lowell's labor and housing markets. Nilda's "choices" are further complicated by some recent events. Both her teen daughters have become pregnant out of wedlock, and her youngest son wants to leave the shelter to join his father in Puerto Rico. Not surprisingly, Nilda is clinically depressed.

Violence, in the home or the neighborhood, is a common theme in the lives of shelter residents. As a result, many become exiles from their own families. The women's poignant stories speak for themselves. Carla, a nineteen-year-old shelter resident, who is five months pregnant, describes her experience with almost clinical detachment.

> It wasn't my choice to leave home at [age] eleven. They removed me from my home. DSS did. Because my two uncles molested me and I needed to get out because I was going crazy inside, and nobody noticed but my schoolteachers, the people that paid any attention to me.
> It was bad. And my sisters knew. My older sister knew, but she never said a word. . . . My uncles used to baby-sit when my mom used to go to take her GED night classes and go to college. . . . My mom was more ashamed of me—because I said something—than sorry for me. Today, I don't know what she thinks. She never said [she was] sorry. She put it all behind her. Not me. I went to a hospital because I had so much built in me that I was in danger of myself at that young age. I was in the hospital for almost two years. Right out of the hospital, they sent me to a foster home and I hated it, so I ran away. And I kept running away every place they put me in. I was twelve years old and I was hanging out with older women. And they showed me the routine. I could stay at their places. The only way I survived in life is by men. Giving up to have a roof over my head. I had a shelter for that night. And food in my mouth. That's how I survived all those years until I was seventeen.

In all these cases, the victim of abuse is the one who has had to leave, with serious psychological and economic consequences—Nilda must leave Puerto Rico, Carla must first leave her family and later on her newfound security, Anette is forced to leave her job, Tatiana and Joannie must leave the state, Vivian leaves school. As one shelter administrator summarized it, "What we often find is that these families face not just one issue, but multiple issues. And it amazes me that [the women] even get out of bed in the morning and start the day, with all the baggage that they have to deal with."

Family violence embodies what the historian Linda Gordon (1990) calls "the less harmonious aspects of family life"—intrafamily conflicts that result from differences in power. Low self-esteem, limited aspirations, and a sense of powerlessness are likely consequences of the violence in the home experienced by many shelter guests. To think that a low-wage job is all it takes to heal is illusory.

Moving On: The Role of Education and Work Experience

I dropped out of school because of a family problem that had to do with my brother.
—Nilda, houseguest

Policy analysts and social science researchers—and economists in particular— highlight the relative contribution of human capital to socioeconomic outcomes; but economic factors, not just "personal" ones, appear to be the most salient in predicting the onset of homelessness. Single mothers for whom monthly rent and utility bills exceed their total monthly income are most at risk of becoming homeless—and that includes high school graduates (or those with a GED) and those with some work experience. The education buffer can do little against rent inflation, years-long public housing waiting lists, a shrinking stock of affordable housing units, and the steady erosion of wages at the lower-skills end of the market. These women's stories also hint at something that classroom teachers have always suspected, that ability is not the only determinant of education attainment, namely, that stability in the home matters.

Melannie was interviewed in late April 1998. She had just come back from taking a placement test at Middlesex Community College (MCC), without the benefit of a night of sleep—she works the third shift at a local hospital, where she is a certified nurse assistant (CNA). At three o'clock in the afternoon, she could not go to sleep until her son got back from school and she had completed her assigned chore at the house for that day.

Melannie would have been an "early exit" in Harris's (1997) typology of welfare-to-work exits, a "short-termer" in Bane and Ellwood's (1994). She uses public assistance as a bridge to get out of a crisis; her relatively more favorable personal resources already made her a more likely candidate to complete a high school education. Melannie's experience lends support to the argument that strategic use of welfare can lead to further education and training. This is precisely one of the options that will no longer be available to Massachusetts's welfare recipients, as education and training can no longer count toward the work requirement.

Even before the latest welfare reform, balancing education and family crises among the poor already meant frequent interruptions and longer completion times for education credentialing. Melannie describes matter-of-factly why she dropped out of school—an event not related to her early pregnancy.

> I was a straight-A student before I went to Lowell High. I went to Lowell High for one year. And I was skipping and skipping 'cause I would get into fights and arguments about my sister. I was always there for her. She always had problems with people in Lowell High because she had a smart mouth. One day, I went to pick up my sister and there was a whole bunch of girls from the high school waiting to jump me. That's when I started skipping school.

One thing that we know about public schools in low-income urban areas is that they experience high turnover rates. We also know that students whose families move frequently have lower test scores, more behavioral problems, and are more likely to repeat grades than their peers who stay at one school. This often is the case in areas with large recent immigrant populations in Boston, Worcester, Lawrence, and Lowell. What we have not looked into sufficiently, perhaps, is how often and why a student who is performing at grade level suddenly drops out. The stories of young mothers in Lowell shelters suggest that family circumstances might be an issue.

Poor families' survival strategies do not necessarily affect all members equally. Moral claims on kinfolk often mean that one family member must sacrifice for other family members to make it through. Twenty-three-year-old Tatiana's is a classic example. "I was sixteen and in tenth grade when my mom asked me if I could get out of school and watch her son. So I did it, as a favor, until she fixed herself up." Nilda (introduced earlier) dropped out of school for reasons that resonate with Melannie's and Tatiana's experience.

> I started working full time before I finished high school. I had a lapse [of time] there between my junior and senior year in high school when a family problem forced me to leave school. I dropped out. My brother was having problems at school and you know that what affects your sibling affects you also; you over-identify with that problem and you want out. I told my dad that I didn't want to go back to school but it wasn't true; I couldn't tell him that my brother's problems were affecting me.

Nilda and Tatiana attempt to come to terms with the decision to drop out of school in their teens by alluding to their altruistic values. Tatiana calls it "a favor" to her mom, but Nilda psychologizes similar circumstances and calls it the result of "overidentification" with her sibling. A generational difference is apparent in their particular choice of words. Nilda, who as a young woman entered a battered women's shelter, emerged from the experience with a politicized vocabulary from the feminist movement of the time that had roots in psychology. The underlying theme in these two women's personal narratives is one of family first, at the cost of personal sacrifice. Ideology, embedded in language, has an effect on how the women tell their particular stories.

Evidence from both quantitative and qualitative studies confirms that work is a relatively widespread economic strategy among welfare mothers (Edin and Jencks 1993; Edin and Lein 1997b; Harris 1993). Work—in particular, low-wage work—also is common among the short-term or cyclical homeless. Qualitative data from the shelter sample tell us how they do it. As Melannie explains,

> I was on welfare when I was sixteen but I got off relatively quick and then I was back on welfare, like, just recently. But throughout the years I just worked like two jobs. I mostly took care of my little sister and worked.
> Every summer I would work at fuel assistance [a job program for youth]. But on regular time I worked at Dunkin' Donuts. I've worked at Dunkin' Donuts for almost all my life. I got paid like $4.50 when I first started and then, like, two or three years ago I was getting $6.25.
> I left the Dunkin' Donuts job about last year. I work third shift at the nursing home now. I've always worked third shift, so that it would be easier for my sister [to baby-sit], because my son would be sleeping.
> It was just like, you know, Dunkin' Donuts was something where I have always been and I was used to it. I guess I was kind of scared to leave it, 'cause I hadn't tried anything else. Now I am signing up to do an RN.

Melannie is a bright and determined young woman. She has beaten the odds against an early birth, dropping out of school at fifteen, and growing up in a poor single-parent household. She would have been less able to make it, however, without her younger sister. Frequently, day-care arrangements falling through keep women with children from holding on to their low-paying jobs. Melannie's personal and family resources suggest that she can successfully make the transition from welfare to work; does this also mean that she can permanently exit homelessness?

When Work Is Not Enough: Day-Care Dilemmas

Tisha is a twenty-seven-year-old mother of two, has a high school education, and completed some college work. When the father of her kids became chronically unemployed yet refused to take care of the children while she worked second shift at a minimum-wage hotel job in Lawrence, she had to quit her job. She was getting unemployment for a while, but things deteriorated rapidly. The father of the kids left and Tisha had to give up her apartment.

> My bills were catching up with me and I just couldn't do it. I was staying in hotels, I was staying with friends, from one house to the next, hoping to get an apartment I could afford. But, apartments, they don't come too quick.
>
> I know I have to get back on assistance; that's one thing. Because in order for me to be able to work, I have to have day care. And that's the hard thing about it. When day care wasn't available to me, I was working. Now, that I am not working, day care is available.
>
> In other words, they'll help you if you are on assistance; they'll pay for day care. But, if you are not getting assistance, then people who are working and not making that much money cannot afford day care.

Tisha's predicament is not unique. Massachusetts families are eligible for subsidized child care if they make less than 50 percent of the state's median income. The state has a waiting list of approximately 13,000 families. The availability of a subsidy, however, does not increase the number of child-care slots, nor does it address quality issues. Access, quality, and affordability issues help explain why most preschool children in the United States today are cared for in either their own home or another home while their mothers work. In 1994, relatives provided care for 62 percent of preschoolers in poor families where the mother worked (Casper 1994).

A pernicious chain of events emerges: the mother with young children cannot work outside the home if she cannot secure child care; but, if she quits her job to take care of her children, or if she gets "on the aid" to become eligible for subsidized day care, she must still find a way to keep a roof over their heads. Whereas she cannot adequately take care of her family with the aid, she cannot do so without it. If she opts for working for wages, she cannot both pay 30 percent to 50 percent of her income on rent and 25 percent on child care and still be able to get by.

Why Work? Perceptions of Opportunity

The clock is ticking and the family cap has already affected some of the guests. I don't know if they are preparing themselves. They don't seem to be scared about it. They don't realize that education and training no longer count towards the work requirement. For the most part, they are in denial.

—Giovanna, shelter program coordinator

Giovanna, program coordinator at one of Lowell's homeless family shelters, notes that a change has occurred both in the demographics of the population at the shelter (a by-product, perhaps, of the new law) and their stated goals. Guests are slightly older. Whereas a couple of years ago guests' stated future goals included, says Giovanna, "getting married,[12] having another child, and getting an apartment," they now talk about "getting a job, getting an apartment, and continuing their education." We do not know to what extent guests' statements are a front; after all, they have learned the weapons of the weak: a surface acquiescence and revealing little about themselves to anybody, but mostly to anybody associated with the welfare bureaucracy, which has an enormous control over their lives. Poverty makes you vulnerable, and "they" can take away your kids.

Personal narratives of women in family shelters suggests that they are not just being canny; in fact, they seem cautiously optimistic. Besides, denial can be an adaptive defense mechanism depending on the situation, how denial is used, and for how long. Denial can be adaptive if it allows for continuing functioning while the women gradually let bits and pieces of the new (and threatening) reality into their conscious awareness. To test their perceptions, guests were asked how they would handle several Lowell work and child-care scenarios.

When staff and guests were asked about work opportunities in Lowell, responses varied, but the strong underlying theme was that "it depends"—on the job, the wages, and the exact location. In the assessments of the local labor market, there was a marked gender difference. John's reply is representative of the relatively few male guests and male staff at the shelter. He is Vicki's partner and the father of her two kids; they have been together for six years. The twenty-three-year-old white male grew up in a single-parent household, between Manchester in New Hampshire and Lowell and Billerica in Massachusetts. John quit school after his junior year because he "had bigger fish to fry; children to support," but, he quickly adds, "I got my GED, so it doesn't matter." John is nonchalant about the job market.

It ain't hard to find a job. You've just got to get off your lazy duff and look for one. Go to McDonald's, Burger Kings. Just start your job history, you know? Go there; they usually hire you. They like people with no experience, because they can show you the right way. It ain't hard; just look. Go to Market Basket, go to Burger King, McDonald's, Wendy's, department stores; go to auto part stores.

Contrast John's assessment of the Lowell labor market with the more cautious statement of the women, both guests and staff.

> BETHANY (twenty-seven-year-old high school graduate): There are not that many job opportunities in Lowell. It really depends on how much education you have and how far are you willing to travel. Not many; mostly temp jobs.
>
> JOANNIE (twenty-one-year-old with a GED): Yeah, there's a lot of temp jobs. Basically the jobs that will hire, like, people without education, like McDonald's and stuff. That and, perhaps, professional jobs like lawyers and dentists, and doctors. I really don't think they have any good jobs. All the guys around here, all they do is sell drugs.
>
> They say that there are so many opportunities; there's not. There's not any opportunities for women with kids because if there was, instead of building beautiful police precincts, they'd be building day cares and they'd be building a center where women could learn anything and everything they want. They wouldn't be building million dollar police stations. They'd be building day cares.
>
> KAYLA (twenty-nine-year-old working on a GED): I don't think that there's really that many jobs in Lowell. Mostly out of town and stuff. And it is hard because I don't have a car. If there's jobs around here, it's mostly at Burger King, McDonald's, Dunkin' Donuts.
>
> Because they're telling me: You've got to get a job; you've got to get a job. I've got to have somebody to watch my daughter, you know? That's the hardest thing. I never had anybody to watch Matty when he was younger, you know.
>
> EMILY (shelter administrator): It seems that there are more jobs out of Lowell, in the suburbs. As far as in Lowell, there are some openings, but our [heads of] families wouldn't qualify for them. For example, there is some demand for substance abuse workers, relief staff, and other [para-professionals], that require at least a high school diploma. But there's no benefits and it is evening work. And that's not something most of them can afford.

Significantly, John speaks in terms of building "a work history," while the women in the sample consistently talk about the desirability of work, particularly work close to home, that will allow them to fulfill their child-rearing and domestic responsibilities. Also noteworthy is that John's frame of reference is other young men, not the young mothers at the shelter. John subscribes to the idea that the man in the family should be the primary earner and provider. He has not pondered, however, about what this means for female-headed families at the shelter. John is an unusual young man in some regards—he worked as both a certified nurse's assistant and as a day care provider before he joined Youth Build and got his present job at a building supplies store, jobs typically sex-typed as female. He is adamant, however, that Vicki does not need to look for a job; that is "his" job. John's ideology of the family stands in stark contrast with the demands of the new economy, where two earners increasingly is becoming the norm, and with the reality of Bethany, Joannie, and Kayla, who must get by on their own.

Stereotyping roles by sex and gender is practiced not only by the men but by the women as well. Women at the shelter report growing more and more exasperated by their male partners' continued dependence on their families of origin, their joblessness or underemployment, and their reluctance to stay at home and take care of the kids while the women work. Isa, for example, is concerned that her partner, Dereck, the father of her two children, won't last too long at the shelter; that his pride won't let him stay—in other words, the shelter is okay for women but not for men. She tentatively reflects on the future.

> I am going to probably have to be the provider of the family once I get my LPN and stuff, which has always been the case, so. . . . That way, if, say, something happens along the road and we're not together anymore, I can take care of myself and the kids. Up to now, I've let him be in control; but not any more. He's going to have to grow up and deal till he gets a Ph.D. and can support us.

Vivian, the twenty-four-year-old mother of five, has always felt confident that she can provide for her kids, but she "wishes that men were men." "I blew up one day and said, 'I'm tired! I am sick of your mother and tired of your brothers. Either you find us an apartment or I'm gone. You are the man in this family, not I!'"

Life After Welfare Reform

They are taking my welfare away pretty soon. And then we are going to be homeless anyway.
—Tatiana, houseguest

We can think of people as having cognitive maps of the job market and how they fit into it or not. Most of the study participants have tried to get, if not hold on to, a job in Lowell; thus their mental map of job opportunities is pretty much in agreement and on target; so are their ideas about the housing market. Yet their personal models of welfare reform vary widely. Respondents for the most part have not yet had a chance of making and matching expectations by the usual trial-and-error process in which we build our mental maps of reality (that is, through experience).

One of the first self-introduction statements by a small minority of respondents alluded to the fact that they were not, at least at the moment, on welfare—that is, they received food stamps and medical care through Mass Health, but they did not receive any cash benefits. Families at the shelter, the women in particular, have more things in common than they care to admit, but some "cope" by emphasizing differences. Isa is an example.

> [Being homeless and in a shelter] is hard because I've always worked and I've never had to, like for a lot of people here, . . . not work. For me, it is very depress-

ing. But I guess it happens to the best of us, you know? So I've been trying to tell myself that the only place from here is up.

In a way, to be downwardly mobile is easier than to be a permanent part of the urban poor. When asked about how they expect welfare reform to affect them and their families, the range of responses vary from "not at all" to "we'll be homeless again."

One way to assess respondents' levels of awareness about welfare reform is to ask them about their short- and long-term plans for income generation, housing, child care, and further education and training. Here is a sample of houseguests' range of responses.

> VICKI: I only get food stamps and Mass Health. I don't think that welfare has anything to do with that.
> JOHN: She [Vicki] doesn't have to work. I make enough money. I do jobs on the side too, which helps.
> VIVIAN: My only concern is child care. Because I've never really depended on cash from AFDC.
> JEANNETTE: It won't [affect me] because, if I finish my GED this year, then, I can go to Middlesex [Community College]. The course I want to take is paralegal; that only takes two years. I have 'til my daughter—who will soon be two years old, 'til she's four years old. So that gives me enough time to study and get what I need to get done done.
> TATIANA: They are taking my welfare away pretty soon. And then we are going to be homeless anyway. But I figure that, if I study, get my income from child support, $110 weekly, and get myself a job, I'll make a thousand or something a month and I can find an apartment. But the thing that kills is day care.
> KAYLA: [My daughter] is going to Head Start in September. So, it's time for me to get a job, you know? Anything, right now. But, something that's going to be steady, and I mean like a forty-hour work week, so I can get off welfare. Because they're only giving me until next September, because my son will be eight and a half then. So, something that I can live on, pay my rent, and have extra money to buy things for my children, and a car.

What most of the stories show is a process of survival and reinvention—from victim to survivor, from dependent to responsible head of household. These women heads of family have confronted serious material hardship and dislocation by constructing an identity as good mothers (just as earlier they were dutiful daughters). Their family responsibilities both constrain and enable them to make rational choices given unreasonable alternatives—for example, leaving an abusive partner to protect the children; or dropping out of school to take care of a parent or protect a sibling. The individual outcomes are not always good. These women's relatively low levels of education and limited skills prevent them from realizing even their most cherished parenting goals in a new economic order that calls for higher skills levels, two adult earners, and provides fewer safety nets for working poor families. Surprisingly, the reigning mood is cautiously optimistic. Yet women's mental maps regarding the future, as their quotes reveal, do not always take into account the steep barriers posed by the new law.

In May 1998, then acting Massachusetts governor Paul Celluci opposed his own advisory board's recommendation to allow welfare recipients to count education and training toward the twenty hours per week work requirement under state welfare law. Obviously, a disconnection exists between what the governor thinks families can do and what they actually can do. The willingness to work is there, but services and resources such as child care subsidies and health care coverage may be required indefinitely to support poor working families. More important, continuing changes in housing assistance programs and the shrinking stock of affordable housing threaten the ability of the poor to work on the goal of autonomy.

This chapter highlights the experiences of one group of poor families who have only recently engaged the consciousness of the American public: women and children without adequate shelter—that is, those precariously housed and the actual homeless. Preliminary findings from ethnographic work and in-depth interviews with shelter residents point at the diversity within this population of primarily young single mothers with small children and recent arrivals to the city—the population most at risk of reaching welfare time limits and experiencing residential instability. Their survival strategies include a fragile set of networks between working poor and welfare poor households that is threatened by recent policy changes.

Time limits threaten to turn families on welfare into homeless families, yet current thinking about welfare reform has been driven by debates about employability. Less attention has been given to the quality of jobs and the need for noncash benefits that only some jobs pay for. The discussion of such benefits, when it occurs, has focused on day care or medical benefits, overlooking the key role of safe, affordable, permanent housing.

Housing is the big, invisible problem for the poor. Poor housing, crowded housing, temporary housing, homelessness, and frequent moves result in instability and the sense of losing control over one's life—a likely recipe for isolation and domestic violence, as the women's stories reveal. Conversely, safe, affordable, permanent housing can instill a sense of autonomy and independence that frees up time and promotes the stability that enables work, improved health, and taking care of family. It is ironic that some women heads of family experience this for the first time in a shelter for the homeless, where one's actions are curtailed and the acquisition of new networks is limited.

In the area of housing, as in the areas of work and education, poor shelter residents are affected ultimately by government policies that shape opportunity. Federal programs to house the poor, for example, have relied on regulatory breaks and subsidies to private real estate developers. In recent years, an upturn in the economy supported strong home buying but undermined rental markets, with rental housing increasingly relegated to the low-income population, continuing to reinforce the economic and spatial divide between affluent and poor households (Harvard University Joint Center for Housing Studies 1997). Rental property owners in Massachusetts responded to changing market conditions by selling off their properties or opting out of programs providing housing to very low-income households and raising rents. Years of federal cutbacks mean that housing subsidy programs, such as Section 8, will be less able to cover the gap in costs, not to mention the shortfall in the supply of affordable units. The Lowell experience shows that even local housing authorities are opting to sell off their property or convert to mixed-income housing developments to make up for the loss in subsidies.

Homelessness is not just a single mothers problem; the elderly, recent arrivals, and working families among the poor also are at risk. This results in the weakening of potential kinship assistance networks. When both housing and income assistance are being cut, and the federal government retreats from its social protection role, single mothers and their children are made particularly vulnerable.

Exchanges among women at the shelter are typically guarded. The welfare system has taught them to live their lives individually, without a sense of common experience. Advocates for the poor in Lowell are beginning to realize that the housing issue affords them the opportunity to successfully integrate homelessness with larger-scale social and economic injustice, and poor families in the community have jumped on the bandwagon. At issue, they claim, is economics and not just one's private fate or willpower, thrift, and personal responsibility. Poor families are not responsible for the erosion of the minimum wage or rent inflation, and they have the right to live without chronic insecurity and uncertainty about their ability to keep their families housed, clothed, and fed.

The basic premise of a welfare state is that government has the ultimate responsibility for the well-being of its residents and that this cannot be entrusted to individuals, private business, or local communities. We know that homeless families often exit emergency shelters and transitional housing programs, just as a significant number of welfare families exit welfare. Government's responsibility for families' well-being is therefore to help them move from temporary exits into permanent ones. Policy analysts and social science researchers point at some of the avenues to accomplish this: a targeted Earned Income Tax Credit (particularly one that is refundable for the lowest-income workers and phased out at higher income levels), food stamps, medical insurance, and child care. This study suggests that stable, safe, affordable housing also is vital. By contributing to self-confidence, independence, and security, housing enables individuals to function effectively as workers and parents—and any policies that seek to promote self-sufficiency among the poor must take these insights into account.

The research reported here was supported by a grant from the MIT Research Support Committee for the Humanities, Arts and Social Sciences Fund.

NOTES

1. The federal law creates a Temporary Assistance to Needy Families (TANF) block grant to states that replaces the federal Aid to Families with Dependent Children (AFDC), the AFDC Administration, Emergency Assistance, and the Job Opportunity and Basic Skills Program (JOBS).

2. As we approach 2002 and welfare reform reauthorization, a new recession is already in the make. Shrinking job opportunities for the less-skilled and educated among current and former recipients, ineligibility for TANF if they have exhausted lifetime limits, and increasing pressure on the states to cut social service programs can lead to increased material hardship for this population, and perhaps a need to rethink the terms of the new law. It will all depend on the severity and the duration of this recession.

3. Massachusetts welfare reform was approved October 31, 1995, and amended April 22, 1996. The state complies with the requirements of the Personal Responsibility and Work Opportunity Reconciliation Act of 1996, with the exception of provisions identified on its 1115 Waiver, implemented November 1, 1995.

4. Only 37 percent of recipients left AFDC as a result of loss of eligibility due to earnings from employment in the year after the reforms went into effect, just as only 37 percent left welfare the year before (Albeda 1997; Johnson 1996). Subsequent drops put the caseload numbers at 73,000 in 1997 and 68,224 in 1998.

5. Although welfare recipients are overrepresented by single mothers who began childbearing as teenagers, caseload records show that most recipients are well past their teenage years (Duncan 1997). Longitudinal studies of welfare receipt, however, suggest that a teenage birth significantly increases the likelihood of long-term welfare receipt (Bane and Ellwood 1994). This is not to say that giving birth as a teen "causes" poorer socioeconomic outcomes (for example, lower rates of labor force participation, lower incomes, higher poverty rates), since we do not know if the outcomes would have been the same in the absence of an early birth (Levine and Whitmore 1997).

6. In the 1990s, the picture becomes complicated by the freezing of government subsidies such as Section 8. The Republican Congress froze the number of vouchers in 1995.

7. *Ideology* refers to those mental frameworks that we use to make sense of the social world around us. Like values, ideologies have a normative or prescriptive character, and like beliefs, they are built on bits and pieces of truth. Ideology inspires attitudes and provides guides for action. An example of ideology is patriarchy. Patriarchy is a family and social system that gives power to the father or the male head of household over women and children, based on his role as family provider and protector. A patriarchal ideology is embedded in the male-headed nuclear family ideal type, the defense of the use of physical force by males as an accept-

able form of social control within the family, or some women's assessment of self-worth based on their ability to attract and retain a male head of household.

8. Twenty percent of Lowell households made less than $10,000 and 43 percent less than $25,000 a year. Overall, about 50 percent of all Lowell households made less than the city's median of $29,000 a year, or about 79 percent of the state's average. The majority of employed residents worked in services (32 percent), manufacturing (29 percent), and wholesale and retail trade (18 percent).

9. In the 1980s, the Southeast Asian population of Lowell experienced a dramatic increase, the result of refugee resettlement and secondary migration. The 1980 census counted fewer than 100 Southeast Asians. By 1990, some 1,000 Vietnamese, 3,000 Laotians, and 25,000 Cambodians were living in the city (Cambodian Mutual Aid Association, cited in Witherbee 1998).

10. Variations in educational attainment cannot be dismissed as merely differences in ability or in parental expectations. The young parents' parents expected their children to do better than themselves. Interview data suggest that other factors might be at play. Several interviewees reported that their mothers had returned to school as adults, to complete a GED or begin a college education, as a result of welfare incentive programs or changes in their marital and parental status.

11. The corresponding figures for the other groups are 44 percent for non-Hispanic whites, 27 percent for Hispanics, and 3 percent for non-Hispanic blacks.

12. Getting married or entering a stable relationship is still high on the list of these single heads of families. Some of the respondents argue that they seek the company and attention more than the financial contribution. Until now, these women have been able to provide for themselves and their children, through welfare if need be. Yet others, however unrealistically, still see marriage as the ticket out of poverty and off welfare.

REFERENCES

Albeda, Randy. 1997. *Welfare to What? A Look at the Department of Transitional Assistance's Report on Families Leaving Welfare*. Boston: Working Massachusetts.

Babson, Jennifer. 1998. "Affordable Housing Crisis Seen." *Boston Globe*, December 10, 1998, B1, 29.

Bane, Mary Jo, and David T. Ellwood. 1994. *Welfare Realities: From Rhetoric to Reform*. Cambridge, Mass.: Harvard University Press.

Bassuk, Ellen L. 1991. "Homeless Families." *Scientific American* 265(December): 20–27.

Bassuk, Ellen L., Angela Browne, and John C. Buckner. 1996. "Single Mothers and Welfare." *Scientific American* (October): 60–67.

Bassuk, Ellen L., and John C. Buckner. 1994. "Troubling Families: A Commentary." *American Behavioral Scientist* 37(3): 412–21.

Bernstein, Nina 1999. "With a Job, Without a Home: Low-Wage Workers Turn to Shelters to Bridge the Gap." *New York Times*, n.d., 1999, B1, 8.

Blank, Rebecca. 1989. "Analyzing the Length of Welfare Spells." *Journal of Public Economics* 39: 245–73.

———. 1996. *It Takes a Nation: A New Agenda for Fighting Poverty*. New York: Russell Sage Foundation.

Boisjoly, Johanne, Kathleen Mullan Harris, and Greg Duncan. 1997. "Initial Welfare Spells: Trends, Events, and Duration, with Implications for Welfare Reform." Working paper 96-22, Poverty, Race, and Inequality Series. Institute for Research on Poverty: University of Wisconsin, Madison.

Boston Globe. 1998. "High Rent Districts." Editorial. n.d., 1998, n.p.

Brelis, Matthew. 1999. "Helter Shelter: Housing Costs Are Out of Control. Does Anyone Care?" *Boston Globe,* January 24, 1999, F1, 2.

Casper, Lynne M. 1994. "Who's Minding Our Preschoolers?" Fall Update. *Current Population Reports,* ser. P70–62. Washington: U.S. Government Printing Office for U.S. Bureau of the Census.

City of Lowell. n.d. *Lowell Opportunity Plan.* Lowell, Mass.: Division of Planning and Development.

Commonwealth of Massachusetts. September 1996. *TANF State Plan.* Boston: Executive Office of Health and Human Services, Department of Transitional Assistance.

Dublin, Thomas. 1992. *Lowell: The Story of an Industrial City.* Washington: National Park Service, Division of Publications.

Duncan, Greg. 1997. "Welfare Reform and Employment: What We Know, and What We Still Need to Know." In *The Urban Crisis: Linking Research to Action,* edited by Burton A. Weisbrod and James C. Worthy. Evanston, Ill.: Northwestern University Press.

Duncan, Johanne, Kathleen Mullan Harris, and Greg Duncan. 1997. *Initial Welfare Spells: Trends, Events, and Duration, with Implications for Welfare Reform.* Poverty, Race, and Inequality series no. WP-96-22. University of Wisconsin, Madison: Institute for Research on Poverty.

Edelman, Peter. 1997. "The Worst Thing Bill Clinton Has Done." *Atlantic Monthly* (March): 43–58.

Edin, Kathryn, and Christopher Jencks. 1993. "Welfare." In *Rethinking Social Policy: Race, Poverty, and the Underclass,* edited by Christopher Jencks. New York: Harper.

Edin, Kathryn, and Laura Lein. 1997a. "Work, Welfare, and Single Mothers' Economic Survival Strategies." *American Sociological Review* 62(2): 253–66.

———. 1997b. *Making Ends Meet: How Single Mothers Survive Welfare and Low-Wage Work.* New York: Russell Sage Foundation.

Finfer, Lewis. 1998. "Homing in on a Crisis in the Neighborhood." *Boston Globe,* December 27, 1998, E4.

Fraser, Nancy. 1989. *Unruly Practices: Power, Discourse and Gender in Contemporary Social Theory.* Minneapolis, Minn.: University of Minnesota Press.

Gordon, Linda. 1990. *Women, the State and Welfare.* Madison: University of Wisconsin Press.

Harris, Kathleen Mullan. 1993. "Work and Welfare Among Single Mothers in Poverty." *American Journal of Sociology* 99: 317–52.

———. 1996. "Life After Welfare: Women, Work and Repeat Dependency." *American Sociological Review* 61(3): 407–26.

———. 1997. *Teen Mothers and the Revolving Welfare Door.* Philadelphia: Temple University Press.

Hart, Jordana. 1996. "Missing Welfare Mothers Sought: Some Teenagers Go Underground." *Boston Globe,* September 13, 1996.

Harvard University Joint Center for Housing Studies. 1997. *The State of the Nation's Housing.* Cambridge, Mass.: Harvard University Joint Center for Housing Studies.

Holzer, Harry. 1996. *What Employers Want: Job Prospects for Less-Educated Workers.* New York: Russell Sage Foundation.

Jencks, Christopher. 1995. *The Homeless*. Cambridge, Mass.: Harvard University Press.

Jensen, Leif, and Yoshimi Chitose. 1997. "Will Welfare Work? Job Availability for Welfare Recipients in Rural and Urban America." *Population Research and Policy Review* 16: 383–95.

Johnson, Jennifer. 1996. "Low Wages, Lousy Jobs and Instability: Why Work Hasn't Replaced Welfare in Massachusetts." Massachusetts Institute of Technology, Cambridge. Unpublished manuscript.

Kalil, Ariel, Mary Corcoran, Sandra K. Danzier, Richard Tolman, Kristen Seefeldt, Daniel Rosen, and Y. Nam. 1998. *Getting Jobs, Keeping Jobs, and Earning a Living Wage: Can Welfare Reform Work?* Discussion paper 1170-98. University of Wisconsin, Institute for Research on Poverty, Madison, Wisconsin.

Kimmel, Jean. 1992. *Child Care and the Employment Behavior of Single and Married Mothers*. Staff working paper 93-14. Kalamazoo, Mich.: W. E. Upjohn Institute.

———. 1998. "Childcare and Federal Policy." *Employment Research* (Spring). Kalamazoo, Mich.: W.E. Upjohn Institute.

Levine, Phillip B., and Diane M. Whitmore. 1997. "Teen Motherhood, Labor Market Involvement and the Receipt of Public Assistance." Paper presented to the Conference on Synthesizing the Results of Demonstration Programs for Teen Mothers, Chicago (November).

Lystad, Mary, ed. 1986. *Violence in the Home: Interdisciplinary Perspectives*. New York: Brunner/Mazel.

Pearce, Diana. 1990. "Welfare is Not *For* Women." In *Women, the State and Welfare*, edited by Linda Gordon. Madison: University of Wisconsin Press.

Pressman, Sylvie. 1996. "Étude comparée de l'immigration ancienne et récente à Lawrence et à Lowell, deux anciens centres textiles du Massachusetts, 1950–1995." [A comparative study of early and recent immigration to Lawrence and Lowell, two older textile centers in Massachusetts, 1950–1995.] Unpublished Ph.D. diss., University of Paris-Sorbonne, France.

Raphael, J. 1995. *Domestic Violence: Telling the Untold Welfare-to-Work Story*. Chicago: Taylor Institute.

Roschelle, Anne R. 1997. *No More Kin: Exploring Race, Class and Gender in Family Networks*. Thousand Oaks, Calif.: Sage.

Rossi, Peter H. 1994. "Troubling Families: Family Homelessness in America." *American Behavioral Scientist* 37(3): 342–95.

Schlay, Anne B., and Peter H. Rossi. 1992. "Social Science Research and Contemporary Studies of Homelessness." *Annual Review of Sociology* 18: 129–60.

Sosin, Michael R., I. Piliavin, and H. Westerfelt. 1990. "Toward a Longitudinal Analysis of Homelessness." *Journal of Social Issues* 46: 157–74.

Tienda, Marta, and Ronald Angel. 1982. "Headship and Household Composition Among Blacks, Hispanics, and Other Whites." *Social Forces* 61(2): 508–31.

Witherbee, Nicole. 1998. "The Lowell Report." In *Communities on the Edge: We Must Find a Better Way*, edited by Vicky Steinitz and Michael Stone. Boston: The HOME Coalition.

Wolf, L. A. 1991. "The Welfare System's Response to Homelessness." In *Homeless Children and Youth: A New American Dilemma*, edited by J. H. Kryder-Coe, L. M. Salomon, and J. M. Molnar. New Brunswick, N.J.: Transaction.

Wong, D. S. 1999. "Families in Mass. Fare Well, Study Says." *Boston Globe*, January 26, 1999, B1, 8.

Chapter 5

Informal Support Networks and the Maintenance of Low-Wage Jobs

Julia R. Henly

The labor market activity of welfare recipients has attracted considerable interest in recent years. This attention is largely due to passage of the 1996 Personal Responsibility and Work Opportunity Reconciliation Act (PRWORA), which increased the employment obligations of parents receiving welfare benefits, emphasized "work first" strategies over education and skills development, and established time limits on the receipt of benefits. Embodied in the welfare reform law is a clear message that recipients are expected to find work as quickly as possible—regardless of individual characteristics and circumstance—and use cash assistance only as a last resort in times of significant hardship. These changes in welfare policy signal a heightened faith in the secondary labor market to meet the needs of welfare recipients.

This chapter explores the role that informal systems of support—that is, social networks of relatives, friends, and acquaintances—play in facilitating the labor market involvement of lower-skilled, low-wage mothers, both with and without welfare experience. A brief summary of the labor market context in which most welfare recipients and other lower-skilled mothers work is presented first. Based on this review, I suggest that alone, jobs in the secondary labor market seldom provide the resources necessary to support a family independently. Next, the proposition that informal systems of support act in tandem with the labor market to supplement low wages and provide work and family supports to low-income employed mothers is explored. Drawing from research on the adaptive strategies of poor families and informal support networks more generally, I discuss the ways in which we might expect informal networks to support low-income, lower-skilled workers and consider the characteristics of networks that may influence how and whether support transactions occur. The relevance of these suppositions about informal helping systems is then examined for a sample of low-income mothers in Los Angeles County, both with and without welfare experience, who were employed in the low-wage labor market prior to passage of the 1996 welfare reform law.

WHAT DO JOBS IN THE SECONDARY LABOR MARKET PROVIDE?

Structural economic changes over the last three decades have negatively affected lower-skilled workers. Increasing skills demands within industrial sectors, geographic shifts in the location of lower-skilled jobs (globally and outside of central cities), the weakening of unions, and changing employer practices regarding the employment of part-time and contingent workforces all have been identified as contributing to the declining wages and more uncertain economic futures of lower-skilled workers (Levy 1998; Blank 1997; Tilly 1996; Danziger and Gottschalk 1995; Freeman 1994). Lower-skilled women have been partially sheltered from these negative economic shifts, but only because they were disproportionately employed in occupational sectors that already paid the lowest wages and offered the least economic security (Blank 1997). Although positive economic trends of late show slight wage gains for the least-skilled workers, continued skills biases in labor market demand suggest that economic growth alone is unlikely to radically improve their economic position (Danziger and Reed 1999; Levy 1998).

Lower-skilled women are disproportionately represented in a few industrial sectors. The majority find work in food service, retail trade, health care, social services, and education, and are employed as office assistants, cashiers, clerks, health aides, teacher's aides, housekeeping staff, and other related positions. Wages are on average less than $8 an hour, and being nonwhite and female continues to be a relative disadvantage even in this lower-skilled sector of the labor market (Holzer 1996). Moreover, workers in these jobs disproportionately face nontraditional work schedules that may include early morning, evening, and weekend hours, split shifts, and frequently changing schedules over which they have limited control (Lambert 1999).

In addition, jobs in the lower-skilled labor market seldom provide formal benefits or supports to facilitate management of work and family demands (Lambert 1999). Indeed, the paucity of employer-based family policy is not only a problem for lower-skilled workers, but affects a much larger proportion of the workforce (Galinsky, Hughes, and David 1990; Glass and Estes 1997). Employer-based policies, when they do exist, are structured such that they make it easier for workers to adjust family life around work rather than adjust work life around family, and as a result, these policies ultimately benefit the workplace more than the family (Lambert 1993).

Existing research establishes that welfare recipients are best thought of as part of, rather than distinct from, the low-wage, lower-skilled labor force (see, for example, Harris 1996; Bane and Ellwood 1994). That is, several studies demonstrate that the majority of welfare recipients either use welfare only briefly or cycle between welfare and employment in the secondary labor market. The problems that welfare recipients encounter in the labor market therefore are likely to be similar to those facing the majority of lower-skilled workers:

low wages, work instability, limited benefits, and minimal job flexibility (Pavetti and Acs 2001). Given the significant labor market involvement of welfare recipients, scholars increasingly recognize the importance of integrating studies of welfare with studies of lower-wage workers more generally (see, for example, Lambert 1999).

INFORMAL SUPPORT AND EMPLOYMENT

How do low-income families get by, given that their jobs are unlikely to prove sufficient for meeting family expenses and caregiving needs? Informal networks of relatives, friends, and acquaintances may play a critical role by supplementing the income of low-income working mothers and offering instrumental assistance (tangible, in-kind help) that reduces the costs of working outside the home.

Informal Support as an Income-Generating Strategy

Low-income parents, whether employed or not, generate income through a variety of means that often include informal as well as formal systems of support. For example, by carefully constructing the family budgets of unemployed mothers on welfare and employed mothers without welfare income, Edin and Lein (1997) conclude that neither lower-skilled jobs nor formal welfare payments are sufficient to meet the expenses of raising a family. They demonstrate that low-income parents receive money from multiple sources and generate income in a variety of ways. These supplements to welfare and to low-wage jobs are primarily informal in nature. In particular, the researchers find that at the same time that mothers are employed in formal jobs or collecting welfare payments, they frequently are participating in the informal economy—earning money through casual, under-the-table jobs. Whereas some of these casual jobs are in established firms where workers are hired illegally and compensated in cash for their services, the informal sector also includes work performed outside of formal-sector establishments—for example, the provision of in-home child care, hair styling, or other services. In addition to work in the informal economy, Edin and Lein (1997) find that welfare and nonwelfare mothers alike supplement income by relying on financial gifts and loans from their informal networks of friends, partners, and relatives.

Informal Support as a Means of Reducing the Costs of Working

Since the expenses of wage-reliant mothers are greater than those of welfare-reliant unemployed mothers, once the additional costs of working outside the home (for example, child care, transportation, health insurance, lost time for participation in other income-generating strategies) are taken into account (Edin and Lein, 1997), decisions to accept employment in the regular economy

/ **181**

may depend on the availability of low-cost ways to meet these new work-based expenses. The assistance provided by informal networks may represent one such low-cost support system. A low-income mother who cannot afford an automobile, for example, may rely on a sibling or neighbor to drive her to and from work. Likewise, this same working mother may have a mother or other relative who is able to care for her children during working hours (see, for example, Brown-Lyons, Robertson, and Layzer 2001; Hogan, Hao, and Parish 1990; Pearson et al. 1990; Jarrett 1994). In this way, in-kind support from informal network members may reduce the costs of working outside the home, making low-wage employment possible for some mothers.

In the case of child care, national studies demonstrate that low-income working parents disproportionately utilize lower-cost, informal child care providers, especially close relatives (Brown-Lyons, Robertson, and Layzer 2001; Hofferth et al. 1991; Institute for Women's Policy Research 1996). In addition to its below-market cost, informal care may fill recognized voids in the formal child care market by providing services to parents of infants or special-needs children and by offering flexible care hours that accommodate the work schedules of low-income parents (Maynard, Kisker, and Kerachsky 1990; Henly and Lyons 2000).

PROPERTIES OF INFORMAL NETWORKS THAT PROMOTE EMPLOYMENT

Drawing from research on social networks and social support, we might expect the informal supports provided by networks to vary by characteristics of the network itself. In particular, whether or how a network is able to assist an employed mother may depend on individual characteristics of network members, structural properties of the network, and expectations that underlie interpersonal exchanges.

Characteristics of Network Members

The ability or willingness of informal network members to provide financial or in-kind support to a low-income working mother is likely to be affected by socioeconomic status. Observed race differences in the amount of support received (for example, Hofferth 1984) indeed may be due in significant measure to socioeconomic differences across networks (Jayakody 1998). Individuals embedded in networks whose members have more economic resources might receive higher levels of support compared with individuals in resource-poor networks (for example, Jayakody 1998; Fernandez and Harris 1992; Antonucci 1985; Thoits 1995). Moreover, the kind of support one can expect to receive also may vary by the socioeconomic characteristics of network members. In particular, research suggests that financial support is more characteristic of informal exchanges within higher-income networks, whereas instrumental assistance is more typically exchanged among members of lower-income networks (Hofferth 1984; Stack 1974; Hogan, Hao, and Parish 1990). Apparently, when money is scarce, people provide direct services in lieu of money—through the provision of child care or transportation, for example, or through extended family household structures.

Beyond the economic capacity of network members, the amount and type of help provided may depend on social roles occupied by members of an individual's network. An individual needing assistance with child care, for example, may be more successful at finding an informal care arrangement if her network includes female friends or relatives (as females are overrepresented as informal caregivers) without employment obligations (as nonworking women may have more time and more flexible schedules to support a working mother). Her chances also may improve if a network includes members who care for their own children at home—a role that may be compatible with providing child-care assistance to others (Henly and Lyons 2000).

Structural Properties of Informal Networks

The type and amount of support one receives from a network also may be conditioned by the particular structure of the network itself. Whereas networks characterized by dense, closely knit ties across members may be particularly important for resource mobilization and exchange (Wellman and Leighton 1979; Bott 1971; Stack 1974), networks that include weaker connections to individuals outside of one's primary social group may provide linkages to a more diverse set of resources and access to novel information (Granovetter 1983). Thus strong ties are recognized for their bonding, support, and coping capabilities, and weak ties for their capacity to bridge members with extralocal resources and opportunities (see Putnam 2000; Sampson 2000).

Several authors have suggested that the close ties exemplified by extended family household structures may be an adaptive response to economic need as well as an expression of long-standing cultural patterns of family formation (for example, Hunter et al. 1998; Hogan, Hao, and Parish 1990). Research demonstrates that families with limited financial resources and African American families (regardless of income) are more likely than families with greater economic resources and white families to form extended households and rely on extended kin for instrumental support.[1] Single-parent families, because they have more limited economic resources and less time to monitor children compared with two-parent families (McLanahan and Sandefur 1994), may compensate for the absence of a partner by forming extended households with nonspousal adults or by relying more heavily on cross-household support.[2] These closely knit, proximate network structures may allow low-income parents to pool scarce resources and reduce expenses, and they also may facilitate the delivery of in-kind supports such as child care.

/   183

Although such structures may operate to reduce expenses and mobilize resource exchange, closely knit structures also may have negative consequences for parents and children (Jackson 1998; Chase-Lansdale, Brooks-Gunn, Zamsky 1994). Extended household structures may increase the caregiving and economic responsibilities of certain household members. For example, a low-income mother whose extended household structure includes an unemployed brother or elderly relative may find herself sharing her already limited financial resources even more widely, and her caregiving responsibilities indeed may increase. Even when additional family members provide important supports to the household such as child care or help with chores, some research suggests psychological costs of coresidence to the parent. Coresiding grandparents, for example, may provide necessary child care but also threaten a parent's parenting autonomy and mental health (Jackson 1998; Kalil et al. 1998; Chase-Lansdale, Brooks-Gunn, and Zamsky 1994). Thus extended household structures may either reduce or increase the burden on employed low-income parents, depending on the characteristics of the members themselves and quality of their relationship with the parent.

Expectations Underlying Interpersonal Exchanges

The support low-income mothers receive—whether financial or in kind—also may depend on the expectations individual network members have regarding their responsibilities to network members. Both equity and exchange theories, while differing in their assumptions about actor motive (for example, fairness versus utilitarian self-interest), assert that individuals seek reciprocal relationships and that patterns of social exchange tend toward equilibrium (Uehara 1995). Moreover, Gouldner (1960) posits that beyond the requirements of reciprocity imposed by systems of social exchange and mutual dependence, a "moral norm of reciprocity" exists that also guides individual behavior and compels individuals to return favors (see also Uehara 1995). The manner in which reciprocal obligations are realized may vary, however, depending on such factors as trust, duration of relationship, and intimacy (Uehara 1990, 1995; Antonucci and Jackson 1990; Ingersoll-Dayton and Antonucci 1988; Rook 1987). For example, whereas immediate and direct returns may be a condition of support from less intimate network members, close network ties that exist over the long term (such as those with family members or fictive kin) can lead to more abstract and flexible definitions of reciprocity that may not require immediate returns of support, or returns in the same domain or even to the same person. That is, within intimate relationships, actors may believe that in the long run everyone is helping everyone, perhaps at different times and in different ways (Antonucci and Jackson 1990; Uehara 1990, 1995).

Whether or not a particular act of support includes an obligation for support in return may depend as well on the type or amount of support being requested. For example, one might expect assistance requests that demand a large investment of resources (such as informal child-care services) to require a return payment of some sort, even when the service is provided by a close network tie whose notion of reciprocity is more abstract. If the support amount is small, or if it does not involve a significant time commitment, neither the person asking for assistance nor the provider may be as concerned about reciprocation, regardless of the nature of the tie.

In practice, these notions of reciprocity translate into bidirectional systems of support, although any particular return transaction may be more or less explicit and immediate depending on the characteristics of the relationship. For example, the mother who lends her car to her daughter may not request reimbursement for gasoline, but she may still benefit from her daughter's unsolicited assistance with grocery shopping, cooking, and housecleaning. A parent who relies on another parent (with whom she does not have a long-term close relationship) to pick up her child from school every day, however, may feel obligated to articulate a clear form of reimbursement for the received services. Thus in our efforts to understand the role informal networks play in supporting working mothers, it is important to consider the working parent's relationship with the support provider and the extent to which the flow of support between them is bidirectional.

THE STUDY

To better understand the role of informal helping systems in supporting the labor market involvement of low-income mothers, semistructured interview data from the Workplace Environment Study, carried out with seventy-four low-income mothers in Los Angeles County, were analyzed.[3] A primary aim of the original study was to improve our understanding of how the overlapping contexts of employment, family, and welfare shape the coping strategies of low-income mothers and their families. In an effort to broaden the focus of inquiry conventionally taken within the welfare literature, the study included low-wage workers both with and without welfare histories.

Two convenience samples of mothers with employment experience in entry-level jobs (a *welfare* sample and *nonwelfare* sample) were deliberately selected. A full description of the sampling strategy is reported elsewhere (Henly 1999). Respondents from both samples lived in Los Angeles County, spoke either English or Spanish, and had some employment experience in an entry-level job in the previous two years. The welfare sample (N = 44) reported at least some AFDC experience in the two years prior to being contacted for study participation, and the nonwelfare sample (N = 30) reported no AFDC experience in the five years prior to being recruited into the study.[4] The welfare sample included respondents who reported simultaneously combining welfare with employment in the regular economy as well as respondents who reported alternating employment and welfare spells.[5]

The study used a semistructured interview protocol including both standard survey items and several less structured items to which respondents provided open-ended, in-depth responses. The interview gathered quantitative and qualitative data about job characteristics and workplace dynamics, household structure and income, family and work demands, and formal and informal sources of support. Special attention is given to the data on informal support in this chapter. (See Henly 1999 and Henly and Lyons 2000 for related papers based on data from the Workplace Environment Study.)

Convenience sampling precluded the possibility of achieving samples that were representative of either the population of welfare recipients or the population of entry-level workers. Moreover, as tables 5.1 and 5.2 illustrate, the welfare and nonwelfare samples differ in important ways other than their welfare histories. The findings reported herein are meant to illustrate the experiences of these unique samples of low-income working mothers and suggest hypotheses for future exploration. Caution must be taken, however, in generalizing the findings beyond the confines of the study itself; and although this chapter will make comparisons between the welfare and nonwelfare samples, these comparisons must be treated with appropriate caution given sampling limitations.

The Sample

As table 5.1 indicates, both the welfare and nonwelfare samples report a mean age of about thirty-five years, and respondents in both samples reported an average of almost two children living with them in their households. Yet those respondents with past welfare experience were disproportionately African American and living without a partner, whereas those without welfare histories were disproportionately Latina and residing with a partner (either cohabiting or married). Both groups were equally likely to live in an extended family arrangement (not shown in table 5.1). Although by study design all respondents had work experience in entry-level jobs across a similar range of occupational sectors, the welfare sample worked in poorer-quality jobs overall.

As table 5.2 indicates, the welfare mothers' wages were significantly lower and their jobs were less likely to offer health benefits than the nonwelfare sample. In addition, the welfare sample was less likely than the nonwelfare sample to be employed at the time of the interview.[6] Thus in the current sample, the welfare and nonwelfare samples differ systematically by race and ethnicity, living arrangements, and job quality. Indeed, these differences may explain welfare use in the first place. Therefore, any dissimilarities uncovered between the two groups may reflect differences on these variables or other unmeasured differences across the two groups.

Table 5.1 / Characteristics of Welfare and Nonwelfare Low-Income Working Mothers, by Age, Race-Ethnicity, Marital Status, and Number of Children

	Total	Welfare	Nonwelfare
N	74	44	30
Age (in years)			
Mean	34.7	34.6	34.8
(SD)	(7.6)	(6.5)	(9.1)
Race-ethnicity (percentage)[a]			
Latina-Hispanic*	47.9	30.2	73.3
African American*	38.4	53.5	16.7
White	12.3	16.3	6.7
Asian-Pacific Islander	4.1	4.7	3.3
Native American	6.8	9.3	3.3
Marital status (percentage)*			
Married-cohabiting	38.9	21.4	63.3
Divorced, separated, or widowed	26.4	28.5	23.3
Never married	34.7	50.0	13.3
Number of children in household[b]			
Mean	1.92	1.95	1.87
(SD)	(1.0)	(1.1)	(.97)
Number of children < age six (percentage)			
One	43.9	44.1	43.5
Two	12.3	8.8	17.4
Three or more	3.5	2.9	4.3

Source: Author's calculations.
Note: Significance level of t-tests and chi-squares denoted with *p < .01
[a]Race-ethnicity categories are not mutually exclusive. Because some respondents classified themselves in more than one category, percentages add up to more than 100 percent.
[b]Children includes respondents' biological and stepchildren; also includes two grandchildren.

THE CONTRIBUTION OF INFORMAL NETWORKS TO THE INCOME-GENERATING STRATEGIES OF RESPONDENTS

Drawing from previous qualitative studies (for example, Edin and Lein 1997), I hypothesized that respondents would generate income through a mix of work-based, welfare-based, and network-based strategies. I find that low-wage workers did generate income in a variety of ways. In fact, only three respondents reported getting by solely on earnings from a job in the formal economy.

Table 5.3 shows the percentage of welfare and nonwelfare respondents reporting each of the three general sources of economic support (transfer

Table 5.2 / Job Characteristics of Welfare and Nonwelfare Low-Income Working Mothers

	Total	Welfare	Nonwelfare
N	74	44	30
Occupations (percentage)			
Teacher aide, child care, health aide, other social service	25.7	31.8	16.7
Retail, food, beverage workers	27.0	27.3	26.7
Production, cleaning, public service	18.9	15.9	23.3
Office, administration	28.4	25.0	33.3
Hourly wage (percentage)			
Mean (SD)**	8.08 (3.5)	7.35 (2.4)	9.12 (4.5)
$6.00 or less	35.1	38.6	30.0
$6.01 to $9.00	39.2	40.9	36.7
$9.01 or more	25.7	20.5	33.3
Hours (percentage)			
30 or less	31.9	38.1	23.3
31 to 40	50.0	45.2	56.7
41 or more	18.1	16.7	20.0
Benefits (percentage)			
Health care for self and or children***	27.0	15.9	43.3
Employment status (percentage)			
Employed at time of interview***	74.3	61.4	86.7
Employed in previous two years	100.0	100.0	100.0

Source: Author's calculations.
Note: Significance level of t-tests and chi-squares denoted with **p < .05, ***p < .01

payments, earnings from employment, money from informal support networks) in the year prior to the interview.[7] The first row of this table concerns informal network income sources and demonstrates that the majority of both welfare and nonwelfare respondents reported receiving economic support in the prior year from at least one informal source (coresiding spouse, nonresidential father, friends or relatives). Not surprisingly, the nonwelfare sample, which was disproportionately married-cohabiting, reported additional income primarily from their coresidential partners (67 percent). Economic support from friends and relatives (13 percent) or nonresidential fathers (17 percent) was less common. Whereas partner income was not available to the majority of respondents in the welfare sample, friends and relatives provided economic assistance to

Table 5.3 / Sources of Income for Welfare and Nonwelfare Respondents: Transfer Payments, Earnings, and Informal Networks in Year Prior to Interview

	Total Sample	Welfare	Nonwelfare
N	74	44	30
Any informal network income	**63.9 (46)**[a]	**52.4 (22)**	**80 (24)**
Coresiding spouse	36.1 (26)	14.3 (6)	66.7 (20)
Nonresidential father	18.1 (13)	19.0 (8)	16.7 (5)
Friends-relatives	23.0 (17)	29.5 (13)	13.3 (4)
Any earnings	**91.7 (66)**	**85.7 (36)**	**100 (30)**
Formal work	86.1 (62)	78.6 (33)	100 (30)
Informal (casual) work	26.4 (19)	35.7 (15)	13.3 (4)
Any transfer payments	**51.4 (37)**	**73.8 (31)**	**20 (6)**
AFDC	38.9 (28)	66.7 (28)	—
Food stamps	36.1 (26)	59.5 (25)	3.3 (1)
SSI	8.3 (6)	4.8 (2)	13.3 (4)
Other transfers	5.4 (4)	6.8 (3)	3.3 (1)

Source: Author's calculations.
[a]Percentage followed by number in each category. Bold text denotes percentage and number of respondents who report any income from the general category.

approximately 30 percent of respondents in this group, and nonresidential partners paid child support to just under one fifth of them.

The different sources of informal network income highlighted in table 5.3 provide markedly different levels of financial support. For example, the income of coresiding partners is substantially higher than the loans and gifts provided by friends and relatives or the child support payments from nonresidential fathers (dollar amounts are not shown on table 5.3). In fact, including the earnings of coresidential partners more than doubles a household's income, whereas considering money from friends and relatives or from nonresidential fathers only marginally improves a household's monthly income. Specifically, those respondents with income from relatives and friends reported receiving an average of $123 in the month prior to the interview from this source,[8] and those with income from a nonresidential father reported an average of $226 in child support payments in the previous month. In contrast, the average earnings of coresiding partners were $1,547 in the month prior to the interview.[9] Of course, other nonspousal adults sharing residence with the respondent also may be working and contributing earned income to the household. Unfortunately, the income of adults other than the respondent's partner were not gathered in a systematic fashion in the study. Overall, financial contributions from friends, relatives, and absent fathers do not match the earnings of employed residential partners.

Consistent with findings from previous studies, the second row in table 5.3 demonstrates that participation in the informal economy also served to supplement earnings from regular work and welfare income. Over one fourth of respondents reported odd jobs (*informal*, or *casual* work) such as "doing hair," caring for the children of friends and relatives, and cleaning houses over the course of the previous year. Some respondents reported carrying out casual work activities in addition to their regular jobs, whereas others reported relying on casual jobs only during periods of unemployment. Like informal support from friends and family, casual jobs did not generate nearly as much income as that provided by a coresiding spouse, nor did the average casual job pay as much as the average welfare benefit or job in the formal economy.

As the second row of table 5.3 also demonstrates, the welfare sample reported greater participation in casual work than the nonwelfare sample (36 percent versus 13 percent). This difference may be due to several factors. As the job characteristics discussed previously demonstrated, the welfare sample reported working in poorer-quality jobs than the nonwelfare sample, which may suggest a greater need for additional earnings even during periods of employment. Moreover, the welfare sample may have had more time to participate in the informal economy, given that they reported less participation in the regular economy. AFDC recipients also faced welfare regulations (during the periods in which they received welfare) that limited the extent to which they could engage in regular work, and these regulations might have increased their incentives to find work in the informal rather than formal economy.[10]

Thus in this sample of low-earning women, respondents with welfare experience (who were disproportionately African American and single) were more economically disadvantaged than their nonwelfare counterparts (who were disproportionately Latina and living with a partner). The greater economic disadvantage was due in part to employment in lower-paying jobs but also the result of minimal contributions from spouses. Importantly, welfare recipients were not able to make up for these deficits in their own and spouses' earnings by additional income generated through casual work, by welfare income, or by financial loans and gifts from friends and family members.

THE CONTRIBUTION OF INFORMAL NETWORKS TO JOB MAINTENANCE

In addition to financial assistance, I hypothesized that respondents would receive in-kind supports that facilitated their work in the secondary labor market. The data suggest that in contrast to their relatively small economic contributions, friends and relatives played a much larger role in providing nonfinancially to respondents. Some of this nonfinancial support served to connect respondents to both formal and informal jobs, thereby contributing indirectly to the aforementioned income-generating strategies, whereas much of it subsidized the costs of working outside the home by providing resources (especially transportation and child-care assistance) necessary to carry out employment activities.

The experiences of Rhonda, a twenty-seven-year-old African American interviewee from the welfare sample, who worked for minimum wage as a cashier and cook at a fast-food restaurant, serves to illustrate the multiple ways in which informal network members can support working parents nonfinancially. Rhonda had found her job twenty months prior to the study interview through information supplied by her cousin, an employee at the restaurant where Rhonda worked. Her cousin informed Rhonda of the position and also recommended her to the manager. In addition to connecting Rhonda to the labor market, Rhonda's family provided significant assistance with the additional expenses that working outside the home entails. Receiving no employee benefits and a minimum-wage salary, Rhonda relied exclusively on her family for meeting both her child-care and transportation needs. She made the twenty-mile trip to and from work each day either by borrowing her mother's car or getting a ride from her mother. Her sister was able to take over caregiving responsibilities for Rhonda's three children (ages nine, five, and three) while she worked the 6 A.M. to 2 P.M. shift at the restaurant. This child-care arrangement involved caring for the older children before they left for school, and providing care to the youngest throughout the day.

Rhonda used her network to find a job, to transport herself there, and to assist with her child care needs. As a whole, respondents described networks that helped out in these three domains to a greater or lesser extent, as is discussed further below.

Nonfinancial Involvement of Informal Networks in Income-Generating Strategies

As the example of Rhonda illustrates, participation in income-generating strategies, whether through the regular or informal labor market, often is enacted through one's social network. Not only can these network members provide financially to low-income mothers, they also can serve as important connections to the labor market. Like Rhonda, just under half (46 percent) of the respondents (both with and without welfare experience) reported being referred to their current or most recent employer by an informal network member, most often a close friend or relative. This finding is consistent with a significant body of literature that demonstrates the importance of informal network referrals to the hiring process, especially in the low-wage labor market (see Granovetter 1994 and Henly 2000 for a review of this literature).

The interviews also suggest that in addition to formal-sector employment, informal jobs also materialize as a result of informal network relationships. For example, the services performed by respondents, such as styling hair, watching children, and caring for an elderly person, typically were provided to friends, neighbors, and relatives, rather than to unfamiliar customers. One respondent, for example, reported providing respite care to her mother for which she was financially reimbursed $110 every two weeks.

Involvement of Informal Network Members in Transportation Assistance

More than one third of respondents (36 percent) reported that, like Rhonda, they did not own a car. These respondents relied either on public transportation, walking, or some informal means (borrowing a car or receiving a ride from a friend or relative) to get to and from their workplaces. Overall, one fifth of the sample relied on one of these informal means, and because welfare recipients were less likely to own their own car, they relied disproportionately on both public transportation and informal network members to get to and from work.

Although many respondents who were without their own transportation had reliable informal arrangements similar to Rhonda's, many others could not rely on informal network members for consistent transportation to and from their workplaces. Some respondents used public transportation, others reported that their means of getting to and from work varied depending on their friends' or families' other obligations, and still others reported relying primarily on one method or another but being without a backup when arrangements fell through. A significant minority (about 40 percent) reported that transportation interfered with their ability to arrive at work promptly, and about half of this group reported being late to work or missing work at least once a month because of a transportation problem.

Involvement of Informal Network Members in Child-Care Assistance

Although informal means of transportation were relatively common in the sample, informal network members played an even larger role in the delivery of child-care services to both welfare and nonwelfare respondents. Consistent with previous research (for example, Hofferth et al. 1991; Institute for Women's Policy Research 1996), informal child care providers were used by the majority of the women in the sample.

Of the fifty-seven respondents with children under thirteen, forty-eight reported a regular child-care arrangement, and almost 80 percent of those with regular care relied on an informal network member. These informal providers were mothers of the respondents in over one third of the cases. Other informal providers included sisters and aunts, and nonrelatives such as friends and neighbors of the respondents. Only 12.5 percent of informal providers were male, and these caregivers typically were relatives of the respondents. Although more than half of both welfare and nonwelfare samples reported using informal child care and at least half of both groups relied on relatives, the nonwelfare sample more frequently reported relatives as caregivers compared with the welfare sample. The greater use of caregiving relatives by the nonwelfare sample may reflect the greater number of Latinas in this group. Previous research demonstrates that Latinos are more likely than African Americans and whites to use relatives to assist with child care, perhaps for cultural reasons or because of more limited child-care options in Latino communities (Fuller, Holloway, and Liang 1996; Kontos et al. 1997).

CHARACTERISTICS OF INFORMAL NETWORK EXCHANGES

These findings reveal the importance of informal support in the form of financial and in-kind (for example, informational job leads, transportation, and child-care) services to respondents, but by no means did respondents receive these supports universally. The review of the social support and social network literature provided earlier suggests that the informal support available from networks may vary depending on the socioeconomic characteristics of network members, expectations that guide support exchanges, and structural properties of the networks themselves.

Although the data do not allow a direct examination of the socioeconomic characteristics of network members, the relatively limited financial assistance from friends and relatives reported in table 5.3 suggests that perhaps respondents were embedded in networks whose members themselves had few economic resources. Respondents living with a partner were likely to benefit financially because of additional income that partners brought into the household. Spousal contributions seldom were matched in amount by other informal income-generating strategies, however, leaving unmarried respondents at a distinct economic disadvantage.

The data are better designed to examine the expectations that guide support exchanges. Overall, it appears that informal supports were received as part of a reciprocal system of exchanges between the respondent and her informal network members. Rarely did respondents report receiving assistance from friends and family without also referring to the contributions they themselves gave to network members. This mutual dependence will be illustrated in two ways. First, a closer examination of informal child-care arrangements reveals that respondents almost always provided compensation to informal caregivers for the services they provided. Second, an examination of household structure suggests that extended household forms represented mutually dependent systems in which respondents both received supports from household members and contributed in return.

In terms of child care, an analysis of respondents' arrangements clearly indicates that informal networks provided the majority of care, but that this care was given with the expectation that it would be compensated, typically monetarily (see Henly and Lyons 2000 for more on child care arrangements of the sample). In fact, respondents with informal arrangements in the current study were just as likely as those with formal arrangements to report providing financial payments to the provider (more than 80 percent of formal and informal providers paid for child care). Of the respondents with paid arrangements, the mean child-care expense was $70.42 per week. In contrast to national data, formal child-care arrangements cost no more than informal child care arrangements; undoubtedly because formal care was used fewer hours per week than informal care (it was especially used by respondents with older children who needed only after-school care), and also because formal arrangements typically were subsidized in this sample.[11]

Although we found no significant difference between the welfare and nonwelfare samples in either the likelihood of having a paid arrangement or the cost of care, the child-care expenses of respondents in the welfare sample consumed a greater share of their total incomes because their earnings were lower and because they were less likely to be living with a spouse (and the additional income contributed by a spouse was significantly greater on average than welfare income).[12]

Even the small group of respondents who reported no financial obligations to their child care providers typically reported nonmonetary obligations, suggesting that they too were embedded in mutual, bidirectional exchanges with informal network members. These nonmonetary payments sometimes were in the same domain (for example, returning child-care services to the provider when she needed care), but also were returned in other ways, by sharing food stamps or groceries with the child care provider. This embeddedness in mutual support systems is exemplified by the comments of Elsa, whose sister cares for her child with no monetary compensation. "I don't pay. We help each other out with our children. I also take care of hers." When asked why she uses this arrangement, she states, "Because we live together and we help each other out. We're very close that way and I trust my sister."

Thus the analysis of child-care arrangements suggests that respondents seldom receive caregiving support without providing something in return, usually money, sometimes in-kind assistance. Importantly, however, the child care "contract," especially for arrangements with relatives, was informal and abstract, and open to negotiation during times when money was particularly scarce. A subset of respondents reported that payments for child care were delayed or forgiven, or providers occasionally would accept in-kind rather than cash compensation. In a few cases, respondents reported that they did not have a standard payment at all, but rather gave the provider "whatever they had to give" at a particular time. For example, Cheryl, a restaurant worker, gave her brother or mother (depending on who watched her children) the sum of her daily tips, which fluctuated depending on the shift and number of hours she worked. The data thus suggest that informal care arrangements can be negotiated and remain negotiable, providing an important source of flexibility to economically insecure employed parents. That such abstract notions of reciprocity were most common in informal care with relatives is consistent with arguments about the prominence of time-delayed reciprocity expectations in close, long-term relationships (for example, Antonucci and Jackson 1990).

Another way in which respondents participated in mutual bidirectional networks—exemplified by Elsa's comments—was through the formation of extended family households. An examination of the living arrangements of respondents demonstrates that most respondents lived in some type of multi-adult household structure—either sharing residence with a partner or relative or both. Whereas one third of the sample lived alone with no other adults, the remainder lived in some type of multiadult structure, either with one other (40.3 percent) or at least two other (26.4 percent) adult members. Almost half (46 percent) of respondents lived in extended household structures—that is, they shared residence with at least one nonspousal adult, typically their mother or other female relative.

Respondents in the welfare sample were less likely than those in the nonwelfare sample to be living with a partner (see table 5.1), and more likely to be parenting alone (45 percent versus 17 percent). Yet both samples were equally likely to live in extended households, and extendedness was only slightly less common among cohabiting respondents compared with single respondents. Thus, rather than serving as an alternative to welfare or to marriage-cohabitation, the formation of extended households indeed may be a complementary strategy that single and cohabiting parents—both with and without welfare—consider.

The current data do not provide systematic information on the reasons for forming extended household structures. An examination of the income of different household types suggests, however, that some respondents indeed may form extended household structures to reduce their economic burdens. For example, respondents who live in extended household structures report lower monthly personal earnings on average ($619.31 for respondents with partners, $633.80 for respondents without partners) than those with partners who do not live in extended structures ($1,218.77). The higher average earnings of respondents who live with their partners but not other adults may lend support to the argument that mothers least in need of economic assistance may choose not to seek out such arrangements.[13] Additionally, though, respondents reporting the lowest earnings ($562.42) also were those who lived alone with their children, which suggests that those most in need of assistance may have been the most socially isolated.[14]

Moreover, data suggest that members of extended household structures took on household responsibilities and reduced the child care burdens of respondents.[15] More than one third of respondents who live with a nonspousal adult report that this person was their children's primary child care provider. Additionally, although most respondents paid for child care, care by household members was twice as likely to be provided at no monetary cost than care arranged with individuals outside of the immediate household. That most nonspousal adults were both female and nonelderly also suggests that these household members may actively contribute to the maintenance of the household. Past research demonstrates that women are more likely than men to contribute domestic labor to the household, and given the close familial ties that household members had with respondents, these individuals seem particularly likely to share in the caregiving responsibilities and tasks necessary to help the respondent and maintain the household.

Many respondents, both with and without spouses, were living in extended households that had the potential to reduce household expenses and increase available supports. Yet many respondents were not living in extended structures, and these respondents may have had less access to informal supports. Low earners who live alone with their children may have a particularly difficult time developing strategies to accommodate family and work demands, as their expenses are likely greater and their resources at home more limited. Overall, the economic situation of respondents living alone with their children may be more dire than that of other respondents. They did not benefit from spousal earnings or the earnings of other adults in the household; their own earnings were low; and although they were more likely to receive welfare income than others, accounting for public assistance payments still does not close the income gap between single and multiadult households.

LIMITS OF INFORMAL NETWORK RELIANCE

Although informal networks provide important supports to most low-income parents in this sample, a system that depends so heavily on these informal exchanges is not without complication. Access to informal systems of support was not universal in this sample. Moreover, support that was available was limited, sometimes unreliable, and required substantial reciprocation (either monetarily or otherwise) from respondents.

Concerning availability, the findings reviewed here demonstrate that more than one third of respondents receive no financial assistance from informal network members, those with the most limited incomes are least likely to benefit from extended household arrangements, and not all who need it can rely on friends and family members for transportation and child-care assistance. These findings suggest that a nontrivial group of respondents may be socially isolated from social networks or are embedded in networks whose members are either unable or unwilling to provide support to them. Efforts to ascertain the size of this group in future studies that include large, representative samples of low-income working parents will be critical.

Moreover, for respondents who did participate actively in informal network exchanges, the support received from these network members sometimes was reported as being inconsistent and unreliable, and data suggest limits to the amount of support respondents could expect to receive. This was most evident in respondents' discussions of their child-care arrangements. Although informal care provided needed flexibility to working parents, respondents reported numerous complications owing to an informal caregiver's other family and work responsibilities. In describing prior child-care situations, respondents frequently reported complications with informal care resulting in a premature end to the child-care arrangement (see Henly and Lyons 2000 for a fuller discussion of informal child care complications in this sample).

This study's findings are not meant to be either conclusive or generalizable to the larger population of welfare recipients or lower-income parents more broadly. Rather, the analysis attempts to add to our understanding of how informal networks can support work in the low-wage economy. The study findings suggest that for this sample, low-income mothers survive in significant measure with the help of their families, relatives, and friends. A coresiding partner's earnings are a particularly important source of network income, yet relatively small amounts of money were provided by nonresidential fathers, or friends and relatives. Unfortunately, the current data do not allow us to directly ascertain the financial well-being of network members, but one might see the limited economic support from friends and family members—especially in light of their substantial tangible assistance—as an indication of economic hardship. That is, low-income employed respondents may, in fact, be embedded in informal networks that are also resource-constrained.

Nonfinancial assistance from friends and relatives was critical to both welfare and nonwelfare respondents. In particular, informal network members facilitated employment by connecting the respondent to employment opportunities; serving as both referral sources and clients in casual work arrangements; providing transportation and the bulk of care to respondents' children during working hours; and by entering into extended family household arrangements that had the capacity to reduce the economic burden and alleviate caregiver responsibilities.

Data further suggest that financial and in-kind supports, which generated income and subsidized employment, were delivered within mutually dependent systems of support. The characteristics affecting network exchanges are worth attending to: they allow us to better understand the context under which both financial and in-kind support is exchanged, and they may affect the type, quality, and stability of the support delivered. Current data suggest that support provided by network members generally was offered within the context of an informal system of mutual, reciprocal exchanges. Whereas respondents relied heavily on network members for support, they also contributed in important ways to these networks. Obligations to return support represented costs and time commitments in addition to the already difficult economic circumstances and harried schedules of respondents. This interdependence of informal network members suggests that not only the kinds of support low-income mothers receive but also the price—monetary or otherwise—that receipt of this support represents to the mother herself is important.

Although the study findings demonstrate the importance of informal networks in the lives of low-income families, they also suggest that informal support was not universally available. Even when it was available, such support could prove inconsistent and unreliable to the parents in the current sample.

Future work might pay greater attention to whether welfare recipients in the labor market have access to the same quality of informal support as their non-welfare counterparts. If respondents with welfare histories indeed have access to more limited resources from informal helping systems, this might help explain why some lower-skilled workers cycle between welfare and employment, whereas other lower-skilled workers remain outside of the welfare system despite working in comparably cyclical jobs. The success of welfare policies that encourage quick labor market attachment may depend on recipients' access to informal means of financial and instrumental support once they enter the workforce and while they are between jobs.

Beyond differences by welfare status, however, these findings question the viability of a system that relies so heavily on social relationships—instead of welfare policy or employer contributions—to improve incomes and subsidize the costs of working outside the home. Although informal networks are important to the well-being of working parents, the amount, consistency, and quality of this kind of assistance is limited, and the secondary labor market alone is unable to meet the needs of low-income mothers satisfactorily.

Portions of this chapter are based on research reported elsewhere (see Henly and Lyons 2000 and Henly 1999). Some of the research reported herein was performed with the permission of the California Department of Social Services (CDSS). The author wishes to thank CDSS for its cooperation. Thanks also for the thoughtful comments and suggestions provided by Yeheskel Hasenfeld, Joel Handler, Michael Sosin, and the members of the Work, Poverty, and Welfare Research Group at the University of Chicago School of Social Service Administration. The Urban Institute Small Grants Program supported the study on which this chapter draws. The opinions and conclusions expressed herein are solely those of the author and should not be considered as representing the views of any agency of the California State Government, the Urban Institute, or individual reviewers.

NOTES

1. The extent to which extended family household structures are an adaptive response to economic need or an example of cultural variations in household preferences has been debated. Yet research (for example, Hogan, Hao, and Parish 1990; Hofferth 1984) suggests that both arguments have merit. Extended structures are more common among lower-income families for blacks and whites, and yet a higher incidence of extended households exists in African American families compared with white families, even after income controls are introduced.

2. Some research suggests that African Americans also may rely more heavily than whites on cross-household support with parenting and other family responsibilities, although whether this racial difference is the result of differences in socioeconomic status, marital status, or culture is unclear (Hunter et al. 1998; Jarrett 1994; Pearson et al. 1990; Belle 1982; Stack 1974).

3. The broader Workplace Environment Study included interviews with both employees and employers in lower-skilled segments of the labor market. This chapter utilizes only data from the employees; analyses of employer data as well as additional analyses of the employee data are reported elsewhere (see Henly 1999 and Henly and Lyons 2000).

4. Access to the welfare sample was granted by the California Department of Social Services (CDSS).

5. Our *nonwelfare* and *welfare* samples are defined differently from Edin and Lein's (1997) *welfare reliant* and *work reliant* samples. Edin and Lein compare women who are working and not working at a point in time. We compare women who share the common experience of work, but who differ in their welfare histories. Thus, unlike Edin and Lein's work-reliant sample, we restricted our nonwelfare sample to individuals with no welfare experience but with work experience in the previous two years. In contrast to Edin and Lein's welfare-reliant sample, our welfare sample is defined by the existence of work and welfare experience in the previous two years. On another note, by design, we did not include welfare recipients without any recent employment experience in our sample because the common experience of employment in lower-skilled jobs was of primary interest to the study. Although the group of welfare clients who have little or no work history is an important subpopulation of recipients to understand, this is not the group of primary interest here, and extensions of study findings to welfare recipients who remain outside of the labor market therefore are inappropriate.

6. Respondents not employed at the time of the interview were queried about their experiences in their most recent job.

7. Respondents in the welfare and nonwelfare samples all had some regular work experience in the last two years by study design. As table 5.3 indicates, the vast majority of these jobs were held in the last year. None of the respondents in the nonwelfare sample had AFDC income by study design. Individuals in this group were not screened for other kinds of welfare income, however, and as the third row of table 5.3 indicates, one fifth of the nonwelfare sample had some transfer income in the last year from either food stamps, disability payments, or other transfer income.

8. Although welfare recipients were more likely to receive income support from friends and relatives, they received it in lesser amounts than that received by those in the nonwelfare sample.

9. Within each of the informal sources of income, the range of income received was substantial. For example, child support from absent fathers ranged from $50 to $475, money from friends and relatives ranged from $25 to $400, and spousal earnings ranged from $200 to $3,200. Three respondents were treated as outliers and excluded from the calculation of sample means.

10. The welfare sample was drawn from participants in both the experimental and control groups of the Cal-WORKS Demonstration Project, and as a result, AFDC regulations were not uniform across the welfare sample. Those who were in the experimental group were subject to a more generous earnings disregard and were not subject to the 100-hour-per-month employment rule. Due to the manner in

which the sample was drawn, to differentiate respondents in the experimental versus control groups of Cal-WORKS is impossible. Given the small sample size, however, the advantage to having access to such information would be marginal.

11. This may also explain why we found no difference in the likelihood of having a no-cost arrangement between formal and informal child care users.

12. For respondents with a partner, their child care burden (child-care expense–income) is reduced by about one half (from .20 to .11) once partner income is considered together with respondents' personal earnings in calculating income, whereas the child care burden of respondents with welfare income is reduced by only about one fourth (from .31 to .23) once AFDC is considered together with personal earnings in the income calculation. Yet one must recognize that in calculating the burden variable for respondents with partners as a proportion of combined personal and spousal income, we assume that respondents and their partners pool their entire earnings and share child-care expenses. In addition, we assume that partners' contributions to child-care expenses are the same across married and cohabiting households. Thus the extent to which respondents' child care burden actually is reduced through their partners' earnings depends on the accuracy of these assumptions.

13. A 2×2 ANOVA, which examines earnings by marital status (partner, no partner) and by household type (extended, not extended), shows a significant main effect by marital status ($F = 5.49$, $p < .02$), but the effect for household type is not significant. The interaction of household type with marital status is significant ($F = 5.60$, $p < .02$)—that is, the income of respondents with partners is higher than the other groups only for those not living in an extended household structure.

14. This assumes, of course, that household structure is an appropriate measure of social isolation. Such an assumption may not be warranted, as previous research suggests that cross-household as well as intrahousehold support exchanges are common in low-income, especially African American, communities (see, for example, Hunter et al. 1998).

15. Extended household members also may have contributed income, but the data do not include systematic information about the income of household members other than coresiding spouses.

REFERENCES

Antonucci, T. C. 1985. "Personal Characteristics, Social Support, and Social Behavior." In *Handbook of Aging and the Social Sciences,* edited by Robert H. Binstock and Ethel Shanas. 2d ed. New York: Van Nostrand Reinhold Co.

Antonucci, T. C., and J. S. Jackson. 1990. "The Role of Reciprocity in Social Support." In *Social Support: An Interactional View,* edited by I. G. Sarason, R. Sarason, and G. R. Pierce. New York: Wiley.

Bane, M. J., and D. T. Ellwood. 1994. *Welfare Realities: From Rhetoric to Reform.* Cambridge, Mass.: Harvard University Press.

Belle, Deborah. 1982. *Lives in Stress: Women and Depression.* Beverly Hills, Calif.: Sage Publications.

Berg, L., L. Olson, and A. Conrad. 1991. "Causes and Implications of Rapid Job Loss Among Participants in a Welfare to Work Program." Paper presented at the annual research conference of the Association for Public Policy and Management, Bethesda, Md.

Blank, R. M. 1997. *It Takes a Nation: A New Agenda for Fighting Poverty.* New York: Russell Sage Foundation.

Bott, Elizabeth. 1971. *Family and Social Network: Roles, Norms, and External Relationships in Ordinary Urban Families.* 2nd ed. London: Tavistock.

Brown-Lyons, M., A. Robertson, and J. Layzer. 2001. *Kith and Kin-Informal Care: Highlights from Recent Research.* New York: National Center for Children in Poverty.

Burtless, G. 1995. "Employment Prospects of Welfare Recipients." In *The Work Alternative: Welfare Reform and the Realities of the Job Market,* edited by D. S. Nightingale and R. Haveman. Washington, D.C.: Urban Institute Press.

Canary, D. J., W. R. Cupach, and S. J. Messman. 1995. *Relationship Conflict.* Thousand Oaks, Calif.: Sage.

Chase-Lansdale, P. L., J. Brooks-Gunn, and E. S. Zamsky. 1994. "Young African-American Multigenerational Families in Poverty: Quality of Mothering and Grandmothers." *Child Development* 65: 373–93.

Danziger, S. H., and Gottschalk, P. 1995. *America Unequal.* Cambridge, Mass.: Harvard University Press.

Danziger, S. H., and D. Reed. 1999. "Winners and Losers: The Era of Inequality Continues." *Brookings Review* (Fall): 14–17.

Edin, K., and L. Lein. 1997. *Making Ends Meet: How Single Mothers Survive Welfare and Low-Wage Work.* New York: Russell Sage Foundation.

Eggebeen, D. J., and D. P. Hogan. 1990. "Giving Between the Generations in American Families." *Human Nature* 1: 211–32.

Fernandez, R., and D. Harris. 1992. "Social Isolation and the Underclass." In *Drugs, Crime, and Social Isolation: Barriers to Urban Opportunity,* edited by A. Harrell and G. E. Peterson. Washington, D.C.: Urban Institute Press.

Freeman, R. B. 1994. "How Much Has De-Unionization Contributed to the Rise in Male Earnings Inequality?" In *Uneven Tides: Rising Inequality in America,* edited by S. Danziger and P. Gottschalk. New York: Russell Sage Foundation.

Fuller, B., S. D. Holloway, and X. Liang 1996. "Family Selection of Child-Care Centers: The Influence of Household Support, Ethnicity, and Parental Practices." *Child Development* 67: 3320–37.

Galinsky, Ellen, Diane Hughes, and Judy David. 1990. "Trends in Corporate Family-Supportive Policies." *Marriage & Family Review* 15(3–4): 75–94.

Glass, Jennifer L., and Sarah Beth Estes. 1997. "The Family Responsive Workplace." *Annual Review of Sociology* 23: 289–313.

Gouldner, A. W. 1960. "The Norm of Reciprocity: A Preliminary Statement." *American Sociological Review* 25(2): 161–78.

Granovetter, Mark S. 1983. "The Strength of Weak Ties: A Network Theory Revisited." *Sociological Theory* 1: 201–33.

———. 1994. "Afterword 1994: Reconsiderations and a New Agenda." In *Getting a Job: A Study of Contacts and Careers.* 2d ed. Chicago: University of Chicago Press.

Harris, K. M. 1993. "Work and Welfare Among Single Mothers in Poverty." *American Journal of Sociology* 99(2): 317–52.

———. 1996. "Life After Welfare: Women, Work and Repeat Dependency." *American Sociological Review* 61(3): 407–26.

Henly, J. R. 1999. "Barriers to Finding and Maintaining Jobs: The Perspective of Workers and Employers in the Low-Wage Labor Market." In *Hard Labor: Women and Work in the Post-Welfare Era*, edited by J. F. Handler and L. White. Armonk, N.Y.: M.E. Sharpe.

———. 2000. "Matching and Mismatch in the Low-Wage Labor Market: Job Search Perspective." In *The Low-Wage Labor Market: Challenges and Opportunities for Self-Sufficiency*, edited by K. Kaye and D. S. Nightingale. Washington, D.C.: Urban Institute Press.

Henly, J. R., and S. Lyons. 2000. "The Negotiation of Child Care and Employment Demands Among Low-Income Parents." *Journal of Social Issues* 56(4): 683–705.

Hofferth, S. L. 1984. "Kin Networks, Race, and Family Structure." *Journal of Marriage and the Family* 46: 791–806.

Hofferth, S. L., A. Brayfield, S. Deich, and P. Holcomb. 1991. *National Child Care Survey, 1990*. Washington, D.C.: Urban Institute Press.

Hogan, D. P., L. Hao, and William Parish. 1990. "Race, Kin Networks, and Assistance to Mother-Headed Families." *Social Forces* 68(3): 797–812.

Holzer, H. J. 1996. *What Employers Want: Job Prospects for Less-Educated Workers*. New York: Russell Sage Foundation.

Hunter, A. G., J. L. Pearson, N. S. Ialongo, and S. G. Kellam. 1998. "Parenting Alone to Multiple Caregivers: Child Care and Parenting Arrangements in Black and White Urban Families." *Family Relations* 47(4): 343–54.

Ingersoll-Dayton, B., and T. C. Antonucci. 1988. "Reciprocal and Non-Reciprocal Social Support: Contrasting Sides of Intimate Relationships." *Journal of Gerontology* 43: 65–73.

Institute for Women's Policy Research. 1996. *Child Care Usage Among Low-Income and AFDC Families*. Research-in-Brief Report. Washington, D.C.: Institute for Women's Policy Research.

Jackson, A. 1998. "The Role of Social Support in Parenting for Low-Income Single, Black Mothers." *Social Service Review* (September): 365–78.

Jarrett, R. L. 1994. "Living Poor: Family Life Among Single Parent, African-American Women." *Social Problems* 41: 30–45.

Jayakody, R. 1998. "Race Differences in Intergenerational Financial Assistance." *Journal of Family Issues* 19(5): 508–33.

Kalil, A., M. S. Spencer, S. J. Spieker, and L. D. Gilchrist. 1998. "Effects of Grandmother Coresidence and Quality of Family Relationships on Depressive Symptoms in Adolescent Mothers." *Family Relations* 47: 433–41.

Kontos, S., C. Howes, M. Shinn, and E. Galinsky. 1997. "Children's Experiences in Family Child Care and Relative Care as a Function of Family Income and Ethnicity." *Merril-Palmer Quarterly* 43(3): 386–403.

Lambert, S. 1993. "Workplace Policies as Social Policy." *Social Service Review* 67(2): 237–60.

———. 1999. "Lower-Wage Workers and the New Realities of Work and Family." *Annals of the American Academy of Political and Social Science* 562: 174–90.

Levy, F. 1998. *The New Dollars and Dreams: American Incomes and Economic Change*. New York: Russell Sage Foundation.

Maynard, R., E. E. Kisker, and S. Kerachsky. 1990. *Child Care Challenges for Low-Income Families*. New York: Rockefeller Foundation.

McLanahan, S., and G. Sandefur. 1994. *Growing Up with a Single Parent: What Hurts, What Helps.* Cambridge, Mass.: Harvard University Press.

Meyer, D. R., and M. Cancian. 1998. "Economic Well-Being Following an Exit from Aid to Families with Dependent Children." *Journal of Marriage and the Family* 60: 479–92.

Mishel, L., and J. Bernstein. 1994. *The State of Working America, 1994–1995.* Economic Policy Institute Series. Armonk, N.Y.: M.E. Sharpe.

Pavetti, LaDonna, and G. Acs. 2001. "Moving Up, Moving Out, or Going Nowhere? A Study of the Employment Patterns of Young Women and the Implications for Welfare Mothers." *Journal of Policy Analysis and Management* 20(4): 721–36.

Pearson, J. L., A. G. Hunter, M. E. Ensminger, and S. G. Kellam. 1990. "Black Grandmothers in Multigenerational Households: Diversity in Family Structure and Parenting Involvement in the Woodlawn Community." *Child Development* 61: 434–42.

Putnam, R. D. 2000. *Bowling Alone: The Collapse and Revival of American Community.* New York: Simon & Schuster.

Rook, Karen S. 1987. "Social Support Versus Companionship: Effects on Life Stress, Loneliness, and Evaluations by Others." *Journal of Personality and Social Psychology* 52(6): 1132–47.

Sampson, R. J. 2000. "The Neighborhood Context of Investing in Children: Facilitating Mechanisms and Undermining Risks." In *Securing the Future: Investing in Children from Birth to College,* edited by S. Danziger and J. Waldfogel. New York: Russell Sage Foundation.

Schilling, R. F. 1987. "Limitations of Social Support." *Social Service Review* 61: 19–31.

Stack, Carol. 1974. *All Our Kin: Strategies for Survival in a Black Community.* New York: Basic Books.

Thibaut, J. W., and H. H. Kelley. 1959. *The Social Psychology of Groups.* New York: Wiley.

Thoits, P. A. 1995. "Stress, Coping and Social Support: Where Are We? What's Next?" *Journal of Health and Social Behavior* 36: 53–70.

Tilly, C. 1996. *The Good, the Bad, and the Ugly: Good and Bad Jobs in the United States at the Millennium.* New York: Russell Sage Foundation.

Uehara, E. 1990. "Dual Exchange Theory, Social Networks, and Informal Social Support." *American Journal of Sociology* 96(3): 521–57.

———. 1995. "Reciprocity Reconsidered: Gouldner's 'Moral Norm of Reciprocity' and Social Support." *Journal of Social and Personal Relationships* 12(4): 483–502.

Wellman, B., and B. Leighton. 1979. "Networks, Neighborhoods, and Communities: Approaches to the Study of the Community Question." *Urban Affairs Quarterly* 14(3): 363–90.

Wentwoski, G. J. 1981. "Reciprocity and the Coping Strategies of Older People: Cultural Dimensions of Network Building." *The Gerontologist* 21: 600–9.

Commentary

The Low-Wage Labor Market and Welfare Reform

Sanders Korenman

According to the Business Cycle Dating Committee of the National Bureau of Economic Research, the 1990s economic expansion began in March 1991. In February 2000, it became the longest expansion since business cycles were first marked in the mid-nineteenth-century. What has been the effect of this expansion on the low-wage labor market? Have the benefits trickled down to the poor? Have sufficient employment opportunities been created for welfare recipients? For less educated workers? For minorities?

First, let us consider the labor market in general. In March 1991, nonfarm payroll employment was 108.3 million (all employment and unemployment figures are seasonally adjusted). Payroll employment continued a gradual decline over the next eleven months, hitting bottom at 108.1 million in February 1992. The data for November 2000 show payroll employment at 131.9 million, an increase of nearly 24 million jobs from February 1992 (see Bureau of Labor Statistics website). Job creation has averaged well above 200,000 jobs per month in this expansion.

Who is getting all these jobs? Since those at the bottom of the labor market are disproportionately unemployed in recessions, they are the disproportionate beneficiaries of employment growth in expansions (for example, Hoynes 1999). Nationally, the unemployment rate fell from 7.4 percent in February 1992 (or a peak of 7.8 percent in July 1992) to 4 percent in November 2000. The unemployment rate has been below 5 percent since mid-1997. Even among adults (age twenty-five and over) with only a high school education, the unemployment rate at the time of this writing is 3.6 percent, down from about 7 percent in the early 1990s. Among those with no high school diploma, the unemployment rate is 6.7 percent. The unemployment rate for black males age twenty and older in November 2000 was under 7 percent, down from 9.5 percent in 1996, and 13.5 percent in 1992. For black females age twenty and over, the November 2000 unemployment rate was 6.3 percent, down from 8.7 percent in 1996 and nearly 12 percent in 1992. The employment-to-population ratio for these women has increased by seven percentage points since the early 1990s, and by four percentage points since August 1996, when national welfare reform legislation was passed.

What about single mothers or welfare mothers, more specifically? Two kinds of information are available on the employment of this population: survey data on employment rates of women who head families, and studies of employment of welfare leavers based on state administrative data, longitudinal surveys, or targeted surveys (Cancian et al. 1999). The first kind of data has the advantage of providing information on the effects of welfare reform on families most at risk of welfare use, rather than recent users. The second are more tightly focused on welfare recipients.

Perhaps the most striking statistic comes from the Bureau of Labor Statistics series on "women who maintain families." Although such women make up only about 6 percent of employment, between November 1998 and November 2000 they accounted for 18 percent of employment growth. In particular, total employment increased by just over three million in those twenty-four months, while employment of women who maintain families increased by 572,000. On average, about 25,000 women who maintain families found employment each month from in 1999 and 2000, whereas the number of families on welfare declined about 31,000 per month during that period. Thus the expansion of employment among single mothers in these two years is consistent with the proposition that a very large number of former welfare recipients and would-be recipients are being absorbed into employment.

More narrowly focused studies of welfare leavers generally confirm this conclusion. Methods vary, but these studies typically find that 50 percent to 85 percent of welfare leavers are employed following welfare exits, with the mode being around two thirds (Cancian et al. 1999).

What about wages? After many years of decline, median hourly wages for men have risen modestly since the mid-1990s (after adjusting for inflation); the median for women has risen fairly steadily in the past twenty years. Evidence also shows that wages at the bottom end of the wage distribution began to rise in the early 1990s (for example, Council of Economic Advisers 1999, 105). Recent studies have identified the decline in the minimum wage as the primary culprit in the decline of wages below the median (Lee 1998). That the reversal of this decline coincides with modest increases in the minimum wage in the mid-1990s therefore is not surprising. In addition to rising wages, the federal Earned Income Tax Credit (EITC) was expanded markedly in the 1990s, boosting the earnings of low-wage workers with children by as much as 40 percent (or by as much as $3,500 annually).

What about the wages and family income of welfare leavers? Families that leave welfare and find jobs are likely to earn more than they would receive in welfare benefits, even if they are able to find only minimum-wage jobs, provided they receive the EITC (Korenman 2000; Kaestner 1999). Moreover, studies find that mean hourly wages exceed the current minimum wage by $1 to $3 per hour. In addition, after adjusting for inflation, both earnings and family income of welfare leavers increase appreciably over time (Cancian et al. 1999; Corcoran and Loeb 1999), whereas welfare benefits clearly do not: indeed, benefits fell in real terms by 30 to 40 percent between the early 1970s and the mid-1990s.

When the economic benefits of formal employment are compared with welfare, child-care costs are critical, as is the ability of women to supplement welfare benefits with income that can be hidden from welfare authorities (Edin, Lein, and Nelson, ch. 3 herein; Edin and Lein 1997; Edin and Jencks 1992). The point here is that while the economic comparison between work and welfare always depended heavily on these two items, policy changes in the 1990s radically shifted incentives in favor of employment (see, for example, Ellwood 1999). The most important policy changes in this respect are the following: an increase in the minimum wage; expanded child support enforcement; a greatly expanded refundable EITC; increased eligibility for public health insurance for poor and low-income children through expansion of Medicaid eligibility and federal funding for state child health insurance programs; and increased funding for child care for low-income women, especially welfare leavers. These carrots to encourage work have received much less attention than the two sticks of welfare reform: work requirements and time limits. The shift to block-grant funding in combination with the marked decline in the welfare caseload has provided states with considerably increased resources (per case), which states are using to provide more intensive services required to help recipients find and maintain work. Whether these changes to "make work pay" outweigh any disadvantages of welfare reform, or if they would have been politically possible without welfare reform, remains an open question.

Yet what about the next recession? One often hears the policy scholar mantra that the real test of welfare reform will come with the next recession. A recession certainly will bring hardship, possibly intensified by welfare reform (owing to time limits on eligibility and block-grant funding); but to say the "real test" is the next recession ignores benefits from greater employment during the many years of economic expansion, or any behavioral effects of welfare reform. Potential advantages linked to formal employment include experience and job-related mobility, employment-related fringe benefits, increased eligibility for unemployment insurance and social security disability, survivorship, and old age benefits. Formal employment may have psychological or behavioral benefits for welfare leavers and their families. Work also may bring employment-related health risks, including stress. Not that formal employment is certainly superior to welfare for all recipients at all times; rather, a real test of welfare reform recognizes a wide range of potential advantages and disadvantages relative to the previous system across the entire business cycle. Effects would include changed incentives related to family formation and dissolution, kin and family network processes, decisions related to fertility, and human capital investment (that is, education, training, health, and migration). Qualitative studies are critical to the analysis of the effects of welfare reform on these family processes. The studies in this volume represent a step in this direction.

Edin, Lein, and Nelson (ch. 3 herein) raise and begin to address an interesting set of questions: What are (and will be) the effects of welfare reform and related policy changes on family processes (broadly conceived) among the poor? How are men and women differentially affected? How do changes in family processes, in turn, affect labor market behaviors and strategies for coping with financial hardship? These authors predict that single mothers who enter the labor force as a result of welfare reform will suffer financially. As a result, they will increase their demands on kin and, potentially, on fathers. Fathers want to support their children, provided they have continuing involvement with and access to their children. A variety of personal and structural conditions, however, prevent their steady employment at decent wages. The authors suggest that coresidence with children could provide an "anchor" that fathers need to maintain stable employment. This conclusion echoes a longstanding and newly revived literature regarding the effects of marriage and fatherhood on men's labor market outcomes (for example, Korenman and Neumark 1991; Akerlof 1998).

Edin, Lein, and Nelson discuss the effects that welfare reform will have on families by lowering the income of single mothers who are forced to leave welfare and enter the labor force sooner than they otherwise would have. Yet there are other possibilities. As noted, at minimum the jury is out about whether those who leave welfare find themselves better off working, and policy developments in the 1990s have changed these calculations in favor of formal employment; and even if single mothers are worse off when they first leave welfare, wages and family incomes appear to increase with time off of welfare.

Because welfare reform further strengthened paternity establishment and child-support enforcement, it also may have reduced a single mother's desire to involve the father. She will be more likely to collect some economic support from the father without his involvement in her or her children's lives—and men's incentives to bear children are certainly altered by improved child-support enforcement.

Henly too concludes with a discussion of welfare reform and family processes (ch. 5 herein). She observes that women on welfare appear to have fewer family or kin network resources available to them than low-income working women not on welfare. Henly interprets this to mean that many women are on welfare because they have fewer family resources to support their employment. While this conclusion is reasonable, we should not assume that those who do not currently receive network support are unable to build such support (Stack 1974). Henly does not observe the availability of an exchange network; rather, she observes actual exchanges. Losing welfare eligibility would lead more women to build and sustain supportive networks. Whether they will be able to do so is an open question that can be answered by additional, careful qualitative research.

Henly also stresses that, although family and kin networks may provide considerable support to the poor, they are no substitute for government support.

Poor people often are embedded in social networks with others who lack resources. Working may reduce their availability to exchange support. Thus, while the demand for network support will rise, women losing eligibility for welfare may not be able to "buy" such support because they may have limited time to engage in reciprocal exchange of services, most importantly, child care.

Buchanan (ch. 2 herein) describes the world of teleservice work. On the upside, it pays fairly well for entry-level work, hours can be flexible, and appearance on the job may be less important than work that requires face-to-face interaction with customers. On the downside, promotion possibilities are limited, work is routinized, job security is limited, and benefits are low. Buchanan points to the "inherent contradictions" of the "demanding nature of 'unskilled' work and the severe personal and financial constraints imposed by flexible employment." High turnover plagues these work environments; these are places where "opportunities are lost, skills are misrecognized, and aspirations are crushed." She urges us to recognize the "perspectives and personhood" of low-wage workers.

Yet what is the alternative? These jobs may not be portals to long-term career paths or vehicles for self-realization, but they appear to be superior in several respects to other entry-level positions. Residents of depressed areas in the United States likely would welcome calling centers. Ironically, some of these establishments are located in Canada by U.S. firms that presumably want a labor force that is relatively well-educated and "middle-class sounding" to speak to a middle-class customer base. If race- or class-based discrimination is at work, odds are that these are reasonably decent jobs that impoverished U.S. communities would value.

Cintrón-Vélez (ch. 4 herein) issues an important warning about the possibility that family homelessness could rise as a result of welfare reform. She ends her chapter with a plea for policy action that could help address this problem:

> Policy analysts and social science researchers point at some of the avenues to accomplish this: a targeted Earned Income Tax Credit (particularly one that is refundable for the lowest-income workers and phased out at higher income levels), food stamps, [housing subsidies,] medical insurance, and child care . . . and any policies that seek to promote self-sufficiency among the poor must take these insights into account.

Yet, with the exception of food stamps, which were restricted for some immigrants and able-bodied adults with no children, all of these recommendations were followed in the 1990s. The refundable EITC was markedly expanded under the Clinton administration. The minimum wage was increased. Medical coverage was expanded through increases in Medicaid eligibility and expanded federal funding for state health insurance programs for poor children. Federal child-care assistance was consolidated and expanded, although whether expansion is sufficient to meet new demand induced by work requirements and welfare term limits is questionable (U.S. Department of Health and Human Services 1999).

Continued qualitative and quantitative research on the interrelated functioning of families and low-wage labor markets after welfare reform clearly is needed. Researchers should sustain a focus on basic research most needed to inform policy debates, and aim for the highest social scientific standards. In this respect, the studies in this book would be enhanced by longitudinal designs that could describe the evolution of kin network structuring over time, leading up to and following welfare exits and greater participation in formal employment. Scholars must examine the increased variety of state welfare programs under the 1996 Temporary Assistance to Needy Families (TANF) block grant that provide rich contextual variation needed to understand the influence of policy regimes on complex family and labor market processes. These research goals are endorsed by leading qualitative and quantitative scholars from widely divergent political positions, as the following passages demonstrate:

> A powerful case can be made for funding basic research in social science as opposed to quick answer–policy relevant research. The misconceptions that motivated many Great Society programs arose as a consequence of the inadequate factual knowledge base about society at large and the effectiveness of government programs in particular. It is unfortunate that in the post–Great Society backlash against social science, funding for basic data collection and evaluation research has been greatly reduced. Social myths thrive in environments without data. Santayana wrote that those who fail to learn from the past are condemned to repeat it. Without an adequate social science factual base and accompanying interpretive framework, we will be unable to learn from the past and are more likely to make fresh errors in designing future policies. (Heckman 1990)

> Our goals should be to identify new objectives, new ways to reduce the numbers of children and families living in poverty, new designs that reform our current benefit structure. To accomplish these goals, we must open up our thinking in order to see accurately intended and unintended consequences of policy. Our efforts to promote social welfare interventions that have a positive effect on the quality of human life rest on two assumptions: that we know what we want the outcome to be, and that we can understand the impact of social programs on individual and collective behavior. These requirements reveal a new set of American dilemmas. We must grapple with a definition of our problems and we must attempt to integrate understandings of the social character of human action and explanation. (Stack 1992)

REFERENCES

Akerlof, George. 1998. "Men Without Children." The Brookings Institution and the Department of Economics, University of California, Berkeley. Unpublished paper.

Cancian, Maria, Robert Haveman, Thomas Kaplan, Daniel Meyer, and Barbara Wolfe. 1999. "Work, Earnings, and Well-Being After Welfare: What Do We Know?" *Focus* 20(2): 22–25.

Corcoran, Mary, and Susanna Loeb. 1999. "Will Wages Grow with Experience for Welfare Mothers?" *Focus* 20(2): 20–21.

Council of Economic Advisers. February 1999. *Economic Report of the President 1999.* Washington: U.S. Government Printing Office.

Edin, Kathryn, and Christopher Jencks. 1992. "Reforming Welfare." In *Rethinking Social Policy: Race, Poverty and the Underclass*, edited by Christopher Jencks. Cambridge, Mass.: Harvard University Press.

Edin, Kathryn, and Laura Lein. 1997. *Making Ends Meet: How Single Mothers Survive Welfare and Low-Wage Work.* New York: Russell Sage Foundation.

Ellwood, David T. November 1999. *The Plight of the Working Poor: Children's Roundtable Report Number 2.* Washington, D.C.: The Brookings Institution.

Heckman, James J. 1990. "Book Review." *Journal of Human Resources* 25(2): 297–304.

Hoynes, Hilary. June 1999. "The Employment, Earnings, and Income of Less Skilled Workers over the Business Cycle." *NBER* Working Paper 7188. Cambridge, Mass.: National Bureau of Economic Research.

Kaestner, Robert. 1999. "Employment Prospects of Welfare Recipients: Another Look at the Data." *Cato Journal* 19(1): 119–41.

Korenman, Sanders. 2000. "Glass Ceilings, Iron Bars, Income Floors." In *Prosperity for All? The Economic Boom and African Americans*, edited by Robert Cherry and William M. Rodgers III (308–12). New York: Russell Sage Foundation.

Korenman, Sanders, and David Neumark. 1991. "Does Marriage Really Make Men More Productive?" *Journal of Human Resources* 26(2): 282–307.

Lee, David. March 1998. *Wage Inequality in the U.S. During the 1980s: Rising Dispersion or Falling Minimum Wage?* Princeton, N.J.: Department of Economics, Princeton University.

Stack, Carol. 1974. *All Our Kin: Strategies for Survival in a Black Community.* New York: Basic Books.

———. 1992. "A Critique of Method in the Assessment of Policy Impact." *Research in Social Problems and Public Policy* 4: 137–47.

U.S. Department of Health and Human Services. October 1999. "Access to Child Care for Low-Income Working Families." Available at *www.acf.dhhs.gov/news/ccreport.htm.*

Part III

PATHS TOWARD CHANGE

Chapter 6

Care at Work

Lucie White

This chapter is based on ethnographic research conducted in a Head Start program in South Central Los Angeles in the early 1990s. Project Head Start is a popular and reputedly successful federally funded preschool program for low-income children and families that was launched by President Lyndon Johnson in 1965 as part of his War on Poverty. My research focused on women who were involved in Head Start classrooms on a daily basis, either as parent volunteers or as low-wage workers who had begun their involvement in the program as parent volunteers, and regarded that involvement as a significant positive force in their lives.

My goal in the project was to listen to how these actively engaged women talked about their experience of volunteering or working in Head Start and what it meant to them. I wanted to understand how these women made sense of the program's effects on the quality and course of their lives. As a scholar of social welfare law and policy, I was fascinated by the local moral and political worlds of Head Start centers. The program first came to my attention in the early 1980s, when clients whom I represented in a legal aid program in rural North Carolina repeatedly told me that Head Start was different from other social programs in which they were enrolled. I became intrigued by how any government program could gain such high regard among these women, who had little reason to place much trust in the state or its law.

Low-Wage Worksite or Place of Care?

Head Start centers are good examples of social institutions that would not exist but for a dense web of federal statutes and regulations that impose dozens of specific commands on local entities such as churches and school systems that receive Head Start funds. Thus the social worlds of street-level Head Start centers are brought into being by law. As Jürgen Habermas reminds us, the rigid processes of modernist public law are not very good at creating life worlds (Habermas 1987). Indeed, those processes are much more efficient at unraveling the intricate webs of human interaction that keep our worlds together. For some of its clients at least, the Head Start program stands out as an exception to Habermas's claim. Although Head Start's law uses many of the same instruments as other social programs, such as command-control regulations and output-oriented performance standards, the end result for many clients is a social and moral space in which they feel that they can thrive, often for the first time in their lives. By looking closely at the interaction between the person, her face-to-face community, and the street-level social setting of the Head Start center, I felt I could learn something about how lawyers who write social legislation can do their work better. Specifically, I was interested in how such lawyers (whom I thought of not as social engineers or policy experts, but rather more as good architects) might create the kinds of legal blueprints—one might call them constitutions—that would promise better worlds.

One might think that this essay on a government-funded welfare program in which much of the frontline work is done by volunteers rather than paid employees has no place in a volume on low-wage work. This conclusion is mistaken for two reasons. First, Head Start is at once a social program and low-wage work site. Examining how Head Start's work environment affects its frontline clients and workers therefore is of interest to anyone who has a wider interest in the shop-floor experiences of all low-wage workers, particularly in the growing sector of the low-wage workforce that provides care services. Furthermore, that Head Start is a government-funded public welfare program does not mean that its relevance for employment policy is limited to public-sector firms. That most low-wage workplaces are said to be private-sector operations is true; their employers are believed to have wide latitude to shape the shop-floor environment without the law's interference. Closer examination, however, shows that such a sharp distinction between public- and private-sector low-wage workplaces is overdrawn. Ethnographic studies consistently show that *all* workplaces—and indeed all street-level social institutions—are shaped through the interplay of public and private law with people's histories, social practices, and cultural commitments. Close study of a work setting such as Head Start, in which the heavy hand of public law appears to be everywhere, can help sensitize us to the law's force in other workplace settings, where its influence, through common-law rules, regulatory practices, and public law norms, though perhaps more subtle, is just as pervasive.

One also might argue that Head Start is of limited relevance to wider discussions of low-wage work because much of the work in Head Start centers is done by volunteers rather than paid employees. In the program researched and discussed herein, only about one third of the active women studied had ever worked in the program for pay. The remaining two thirds worked on a regular basis in Head Start classrooms without receiving any wage. Given that all of these women were very poor, I expected to find the difference between working for love and working for money to be very important to them, and it was. Yet at the same time, the boundary between wage workers and parent volunteers was a good deal more blurred than I had expected. Although only a third of the women studied had eventually made the move into the ranks of paid employees, such former volunteers made up about 70 percent of the program's paid staff, which included teachers, assistant teachers, social service aides, kitchen staff, janitors, and the like. Once hired, these former volunteers often moved back and forth between paid and volunteer positions as their family obligations shifted and welfare eligibility rules changed. Moreover, whether or not they were sometimes paid a wage, all of the actively involved women in my study tended to discuss their work at Head Start in similar terms. Sometimes they would talk about it in the instrumental language that I had expected: working at Head Start was a safe, sometimes pleasant, always boring, and often stressful way to get a minimum-wage paycheck and a few job skills. Yet these Head Start women would also talk about that work—in intense and even impassioned terms—as a critical source of social support, a nurturing or life-changing personal experience, and a spiritually meaningful vocation. Understanding how Head Start's shop-floor environment brings forth such feelings among its paid and unpaid workers might suggest specific practices through which other low-wage work sites can enable their workers to feel safe and even on occasion to thrive. Thus we now turn to the question of how Head Start brings forth such feelings in both parent volunteers and paid workers.[1]

Stories of Change

In their interviews, Head Start women related many things about their lives. They talked about their everyday frustrations with coworkers, supervisors, troubled Head Start parents, and the children. They told of the despair they often felt, especially on "blue" days, when faced with the endless tasks of caring—wiping up runny noses and tears and vomit, scrubbing down floors after lunch, swabbing the chewable toys with alcohol after the kids had gone home. They told of the anger they felt when they got their paltry paychecks, or in the case of volunteers, when they did not get any paycheck at all. And they talked about the stress of keeping body and soul and budget together as single mothers.

At the same time these stories told of an endless flow of troubles, they also painted a picture of Head Start as a powerful force of change. In spite of their frustrations, Head Start women consistently described the program as a place where they felt cared for, respected, and competent. They described how the program helped them to become stronger, more clearheaded, and more outspoken. They told how these changes carried over into other settings, such as their families, children's schools, churches, and civic or community organizations. They spoke of how Head Start helped them make hard changes, such as leaving an abusive partner, returning to school, or seeking a more challenging job.

As I spent more time with these women, I picked up on a feedback loop that helped to explain the intensity of these reported feelings. The loop went as follows. Women who already were poised—owing to such factors as childhood experience, cultural affiliations, moral values, personal history, temperament, and tastes—to use Head Start as a source of social support for making personal changes were the most likely to get drawn into active involvement in the program. Their involvement, in turn, engendered an emotional investment that led them to view the program in idealized terms. This idealized attachment gave these women an internal source of support for making the changes they sought. As they felt these changes taking place, their already high regard for Head Start's "power" intensified, and their loyalty became stronger.

The passion with which these actively engaged women describe Head Start is hard to convey without lapsing into overblown rhetoric. Yet such rhetoric is commonplace among women for whom the program has been a place of personal change. My research on Head Start's legislative history has uncovered public testimony from literally hundreds of women who credit Head Start with changing their lives. Indeed, in its Final Report, President Clinton's 1993 Commission on Head Start Quality and Expansion briefly addressed the phenomenon—widely recognized among Head Start administrators and practitioners, but rarely taken seriously by researchers—to which this testimonial record speaks. The preface to the commission's report quotes a Head Start woman who testified that through her involvement, "I learned to live again, not just survive" (U.S. Department of Health and Human Services 1993, iv). The report then notes that many active Head Start parents report such experiences, and observes that these parents' own voices may "best tell the story" of Head Start's extraordinary impact on many women's lives.

The hundreds of testimonials by Head Start clients in the records of congressional oversight hearings give us a wider perspective on how actively involved Head Start clients experience the program's effects. This testimony surely was scripted with help from professional advocates. Yet these public testimonials use the same images and storylines often heard in candid conversations with active Head Start women. To convey the intensity and indeed the spiritual quality of those conversations, I quote excerpts from these public records. The excerpts are grouped into five themes, arranged to suggest a storyline that women repeatedly used to describe the process as well as the quality of the change they experienced. This storyline locates the Head Start woman as a lucky *object*—or chosen vessel—rather than a struggling human *agent* of change. As my relationships with individual women evolved, sometimes they would depart from this formulaic plotline, groping for words to convey a more active process of change—one that was slow, uncertain, haunted by loss, and embedded in their everyday routines and relationships rather than ordained by some overarching "Head Start power."

A Safe Place

Starting to work with Head Start made me find my place (Stewart 1990, 103). . . .
I have a place to go. It's a place to get together . . . to gossip and lose your tensions.

You find out that other people have the same tensions as you. . . . [Y]ou can get together and talk. (O'Keefe 1979, 25)

Twenty years ago without speaking English with a 4-year-old child I walked into a small classroom and immediately I felt very welcome. . . . There is not the language barrier. It doesn't matter if we don't speak the language or we have an accent. There's always a place for us. . . . These are the kinds of programs that we need . . . programs that don't judge us . . . [p]rograms [in which we] have the opportunity to educate ourselves. (Romero 1993, 39)

I encountered many friendly faces with smiles . . . . I did not need to be afraid of saying the wrong things (Abu-Tayeh 1993, 54).

They were friendly and understood where I was coming from. It wasn't like walking into a bunch of strangers. . . . They'll work with you instead of against you. (Hale 1990, 108)

A Stirring of Hope

When I came . . . my self-esteem was real low and I looked at myself as a little bud, but the flowers were wilting instead of growing. . . . But as I got more involved in Head Start . . . I got the Head Start feeling. (Norwood 1993, 61)

I felt a sense of despair, with little self-esteem. . . . I thought my life was without meaning. One day I heard there was a Head Start class down the street, at a time when I had lost all hope of ever being anything but an outcast . . . . I learned that I was not the only young mother or dropout. I started putting time in at the class. The teacher would give me work to do with the children. I remember picking up a book to read to the children and the fear I felt. I realized that I needed a Head Start. (Malone 1990, 97)

God . . . gave me a beautiful family. My mother immediately adopted me and soon began to feed me all the nutritional things that I needed. She . . . pulled me from under a rock. With loving care she spoke the beauty of understanding and accepting all things. She said that everything had a reason for being. . . . My mother would always pick me up when I fell down and then I looked around and said, "Is my adopted mother here?" Yes, of course. It's Head Start. (National Head Start Association 1990, 17)

Gaining Voice

Before I entered the Head Start Program, I was afraid. I wouldn't talk; my voice got shaky, and my knees would tremble. . . . I couldn't talk in front of anybody. I was afraid to open my mouth. But my program director pushed me. She told me I could do it . . . and I kept trying. I kept getting up. She kept pushing me and I didn't stop trying. Today, I'm a new person. . . . I'm not afraid to talk anymore. (quoted in O'Keefe 1979, 25)

I began writing poetry. I was never interested in writing before, but the frustration of a bad marriage, a houseful of babies . . . needed a mode of expression. . . . The staff at Head Start found out about [my poems] and I gave them permission to print them in the Head Start parent Newsletter. . . . I had to give up my dreams once again and concentrate on providing them with basic needs. Head Start was there once again, providing outlets for my frustrated, creative urges. . . . Having a voice is one thing, but being able to express that voice is another, and having someone to listen when you express your opinion is the greatest success of Head Start. They listen! (Andrews 1990, 105–6)

Reaching Toward Others

Ms. Boyd enjoyed her experience so much that she helped to recruit other parents so they could share the joy.

"You feel good because you give yourself." (Boyd 1990, 97)

I love getting the chance to help other people the same way I was helped. (O'Keefe 1979, 25)

The moral support I got from Head Start down through the years has helped me to climb up the ladder. Many times it seemed like the next rung was missing or would break under the pressure—but I could always count on . . . Head Start to be there . . . I think the most important thing . . . [is] that through the support I have received, I have learned how to support others. (Andrews 1990, 106)

Head Start treated me with respect and provided we with opportunities to grow, through training and support. As I continue to grow . . . I am able to offer other low-income parents the same kind of opportunities for training, employment, and self-realization. (Dillon 1990, 189)

Head Start helps you to get involved in your future. It's because of Head Start that I am training other people in assertiveness, leadership, and politics. Head Start has helped me to reach people, to encourage them. It makes me feel good to help others. (Reyes 1990, 46–47)

Making Real Change

If it had not been for Head Start . . . I might still be a maid. . . . Head Start gave me the first job I ever had that did not include pushing a mop. (King 1984, 35–36)

Seeking the Source of Care

In conversations with active Head Start women, both paid workers and parent volunteers often told of how their involvement with the program made them feel nurtured and strong. Both workers and volunteers reported these feelings. I could not help but wonder who was *providing* all of this care. Was there some fifth column of invisible care workers behind it all, secretly holding people's hands? From the zero-sum perspective of conventional labor economics, this idea, though outlandish, seemed almost plausible. As preschool teachers, home health aides, psychotherapists, and parents know well, the effects of care do not simply happen: such results take a lot of artful and exhausting work. Somewhere behind all of the psychological benefits that Head Start women reported from the program, there had to be workers who were producing those benefits by, to quote the anthropologist Karen Sacks (1988), "caring by the hour."

Only gradually did I realize that the dynamics of this care system were not so simple. For actively engaged women, Head Start was not a zero-sum world in which care outputs were *produced* by the efforts of care workers. Rather, Head Start was a more complex world, where such effects were produced through webs of mutually enabling relationships that were brought forth in its ground-level social environment. In Head Start, I found care coming out of a dynamic system, in which intense mentoring relationships among women (one woman called them "mother friendships") offered the kinds of listening, dialogue, action, and reflection that started virtuous circles of personal growth, relational trust, social competency, and civic engagement. The fact that good caring relationships promote virtuous circles of well-being, personal growth, and social cohesion is commonplace to people who have experienced such relationships in the context of the family, the workplace, civic organizations, or faith communities. This also is a key finding in research on the effects of "social capital" on individual well-being and political culture (Putnam 2000). The following account teases out the features of Head Start's ground-level culture that help such generative caring relationships, and the good effects that follow from them, get off the ground.

First, Head Start's legal framework mandates that clients be offered many opportunities for active involvement in the program, as classroom volunteers and observers, participants in education enrichment activities, members of the program's parent policy council, and candidates for staff positions (U.S. Office of Child Development 1970). This legal framework and the program's public culture and street-level institutional practices come together to encourage Head Start's workers to invest themselves deeply in their work. They understand this work to include that of mentoring and supporting other women, particularly the new parent volunteers. Intense, caring relationships thus form between coworkers. In particular, intense relationships often form across two generations, as experienced older teachers work with parent volunteers, younger teachers, classroom aides.[2]

These relationships sometimes encourage personal growth in one or both partners. This happens gradually, from a ground of daily interaction, conversation, and emotional support. As conversations continue over several months, each partner gains new insight about the value of her Head Start activity. In the best scenarios, the relationship eventually gives each partner an active, challenging listener with whom to find the words for relating her Head Start experience to her overall life path. Thus the relationship can give a woman a place to *story* her Head Start experiences, through dialogue, into accounts of moral, spiritual, and political change.

In the language of linguistic philosophers, this kind of dialogue is performative as well as descriptive: it does not merely report on changes that took place before the conversation. Rather, such dialogue creates the changed subjects of which it speaks, through the relationships that such conversation creates. Such relationships give each woman the support and encouragement to undertake new projects and, through continued dialogue, to infuse these projects with moral and political value. Thus my research suggests that Head Start does not care for its clients through the menial labor of its workers. Rather, the program draws women into generative caring relationships that support *both* partners along paths of moral and political change.

Such relationships do not develop easily among Head Start women. These relationships inevitably encounter resistances which are only overcome by a favorable confluence of circumstances, timing, and luck. The most fine-grained analyses of mentoring relationships among low-income women have shown that a woman's capacity to enter such a relationship is affected, but never determined, by the elusive moving picture we might call temperament, personality, or character. Her likelihood of sustaining the relationship—particularly as mutual trust develops—is affected but not determined by how she remembers her childhood connection with her own primary caregivers, as well as a myriad of other factors. As theorists of development in relationships teach us, the ultimate task for public policy in this domain is to design social settings and practices that will make successful generative relationships more likely to thrive among a wider range of subjects. Owing to the complexity of the systems in question, this task cannot be accomplished through conventional methods of policy analysis and design. Rather, the task must be approached through an iterative method, which moves back and forth between thick descriptions of successful practices and analysis of the factors that are most critical to replicating them.

We do not yet have a baseline of case studies from which to tease out such factors except in the most general way. Every Head Start must comply with uniform federal requirements. As discussed above, some of these requirements seem particularly important in enabling generative caring relationships to develop among women who are poised to enter into them. Particularly important is the federally mandated requirement that local programs grant a preference to parent volunteers when hiring staff members. This requirement is critical, because it increases the chance that a young volunteer will encounter an older Head Start teacher who started out as a parent volunteer herself. Some of these teachers can claim to have been there—that is, to have lived through such experiences as race discrimination, workplace exploitation, domestic and community violence, exhaustion, and despair.

Yet federal requirements alone cannot ensure that a Head Start center will offer a setting where generative caring relationships can flourish. Such relationships are more likely to blossom in programs in which parent involvement is specifically valued and supported at the local level. Head Start's law gives each grantee great latitude to define its own priorities and custom-design its day-to-day practices to reflect them. Some programs, such as the Los Angeles program studied here, have designated the support and development of *adults* as a key objective, and then backed up that priority with programming and resources targeted specifically to adults' well-being and needs. Such local priorities increase the chance that a program will draw and keep teachers who have the life experience, therapeutic know-how, and commitment to take part in the kind of relationships that seem to be at the crux of women's experiences of change.

This last point is critical. Even in the occasional Head Start program where the local setting is optimal, there is no guarantee that any particular woman will get drawn into a sustained caring relationship that enables her to change. Sophia Bracy Harris, an activist who has been awarded a MacArthur Fellowship for creating transformative early care and education work settings for African American women, has written a book about the potential synergies between care-work settings, webs of social interaction, and moral or political change. Harris aptly named her book *More Is Caught than Taught* to underline two ideas. First, the critical moments through which a good relationship takes hold are bound up with the mystery of human agency itself. Second, that mystery transpires, through time, with the simple elegance of two actors on a field that their own movement continually reconfigures.

Listening to the Dance

Analytical tools are too blunt for teasing out all that must come together to catch and throw a ball. Thus, to go further in exploring the interaction between Head Start's legal framework, street-level social ecologies, and interpersonal relationships, we now turn from categorical to qualitative representation. Can Head Start's widely touted power to *enhance* adults' well-being and moral imagination be caught in action under the ethnographer's lens? Can looking closely at Head Start's shopfloor culture help us learn something about how law can interact with shop-floor practice to increase the chance that workers will feel more connected, more competent, more hopeful, more alive, in their jobs and lives?

In the second part of this chapter, we enter the world of Los Angeles's Education and Training Institute (ETI) Head Start program, to look closely at a generative caring relationship between two women.[3] The younger woman, E.M., is the mother of Lavinia, a three-year-old student at ETI's Church of the Redeemer Head Start site. The older woman, J.G., is the site's head teacher as well as the mother of three grown children who had attended ETI Head Start two decades earlier. Using field notes, interview transcripts, and my own interpretations, I seek to convey something of the rhythm and texture of the relationship between these two women over the course of a year. I focus particularly on E.M.'s own account of the changes that she experienced in Head Start, as well as her reflections on how and why those changes took place.

SCENES FROM ETI HEAD START:
SOUTH CENTRAL LOS ANGELES, 1992

The Setting

It is one of those rare clear mornings in early June. At this time of year the smog usually doesn't clear until about noon, especially so close to the ocean. Three women in their mid-thirties, white, dressed in suits, low heels, light makeup, hover over a pile of papers at the heavy wooden table that almost fills the conference room of the ETI Head Start's main office in Inglewood, one of several municipalities on the margins of South Central Los Angeles. The women are state employees, down from Sacramento for the day. They have just driven in from the airport in a blue-gray 1991 Legacy sedan, rented from Avis for the occasion. Their mission is to audit a grant that the ETI Head Start program gets from the state to buy food.

ETI Head Start traces its roots back to the early days of the War on Poverty. Several of the women who started it still are very much present in the program's day-to-day life, even though most of them are now retired from teaching or staff roles. They describe how they started the program in a ball field next to the Lincoln Terrace Housing Project in the summer of 1965. They got the program up and running before the promised summer money arrived from the federal government. Their husbands and boyfriends made tables for them out of scrap lumber. They gathered old magazines for art and pots and pans from their own kitchens for music, and stored them at night in the ample trunk of one woman's 1960 Chevrolet.

The children would gather in a circle every morning in the shade of a big eucalyptus tree. The women would sit with them, singing and laughing and clapping hands. These women's mothers and aunts had brought them across the country in the years after World War II, on trains and in Greyhound buses and family pickups, along circuitous paths that took them through St. Louis and Sacramento and Chicago before coming to rest, among family, in the cool blue low-rise public housing projects of Watts. They came from Alabama, Louisiana, Mississippi, looking for work, and the ocean, and seeking to leave their white folks' dirty laundry behind.

The work they made for themselves during that first summer of ETI's Head Start program was reassuring, exhausting, familiar work. It was also angry, defiant, determined work—this work of making home on foreign soil. Their mothers and grandmothers had been doing this work for as long as they could remember—schoolmarms, healers, sisters, daughters, wives. Only the backdrop looked different—a pale blue, discolored slab of California-style public-housing-project concrete, rather than the dark pine slats of the farmers' cabins, rural schoolrooms, and churches where kids had been cared for before the Great Society came along.

By June 1992, ETI's Head Start program has spread out over an eleven-mile radius, from its central office in the working-class enclave of Inglewood down into the largely Latino municipalities of South Gate and Huntington Park and then back east toward the program's original site at Lincoln Terrace. To get from the administrative office in Inglewood over to Lincoln Terrace, you have to head seven miles due east, from where Century Boulevard begins at LAX (Los Angeles International Airport) and the ocean to where it ends abruptly just over the boundary line between Los Angeles and Watts. You have to pass by blocks of once-neat stucco bungalows, now laced with graffiti on the walls and wrought iron on the windows. You have to pass by the blackened frames of corner liquor stores, scorched and looted just a month earlier in the most recent riot—upheaval, insurrection—the one that was captioned a "post-modern food riot" by trendy L.A. pundit Mike Davis, and that played, to the people I talked to, like a spasm of displaced, dispersed graspings for justice. You have to pass by parks and community centers that had been built on the ashes of an earlier, more focused conflagration. You have to pass by the cement play yard of a fenced-in, floodlit, twenty-four-hour-a-day-security-guarded parochial school, and pawnshops, auto body shops, taquerias, Church's Fried Chicken, but not a single pharmacy or grocery store or laundromat. You have to go clear to the end of Century Boulevard, under the Harbor Freeway, over the Long Beach railroad track, beyond the point where the six-lane urban boulevard becomes the pebbly trickle of an inner-city street. Finally, if you go far enough, you will run literally head-on into the side yard of the Lincoln Terrace Head Start Center.

The three women who are auditing ETI's food accounts for the state have been instructed to do a few spot checks of ETI Head Start classrooms after they finish their paperwork. That way they can see firsthand whether or not the money that the program has purportedly spent for lunches is in fact getting translated into good, hot, healthy food.

The three women finish working through the books at the main office at about 10:45. Lunch is served to the Head Start children at about 11:15. The program's associate director urges them to do their site visit at Lincoln Terrace and the other two ETI sites in Watts, because at those sites, rather than in the slightly better off neighborhoods of Inglewood, Huntington Park, or South Gate, the hot lunches served at Head Start make the greatest difference. The three women seem uneasy when the director makes this proposal. Mustering all of their bland, bureaucratic tact, they explain that they would rather do their site visit at ETI's Inglewood Head Start Center, just a couple of blocks from the central office. With their late-model rental car, and with all three of them white, visions of Reginald Denny, Crossroads, bright-eyed, fair-skinned, good-hearted intruders being stoned flicker at the margins of their minds. With a plane to catch at five, and kids back home in Sacramento to feed and bathe and put to bed, they really should do their site visit somewhere closer at hand.

Maybe another time they can go have lunch with the kids and their mothers at Lincoln Terrace and the Church of the Redeemer.

The Actors

I first met E.M. on a rainy morning in February 1992, four months before the auditors came from Sacramento to check out the ETI program meals. We both were attending an ETI-sponsored nutrition class for Head Start parents at South Central Los Angeles's Westside Community Center.

My field notes describe the encounter:

> It is raining. Westside Community Center is a low-slung, warm toned, tasteful public building set inside an eight foot high wrought iron fence on a full block of dark green, richly shaded ground. It has a day care center, a soul food cafe, lots of offices, and a large function room with a basketball court painted on the floor, a stage at one end, and a kitchen off to the side. Although the building's sleek facade is well maintained, the interior has the unmistakable mark of an aging public building. The nutrition class meets in the large function room with the basketball court painted on the floor. A woman from the University of California Agricultural Extension Service, Margaret, is teaching the class. It seems like she had been doing so for years. She conducts the class in a very "rote" way, relying very heavily on the handouts that the Extension Service provides. The women are remarkably patient: they seem both relaxed and bemused. The whole scene reminds me of a benign high school home economics class, where you really like the teacher, but recognize that she is a little out of it.
>
> Margaret never gives us a chance to talk about our own issues—most of us think we have weight problems—or about the hassles of fitting all of our required daily nutrients into a McDonald's and doughnuts diet. Nonetheless, the women express a sense that the class is worthwhile. At the end of class, we sample a black eyed pea salad that one of the women has prepared. Several women cannot eat the salad without salt, so they eat chips instead.
>
> After the class, Jewel, a staff person from Westside, requires everyone, including me, to fill out an income eligibility form for the City of Los Angeles. She tells us to bring a xeroxed piece of identification to attach to next week's form. She assures us that no one will check up on what we write down. Nevertheless, there is something chilling to have such an intrusion follow on this very easy-going session. Jewel asks me several times to fill out the form, even after I mumble that, as a law professor, I don't think I am eligible for services under the City's poverty guidelines.
>
> Among the women in attendance is E.M., who has brought her two-year-old son Peter with her. Peter sat in her lap through the entire class. He was remarkably well-behaved.

After the nutrition class, E.M. bundled Peter into his rain gear and buckled him into the car seat of her late-model Monte Carlo. The car had a broken right front window and a FOR SALE sign taped to the dash. She had decided she could not afford to keep it. E.M. invited me to share the front seat with her. I left my aging Mazda in one of the ten parking spaces for Westside's staff, which was well within the perimeter of the building's ten-foot-high wrought iron fence.

The drive to the Church of the Redeemer did not take more than five minutes. You had to make a big circle around Westside's lawn, swing by the Martin Luther King Shopping Mall, and then go south for a few blocks down 103rd Street. The Head Start classroom was in a blue prefabricated building adjacent to a small church. Its fenced-in play yard abutted a gravel parking lot that was bounded by the Blue Line, the recently constructed commuter rail line from Long Beach to downtown L.A. Although the classroom was designed for twenty children, it currently served sixty-four African American and Latino children in two three-hour shifts. Inside, the telltale rug-paved rectangular "circle" signaled that you were in a nationally certified center for the education of young children. One side of this circle was bounded by a blackboard that was bordered, both above and below, by parades of alphabet cards in bright block letters. The opposite side was bounded by a wide strip of mottled, gray-brown linoleum on which three knee-high rectangular children's tables were framed by tiny chairs.

By the time we arrived at the site, according to my field notes, the children were already seated, six to a table, eating baked chicken, steamed carrots, cabbage, bread, and peaches for dessert. On entering the classroom, E.M. set her son, Peter, down on the rug so she could load up two plates of food. One of the perks of volunteering in your child's Head Start classroom, which E.M. did on a daily basis, was that the program would feed you and your younger children a hot meal. When he hit the carpet, Peter toddled straight for the table where his three-year-old sister Lavinia was eating and sat down beside her to join the meal. E.M., taking Peter's lead, brought their plates to Lavinia's table, sat down beside her children, and started her meal. I brought my own plate to the table and we began to talk.

Most of the children were silent. Some earnestly sawed away at their chicken with plastic spoons. Others traded fork for fingers, carefully wiping up afterward on a napkin or shirt. Their faces looked distant, deliberate, as their forks worked in circles on carrots, then chicken, then cabbage. A few ate quickly, announcing themselves as future leaders by the daunting way they wielded their spoons. Most of the children were more cautious, however, laboring to get each morsel of cabbage and chicken and carrots securely in their mouths. One or two of the children sat perfectly still amid this flurry of eating. Their fingers were quiet; their eyes were dark pools. After the rest of the children had finished, their plates, though still full, were removed.

Conversations with E.M.

E.M. came to Lavinia's Head Start classroom every day. She worked alongside the teachers and aides, engaging in the thousands of small, face-to-face interactions that produce care. My longest taped conversation with E.M. took place at the Westside Community Center on July 2, 1992. By this time, we had spent many hours together in Lavinia's classroom. The neighborhood was starting to rebuild after the Rodney King fires. My field notes describe the scene:

> This morning I went to Westside to interview E.M. She arrived at 10:00, right on schedule. We went to the Center's pre-school, which was closed for the summer. There, seated next to each other on a couch, we talked for about an hour and a half.
>
> I was struck by how she seemed to get more and more relaxed as we talked, so that she seemed able to express deep and complex feelings much more openly near the end of the interview. She always talked about her husband's violence indirectly, by saying "he got physical," rather than giving any detail. She said several times that Lavinia's teacher, J.G., could sense what she was going through with her husband, without her ever having to put it in words. This seemed to be a quality that was very important for her.
>
> At the point in the interview when E.M. tried to explain what was so "therapeutic" or satisfying for her about working every day in Lavinia's Head Start classroom, she started to cry.

One of the first things that E.M. wanted me to understand was that, as a veteran client of government-funded social programs, she did not come to Head Start with very great expectations:

> E.M.: I'm on welfare, you know. I was ashamed, because I had worked since 1977. Then I had to ask for help. . . . Those people up there are not nice. I don't care for them. They don't care for us.
>
> L.W.: How are they not nice?
>
> E.M.: They treat you like dirt. They don't even know you, and they treat you like dirt. The first day I applied, this woman had never met me. She didn't know me. And she treated me like I was somebody on crack . . . just like a nobody . . . like I was nothing. And I don't like being treated like that. . . . I didn't feel like I should have been treated that way, or anybody else should be treated that way. . . . [T]hey don't care. They just don't care.

Yet from her first contact with Head Start, things seemed different:

> When I first took Lavinia [to Head Start], she cried for two or three days, which they all do. . . . I signed a paper saying that I would volunteer at certain times. But I had my small child Peter . . . I thought that I would have to make arrangements for Peter to be taken care of while I go up there to volunteer. . . . I didn't know that I could volunteer with him until a week and a half [later, when] I took him in one day and I saw another lady there with her smaller child. . . . And so I asked the site director, J.G., "Is she volunteering?" And she said, "Yeah." And I told her, "Well, I didn't know you could bring your smaller children." She said, "Oh yeah. You can bring him. You just have to watch him. You have to take care of him, and otherwise you can come in and volunteer. There's no problem there."

J.G.'s voice had a quality of warmth that drew E.M. out of herself and into the classroom. "So I went there the next day, and I have been going there every day since" (E.M., Int. A, 16). E.M. thus joined a small group of mothers, grandmothers, aunts, older sisters, and friends of Head Start children who volunteered in ETI Head Start classrooms every day.[4]

In my conversations with E.M. and the other regulars, I tried to understand their motivation. Echoing Head Start's official rhetoric, E.M. often told me that she worked in the classroom to improve her own parenting skills and thus to help her children. This trickle-down theory for parent involvement is the most familiar in Head Start policy circles: getting parents to volunteer in Head Start classrooms is a "back door" way for the state to improve the home environment of poor children. A second reason E.M. gave for her involvement, however, did not fit so easily with this theory, or with her own expectations; it was more "selfish." "I love kids, but after having three children you never dream that you'd want to be bothered with a class full of children. But I enjoyed it! . . . I was able to get away from home" (E.M., Int. A, 13). Most of the regular volunteers expressed similar feelings as I talked with them at length. For instance, J.P., a bus driver who was on temporary disability for job-related stress, when asked why she volunteered in her child's Head Start classroom every day, said, "A lot of parents don't really get involved in the program. But it really does me good; it really makes me feel good to be helping the children. It's really inspiring; you have to understand what it does to me."

As I came to know E.M. more intimately, she began to say more about what lay behind her own "selfish" motivations for classroom volunteering:

> My husband and I got married in 1983. . . . We moved to Seattle, Washington . . . in 1977. . . . We both worked when we left [for] Washington. I worked for General Telephone . . . in West Covina. . . . And he's been in the military for twelve [years]. He got out of the military, got into the Reserves, and . . . got a job at a state corrections facility, a prison. . . . We had our first child, and then we had our second, and our third. . . . At first we were pretty happy. We argued like everybody else and wouldn't speak for a couple of days, but basically we had a good marriage.

Then, in the recession of the 1980s, her husband lost his job. Over his wife's objection, he decided to move the family back to South Central L.A., their childhood home. The area had become more violent in the decade since they had left:

> There's a lot of shootings and stuff that go on over here, and gangs and all of that. I was kind of afraid when I first moved back, you know, . . . and I live here. I grew up here. . . . When we moved we had our house in bars, and it took me a while to get used to that. . . . And the sirens and the shootings and all of that.

Soon after they returned, things started to fall apart:

E.M.: [When] we moved here, I don't know what happened. The bottom just fell out. Things just started to change, and he treated us like a second family. . . . He just changed. He didn't want to work. . . . He wanted me to get on welfare, so I got on welfare. . . . He decided that he didn't want to work. Just like that. We had just had our last child.

L.W.: Why do you think he decided he didn't want to work anymore?

E.M.: I don't know. He's a complicated person . . . and confused. He has some emotional problems, and I think they stem from childhood, and he's also an alcoholic, and he doesn't want to believe that. . . . So he kind of decided he had enough with work. . . . And then he came back here and got with the same old crowd, and you know, when you leave and you come back, and the same people are doing the same things that they did when you left. . . . He just got in with the same crowd. . . . He wanted everyone to kind of take care of him. . . . The drinking got worse, a lot worse. He went in for one interview for something, for the post office, I believe. He scored high on the test, but they checked his background and he had had two arrest records since we've been there. . . . For disturbing the peace and drunk driving. . . . So they didn't hire him. And he felt like, well, I'm not going in for any more interviews. . . . He just wanted me to work, and he didn't want to work. And things just got bad.

Gradually, her husband's stress began to turn to physical abuse. "He got physical, . . . violent." E.M. came to Head Start for the first time during a period when her husband's increasing violence had begun to drive her into depression and withdrawal:

I stayed home. I was always depressed. I was a really depressed person. I had lost, I had lost . . . I'm small. You know, my normal weight is about 115. And I had gone down to 98 pounds, you know, going through this. But my daughter got with Head Start and I started volunteering, and the place really kind of saved me in a way.

Observing E.M. in the Classroom

The center of E.M.'s Head Start experience was her day-to-day work in Lavinia's classroom. In our July 2 interview, E.M. found it hard to find words to describe the changes that she felt from that experience, because so much of what mattered most seemed very small. My field notes from a typical day are perhaps the best way to convey my own impressions of the scene:

This morning I went to the Church of the Redeemer. I arrived at about 10:00. J.G. was with the children in the play yard. The other two teachers were in the classroom, with the parent volunteers. B.T. [another parent] was cutting out newsprint and stapling it into individual copy books for each child. E.M. was talking with the two other parent volunteers. I returned to the play yard to talk with J.G. She is very concerned about the shrinkage of primary health care facilities in the neighborhood, but has inexhaustible faith in Head Start, and seems confident that things will eventually improve. When we returned to the classroom, E.M. and I helped a table of kids cut and paste a construction paper Halloween scene. The shapes had all been cut out by parent volunteers. We helped the kids paste the shapes onto construction paper to make a scene of a haunted house, a ghost, a pumpkin, etc. E.M. and I helped spoon out globs of glue and make sure that the kids pasted the shapes appropriately on their pages.

After this exercise was completed, we lounged around on the rug while the kids helped serve up lunch. For lunch they had chicken, collard greens, cantaloupe (cut by B.T.) and cornbread. J.G. explained that it was a real southern meal.

In our conversations, E.M. gave her own perspective on this routine:

> We help with the activities. Like if they are doing coloring at the table, if they're doing cutting activities, [we] teach them how to cut with scissors . . . and their shapes and numbers and all kinds of things. We're broken up into groups. So there may be three or four tables of children. Half the class will go outside and play and the other group will stay in. Two teachers have to be outside . . . and two teachers have to be in the class. . . . So if there's two parents, one parent will go outside with the two teachers and one will stay in with the other two teachers. And so we help . . . the teachers at the table, helping the kids. . . . [W]e have song time. That's in the morning when they first get there. They have a light breakfast when they get there and then they play outside and [do indoor activities] at the same time and then they'll switch off. . . . And then they have games that they do or they'll talk about the animal sounds and we'll wash up and get ready for lunch. And they help with lunch. I help with lunch.

Preparing and sharing meals with the children was a central theme in E.M.'s account of her work:

> E.M.: I help prepare and fix the plates. And the kids would come up to the tables and we fix the plates and they would set them on the table, learn how to set the table. [O]ne parent is allowed to be served lunch, but if there's enough food to go around then the other parents and the children can get to have lunch too.
>
> L.W.: Would you usually end up getting lunch?
>
> E.M.: Yes, yes I would. Because I was usually there every day.
>
> L.W.: And what about your little one?
>
> E.M.: We would share a lunch. . . . The food was good, excellent. It was good. They had ham. They had baked chicken, macaroni and cheese, turkey, well, chicken, and dressing. Beef stroganoff, which I went home and duplicated the recipe. I tasted it, tried to find out what was in it. And I duplicated it. Pretty good! . . . They have tacos and burritos and enchiladas and greens and cabbage and brussels sprouts, and—I love vegetables—and corn and all kinds of stuff. . . . And it's good food. It's good. I thought it was like cafeteria food, but it was good food.

A Relationship Begins to Form

As E.M. continued to talk about her day-to-day routine in the classroom, she began to tell me about her relationship with J.G.:

L.W.: Did you get close to any of the teachers over the year?

E.M.: Yes. I did. I got very close with J.G.

L.W.: Did you get close so you could actually talk to her?

E.M.: Yes . . . I got a little close with all of them, but J.G. was the one, she's the same age as my mother, so she was more like a mother friend, so I really got close with her.

L.W.: What kind of role would you say she played in your life over the year?

E.M.: [S]he knew the problems that I was having, even before I came out and told her, because she's been through similar things, so she said she kind of had an idea. I think she saw that I needed a little help at the time. You know, if it was nothing but ah, not a shoulder to cry on, but just an ear, you know, and to tell me that things would be all right. Because, like I said, I was depressed when I got there. I really was. And I, um, didn't have a lot of self-esteem. I still have a long way to go. In a lot of ways I just felt like my whole world had just come to an end. And so she just kind of talked to me, and let me know that things don't stay the same, and that, you know, people do survive, and you just have to basically be there for your children and yourself, you know. You just have to live for yourself and your children. You don't have any control over anybody else. . . . I can relate to her. . . . Besides that, me getting involved with the classroom was therapeutic. She kept me busy. I was always busy.

L.W.: When would you find time to talk with her during the day?

E.M.: When we were out in the yard. Or sometimes I would just hang around after class was over, until the next class started, and we talked, you know. Mainly when we were outside in the yard watching the children, we'd walk around, and we'd just talk. She was a big help.

L.W.: What do you think it was about her that enabled you to do that?

E.M.: She's not afraid to show feelings and emotions and she's not afraid to say "I've been there" and "I know what it's like." And she's a very compassionate person and real warm. . . and she's real honest.

L.W.: Honest in what sense?

E.M.: Just about everything. I mean, what she has to say, she doesn't bite her tongue, so I know she's going to tell me the truth. She'll just come out and say it, you know. And sometimes truth hurts, but you need the truth.

L.W.: And you're saying truth about what she thought was going on with you?

E.M.: Yeah, what she thought.

L.W.: Thinking back on it, how would you say you approached her?

E.M.: She approached me first, I believe.

L.W.: And you think she perceived that something was going on?

E.M.: Yeah. She could see. I don't know. I don't remember how we first started talking about it. I don't remember. All I know is it came up and. . . . Well, she may not have really approached me, but she treated me like she knew. Some days I really didn't walk in with a long face or anything like that. I carried on my day and I was happy while I was there, but when it got time to go home I wouldn't want to go home. I'd kind of hang around. And so she might have picked up there too. . . . And then a couple of times I had to walk or catch the Blue Line, and I would call and tell her we would be late, because my husband had gotten mad and took the car or something like that, and she probably thought about that too. . . .

L.W.: And sort of put stuff together?

E.M.: Yeah. I don't remember when we really started talking about it. I might have said something like, "I'm having problems." And she said something like, "Yes, I know. I already know you're having problems." Or she would just come over to me and just put her arm around me and tell me things are going to be all right without me saying anything.

Changes Begin to Happen

After E.M. became a regular volunteer in the classroom, J.G. urged her to run for a position on the ETI Head Start's policy council.

> I volunteered to be elected to run for secretary. [N]obody else was going to do it from our area. And somebody from our area has to run for something. So I said, "Well, I'll do it." I didn't expect for them to choose me. . . . I didn't know these women. This is my first year. I didn't run for chairperson, because I thought, "I'm not qualified to be a chairperson." You know, I mean, that's the way I think. . . . That's the way I was thinking. So I ran for secretary. And I got chosen! . . . I was really surprised.

Although E.M. had done clerical work for twelve years, serving as the secretary of the policy council took on a meaning that exceeded the scope of the duties she was required to perform. Her voice was playful as she told me how keeping the minutes for the policy council had helped turn her back from despair:

> I had a job to do. I had duties. I had a format to follow. I had responsibilities, you know, that people were depending on me to do. I felt good. . . . You see, I'm good with paperwork. I'm good. And I got my notebooks together. And I got the plastic covers, the little covers for every paper, and I had categories set up, and I had it just perfect. My little notebook. Oh, I was so proud of that notebook. I mean I had it together! So when I was there I conducted my little position like a professional. I thought I was somebody, so it was fun.

As my interview with E.M. continued, she became more and more focused on trying to convey her internal process of change:

> E.M.: I was being assertive. I started being assertive. I started feeling like somebody again. And also, I think the reason that my husband started getting violent, which has been . . . we've been having problems since we moved here, but he really started getting violent within the last year, I think, because I started doing what I wanted to do. I used to [do] whatever he wanted me to do. But it worked okay before. It was all right. I was happy. He was happy, you know. And now it was like, if he told me to do something, and I didn't agree with it, I would question him about it or say, "Well, look, I don't know, I don't agree with that. I don't want to do that." And he didn't know how to handle that, so that's when he started. It was in stages. First he got verbal.

Like the first time he ever called me out of my name . . . he just might as well have kicked me, because he had never called me out of my name. Then he got worse. Then he got really verbal. And then he got a little physical, and then he got really physical. He started getting really physical when he could not control me any more.

L.W.: And you're feeling like your experience at Head Start and your having responsibility was making you more assertive?

E.M.: I started to change too, because I wasn't the same little wife that would just follow his orders, which I did before. . . . But then he just started demanding impossible things out of me, things that I really didn't agree with at all. . . . It wasn't like he would ask me, "Well, don't go out to party." It wasn't that type of thing. Because I don't party. . . . It was just like, he may have said, "Go do this. Go to the store and do this and do that." And I may have said, "Well, I have something else to do right now. You'll have to do it yourself." And that was like, "What? I told you." "Well, I don't care what you said. You can do it. If you want me to do it tomorrow, when I have free time, I will do it, but I'm not going to do that right now." That's just an example of things, you know. And he just couldn't deal with it. . . . I'm still a little emotionally tied. I mean, I don't love him. I don't love him like a husband and wife. I care for him, because he's my children's father, and I thought I would never say this, because I loved him with a purple passion. I mean, I just, you know, but it, it just died. He just killed . . . each day he was being, you know. And so I finally . . . and that was the only way. I would have never moved. I would have taken abuse until I got to that point. . . . It just finally got to the point where I did not love him any more and that was the day that I walked out. I couldn't see any reason staying taking that.

L.W.: So it sounds like Head Start for you was at the same time a place where you had opportunities to . . .

E.M.: To get myself together . . .

L.W.: . . . and also a support as the change was happening?

E.M.: Ah, oh yeah. Yeah. A big support. Yeah.

Finding Words for the Process of Change

The first time I talked to E.M. about Head Start, she spoke about its impact in language that I found vague, "pumped up," and familiar. She told me that Head Start had saved her life. As I heard a more detailed account of her involvement in the program, I gained a new respect for the spiritual rhetoric that she and other Head Start women so often have turned to in an effort to find words for their experience. The transformation E.M. experienced through Head Start was multidimensional in both its dynamics and its effects.

In terms of effects, we might begin with the notion that identity does not remain fixed in the course of different relationships. Rather, a person has many potentials, which come in and out of focus as he or she interacts with different people in different social domains. With respect to Head Start's effects on E.M., we might say that several of these potential identities experienced significant change.

Thus we might see E.M. as a victim of intimate violence. From this perspective, change is straightforward: a woman subjected to verbal and physical abuse finally gained the self-confidence to leave a violent but emotionally entangling relationship. We might also see E.M. as a person with diagnosable psychiatric disorders. Her involvement in Head Start alleviated symptoms of severe depression, anorexia, and suicidal ideation. She also was a woman in extreme psychological distress. Her work in Head Start helped her repair an eroded sense of self-esteem and strengthened her capacity to assert her needs and desires. From an employment perspective, she was a woman with substantial job experience but with limited higher-level job skills and limited vocational confidence. Her work in the classroom and on the policy council helped her back on her feet. She got a chance to brush up on old job skills in a supportive setting, as well as an opportunity to learn new ones. The satisfaction she found in the classroom led her to formulate new and more challenging vocational ambitions. Finally, when E.M. enrolled her daughter in Head Start, she was a woman in spiritual turmoil. Her involvement in Head Start helped her come through that crisis. Particularly through her work in the classroom, E.M. recovered a sense of moral agency.

As I worked with E.M. over the year, I slowly gained an understanding of the process through which these multiple changes took place. E.M. was deeply involved in three critical relationships during her year in Head Start. The momentum for change came from within each relationship, as well as through the interplay among them. These relationships were settings for intense, trusting conversation and a focus of dialogue and self-reflection. Through that reflection, the moral significance of each relationship was enhanced. E.M. seemed to turn the work that she was doing in the classroom into a mirror, or a map, of her own path of change.

The first of these relationships was between E.M. and the informal community of other active parent volunteers in her daughter's Head Start classroom. Through them, E.M. found a place to get basic social support around the day-to-day stresses of her life. These relationships also initiated E.M. into Head Start's workplace culture. By working side by side with other parents, E.M. learned the routines of the Head Start classroom—how to keep peace on the playground, how to get the kids to settle down for quiet activities, how to tell when a child needs to make an emergency trip to the bathroom, how full to fill their milk cups to cut down on spills. By gossiping with these other women in the play yard, E.M. learned the secrets of the workplace social setting: which parents were having affairs with local community organizers, which teachers were the hardest to work with, which field administrators had the most clout in the central office when you wanted to get a real Head Start job. By taking part in official parent involvement events with these other women—from nutrition classes to diversity awareness days to policy council meetings—E.M. learned the special language that Head Start women use, the stories they tell, to convince themselves and each other that they are indeed being changed. In much the same way that other change-oriented social settings have been recognized to work, the Head Start parent community initiated E.M. into Head Start's narrative culture. Through these connections, E.M. was shown and told what kind of life changes to expect from the program; she was encouraged to look for those changes in herself; and she was taught the stories and images and rituals to use to testify to those changes, thereby confirming that they are indeed real.

Thus described, the informal Head Start parent community has an almost cultlike quality. One can easily imagine a vulnerable woman connecting herself to such a community in a passive and even an addictive way: reciting the boilerplate rhetoric that Head Start "saved" her, falsely assuring herself that real change has magically happened without any pain. Based on my research in Head Start programs, I have no doubt that some of the most vocal boosters among Head Start parents do just this. They have learned from other parents how to "talk the talk" of personal transformation, but have not found their way to the intensive personal relationships that must go along with these public practices in order for sustained intrapsychic change to occur. E.M. found such relational anchors in her "mother friendship" with J.G. and her "therapeutic" relationship with two Head Start children. Through these two relationships E.M. was able to move beyond an easy insistence that change had occurred into the more difficult moral space in which change is not so certain—and therefore, perhaps, a little more possible.

The Mother Friendship

I had my most extended conversation with J.G., on an afternoon in mid-June 1992, a few weeks before my long conversation with E.M. at the Westside Community Center. The second shift of children had just gone home. Two weeks remained in the regular academic year. J.G. had just learned that the emergency funds that had been promised from the federal government to keep the program open for six weeks during the summer would not be coming through.

> I'm from Birmingham, Alabama. I have two brothers and I have no sisters. My father died when I was a year old, and I was raised by my mother, a single parent.
>
> Coal and iron is the state of Alabama. That's where the money comes in, is coal. My grandfather worked at a place that's called Flattop, Alabama. It's one of them little coal mining towns. He was a coal miner and a gambler, and my grandmother [Grandma Alice] was born in Montgomery, Alabama . . . and she had only one child, which was my mother. She was working in the laundries, because that was the only jobs back then. You either worked in a laundry or you worked in the houses . . . in housekeeping. There was no other jobs for you to do back there. And so my mother had worked in the laundry also, and then my mother . . . took sick, and then she became a domestic worker. . . . She was a domestic worker and I became a baby-sitter. . . . I was the type of baby-sitter that, like for summers, when people would go out of town, I would travel with them to take care of their children. (J.G., 1)

J.G.'s mother had one family in particular for whom she worked, the Tutweilers. Her mother had a house on the Tutweiler property where she and her children lived with J.G. and her other children during the week.

[W]e were all raised up together because my mom had to keep all of us together. . . . My mother would stay there. . . . The house wasn't that far. It was in the community. I worked with these people the whole [time] I was in school, baby-sitting and helping, and my mother did the cooking, . . . and she was responsible for the children. (J.G., 3)

The most important figures in J.G.'s childhood were her mother and Grandma Alice, a midwife and healer.

Grandma Alice! [A]ll I can remember, she was Cherokee Indian. She was ninety percent Cherokee Indian. She was a reddish color, with straight hair, and she said her father was black, and her mother was Cherokee Indian. It's all I can remember . . .

She was a doctor in a sense of speaking. She took care of the little kids when they were sick. If someone needed to talk to somebody, if you had a problem, you could go and say, "Well, I'm going to talk to Grandma." My grandma would sit on the porch and the kids would sit around her feet and she would talk to us. If a child would get hurt or something, she would come. She would always tell us that her mother was an Indian, Cherokee Indian, and that she had healing powers. . . . [S]he told us that she had been blessed with these healing powers. And she would go to the yard and get these weeds, and make this medicine out of these things. Not store bought medicine. . . . She believed in herbs and vinegar and garlic and stuff like that. She was a midwife also, and she would deliver the babies. Most of the little children in the neighborhood, even the white, she had delivered a lot of the kids. So they looked upon her as Grandma Alice. (J.G., 13)

J.G. learned a hard but critical lesson from Grandma Alice:

Growing up as a child, I think my love of children and people grew from . . . my grandmother having a lot of love for everybody. And as children we had so many children around us, all children. We had so much love. We were very poor people, but we had something that money couldn't buy. We had a lot of love. . . . That's one thing nobody can take from you. And that seems to work in my everyday life now too. (J.G., 5–6)

From childhood, J.G. wanted to spend her life doing the kind of work that she learned from her mother and Grandma Alice and already had been called on to do. She called it "being the mother." This might have been called care work, or in more familiar language, domestic service.

I've wanted to work with people, children, for the simple reason, when I was coming up as a young girl in the South, young kids were given a responsibility, in somewhat an adult capacity. My mom took very ill when I was very young, and I had to take over like I was the mother of the house. And so I gained this responsibility of . . . being the mother and things like this. So I always said that when I get to be grown I was going to be a social worker and I was going to work with children and older people. (J.G., 1)

Life for J.G. in Alabama in the 1950s was not all harmony:

[T]here was white kids and there was black kids. . . . I knew you were different. I just knew you was just lighter, and your hair may have been a little bit different . . . and there were a lot of little Jewish kids. . . . But by my mother working around children, and we living in the same house, my mother never did allow us to be name calling. (J.G., 6)

As soon as she finished high school, J.G. married a brother of one of her favorite high school teachers. A year later, she had her first baby, a daughter. Then, in 1963, she and her baby boarded a train to join her husband in Los Angeles.

Someone told my husband to come to California, because this was the land of milk and honey. And he came out here and had to sleep in the mission. . . . He got here and there was no job. . . . So he calls me and says, "Come to California baby. I can't live without you." My mother says you have to go wherever your husband is. You're married now. If he's in a tent, you got to sleep in that tent. So I grab my baby and gets on the train and I come to California. (J.G., 23)

When she arrived, he was sleeping in an apartment with no lights and no furniture.

I came from a family where we didn't have everything. And I made the best of it. I got in and did what I had seen my momma do. If we had a little vegetables or something, we shared them among each other. I got candles and I used them for lights. I went to the market and got a fifty pound bag of ice, and put it in the sink, and wrapped it up with rag and put my baby's milk on it. . . . Because I had learned to live with less, and be happy, and go to bed and count my blessings and be content with it. And I stayed on, and the first paycheck he got working at Bullocks in the restaurant, we got the lights turned on, . . . and we got our first chicken. . . . We didn't have anything to cook it in. I went to the secondhand store and bought pots and pans, so that we could have some things to cook, and I cooked them their first meal. We had no furniture. I went in this furniture store they'd just burned in Compton . . . I said, you know, we're trying. One dollar we gave the man, and we got three rooms of furniture. . . . I wasn't working because I had the little baby. . . . So I called my mother, and I asked my mother if I saved up enough money, a bus ticket, would she come and stay with me until I could try to find me a job. (J.G., 25)

Two years after J.G. came to Los Angeles, the first Watts riots swept through her neighborhood. When I talked with her, the memories, recently reawakened by television images of the Rodney King fires, still burned in her mind. During the first decade that she was in L.A., she had a history of increasingly unskilled jobs in the Southern California industrial corridor. Then she got a stable job.

> I knew I had to work hard to get enough money for my family to survive. And I kept saying, "I got to make enough money." I worked hard. I said, "If you get my foot in the door they are going to let me work on. I'll mop the floors, I'll clean the toilets, I'll wash the windows. There's nothing that I won't—within rights—that I won't do to earn a living. Because you always got to start at the bottom and go to the top." And I worked myself up to be supervisor. I worked for that company for fifteen years. (J.G., 27)

The job required her to commute between one and two hours each way to work. After her son was badly injured by a distant relative who was caring for her children while she worked, she quit and began drawing AFDC. Just like most of the women with whom I talked, J.G. had nothing good to say about AFDC. She told me, "they treat you like dogs."

Eventually J.G. enrolled her youngest child in Head Start. Like E.M. two decades later, she got hooked on the daily ritual of volunteering in her child's Head Start classroom. After three years as a parent volunteer, she was hired as a teacher in the program. From the outset, she regarded one of the most important features of her job as a Head Start teacher to be her work with parents. She credits two figures, her child's first Head Start teacher and her own Grandma Alice, with teaching her how to work effectively with Head Start parents.

The Teachings of Grandma Alice

When I asked J.G. to tell me more about what she had learned from Grandma Alice, her voice changed. She stopped chatting with me in the easygoing way that had made me feel like her sister, and began to chant like an old woman in mourning. She spoke the words through her body—her eyes and her hands and her breathing—as much as her voice. What follows are excerpts from what she told me.

> I was in Birmingham on the same street when they threw the bomb in the church and burned up the little girl. . . . I couldn't, you know. I couldn't understand. I knew there was a lot of prejudice and a lot of things was going on. Plus I knew a lot of people who was KK [Ku Klux Klan] members. I knew them . . . from my mother . . . from my grandmother. . . . My grandmother knew them all.
>
> And [Grandma Alice] told us about the time when they came to our house when we were little to burn our house. And they had burned a cross in front of our door. And my grandmother had told us that they had came.
>
> I must have been a baby. And when the guys all came and the guy that came up and had burned the cross and he was making my granddaddy and everybody come out of the house, and my grandmother got up out of the bed, and came to the door with the ax in her hand.

And when she came to the door the guy who was in the front, he says, "Oh, my God. No. No. Do you know who that is?"

And she walked up and she says, "And I know every one of you." . . . She delivered the majority of them.

And he says, oh, he says, "Ooh, oh, Granny. I'm sorry, I'm sorry, I'm sorry. Oh Granny, I'm sorry. I'm sorry. Please forgive me. I'm sorry, I'm sorry, I'm sorry."

And she said, and she, you know, she's an old lady, and she says, "And then I'm going to tan your hide."

And these were grown men. But she just . . . she was . . . my grandmother was that kind of person. She wasn't afraid of anybody. Any color. Because she said, "Every one of you, I brought you here, and I'll take you away." She said, "Every one of you. I gave you life, and I'll take your life away from you."

But she was that type, until the day she died. My grandmother was that way. And when, the day of her funeral, the whole front of the church . . . there was more whites in the church than there was black. Because she had, she was that kind of a lady. She had love and compassion and justice for everybody.

E.M. never told me that J.G. had shared this childhood story with her on their walks in the Church of the Redeemer's play yard. Yet E.M. told me how J.G. taught her and other Head Start women, by her example as well as her words, how to face up to the people in South Central Los Angeles who threatened their dignity, in welfare offices, retail outlets, police stations, and on the streets.

The Children

The third relationship that helped enable E.M. to change was with two Head Start children. Early on in our interview, on July 2, E.M. described her work with these children as "therapeutic." Near the end of the interview, I asked her why she had used that word:

Because . . . in every class there's some children that are not too receptive. Or children that are problem children. Like there was these two, sister and brother. Well, the brother was really having problems at home and at school since he was a little kid. . . . He was kind of bad.

She went on to describe a process of working with this boy that mirrored the work of listening that J.G. was doing with her. She engaged him in activities. She gave him the chance to talk to her. She tried to let him know that she was seeking to understand:

But you had to understand why. So, my thing was to get to be friends with them and break this barrier, and try to, you know, um . . . I can't even think of the word, just . . . just to see him, to see if he can act like the other kids. Not to be so disturbed at school. Or behave . . . it's hard to explain. But we became really good friends. . . . Every morning, he would say good morning to me, and he would want to know what you know. He'd tell me my earrings were pretty, or what I have on is pretty, and he would just touch my face, touch my hair. And that, that was so rewarding, because here's this kid that everybody said was bad, and he would do all sorts of things for attention . . . that would get on your nerves. I wanted to see if I could bring him out of that . . . not completely, but while he was there . . . have him act not so wild.

The second Head Start child that E.M. worked with was a young Latina girl.

E.M.: And then there was this other little girl that came in, her father committed suicide in front of them. In front of the children.

And she came and she cried everyday. You couldn't get her to walk. You'd have to walk her. You couldn't get her to color. You'd have to take a crayon, put it in her hand, hold her hand. You couldn't get her to eat. You would have to feed her. Open her mouth, put the food in it. She just would not respond to anything.

And that was my mission. I was going to help that little girl. I was going to be her friend. And I was going to see if she would start coloring by herself, if she would eat.

When I would come in everyday, when the kids would play, she wouldn't play. But I would take her by the hand and we'd walk around the playground. Just walk. And I'd just talk to her and just point out different things, and just walk. She'd never say anything, but she would walk with me.

And after that she would, when she'd leave, her mother would pick her up, I'd wave to her. She'd wave or she'd smile. And then the crayons, finally instead of me getting the crayon, picking the color for her, because I would ask her what color do you want. She would not respond. She wouldn't even look. But, after a while, I would ask her what color do you want. She would tell me. Then I would get it. Put it in her hand and we would color together.

Well now, I ask her, what crayon do you want. She would say blue and get it herself and start drawing.

I mean, anybody could have done that. I didn't do anything that anyone couldn't have done, but it was just that was something at the time that I needed to do as well as needed to help her do, because it helped me too. It made me feel so good.

L.W.: Tell me how was working with these two kids therapeutic for you?

E.M.: That, that I was able to help somebody, because I, you know, the past few years it seemed like I couldn't help anybody. I couldn't help myself. . . . I didn't think too much of myself [so] I couldn't help anybody. Let alone myself or my kids. I was just there.

I went to this school, and these kids are having problems. I'm having problems. I'm working with them and they're making some effort, I mean some progress. And at the same time I am too, because I'm being like pumped up in a way, but it's a good pump up, because . . .

You know, you get nothing out of it other than a smile. I'm not getting paid for this, . . . for making it a challenge for me to go after a certain child and work with them. But I am getting paid in another way. I really get choked up thinking about it. It's just so rewarding. Well . . . I'm sorry . . . [She starts to cry].

In our conversations over the year, E.M. told me how working with these children gave her some hope that she could make changes in her own life. If these two children could overcome the violence that had overwhelmed their lives, then surely E.M. could face her own predicament. Her work with the children helped her regain a sense of her capacity for moral agency, even in the face of world-shattering violence. The gradual responsiveness of these children to her efforts at connection gave E.M. living proof that she had, or could bring forth from herself, what it took—the creativity, the patience, and the sheer, groundless hope—to be an effective agent of change. The fascinating thing about her experience is that through her work with these children, she was able to bootstrap the kind of foundational self-confidence that both motivated and enabled her to change her own circumstances.

Finally, her work with the children gave her a new perspective on social loyalties and cultural conflicts that had blocked her motivation to seek change in her own life. The self-confidence that she gained through her work with the little girl helped her find the power to stand up to her husband, even as his violence escalated in response to her newfound assertiveness. At the same time, her painstaking work of reclaiming the voice of the little girl gave her a new sense of self-respect, and indeed, of awe, as she felt her own voice gain strength, even in the face of violence. Thus she eventually was able to *feel*, as well as know, that she no longer loved her abusive husband, and therefore could walk away.

E.M.'s relationship with the little boy may have been even more critical in enabling her to leave her husband. That relationship focused on two related strategies. Like so many other low-income African American boys, this child already had been labeled as "bad," even by the teachers and parents who were seeking to nurture him—and like so many children who are so labeled, his behavior had begun to shape itself, Pygmalion-like, to fit that expectation. E.M.'s first strategy was to assure this young boy, through gentle body language, that she would not accept the pervasive societal assumption that he was destined for violence. Her second strategy was to respond to his impulsive energy with playfulness and creativity, rather than the rejection that read it as a precursor of violence. By using these two methods day in and day out for a year, she was able to bring forth palpable changes in this boy's self-concept and behavior. She was able to help redeem this young boy from the fate of her husband, in which the line between personal moral failure and societal injustice could not be drawn.

By working with a young African American boy, E.M. gradually found it possible to walk away from her husband. Because she identified herself so deeply with the African American community, it was not possible for E.M. to leave her husband without feeling a sense of betrayal. Even at the height of her husband's violence, E.M. felt a blood loyalty toward him that seemed to run deeper than her own safety. She saw him as a man whose life chances were eventually ruined by the shadow that remains, in the suburbs of Portland as much as the streets of Watts, from our country's history of slavery. Yet through the hope that came from her work with this little boy, she gradually became able to feel, condemn, and finally resist her husband's violation of her body, even in the face of that truth.

E.M.'s relationship with these two children bears a fascinating similarity to J.G.'s relationship with her. In the texture and flow of the interaction, these relationships—one a mother-friendship between two women and the second a pair of therapeutic relationships between the younger woman and two children—mirror one another. The dance of these two very different relationships leave strikingly similar traces over the course of time. This congruence is particularly apparent if we compare J.G.'s work with E.M. with E.M's work with the little girl.

World Making

In our July 2 interview, E.M. described the method and course of her work with the little girl with remarkable precision. Both she and J.G. gave accounts of the relationship between them. Both relationships were anchored in mutual presence. E.M. spent her first few months with the little girl simply being in the young girl's presence, walking with her on the playground, sitting with her on the rug and at the table. J.G. made herself present to E.M. by small, unobtrusive actions, such as greeting her by name every morning and inviting her son Peter to stay with her while she volunteered. These gestures made E.M. feel both welcomed and recognized as an individual, without feeling pressured either to disclose her "needs" or to perform any tasks. In both relationships, walking together on the playground without exchanging words became a way to deepen the sense of safety that comes from mutual presence, while getting to know the rhythms of the other's body. Her embodied knowledge of the little girl's movement was something upon which E.M. drew as she began to coax the child into more sustained interaction. In the relationship between E.M. and J.G., the walks were a way for J.G. to sense that E.M. was in trouble, and for E.M. to realize that J.G. knew what she was going through, without words having to pass between them.

With this foundation of trust, the relationships could move into a phase of more intensive interaction. As the bond between E.M. and the child began to grow, E.M. found her way into games of give and take in which she could gently mirror the child's own actions. Through that play, E.M. received these halting gestures as the girl's desire for language, and thereby encouraged the child to feel that she had the capacity to say more. In her work with E.M., J.G. looked for ways to hint, through a joke or a hug or a word, that she had "been there," and therefore might be someone to talk with about troubles at home. J.G. also noticed—and praised—the subtle features of E.M.'s work in the classroom that showed that the younger woman had not entirely forgotten her past competencies, and that pointed toward skills she could develop in the future. Finally, J.G. began to use her irreverent humor as their relationship strengthened to cajole E.M. to take risks, such as running for the policy council, that might help her regain self-confidence.

Through months of gentle but rock-solid presence, J.G. and E.M. both attuned themselves to the shattered rhythms of another person's world of pain.

At the same time, each woman cast a third eye for paths of growth that the other might take from the safe place they had made together. These relationships evoke the freeze-frame photographic records that attachment theorists have made of the rhythms of empathy and distance between an infant and her caregiver. They also evoke accounts that the British pediatrician and psychoanalyst D. W. Winnicott has given of his clinical work with troubled children and adults. Moving to a very different social universe, these relationships evoke successful support programs for low-income women. Mary Belenky, for instance, who founded the Listening Partners program for low-income women in Vermont, and Toby Herr, who founded Chicago's widely acclaimed Project Match, both describe the crux of their programs as long-term mentoring relationships for individual women in a context of intensive vocational coaching and peer-group support. Psychiatrists, attachment theorists, and more recently, social support practitioners all use the verb *mirror* to describe one of the most basic moves in generative caring relationships that seem to enable human beings, at any age, to grow.

Through her conversations with J.G., E.M. came to understand her relationship with the two children as a political and, indeed, a spiritual project, with meaning that reached further than the four walls of the Church of the Redeemer's Head Start classroom. E.M.'s yearlong dialogue with J.G. enabled the younger woman to understand the day-to-day work she did with these children as redemptive labor, that looks toward a hope that wrong can be condemned in ways that even those who inflict it can come to understand. Another Head Start woman called this the work of "learning to live again, not just survive." Martin Luther King, Jr., might have spoken of this work as moving beyond the "chain of hate" toward "beloved community."

Elaine Scarry, the literary critic and author, came up with a simple phrase to describe the relationships that E.M. made with these children: it is the work of remaking the world (Scarry 1985). How did a Head Start classroom become a setting for this moral project? How can the women who are doing this work at the grassroots level gain a greater voice in shaping the moral environment of workplaces and other street-level social institutions, and in changing the ground rules of our democracy so that their voices are more respected in the processes through which social policy is made?

Other chapters in this volume have documented that caregiving is becoming an increasingly important sector of the low-wage labor market, particularly for marginalized women. An increasing percentage of the lowest-wage workers in this country are required to put their human emotions on the line at the workplace, to provide goods such as day care for children, home care for the elderly, hospital care for the acutely ill, long-term care for the severely disabled, and community-based care for those with psychiatric or developmental impairments. Might the shop-floor environment in this sector be designed to foster, rather than obstruct, the sorts of relationships that can both replenish the psychic energy of the caring workers, and enable those workers, as well as their clients, to grow?

This chapter has sought to show that some women find their Head Start centers to be places where generative caring relationships can flourish. This implausible but well-documented reality opens up many questions. What would it take to replicate and sustain such relationships in other social settings? Can new workplace policies help to bring such a culture into a wider array of work environments? And with regard to care-work in particular, can a work-culture that promotes the emotional well-being and personal development of the workers enhance their capacity to do the work, or does such a culture breach a sensible boundary between personal and workplace identities? My work on Head Start has shed some oblique light on these questions. More sustained research clearly is in order.

Substantial portions of the ethnographic data and interpretations that I set forth in this chapter were presented as part of a Symposium on the Structure of Care Work, sponsored by the *Chicago-Kent Law Review* (see White 2001).

NOTES

1. The question of how the experience of working as a volunteer, as opposed to working for wages, affects one's attitude toward the workplace experience is a subject that warrants further study.

2. Recall that of the paid workers in the two programs researched, 70 percent had begun their work for Head Start as parent volunteers. Many active Head Start parents both volunteer in the classroom and participate in enrichment activities.

3. ETI, along with other names and identifying details used in reporting on my ethnographic research, is fictitious. In addition, portions of transcripts and field notes were edited to make them more readable.

4. I include other primary caregivers because at the most socioeconomically stressed sites, such as Lincoln Terrace and the Church of the Redeemer, as many as a quarter of the children's legal custodians were grandmothers, older sisters, foster parents, or others, rather than a biological parent.

REFERENCES

Abu-Tayeh, Pauline. 1993. *Oversight Hearing Regarding the Head Start Program Before the Subcommittee on Human Resources of the House of Representatives Committee on Education and Labor*, 103d Cong., 1st sess. 61.

Andrews, Myrtha. 1990. *Head Start Reauthorization Hearing before Subcommittee on Children, Family, Drugs, and Alcoholism of the Senate Committee on Labor and Human Resources*, 101st Cong., 2d sess. 97.

Boyd, Eliza. 1990. *Head Start Reauthorization Hearing Before Subcommittee on Children, Family, Drugs, and Alcoholism of the Senate Committee on Labor and Human Resources*, 101st Cong., 2d sess. 97.

Dillon, Alyce. 1990. *Hearing on the Reauthorization of the Head Start Act Before the Subcommittee on Human Resources of the House of Representatives Committee on Education and Labor*, 101st Cong., 2d sess. 189.

Habermas, Jürgen. 1987. *The Theory of Communicative Action*. Vol. 2, *Lifeworld and System: A Critique of Functionalist Reason*. Translated by Thomas McCarthy. Boston: Beacon Press.

Hale, Dolores. 1990. *Head Start Reauthorization Hearing Before Subcommittee on Children, Family, Drugs, and Alcoholism of the Senate Committee on Labor and Human Resources*, 101st Cong., 2d sess. 97.

King, Frankie. 1984. *Reauthorization of the Head Start Act, 1984 Hearing Before the Subcommittee on Family and Human Services of the Senate Committee on Labor and Human Resources*, 98th Cong., 2d sess.

Malone, Lula. 1990. *Head Start Reauthorization Hearing Before Subcommittee on Children, Family, Drugs, and Alcoholism of the Senate Committee on Labor and Human Resources*, 101st Cong., 2d sess. 97.

National Head Start Association. 1990. *Head Start: The Nation's Pride, A Nation's Challenge. Recommendations for Head Start in the 1990s.* The Report of the Silver Ribbon Panel, A Project of the National Head Start Association. Washington, D.C.: National Head Start Association.

Norwood, Carlis. 1993. *Oversight Hearing Regarding the Head Start Program Before the Subcommittee on Human Resources of the House of Representatives Committee on Education and Labor*, 103d Cong., 1st sess. 61.

O'Keefe, Ann. 1979. *What Head Start Means to Families*. U.S. Department of Health, Education, and Welfare. Office of Human Development Services. Administration of Children, Youth, and Families. No. 79-31129, Washington, D.C. (September).

Putnam, Robert. 2000. *Bowling Alone: The Collapse and Revival of American Community*. New York: Simon & Schuster.

Reyes, Blas. 1990. *Head Start Success Stories*. CSR, Inc. Region V Head Start Training and Technical Assistance Resource Center.

Romero, Alma. 1993. *Oversight Hearing Regarding the Head Start Program Before the Subcommittee on Human Resources of the House of Representatives Committee on Education and Labor*, 103d Cong., 1st sess. 39.

Sacks, Karen. 1988. *Caring by the Hour: Women, Work, and Organizing at Duke Medical Center*. Urbana: University of Illinois Press.

Scarry, Elaine. 1985. *The Body in Pain: The Making and Unmaking of the World*. New York: Oxford University Press.

Stewart, Earnistine. 1990. *Head Start Reauthorization Hearing Before Subcommittee on Children, Family, Drugs, and Alcoholism of the Senate Committee on Labor and Human Resources*, 101st Cong., 2d sess. 97.

U.S. Department of Health and Human Services. 1993. "Creating a 21st Century Head Start: Final Report of the Advisory Committee on Head Start Quality and Expansion." Washington, D.C.

U.S. Office of Child Development. Head Start. 1970. "Head Start and the Parents." Transmittal Notice 70.2 for Instruction I-30, Sec. B-2 (August 10).

White, Lucie E. 2001. "Raced Histories, Mother Friendships, and the Power of Care: Conversations with Women in Project Head Start." *Chicago-Kent Law Review* 76: 1569.

Chapter 7

Who Counts? The Case for Participatory Research

Frances Ansley

By now in most polarized societies the gap between those who have social power over the process of knowledge generation, and those who have not, has reached dimensions no less formidable than the gap in access to the means of physical production.
——Mohammad Anisur Rahman (1991)

Anyone who claims that good research is not political is just plain wrong. . . . Research can be political in two ways. First, it can be related to the external political process; the decision to research a certain issue will potentially influence public policy debates in broader society. Second, there are internal political processes within the research process itself. The relationship between the researcher and the organization or people to be researched is also a political relationship.
——Philip Nyden and colleagues (1997b)

Scholars who study and write about poverty and low-wage work in early twenty-first-century America face important challenges in conducting and disseminating their research. The growing divide in wealth, life chances, and basic security that has become so pronounced in our country in recent decades increasingly distances university-based poverty researchers from some of their most important "subjects." Meanwhile, the academy's scramble to reinvent itself in the changed post–cold war funding environment means that scholars' ability to command respect within their institutional settings frequently hinges on how successful they are at marketing their projects and capacities to external entities that are in a position to pay for scholars' research services.

Participatory research is an alternative to reigning research methodologies that offers distinct advantages to scholars who are troubled by these developments.[1] This type of investigation emphasizes the involvement of people and communities normally excluded from the research process and the world of policy making. In the model's strongest form, participation occurs at every stage of the research endeavor, from the initial framing of research questions to the dissemination of results and the carrying out of social action based on the project's findings.

Participatory scholars themselves are a variegated lot, with roots in disparate settings that range from human resource management projects in manufacturing facilities in the world's north, to insurgent organizing among landless peasants in the global south (Greenwood and Levin 1998; Cancian and Armstead 1992; Reason and Roward 1981). My own values and experiences have brought me to the conclusion that the strands of participatory research that offer the most promise for meaningful work are those that first emerged from contexts of heated social contestation in Latin America, Asia, and Africa. These strands are importantly marked by their uneasy encounters with mainstream, postcolonial "development" practice in Third World countries. Researchers working in this vein have articulated sharp critiques of antipoverty projects imposed from above or abroad, and have produced a compelling literature about the ways that expert-led knowledge systems and expert-led projects—sometimes intentionally and sometimes not—tend to reproduce and reinforce existing relationships of power (Rahman 1993; Fals-Borda and Rahman 1991; Chambers 1983; Tandon 1982).

Whether north or south, the advantages of participatory research methods over traditional ones are several. Participatory approaches are linked more reliably to issues and situations that are defined as worthy of study by those directly affected. Lay participants often bring to the endeavor crucial knowledge and ways of knowing that otherwise would be inaccessible to the research team. The quality of research is increased by midcourse corrections that are a natural corollary of feedback and consultation built into strongly participatory projects. The results of participatory research achieve better-targeted diffusion because they are "self-disseminating" to participants and their immediate communities. Participatory research is more readily translated into grassroots social action. Finally, the process of designing, carrying out, and disseminating participatory research itself builds human and social capital—that is, it increases the individual and joint capacity of academic and nonacademic participants to understand and act on their material and social environment. Those participatory projects that involve partnerships between university-based researchers and socially disadvantaged or marginalized communities have another advantage: they help to build vital bridges of communication and cooperative action across the growing socioeconomic divide that so marks our present situation.

This chapter will briefly introduce the body of theory and practice now emerging under the banner of participatory research, and will argue that investigators working on issues of poverty and low-wage labor should add some version of participatory research to their list of professional competencies. In issuing this call, I do not underestimate either the potential rewards or the tough challenges. Greater use of participatory and community-based methods can improve the quality of what poverty scholars do, and for many of us, it can bring our work into better practical and ethical harmony with our own analyses and aspirations. A serious embrace of participatory methods and values, however, would require a radical reorientation of our current practice, because it depends on our taking the simple but giant step of including no- and low-wage workers themselves within the close circle of our research collaborators, and within the larger circle of key audiences we regularly strive to reach. Such a choice would require us to do nothing less than democratize our own research practices.

ROOTS OF A MOVEMENT

Worldwide, there is a growing recognition of the need to develop research capacity and to carry on research activity beyond the bounds of the academy and outside of traditional academic disciplines and folkways. Adherents of participatory research have criticized traditional approaches for failure to produce practical, useful results and for a tendency to reinforce existing power relations and social structures. They also point out that traditional research seldom does anything to increase the capacity of oppressed communities to engage in political or economic self-help. Along with advocates for the closely allied and overlapping practice of "community-based research" (Sclove et al. 1998; Murphy et al. 1997; Nyden et al. 1997a), these critics have attempted to invent, refine, and promote other ways of producing and disseminating knowledge.[2]

The emerging participatory research tradition has some of its most important roots in social conflict in the global south among scholars and community leaders who believe that the research enterprise properly understood includes not only the production of knowledge, but also two further imperatives: education and social action.[3] For instance, the Colombian sociologist and activist Orlando Fals-Borda (1991), a leading theoretician and practitioner of participatory methods, has observed, "It is useful to recall from the beginning that [participatory research] is not exclusively research oriented, that it is not only adult education or only sociopolitical action. It encompasses all these aspects together as three stages or three emphases." John Gaventa (1991), a northern researcher deeply influenced by the practice and theory of southern colleagues, similarly observes,

> Participatory research attempts to break down the distinction between the researchers and the researched, the subjects and objects of knowledge production, by participation of the people-for-themselves in the process of gaining and creating knowledge. In the process, research is seen not only as a process of creating knowledge, but simultaneously, as education and development of consciousness, and mobilization for action.

Participatory research projects identified with this southern strand take many different forms, but all are conceived as democratic social practices that build various capacities for improvement and self-governance within the communities or organizations that are collaborating on the research. The following illustrate the variety of research projects that exemplify these practices.

A network of villages in southwest Colombia got together to protest fraudulent billing practices by a coal utility. When the company claimed that the bills were computer generated, and were therefore immune from patterned error or intentional misrepresentation, the villagers worked with outside researcher-facilitators in a decentralized effort to collect and document family utility bills over time, and to plot them against actual energy use. They were able to trace and record patterns that revealed quite clearly that the company's customers were being unfairly billed, thus successfully challenging the expertise and neutrality of the computer system, and eventually winning a degree of restitution. Meanwhile, the collective sense-making activity had a strong impact on participants and strengthened the communities' network of social capital. (De Roux 1991)

A coalition of community-based organizations in Appalachia, in collaboration with a handful of regionally-based researchers working outside the academy, conducted a multi-state, multi-year study of absentee land ownership in Appalachia. The project trained lay people and community activists to gather local data from individual county courthouses. The community teams added their local knowledge as an aid in data interpretation, and results were collated and fed back to grassroots economic and environmental justice groups at the base. Those groups in turn were able to use the information to further their work. Groups pushed for a fairer and more realistic taxation of mineral holdings in impoverished coal counties where the tax base was virtually nonexistent, and they raised questions about the efficacy of local economic development strategies that failed to address the dominance of absentee ownership. The study challenged the prevailing wisdom that Appalachia's problems were a result of land *settlement* patterns (seen as the result of "bad choices" by too many of the region's low-income individuals), and pointed instead to land *ownership* patterns, characterized by intense concentration of land holdings in the hands of absentee corporations. (Gaventa and Horton 1981)

Janitorial service employees in Los Angeles worked with researchers from UCLA to document hazardous elements in traditional cleaning products, to design a method for gathering information on risks and risk perception, and to develop a system for evaluating cleaning products proposed for use on the job. (Gottlieb 1997)

A group of maquiladora workers from across northern Mexico met with a physician and health educator for a weekend workshop where they received an orientation on varieties of physical, chemical, and psychological risk common in Mexican factory work. They next broke into smaller groups by work site and were set free with butcher paper and art supplies, instructed to create detailed "risk maps" of their different factories. Shy and subdued up to that point, when given the map-making task, the workers at the gathering came alive. Two hours later they had produced a set of charts and diagrams, and had shared with each other a set of vivid narratives about a wide array of occupational hazards. The physician returned to her work with a more sophisticated understanding of work in the maquilas, together with a number of new research questions. Each work group returned to its home town with a better understanding of how its own plant fit into a broader context and with an action plan for tackling at least one of the risks the group had identified in the mapping exercise.[4]

Middle school, high school, and college students in urban projects around the country worked together to take systematic soil samples and plotted them on neighborhood maps in order to identify, publicize and abate lead hazards in their communities.[5]

Members of a labor union in the southeastern United States received training in how to detect early warning signs of an impending plant closing in a legal environment where the law gave them little right to timely information about the future of their jobs. Later they used their access to company garbage cans, to shipping documents, and to contracted truck drivers to anticipate shifts in production and the closing of facilities, thus enhancing their ability to organize around or bargain over their employer's siting decisions.[6]

A group of formerly homeless women, who were enrolled as college students in an urban university, decided to conduct a project interviewing mothers who were then on the street or in shelters. They talked extensively among themselves about their own experiences before deciding on a format and focus for the interviews, and they worked hard to design a process well-informed by their own memories and perceptions of being homeless. (The group, however, rejected the word *homeless,* redubbing their previous condition as "roofless." They recalled with stubborn pride and no little anger that they had always managed to make *homes* for their children, even when they were without physical shelter, and they wanted that achievement recognized.) After the interviews were done, the students and their professor felt that the project design was fully vindicated by the quality of the responses they elicited from interviewees. The students were also committed to doing their own data analysis, and planned to use the interviews to strengthen a campaign around the need for affordable housing and better transitional shelter for women in the era of welfare "reform."[7]

As these examples suggest, the form and concrete focus of participatory research projects in this southern tradition vary greatly. Despite their variety, most also share some important objectives. A long-term goal repeatedly voiced by this school of researchers is egalitarian social change. They stress that the participatory research they are seeking to advance is more than methodology— it is a value-laden activity aimed at serving the community's desire to bring about a more democratic and just society. An important short-term goal linked to that long-term aspiration is to strengthen the capacity and social agency of participating communities through ongoing cycles of action and reflection in which the community itself is actively engaged.

Such a process is in sharp contrast with the unilateral, extractive dynamic that marks most traditional research on disadvantaged communities. A poverty researcher applying a traditional methodology, for example, might conduct interviews with poor people, take tapes back to an academic lair for transcription and analysis, and then cut, paste, and weave the voices of informants into a text, perhaps even with the conscious desire to "give voice" to people often excluded from the discourse of poverty policy. Likely work products—perhaps a doctoral dissertation, an article for a disciplinary journal, or a book published for academic or other highly literate audiences—are dictated at least in significant part by the career demands or professional ambitions of the writer, rather than the interests, literacy levels, or self-identified priorities of the individual and organizational research subjects.[8] The desire to help people in need by quoting them and calling attention to their problems in print certainly is not a bad thing in itself. Even in the best case, however, it is not enough, and in the worst case, it can obscure for the well-intentioned researcher her or his own elitist assumptions, self-interest, and failure to ask thoroughgoing questions about the relationship of her or his own work to the achievement of meaningful social change. The participatory research ethos suggests that one way researchers can avoid such disappointments is to move beyond scholarship that is simply *about* or *for* the poor, and instead to develop projects that are *with* and ultimately *by* those at the heart of the enterprise.

LIMITATIONS OF THE TRADITIONAL RESEARCH PARADIGM

Academic researchers who undertake participatory research no doubt will encounter difficulty. Scholars are likely to face substantial resistance if they move to include no- and low-wage people among their research collaborators on questions of poverty and low-wage labor markets. Those who make it a regular practice to devote serious time to writing up or presenting their research results in ways that are widely accessible to low-wage workers and other poor people are also likely to face opposition.

Career pressures can bear heavily on researchers in a way that discourages serious attention to low-wage audiences. Academics typically address their work to experts in their field, presumed to be the scholar's only true "peers." These are people usually within the writer's own discipline, heavily credentialed readers who by definition have shown themselves capable of adapting to and thriving in academic culture. Formal and informal ranking schemes within disciplines often intensify scholarly striving for well-placed readers.

The scholar who would work with grassroots collaborators or address grassroots audiences confronts other obstacles as well. Few universities offer serious training in participatory methods. Academic evaluation and reward systems are keyed to the academic year rather than to community rhythms. Regulatory regimes, such as the rules pertaining to human subjects, operate on assumptions ill-suited to partnering with community-based organizations.[9] The complexities and politics of managing and completing a collaborative endeavor with a nonacademic grassroots partner can make a traditional research project look like a picnic (Nyden and Wiewel 1992). Moreover, universities are thoroughly embedded in existing relationships of local and more distant power (Press and Washburn 2000). In some circumstances, these relationships can make themselves strongly felt in ways that disrupt, limit, or punish those projects of university-based researchers that have threatened to question or upset such ties (Joy 1999; Soley 1995; Burd 1994).[10]

The foregoing discussion should not, of course, obscure the fact that institutional constraints and personal ambition are only part of the reason why academics might spend so much energy aiming toward high places. In many cases, researchers *choose* elite audiences and conventional topics and methods precisely because they want to influence policy.

Many of these impulses are unexceptionable. Scholars studying poverty, low-wage work, and social retrenchment, for instance, surely should move beyond academic audiences and be appropriately aware of readers who currently have the recognized power to make and authoritatively interpret policy. Certainly, poverty researchers who hope to make a difference must resist being contained by the isolating discourse of the disciplines, and should strive for visibility and real impact on public decision making.

Nevertheless, strategies that stress persuasion of elites as the primary avenue to meaningful changes in the real world may have limited efficacy. In a social order that encompasses increasingly extreme differences of wealth and power, projects aimed primarily at elite audiences can further isolate researchers from crucial experiences and resources located in relatively poor and powerless communities. Concomitantly, an orientation toward persuasion of elites can create too cozy a relationship between scholars and those in dominant policy positions—one that domesticates researchers and discourages them from turning too harsh or searching a gaze on the practices and holdings of those in power.

Further, targeting elites as the audience for research implies that important changes can—indeed must—come from above, and that elites are best motivated to implement those changes when highly trained professionals (who are dependent in various ways on favorable relationships with well-regarded academic institutions) present them with accurate facts and persuasive arguments. Yet some scholars believe to the contrary—that those without much immediate or evident institutional power are precisely the ones who must envision and demand redistributionist and liberatory change if it is ever to occur. In this sense, paradoxically, the powerless indeed may hold an indispensable key to social transformation and a deep reordering of power relations. To be sure, today's policy makers and power brokers could stand to be better educated and informed, and progressive intellectuals at times should attempt to do that educating. During the Clinton administration, for example, it struck me quite forcefully that the president of the United States was much more significantly constrained by an electoral system dominated by powerful entrenched interests than by a lack of accurate information or paucity of good ideas. Similarly, business and media executives usually are too wedded to their short-term self-interest, as framed by present social arrangements, to alter course voluntarily.

Some social theorists have suggested that power in contemporary society rests importantly on the capacity to induce acquiescence among those disadvantaged by existing arrangements (Fay 1987; Lukes 1974; Gaventa 1980). Others have said that the post-1989 trend away from regimes openly and heavily reliant on naked coercion of their own citizens has made persuasion and consent all the more dominant as a method of maintaining order (Robinson 1996). If these observations are accurate, then those interested in altering the distribution of power and resources need to find ways to promote critical questioning, expose and interrupt regressive consensus, and push for strong rather than weak democracy (Barber 1994). Participatory research can play an important role in such a process.

Participatory research promises a more effective role for the researcher concerned about the future of powerless communities and interested in unsettling popular acquiescence and despair. Through the participatory research process, researchers can pose questions about accepted social and political practices in ways that have the potential to reframe debates. If researchers work in participatory modes, they can help to pose these questions and raise discussions in ways that are linked to people's own experience, that more readily translate into vibrant and sturdy social movement, and that carry the power and conviction of experiential learning—that is, fully rooted and embodied in particular contexts that people have come to know and understand with subtlety and self-confidence.

In addition to the foregoing practical and strategic reasons for including low-income people on research teams and in intended audiences, ethical imperatives may also compel such moves. Beyond the simple ethical notion that advocates of democracy should practice what they preach, antipoverty researchers who study the poor may have additional ethical concerns arising from the information-gathering activities they carry out. Many participatory researchers say that those who conduct research on socially subordinated groups have an ethical obligation: first, to return the research to its source in disadvantaged individuals and communities, and second, to recognize a right in those sources to exercise control over the sharing and use of the research.

Scholars who study the poor should assume more often the obligation of creating a circuit of return to their sources. Scholars who work with people who are from socially marginalized or disadvantaged communities should assume more often the obligation of sharing control over research findings—even sometimes of yielding it altogether—to the subjects of their research or to their grassroots collaborators.

A first level of return might be to share with interviewees the work product that the researcher has created from their words, including copies of interview transcripts, drafts, and final publications or releases. This level alone would represent a substantial commitment, especially if translation was required. Yet a thoroughgoing participatory protocol would require more than this sort of one-directional, first-level sharing, at least as to those interviewees who are participants in the endeavor. Involvement would be required at a point much earlier than the interview (or other form of data collection), ideally at the stage when goals and research questions are defined. Participation would continue thereafter as information is gathered and analyzed, as various kinds of reports and products are developed, and as resulting plans for action are made, carried out, and evaluated. In other words, a participatory model would aspire to involvement of research subjects "at every step of the process until the publication of results and the various forms of returning the knowledge to the people are completed" (Fals-Borda 1991, 7–8).[11]

This level of participation imposes formidable demands, and foreseeably enough, many efforts end up by choice or necessity as a hybrid of participatory and more expert-led components. Further, my organizer colleagues in grassroots groups often are the first to point out that participatory methods are not appropriate for all research projects.[12] The participatory model, however, would start with at least the aspiration that members of a fully participatory project will function as active collaborators, designers, analysts, censors, and creators, and not simply as passive recipients of knowledge decanted into their waiting heads—or even implemented behind their oblivious backs—by a so-called expert.

A CALL TO MORE DEMOCRATIC PRACTICE

For the foregoing practical and ethical reasons, we poverty scholars should pursue our research both with and for those who most need antipoverty reform. Such people are seldom invited to participate in policy debates or contribute to or reflect on current theories about the economic and social order. Nevertheless, they are the main players whose quiescence or resistance creates the climate in which political and economic decisions are made, the ones whose passivity or action can naturalize or challenge existing social arrangements.

Although subordinated communities possess strategic advantages that should make us eager for collaboration and access, they also suffer from strategic disadvantages as potential change agents and transformers of policy. Some of these disadvantages could be offset, at least in part, by change-minded scholars willing to put a priority on collaborative and participatory work. For instance, poor and working people need better access to each other, fuller knowledge of their own and their peers' histories, well-documented studies of the concrete and changing operations of local and global power, alternative sources of reliable information and analysis, sturdier alliances and coalitions, and better opportunities to educate and pressure elite policy makers.

In sum, researchers have an ethical obligation to recognize the individual vulnerabilities and social needs of subordinated people whom they study or with whom they conduct collaborative investigations. These ethical concerns bolster the practical and strategic reasons why poverty scholars should use participatory methods and seek popular audiences for their work more often.

Participatory methods provide useful tools for those who want to move in this direction. They often are able to lay the foundation for policy proposals that are legitimate, comprehensible, and workable to those directly affected. Since such methods require concrete involvement, they also are particularly likely to create educational experiences that help groups of marginalized and quieted people move into action. The following sections set out the case for each leg of the "triad of advantage" claimed by advocates of participatory research: that is, that participatory methods can improve the quality of research results; provide meaningful occasions for experiential learning and popular education; and enable bottom-up action for social change.

PARTICIPATORY RESEARCH AS MORE EFFECTIVE INVESTIGATION

Teaming with the subjects of one's own research is a concept in some tension with conventional research protocols, as adherents of the insurgent strand of participatory research have been quick to concede and affirm.

> The generation of scientific knowledge does not require the method of detached observation of the positivist school. Any observation, whether it is detached or involved, [is] value biased, and this is not where the scientific character of knowledge is determined. The scientific character or objectivity of knowledge rests on its social verifiability, and this depends on consensus as to the method of verification. There exist different epistemological schools with different respective verification systems, and all scientific knowledge in this sense is relative to the paradigm to which it belongs and, specifically, to the verification system to which it is submitted. (Rahman 1991, 14–15)

Far from being apologetic, proponents of participatory research are convinced that in some instances their methods offer epistemological advantages over traditional ones. Sometimes people directly affected have access to knowledge uniquely available to them by virtue of their situation or inherited and accumulated experience, an advantage that even traditional paradigms would recognize, at least once strongly demonstrated (Greenwood and Levin 1998). Striking descriptions along this line come from development practice in the Third World. The following classic rendition by Robert Chambers (1983, 85–86, 98) is illustrative.

Many of the practices of small farmers which were once regarded as primitive or misguided are now recognized as sophisticated and appropriate. . . . Mixed cropping has been and remains a widespread technique in small farming in tropical Africa and elsewhere. Yet for many years it was regarded as backward. Since agricultural research was confined to pure stands of crops, it was only natural that the advice emanating from research stations and conveyed to farmers was also to plant pure stands. When small farmers continued to plant mixtures, they were branded as primitive, conservative, ignorant, lazy, and unprogressive.

With hindsight, the agricultural researchers and extensions staff are easily condemned. But there were many reasons for their behavior. Many of the researchers were foreigners with a background and training in the agriculture of temperate climates. . . . The agricultural development policies of the colonial countries where they worked aimed to increase the output of single crops, mostly cash crops for export. . . . Monoculture was practiced by large (plantation, European settler) farmers who influenced research policy. The organization and rewards of agricultural research also pushed researchers towards work on only one crop at a time: crop-specific teams were, and still are, a simple way to organize research. . . . On top of all this, in most of Africa, expatriates conducting agricultural research suffered from cultural conditioning, which made it difficult for them to see indigenous farming as anything but backward. The model in their minds was a tidy, geometrical, mechanized field in Europe or North America. The higgledy-piggledy muddle (as it seemed) of mixed cropping on African farmers' fields scarcely appeared a place to learn anything.

And yet it was . . . . Not only have many of the supposedly irrational and wasteful practices of traditional African farming been found to be prudent and sound, but mixed cropping has been shown to have many advantages. . . . Small farmers are, after all, professionals. They cannot afford not to be. And as professionals they have much to teach.

For originators and bearers of modern scientific knowledge, it requires a major effort to recognize that rural people's knowledge exists at all, let alone to see that it is often superior. The arrogance of ignorant educated outsiders is part of the problem. They do not know what rural people know and do not know that not knowing matters.

Note that Chambers does not claim across-the-board superiority for the small farmers. Elsewhere he speculates with attentive interest as to why (at least in his own view) rural people's knowledge tends to be demonstrably superior to that of outside experts in matters of the environment and farming practices, but substantially less so in health and nutrition. "Both outsiders' knowledge and the knowledge of rural people can be wrong. The key is to know which is wrong when" (Chambers 1983, 96–97).

In some situations, participatory research will be one among several reasonable options, or it may serve as a crucial complement to conventional methods. Sometimes it will be clearly ill-suited to the task. In other cases, however, participatory approaches will prove empirically superior because they will allow access to and creation of knowledge unavailable through other means.

PARTICIPATORY RESEARCH AS POPULAR EDUCATION

A second advantage that participatory research offers for poverty scholars is its educational power. It is no accident that strands of participatory research rooted in the global south bear a close relation to the equally lively southern tradition of adult education for social change. Latin America, Africa, and Asia—home to many experiments with participatory research—also have been a fountain of practice in the field of "popular education," or in Spanish, *educación popular*. The phrase signifies not education that would win a popularity contest, but education that is of the people, that draws on populist energies.[13]

Both phenomenologically and analytically, popular education in the global south is connected intimately to participatory research. The two practices and concepts are interpenetrating in many cases. Popular education is a primary method by which participatory researchers fulfill the mandate of returning their research to its source. In addition, participatory research is a primary method by which popular educators encourage their students to learn about something by investigating and trying to change it. Popular education is a bridge from the first to the third leg of the triad—from research to education to social action.

What popular education brings to the three-legged enterprise is a rich history of experimentation and learning about adult education with marginalized and oppressed people, most often in situations of social conflict. The famous Brazilian educator Paulo Freire began to develop a methodology of transformative teaching and learning in the 1960s when he was a literacy teacher with Brazilian peasants who were struggling for land reform. In writing about this education process, Freire stressed the importance of engaging students in a series of action-reflection cycles that use material from their everyday lives. He maintained that liberatory knowledge could be built only through a process of critical reflection on one's own experience, and that educators had to learn to recognize the power that lay within their students to construct the knowledge they needed for the tasks that confronted them (Freire 1970).[14]

Though Freire often is cited as a founding figure in popular education, there are antecedents of the approach on all continents. Europe has long had lively popular education practitioners at work (Almas 1988). North America has its own traditions, with Tennessee's Highlander Folk School—later called the Highlander Research and Education Center—having a particularly high profile (Lewis 1998; Nadeau 1996; Park 1993; Horton 1998; Horton and Freire 1990; Glen 1988; Clark 1986; Arnold, Barndt, and Burke 1985; Phenix 1985; Adams 1975). National liberation movements and grassroots organizations of the past in Central and South America, Mexico, India, the Philippines, southern Africa, and elsewhere often incorporated popular education into their organizing and mobilizing activities. Today in the global south, popular education continues to be a characteristic practice among grassroots movements that are responding to poverty and the pressures of globalization (Inter-Church Coalition on Africa 1993; Riano 1991; Núñez 1990; IMDEC 1989; ALFORJA 1988; Hope and Timmel 1987; Barndt 1980).

Popular education events and materials often are recognizable across languages and cultures, partly by virtue of common techniques. For instance, popular education workshops are very likely to include work in small groups, and to call for activities that use forms and materials (such as pictures, maps and charts, theater, music, and games) that do not require writing but rather various forms of interaction, expression, and bodily movement. Participants at a popular education event, whether literate or not, bring their own stories and experiences into an interactive process where they are at the center of the enterprise.

At their inception, most strands of popular education practice were keenly attuned to problems of economic class. Since then, popular education—like other forms of progressive theory and practice—properly has been subjected to continuing rounds of examination and critique about the extent to which it has or has not accounted for the claims of gender, race, sexual orientation, and other important categories of identity and difference (Maguire 1997; Doerge 1994). Most popular education events and materials now display increasing awareness and sophistication about ways of creating just and inclusive learning environments, but the process of challenge and reflection is certainly not complete.

In any event, most practitioners view popular education as more than a pedagogical process and more than a collection of exercises or workshop methodologies.[15] They see it as resting on the premise that present social arrangements are unjust, and that authentic education works to inspire and empower people to challenge those arrangements. Popular educators also tend to believe that people themselves are the best experts on the injustices they confront and are best situated to understand obstacles and develop viable solutions. To do so they need resources, to be sure: space and time for reflection, judicious challenge and support from educator-animators, and an opportunity to learn from and with their peers.

Academics in the United States who are interested in working on problems of poverty should give serious thought to joining the worldwide current of intellectuals working with and in the traditions of popular education. The methods and experiences of popular educators might help scholars of poverty to imagine ways of making our research and theory more understandable and accessible to poor people themselves. The standard this goal suggests is a high one for those who undertake to democratize their work at the dissemination phase. As one practitioner (Fals-Borda and Rahman 1991, 4–5) of participatory action research (PAR) once described his practice,

> Production and diffusion of new knowledge [is a] technique . . . integral to the research process because it is a central part of the feedback and evaluative objective of PAR. Although PAR strives to end the monopoly of the written word, it incorporates various styles and procedures for systematizing new data and knowledge according to the level of political conscience and ability for under-

standing written, oral, or visual messages by the base groups and public in general. . . . Four levels of communication are thus established, depending on whether the message and systematized knowledge are addressed to pre-literate peoples, cadres or intellectuals. A good PAR researcher should learn to address all four levels with the same message in the different styles required if he is to be really effective in the written, auditory, or visual communication of the thought or message.

Such a discipline would require us to spend as much time working to create materials and events for popular audiences as we spend working up the same research for scholarly publication and dissemination within academe. Perhaps such creations might take the form of popular education curriculum units, comic books, plays, or videotapes. Perhaps they would be more traditional booklets and presentations, but pitched at a literacy level and written in or translated into languages that made wider access possible. This is a modest proposal, after all: it calls simply for the scheduling of time and care for this kind of work equal to that which we routinely lavish on more privileged and privileging audiences. Yet I suspect that for most of us, this allocation of time would represent a radical break.

The needs and opportunities are all around us. Welfare mothers know a lot about the conditions they face and manage every day, but they could benefit enormously from the chance to *systematize* their knowledge.[16] They need to compare their knowledge with that of others, and hear about larger patterns. They need to develop and learn vocabularies and categories that make sense of such things as the growing isolation of the low-wage labor market, the gender segregation that remains characteristic of the U.S. economy, the history of poor relief, and current thinking behind the minimum wage. They need to have greater general economic literacy.

Likewise, prisoners need to understand more about the emergence of a new prison-industrial complex, and the history and demographics of the criminal justice system. Rank-and-file unionists need to understand more about labor history, the role of race in structuring the labor force and undermining worker organizations, the value and functions of women's unpaid work, and the dynamics of the new global economy. Immigrants studying for the U.S. citizenship exam and those taking classes in English for Speakers of Other Languages need to know more about the history of this nation's immigration law, the slave trade, international human rights, and the role that past immigrants have played in building the U.S. economy. Gang members and other youth need to know more about the history of vagrancy laws and their rights (or lack thereof) in relation to the police.

Obviously, such a list could go on. Equally obviously, each of the constituencies named has much to teach academics and others about the situations, experiences, and perceptions of its members. To the good fortune of academic researchers, finding ways to link with such people is not hard. Many already belong to organizations or are located in institutions where mutual teaching and learning on these issues can be convened. Many of their organizations and institutions are hungry for curricula, educational ideas, and substantive information about the local, regional, or national scene—in other words, for things that academic collaborators (and their students) should be able to provide. Many have research needs that are going unmet because they lack the ability to pay the going rate in the existing market for research services.

Of course, not everyone will choose to devote serious energy to reach such lay audiences, create more accessible texts, or disseminate them through more grassroots channels. More of us should do so, however, and perhaps some of our institutions and disciplines, if tested more assertively, will prove open to faculty movement in this direction. After all, the air is thick with talk of the importance of "civic engagement" (National Commission on Civic Renewal 1998; Barber 1998; Ehrlich 2000; Boyte and Kari 1996; Fear and Sandman 1995; Boyer 1990). Americans in particular have traditions in higher education that we can call on to justify a more democratic vision of the scholarly mission. Yet few universities have built much in the way of a reservoir of good will with ordinary citizens (Mathews 1996). In any case, we cannot know how our institutions will respond unless we put them to the test.

PARTICIPATORY RESEARCH AS SOCIAL ACTION FOR CHANGE

Social action is the third leg of the participatory research triad. In addition to challenging traditional epistemological assumptions, advocates of participatory research criticize the extent to which standard research practices tend to reinforce existing assumptions, institutions, and social structures. They maintain that the independent conservation and production of knowledge by disadvantaged or marginalized people is necessary to the project of changing present power relations. Building people's capacity to pursue organized inquiry and disseminate findings to strategic audiences is a vital component of movements for social change in the knowledge economy (Rahman and Fals-Borda 1991, 30–32; see also Hall 1979; Tandon 1982, 79).

> [W]e can see that a key weapon in the hands of the elites to make the people wait upon them for leadership and initiative, whether for "development" or social change, has been the assumed superiority of formal knowledge. Of this type of knowledge, the elites have a monopoly, unlike popular knowledge . . .
>
> [Participatory methods] should give the common people—as the very subject of history—greater leverage and control over the process of knowledge generation.

Similarly,

> [D]omination of masses by elites is rooted not only in the polarization of control over the means of material production but also over the means of knowledge pro-

duction, including control over the social power to determine what is useful knowledge. Irrespective of which of these two polarizations sets off a process of domination, one reinforces the other in augmenting and perpetuating this process.

In order to improve the possibility of liberation, therefore, these two gaps should be attacked simultaneously wherever feasible . . . [I]t is absolutely essential that the people develop their own endogenous consciousness-raising and knowledge generation, and that this process acquires . . . social power. (Rahman 1991, 14)

Almost by definition, a successful participatory research project should lead to social action, though the nature and the scale of this action is hardly uniform. Bottom-up strategies for social change may center on protests against injustice, direct action to disrupt or supplant business as usual, the negotiation of incremental reforms, or the creation of new alternative institutions. Participatory research can play an important role in these strategies, alone or in hybrid combinations. For instance, *popular epidemiology*—often judiciously joined with raucous troublemaking and public-interest litigation—more than once has led to environmental cleanup and compensation for injuries after environmental insults (Cole and Foster 2000; Brown and Mikkelson 1990; Merrifield 1979). In the case of the citizens' health movement that sprang up in the context of AIDS activism, participatory research and popular education carried out by and within the AIDS community led to radical restructuring of drug trials and significant increases in government funding for AIDS research (Epstein 1991). An aboriginal research project in Northeast Arnhem Land in the Northern Territory of Australia led to changes in the schooling of local children and a transformed role for the school in the community, with an indigenous governance structure, curriculum, and pedagogy (Marika et al. 1992).

In these cases and others, so-called "human subjects" of a research enterprise become collaborators in a joint endeavor, educators of their peers, and active participants in demanding change or reconstructing institutions. The process of investigating a shared problem also serves as an exercise in civic muscle building: it improves the skills, self-confidence, and engagement of participants, and in this sense is often correctly seen as more important than the immediate informational product created by the research.

For many practitioners of participatory research, the commitment to action that challenges and transforms existing relationships of power is at the heart of their theory and practice. Today, when even major international development agencies are rushing to embrace the virtues of participation (World Bank 1995), concerns about cooptation have begun to figure prominently in discussions about how and for whom to pursue this kind of work. Participatory researchers who identify with the insurgent southern strand of the tradition have begun to insist even more sharply than before that a demonstrable link to social change is indispensable to authentic participatory work. At a recent world gathering of participatory researchers, attendees conceived of participation "as a struggle against political and economic exclusion from exercising control over public resources," and rejected definitions that "reduce participation to a simple manipulation of the masses to obtain support for government proposals designed to maintain the status quo" (Fals-Borda 1998a, 161).

As researchers, those of us in academia live and work in a force field deeply structured and influenced by powerful elites. We find that our lives, our research projects, and the audiences we choose to write for are undeniably affected by the systems of power and status within which our lives and work are embedded. That so few of us undertake the intellectually arduous work of translating our theories and knowledge into accessible language that can be understood— then challenged, refined, debunked, debated and acted on—by those most directly affected is scandalous. Further, for those of us who do attempt this kind of work, the lack of collegial discourse about how to do it with excellence prevents us from evaluating and improving our practice in the ways we want.

Participatory and community-based projects often seem small and lowly in relation to the scale of the relevant problems.[17] Certainly the majority of participatory research efforts are mounted locally, and there is no denying that local research and organizing need a broader horizon of theoretical analysis and a broader field of practical alliances, networks, and institutions if they are to achieve widespread change or build meaningful alternatives. In the United States, the startling disconnect between myriad forms of local organizing now flourishing and the vacuum where an effective and well-rooted national movement for egalitarian social change should be must give any poverty scholar or strategist serious pause.

Yet real shortcuts to power are few. In the current climate, where effective strategies for combating poverty are so unclear, a multitude of small efforts linked to particular settings, and drawing deeply from local experience, often prove more promising than less rooted, more abstract efforts parachuted in from on high. Indeed, despite years of effort and rivers of money, more conventional types of research and policy making cannot point to a successful track record of poverty reduction launched from some higher level or enabled by a better-elaborated theory. Participatory researchers around the world continue to struggle with the need to generate theory, create larger networks, and achieve measurable results, but the challenge of achieving effective change is no more severe for them than for others attempting to address problems of poverty and low-wage work.

Accordingly, despite the difficulties confronting them, more scholars of poverty should undertake participatory research projects with organized community collaborators. More of us should share our findings in creative ways with popular audiences. And more of us should work in alliances with practical organizing efforts to achieve the needed changes suggested by our findings.

Participatory projects often produce more useful information than conventional ones. In many instances, research linked to community concerns and community action has a better chance of changing public discourse, because in some important ways it demonstrably *comes from* the public. Such projects also create social space for education, settings where people can start learning about their ability to define and investigate social problems, where they can cultivate their ability to make persuasive arguments to their fellow community members or to authorities, and where they can gain practice in studying local conditions, participating in local struggles, and analyzing local—and distant— power relations.

Participatory and popular methods make sense on a practical level for those who want to see a more democratic and egalitarian order. Significant and lasting social change in this direction simply cannot happen unless people are more educated, organized, and in motion about the issues and players affecting their lives. This approach also makes sense on an ethical level, because participatory methods better comport with avowed commitments to democracy. Further, these methods can better establish relations of mutual respect and recognition between the researcher and researched. Participatory and popular methods enable the return of knowledge gleaned from subordinated people and constructed with their help. Finally, they build bridges across the divide now growing between those (like most academics and policy researchers) who live in relative comfort and security, and those people in "the rest of the world" who do not.

None of the foregoing discussion means that no role exists for expert-led research. Participatory research is hardly the only tool or approach that might prove useful to a scholar who wants to reach out to nonelite audiences, nor is it the only approach that allows adherence to ethical principles of democratic respect and care. Many groups of poor people and low-wage workers will be interested in knowledge produced by traditional research protocols if researchers take the trouble to develop better methods of dissemination. Moreover, a project that involves nonparticipatory modes of research design or data gathering can do a perfectly fine job of taking results back to informants for review and can include them in decision making about next steps. In even the most traditional project, the "human subjects" play a key role by contributing information to the endeavor. Even the purest participatory undertaking entails some degree of role differentiation between people with different sorts of training, skill, personality, and perspective.

Neither should the foregoing discussion be taken to deny that participatory research can be carried out in ways that are corrupt and cooptational. Technical methods and processes can be used for diverse ends, and high aspirations can founder on many kinds of weaknesses (Gaventa 1998; Chambers 1997, 211–14 and passim). The point is not that one method or approach is always better than another. Nevertheless, both the push and the pull toward elite audiences are so great for most professional researchers that even the strongest counterpressure in another direction, the most impassioned calls, and the most elaborate preparations and reinforcements will not be disproportionate or unwarranted.

AFTERWORD

What if we who have contributed to this volume were to take up the challenge of translating its theory building and fact gathering into a form that would be interesting, accessible, provocative, and useful for unwaged and low-wage mothers most directly affected by welfare reform?

Where would we start? How would we plan and prepare our research in a way that included meaningful consultation with no- and low-wage workers? How would we disseminate our findings? What other relationships—with poor people and their organizations, adult basic education teachers, citizenship tutors, poverty lawyers, vocational trainers, community organizers, child care providers, battered women's advocates, artists, trade unionists, youth leaders, venturesome publishers—might we need to build in order to imagine and carry out an effective project that was participatory and broadly shared with strategic, hard-to-reach audiences? If we attempted such a project in a coordinated way, or with a single product in mind, what sorts of political discussions and disagreements might it stir up among us that would be different from merely thinking about a book aimed at academics and policy makers?

Most likely, within our group we already have a number of connections to relevant people and organizations, though I imagine we would need to build more. Many contributors to this book likely are already involved in nascent or explicit popular education efforts pieced together with scraps of leftover time at the margins of *real* scholarship. Yet if we brought such an effort more to the center of our professional attention, treated it as a legitimate and necessary part of our central mission, defended these choices to our deans and faculty rewards committees, publicly recognized each other for the importance and intellectual rigor of such work properly done, pushed publishers and foundations about what they could contribute to such a democratized research endeavor, ran regular reality checks with hardnosed antipoverty and labor organizers—if we really gave it our best shot—what might it look like?

I cannot possibly name all of the people who have helped me with the ideas developed in this chapter. Most crucially, a number of people and groups worked with me on a series of cross-border investigations over the past decade, an ongoing project that represents my own most direct and extended experience with collaborative and participatory research methods. Primary among them are the blue-collar workers in Tennessee and Mexico who participated as hosts or travelers on cross-border exchanges and who shared themselves and their perspectives so generously. In addition, staff members of collaborating economic justice groups on both sides of the border have been a joy to work with. Special institutional thanks are due to Appalshop, the Highlander Research and Education Center, and the Tennessee Industrial Renewal Network. The University of Tennessee College of Law, the university's campuswide faculty development program, the U.S. Department of Housing and Urban Development, the Fund for Labor Relations Studies, and Canada's Social Sciences and Humanities Research Council provided support for my time on some of these same investigations. All errors and weaknesses are, of course, my own.

NOTES

1. For purposes of this chapter, a broad array of theories and practices are grouped under the term *participatory research.* The literature is growing fast. Additional references appear in the text and notes herein, but for some helpful entry points see Williams 1996.

2. Various labels and schematics have been proposed for distinguishing different currents within participatory research and its allied methodologies, and various histories are in circulation. (See, for example, Park 1993; Reason 2000; Kemmis and McTaggart 1988; Kemmis 1988). Some strands of participatory research (PR) are less critical of existing arrangements, less insistent on the need for broad social transformation, and generally less interested in issues of power than those with roots in embattled communities of poverty in the Third World. Most all variants of PR, however, are still unconventional in their recognition that active involvement of research subjects can yield results more likely to make a difference in actual institutions. The number of arguably related schools and practices—many of which have their own literatures, acronyms, and leading lights—is large. Some of the types of inquiry often counted as participatory research include research in organizations (for example, William Foot Whyte), in community development (for example, Orlando Fals-Borda, Budd Hall, Patricia Maguire, and Rajesh Tandon), in schools (for example, Michelle Fine, Stephen Kemmis, Robin McTaggart, even John Dewey), with farmers (for example, Robert Chambers), and in evaluation (for example, Jennifer Greene and Lawrence Salmen).

3. See Green et al. 1997. For more on the connection between research and education see Freire 1982.

4. Observations of author, Ciudad Juarez, Mexico, March 1993.

5. See, for example, a report from high school students enrolled in an Upward Bound program at Oberlin College, posted at *http://sites.netscape.net/upwardboundsophs/ homepage* and at *http://sites.netscape.net/upwardboundjrs/homepage* (last visited 7–29–99).

6. Observations of author, Knoxville, Tennessee, 1991 to 1996. See also LaBotz 1991.

7. Personal interviews with Delores Bell, Brenda Farrell, Catherine Ferreira, Marie Kennedy, and Betsy Santiago, in New Market, Tennessee, June 1996. See Williams 1997b.

8. Examples of my own work that conform to this model include Ansley 1993, 1995, and 1998.

9. Some institutions and groups are attempting to develop guidelines for participatory research that will in some way relate to existing regulatory structures. See Detroit-Genesee County Community-Based Public Health Consortium 1994; Graber 1994.

10. Despite these formidable pressures are countertrends, fraught with their own complexities. See Ansley and Gaventa 1997, and Nyden et al. 1997a.

11. Defining the endpoint of a participatory project can be difficult, and "returning the knowledge to the people" may not be the last step but simply another stop along the way. At any rate, some participatory researchers stress the practical and ethical importance of planning for the researcher's own individual "exit" in a transparent, thoughtful—and participatory—manner.

12. Bob Becker, for instance, an organizer for the Tennessee Industrial Renewal Network, has on more than one occasion said something like the following to me and other university colleagues in discussions of participatory research: "Sometimes, you all, we just want a good competent academic researcher to go out there and get some information for us and give us the answer to our question without a whole lot of lip! We don't always have the time to mount a big participatory project, and we don't always believe that research is the best use of our time." Bob Becker, interviews with author, Knoxville, Tennessee, in various years, over various sorts of beverages, and across various sorts of tables.

13. I have briefly discussed popular education elsewhere, in the context of its applications to law school pedagogy. See Ansley 1994.

14. Paulo Freire died in 1998, and a recent double issue of the journal of the International Council for Adult Education is a tribute to him, with contributions from a wide range of educators all over the world. See "A Tribute to Paulo Freire," *Convergence* 21 (1–2, 1998).

15. A Canadian popular educator tried to draw the line as follows (Nadeau 1996, 4–5):

    The recent "popularity" of popular education brings with it the risk that it will be reduced to group dynamics and participatory training techniques. This is a misuse and a misreading of what popular education is about. Popular education is part of the wider process of organizing for social change and movement building.

16. The reference here is to a concept common among popular educators and activists in Latin America: *sistematización*. The term refers to a process of analysis built by reflecting on one's own individual or collective experience, seeking patterns and connections, and working to situate the immediate experience under consideration within a larger spatial and temporal frame.

17. For a reflection on the felt need of the international participatory research community to confront questions of scale see White 1998.

REFERENCES

Adams, Frank, with Myles Horton. 1975. *Unearthing Seeds of Fire: The Idea of Highlander.* Winston-Salem, N.C.: John F. Blair.
ALFORJA. 1988. *Técnicas Participativas para la Educación Popular, Tomo II.* San José, Costa Rica: Centro de Estudios y Publicaciones.
Almas, Reidar. 1988. "Evaluation of a Participatory Development Project in Three Norwegian Rural Communities." *Community Development Journal* 23: 26.

Ansley, Frances Lee. 1993. "Standing Rusty and Rolling Empty: Law, Poverty, and America's Eroding Industrial Base." *Georgetown Law Journal* 81(5): 1757–1896.

———. 1994. "Starting with the Students: Lessons from Popular Education." *Southern California Review of Law and Women's Studies* 4: 7.

———. 1995. "The Gulf of Mexico, the Academy, and Me." *Soundings* 78: 68.

———. 1998. "Rethinking Law in Globalizing Labor Markets" *University of Pennsylvania Journal of Labor and Employment Law* 1(2): 369–427.

Ansley, Frances, and John Gaventa. 1997. "Researching for Democracy and Democratizing Research." *Change Magazine* (Symposium Issue on Higher Education and Rebuilding Civic Life) 29(1): 46–53.

Arnold, Rick, Deborah Barndt, and Beverly Burke. 1985. *A New Weave: Popular Education in Canada and Central America.* Toronto: CUSO/OISE.

Barber, Benjamin. 1994. *Strong Democracy: Participatory Politics for a New Age.* Berkeley: University of California Press.

———. 1998. *A Passion for Democracy: American Essays.* Princeton, N.J.: Princeton University Press.

Barndt, Deborah. 1980. *Education and Social Change: A Photographic Study of Peru.* Dubuque, Iowa: Kendall/Hunt.

Boyer, Ernest. 1990. *Scholarship Reconsidered: Priorities of the Professoriate.* Princeton, N.J.: Carnegie Foundation for the Advancement of Teaching.

Boyte, Harry, and Nancy N. Kari. 1996. *The Democratic Promise of Public Work.* Philadelphia: Temple University Press.

Brown, Phil, and Edwin J. Mikkelson. 1990. *No Safe Place: Toxic Waste, Leukemia and Community Action.* Berkeley: University of California Press.

Burd, Stephen. 1994. "Scientists See Big Business on the Offensive: Researchers Say Industry Uses Federal Rules on Misconduct to Attack Findings It Doesn't Like." *Chronicle of Higher Education,* December 14, 1994, A26.

Cancian, Francesca M., and Cathleen Armstead. 1992. "Participatory Research." In *Encyclopedia of Sociology,* edited by Edgar F. Borgatta and Marie L. Borgatta. Vol. 3. New York: Macmillan.

Chambers, Robert. 1983. *Rural Development: Putting the Last First.* Burnt Mill, Harlow, Essex, U.K., and New York: Longman Scientific and Technical/Wiley.

———. 1997. *Whose Reality Counts? Putting the First Last.* London: Intermediate Technology.

Clark, Septima, with Cynthia Brown. 1986. *Ready from Within: Septima Clark and the Civil Rights Movement.* Navarro, Calif.: Wild Trees Press.

Cole, Luke W., and Sheila R. Foster. 2000. *From the Ground Up: Environmental Racism and the Rise of the Environmental Justice Movement.* New York: NYU Press.

De Roux, Gustavo I. 1991. "Together Against the Computer: PAR and the Struggle of Afro-Colombians for Public Service." In *Action and Knowledge: Breaking the Monopoly with Participatory Action-Research,* edited by Orlando Fals-Borda and Mohammad Anisur Rahman. New York: Apex Press.

Detroit-Genesee County Community-Based Public Health Consortium. 1994. "Community-Based Public Health Research Principles and Application Procedures." (On file with author.)

Doerge, Suzanne. 1994. "Feminist Popular Education: Transforming the World from Where Women Stand." OISE Papers. Ontario Institute for Studies in Education, University of Toronto.

Ehrlich, Thomas. 2000. *Civic Responsibility and Higher Education*. Phoenix, Ariz.: Oryx Press.

Epstein, Steven. 1991. "Democratic Science? AIDS Activism and the Contested Construction of Knowledge." *Socialist Review* 21(2): 35–64.

Fals-Borda, Orlando. 1991. "Some Basic Ingredients." In *Action and Knowledge: Breaking the Monopoly with Participatory Action-Research*, edited by Orlando Fals-Borda and Mohammad Anisur Rahman. New York: Apex Press.

———. 1998a. "Theoretical Foundations." In *People's Participation: Challenges Ahead*, edited by Orlando Fals-Borda and Immanuel Maurice Wallerstein. Bogotá, Colombia: Tercer Mundo Editores.

———. 1998b. "Cooptation and the New Scientific Paradigm." In *People's Participation: Challenges Ahead*, edited by Orlando Fals-Borda and Immanuel Maurice Wallerstein. Bogotá, Colombia: Tercer Mundo Editores.

Fals-Borda, Orlando, and Mohammad Anisur Rahman, eds. 1991. *Action and Knowledge: Breaking the Monopoly with Participatory Action-Research*. New York: Apex Press.

Fals-Borda, Orlando, and Immanuel Maurice Wallerstein, eds. 1998. *People's Participation: Challenges Ahead*. Bogotá, Colombia: Tercer Mundo Editores.

Fay, Brian. 1987. *Critical Social Science: Liberation and Its Limits*. Ithaca: Cornell University Press.

Fear, Frank A., and Lorilee R. Sandmann. 1995. "Unpacking the Service Category: Reconceptualizing University Outreach for the 21st Century." *Continuing Higher Education Review* 59(3): 110–22.

Freire, Paulo. 1970. *Pedagogy of the Oppressed*. New York: Continuum.

———. 1982. "Creating Alternative Research Methods: Learning to Do by Doing It." In *Creating Knowledge: A Monopoly? Participatory Research in Development*, edited by Budd Hall, Arthur Gillette, and Rajesh Tandon. New Delhi: Society for Participatory Research in Asia.

Gaventa, John. 1980. *Power and Powerlessness: Quiescence and Rebellion in an Appalachian Valley*. Urbana: University of Illinois Press.

———. 1991. "Toward a Knowledge Democracy: Viewpoints on Participatory Research in North America." In *Action and Knowledge: Breaking the Monopoly with Participatory Action-Research*, edited by Orlando Fals-Borda and Mohammad Anisur Rahman. New York: Apex Press.

———. 1998. "The Scaling Up and Institutionalization of PRA: Lessons and Challenges." In *Who Changes? Institutionalizing Participation in Development*, edited by James Blackburn with Jeremy Holland. London: Intermediate Technology.

Gaventa, John, and Billy D. Horton. 1981. "A Citizens' Research Project in Appalachia, USA." *Convergence* 3: 30.

Glen, John M. 1988. *Highlander: No Ordinary School, 1932–1962*. Lexington: University Press of Kentucky.

Gottlieb, Robert. 1997. "Janitors and Dry Cleaners: Constructing a Collaborative Model for Environmental Research." In *Building Community: Social Science in Action*, edited by Philip Nyden et al. Thousand Oaks, Calif.: Pine Forge Press.

Graber, Glen. 1994. "Participatory Action Research: The Regulatory Challenge." (On file with author.)

Green, L. W., et al. 1997. "Background on Participatory Research." In *Doing Community-Based Research: A Reader*, edited by Danny Murphy, Madeleine Scammell, and Richard Sclove. Amherst, Mass.: The Loka Institute.

Greenwood, Davydd J., and Morten Levin. 1998. *Introduction to Action Research: Social Research for Social Change.* Thousand Oaks, Calif.: Sage.

Hall, Budd. 1979. "Knowledge as a Commodity and Participatory Research." *Prospects* 9: 393.

Hope, Ann, and Sally Timmel. 1987. *Training for Transformation: A Handbook for Community Workers.* Guero, Zimbabwe: Mambo Press.

Horton, Myles (with Judith Kohl and Herbert Kohl). 1998. *The Long Haul: An Autobiography.* New York: Teachers College Press.

Horton, Myles, and Paulo Freire. 1990. *We Make the Road by Walking: Conversations on Education and Social Change,* edited by Brenda Bell, John Gaventa, and John Peters. Philadelphia: Temple University Press.

Instituto Mexicano para el Desarrollo Comunitario (IMDEC). 1989. *Punto y Seguido: Los Primeros 25 años de IMDEC.* Guadalajara, Jalisco, Mexico: IMDEC. (Available from IMDEC, the Mexican Institute for Community Development, in Guadalajara)

Inter-Church Coalition on Africa. 1993. *To Be a Woman: African Women's Response to the Economic Crisis: Video and Resource Guide.* Toronto: Inter-Church Coalition on Africa.

Joy, Peter. 1999. "Political Interference with Clinical Legal Education: Denying Access to Justice." *Tulane Law Review* 74: 235.

Kemmis, Stephen, 1988. "Action Research in Retrospect and Prospect." In *The Action Research Reader,* edited by Stephen Kemmis and Robert McTaggart (27–39). Victoria, Australia: Deakin University Press.

Kemmis, Stephen, and Robin McTaggart. 1988. "Introduction." In *The Action Research Reader,* edited by Stephen Kemmis and Robert McTaggart. Victoria, Australia: Deakin University Press.

LaBotz, Dan. 1991. *The Troublemaker's Handbook: How to Fight Back Where You Work—and Win!* Detroit: Labor Notes.

Lewis, Helen. 1998. "D. Myles Horton." In *People's Participation: Challenges Ahead,* edited by Orlando Fals-Borda. Bogotá, Columbia: Tercer Mundo Editores.

Lukes, Steven. 1974. *Power: A Radical View.* London and New York: Macmillan.

Maguire, Patricia. 1997. *Doing Participatory Research: A Feminist Approach.* Amherst: Center for International Education, University of Massachusetts, Amherst.

Marika, Raymattja, Dayngawa Ngurruwutthun, and Leon White. 1992. "Always Together, Yaka Gana: Participatory Research at Yirrkala as Part of Development of a Ylngu Education." In *A World of Communities: Participatory Research Perspectives,* edited by James S. Frideres. North York, Ontario: Captus University Publications.

Mathews, David. 1996. "The Public's Disenchantment with Professionalism: Reasons for Rethinking Academe's Service to the Country." *Journal of Public Service Outreach* 1: 21.

Merrifield, Juliet. 1979. "Putting Scientists in Their Place: Participatory Research in Environmental and Occupational Health." In *Voices of Change: Participatory Research in the United States and Canada,* edited by Peter Park et al. London and Westport, Conn.: Bergin and Garvey.

Murphy, Danny, et al., eds. 1997. *Doing Community-Based Research: A Reader.* Available from the Loka Institute at: *www.loka.org.*

Nadeau, Denise. 1996. *Counting Our Victories: Popular Education and Organizing—A Training Guide on Popular Education and Organizing.* Toronto: Repeal the Deal.

National Commission on Civic Renewal. 1998. *A Nation of Spectators: How Civic Disengagement Weakens America and What We Can Do About It.* College Park, Md.: National Commission on Civic Renewal.

Núñez, Carlos. 1990. *Más Sabe el Pueblo: Anécdotas y Testimonios de Educadores Populares Latinoamericanos.* Guadalajara, Jalisco, Mexico: Instituto Mexicano para el Desarrollo Comunitario (Mexican Institute for Community Development). Available from IMDEC in Guadalajara.

Nyden, Philip, Anne Figert, Mark Shibley, and Darryl Burrows. 1997a. *Building Community: Social Science in Action.* Thousand Oaks, Calif.: Pine Forge Press.

———. 1997b. "University-Community Collaborative Research: Adding Chairs at the Research Table." In *Building Community: Social Science in Action,* edited by Philip Nyden et al. Thousand Oaks, Calif.: Pine Forge Press.

Nyden, Philip, and Wim Wiewel. 1992. "Collaborative Research: Harnessing the Tensions Between Researcher and Practitioner." *American Sociologist* 23(4): 43–55.

Park, Peter. 1993. "What Is Participatory Research? A Theoretical and Methodological Perspective." In *Voices of Change: Participatory Research in the United States and Canada,* edited by Peter Park et al. London and Westport, Conn.: Bergin and Garvey.

Phenix, Lucy Massie. 1985. *You Got to Move: Stories of Change in the South.* (A film available on video from First Run/Icarus Films and in many public libraries.)

Press, Eyal, and Jennifer Washburn. 2000. "The Kept University." *Atlantic Monthly,* March.

Rahman, Mohammad Anisur. 1991. "The Theoretical Standpoint of PAR." In *Action and Knowledge: Breaking the Monopoly with Participatory Action-Research,* edited by Orlando Fals-Borda and Mohammad Anisur Rahman. New York: Apex Press.

———. 1993. *People's Self-Development: Perspectives on Participatory Action Research.* London and New Jersey: Zed Books.

Rahman, Mohammad Anisur, and Orlando Fals-Borda. 1991. "A Self-Review of PAR." In *Action and Knowledge: Breaking the Monopoly with Participatory Action-Research,* edited by Orlando Fals-Borda and Mohammad Anisur Rahman. New York: Apex Press.

Reason, Peter. 2000. "Three Approaches to Participative Inquiry." In *Handbook of Qualitative Research,* edited by Norman K. Denzin and Yvonna S. Lincoln. Thousand Oaks, Calif.: Sage.

Reason, Peter, and John Roward. 1981. *Human Inquiry: A Sourcebook of New Paradigm Research.* London: John Wiley & Sons.

Riano, Pilar. 1991. *Women in Grassroots Communication.* New Westminster, British Columbia, and Thousand Oaks, Calif.: Repeal the Deal Productions/Sage.

Robinson, William. 1996. *Promoting Polyarchy: Globalization, U.S. Intervention, and Hegemony.* Cambridge: Cambridge University Press.

Sclove, Richard, et al. 1998. *Community-Based Research in the United States: An Introductory Reconnaisance.* Available at: *www.loka.org.*

Soley, Lawrence. 1995. *Leasing the Ivory Tower: the Corporate Takeover of Academia.* Boston: South End Press.

Tandon, Rajesh. 1982. "A Critique of Monopolistic Research." In *Creating Knowledge: A Monopoly? Participatory Research in Development,* edited by Budd Hall, Arthur Gillette, and Rajesh Tandon. New Delhi: Society for Participatory Research in Asia.

White, Lucie. 1998. "Facing South: Lawyering for Poor Communities in the Twenty-First Century." *Fordham Urban Law Journal* 25: 813.

Williams, Lee. 1996. "An Annotated Bibliography for Participatory and Collaborative Field Research Methods." Knoxville: Community Partnership Center, University of Tennessee.

———. 1997a. *Grassroots Participatory Research: A Working Report from a Gathering of Practitioners.* Knoxville: Community Partnership Center, University of Tennessee.

———. 1997b. "Roofless Women's Action Research Mobilization." In *Grassroots Participatory Research: A Working Report from a Gathering of Practitioners,* edited by Lee Williams. Knoxville: Community Partnership Center, University of Tennessee.

———. 1997c. "Maquiladora Worker Exchange Project, Tennessee Industrial Renewal Network." In *Grassroots Participatory Research: A Working Report from a Gathering of Practitioners,* edited by Lee Williams. Knoxville: Community Partnership Center, University of Tennessee.

World Bank. 1995. *Putting People First.* Washington, D.C.: World Bank.

Commentary

Quiescence: The Scylla and Charybdis of Empowerment

Joel F. Handler

T he essays in this book are part of a long tradition of ethnography of the poor. Being somewhat arbitrary, the more recent period could start with Elliot Liebow's *Tally's Corner* (1967), which reported on the lives of African American men who would gather on a street corner in Washington, D.C. The book is important because its subject is the African American male, usually ignored in academic research (or when discussed, usually in severely negative terms). Moreover, the men come through as people who try to cope in the face of a harsh society and, contrary to the popular stereotype, care about their partners, families, and friends. Liebow documents the point that dysfunctional, negative, culture-of-poverty behavior in the eyes of middle-class observers in fact is functional behavior in a hostile environment. One example is the then popular deferred gratification theory, which held that the poor could not save money because they cannot defer their gratification (in the manner, that is, of the sober, debt-burdened middle class). Liebow points out that quickly converting cash into durable goods is a way of avoiding the inevitable, hard-to-resist requests for loans. In other words, spending for durables is a method of saving in the inner city. This is strategic coping behavior, not pathology.

Over the years has been a steady stream of excellent studies that document similar behavior. In addition to the work of Elijah Anderson, Katherine Newman, Kathryn Edin and Laura Lein, to mention only a few—for example, White (1990), Sarat (1990), Ewick and Silbey (1998), and Gilliom (1997)—are many others. Aside from the rich, detailed, informative discussions in these works of people who normally appear only as survey statistics, the important message that comes through is that many of the poor are not passive, dependent, weak objects. Instead, they show resilience, intelligence, and courage as they are forced to cope with multiple, adverse conditions ranging from family and friends and neighborhoods to scores of public and private agencies.

The ethnography expands on the basic point Liebow makes—that many of the poor are adept at a variety of survival skills. Yet they also make the additional point that in many instances, the seemingly downtrodden not only are able to resist harsh and punitive measures, but also to manipulate these systems for their advantage. The portrait that emerges is one of subjects rather than objects, that the poor (or at least the subjects of the various studies) are knowledgeable, active people who, at least to some extent, have control over their lives. *Resistance* is a key concept. A favorite example is the ability of welfare families to increase their well-being through various kinds of unreported income (Gilliom 1997). This ethnography tradition is important; it not only is humane but crucial for our understanding and our policy choices to recognize that the poor are subjects (Handler 1990). To try to understand *their* world and to build on their capacities is important.

I would like to raise a cautionary note. Romanticization is a concern. In the celebration of the struggles and apparent successes, are we forgetting that when the day is over, the poor still are trying to cope under severe conditions, they remain in poverty, and despite acts of resistance, they continue to be very dependent? The worry is that in the celebrations, we go overboard in believing that change will come from the bottom, and that we do not pay sufficient attention to difficulties of empowerment. For example, Stephen Winter (1996, 721), in discussing Foucault's understanding of power as a system of relations, writes,

> The second advantage of this reconception of power is that *it is, in a profound sense, empowering*. To understand power as a property of a social system of relations is to see power as a shared resource that can be activated from many different positions within that system. Once power is understood as relational, it becomes apparent that at least some of what the dominant "have" must already be available to the subordinated. . . . The deconstruction of power is also the deconstruction of agency and autonomy of the traditional liberal subject. This means that responsibility for subordination and inequality cannot be localized in certain identifiable agents; it is widely distributed throughout the social network. To the exact degree that this understanding of power diminishes the agency of the dominant, it amplifies the agency of the subordinated. What it subtracts from one part of the network, it necessarily redistributes to the other.

We will return to this quote subsequently, but aside from the concluding statement, "Still, transformation is not going to be easy," there is no discussion of empowerment. This is fairly typical. The men in *Tally's Corner* become subjects, they can cope, which is important and valuable, but at the end of the day they cannot escape.

This concern is best illustrated by discussing the problem of quiescence. The informed citizen model is that if the citizen acquiesces in a decision affecting his or her interests, the citizen agrees with the decision. This is true even for quiescence, which often is construed as silent acceptance. In principle, we know that this is not necessarily true, but in practice, we often act as if it were true. While quiescence—indeed, the informed citizen or consumer—presents difficulties for the educated middle class, it is especially troublesome as one moves down the socioeconomic ladder. For the poor, alternatives and life chances are more limited. In Cintrón-Vélez's chapter on homeless families in three shelters (ch. 4 herein), many public and private agencies are involved in the lives of these families: public and private housing, child protection services, police, welfare, food stamps, Medicaid and health services, education and training, day care, employers, as well as others. The other chapters report similar dense relationships. How much understanding do the poor have of the rules and regulations, of the reasons for decisions that are made?

Consider some issues that have arisen as part of the current welfare reform—the unexpected, large declines in food stamps and Medicaid enrollments even though families who lose welfare still are eligible for these two programs, and the significant decline in new cases (Brito 2000). Are those who fail to sign up being deliberately misled? Are they under their own mistaken assumption that they no longer are eligible? Or have they decided independently that they no longer want "welfare"? At the present time is only silence. What does it mean? How their silence is interpreted—whether society will even bother to find out—depends initially on conceptions of not only who the poor are but also what we understand about power and empowerment. Another issue involves the use of sanctions. In a current study of welfare sanctions, counties have provided a list of recipients who have been sanctioned; yet in telephone interviews, the recipients were unaware that they were sanctioned. They viewed the changes in the grant amounts as another example of the unfathomable, bewildering bureaucracy.[1] Coping and resistance is empowerment. Empowerment requires not only feelings of self-efficacy but also an understanding of the environment and a vision of feasible alternatives.

Let us consider one more illustration from the past. During the War on Poverty, when the government still was interested in building housing for the poor, a group of reform-minded architects decided to ask the prospective tenants what kind of apartments they would like. To the dismay of the architects, the residents described "railroad" apartments—rooms positioned end to end. These were the apartments in which they grew up, in Chicago. The architects then decided to construct models of apartments. This time, the tenants selected the models. The easy point, of course, is that in the first go around, the tenants had no experience with a different style of apartment. Here the architects had the sense and values to ask the tenants, and the means to present alternatives. Yet this kind of sensitivity and ability to present alternatives may be rare. In other scenarios, those in power do not care what the tenants want, or they think they know what the tenants want, or they take the tenants at their word. The first two examples are familiar exercises of power, but how to interpret the last? Are the tenants empowered when they are given limited choices? Isn't second-guessing the tenants paternalistic?

This leads to a discussion of power. How is power structured in the lives of the poor, who must cope with dozens of agencies for their daily existence? Power is not always direct and observable; often it is subtle and manipulative. The standard definition of power is: A has power over B to the extent that A can get B to do something that B would not otherwise do.[2] At first blush, this defi-nition seems unproblematic, especially in the context of the dependent bureau-cratic client. The client, as the price of receiving something needed, has to do something that the official insists on, such as participate in a work program, reveal a matter of privacy, or engage in other kinds of behaviors. The model assumes an objective conflict of interests, with a direct exercise of power and a knowing, albeit unwilling, submission.

Suppose, however, that the client willingly submits. Has power been exer-cised if B *appears* to do what A wants? Now the situation becomes more prob-lematic. What does consent or quiescence mean in a hierarchical relationship? Can we take the client's position at face value? What other choice do we have? Steven Lukes (1974) argues that there are three dimensions of power. The one-dimensional approach is the example just given, where A gets B to do some-thing B otherwise would not have done. This dimension focuses on observable behavior; as such, it assumes that grievances and conflicts are recognized and acted on. Nonparticipation or inaction can be seen as consent or alienation. Qui-escence lies in the characteristics of the victims; it is not constrained by power.

The two-dimensional view of power seeks to meet this last point. Barach and Baratz argue that power has a "second face" by which it is not only exercised upon the participants within the decision-making arenas but also operates to exclude participants and issues altogether: that is, power not only involves who gets what, when, and how, but also who gets left out and under what circum-stances (Barach and Baratz 1962; Barach and Botwinick 1992). Some issues never get on the political agenda—for example, the issue of pollution in a com-pany-dominated town. The study of power also must include barriers to the expression of grievances.

According to Lukes, the two-dimensional view, while a considerable ad-vance, does not go far enough; it fails to account for how power may affect even the conception of grievances. The absence of grievances may be due to a manip-ulated consensus. Furthermore, the dominant group may be so secure that its members are oblivious to anyone challenging their position: "the most effective and insidious use of power is to prevent . . . conflict from arising in the first place." This is the third dimension of power. A exercises power over B not only by getting B to do what he does not want to do, but A "also exercises power over him by influencing, shaping or determining his very wants" (Lukes 1974).

An important characteristic of the three-dimensional view is that it is not confined to looking at the exercise of power in an individualistic, behavioral framework; rather, it focuses on the various ways by which potential con-flicts are excluded. This view is much more sociological than either the one-or perhaps the two-dimensional view. In three dimensions, two theoretical approaches are combined—the hegemonic social and historical patterns iden-tified by Gramsci and the subjective effects of power identified by Edelman.[3]

What are the mechanisms of power in the three dimensions? In the first dimension are the conventional political resources used by political actors—

votes, influence, jobs. The second dimension adds what Barach and Baratz call the "mobilization of bias." These are the rules of the game—values, beliefs, rituals, as well as institutional procedures—that systematically benefit certain groups at the expense of others. The mobilization of bias operates not only in the decision-making arenas but also—in fact primarily—through "non-decisions" whereby demands are "suffocated before they are voiced, or kept covert; or killed before they gain access to the relevant decision-making arena; or failing all of these things, maimed or destroyed in the decision-implementing stage of the policy process" (Barach and Baratz 1962).

Three-dimensional mechanisms of power include not only the control of information and socialization processes, but also fatalism, self-deprecation, apathy, and the internalization of dominant values and beliefs—the psychological adaptations of the oppressed to escape the subjective sense of powerlessness. Voices become echoes rather than grievances and demands. As Paulo Freire puts it, because dependent societies are prevented from either participation or reflection, they are denied the very experience necessary for the development of a critical consciousness; instead, they develop a "culture of silence" (Freire 1970; see also Bumiller 1988; Gaventa 1980). Moreover, the culture of silence may lend legitimacy to the dominant order. Finally, if the dependent voices do emerge, they are especially vulnerable to manipulation by the powerful.

While Lukes's three faces of power is very influential, this model has been criticized as presenting a view of power that is overly monolithic, sovereign, top-down—in short, hegemonic. Such a view emphasizes negative, prohibitory power, the denial of sovereignty to sovereign individuals. Poststructuralists argue that power is never so complete, that a dialectic always exists between agents. (Clegg 1989). Power, according to Foucault, is "four dimensional": it is not a "thing" possessed solely by individual agents (the powerful), but rather a dynamic system of "performances"; and "the powerful, too, are subjects produced by the operations of power." According to Winter (1996), Foucault argues that every one—the powerful and the seemingly powerless—is "constructed by the processes of power. But it is not all-determining precisely because it is a process. . . . As Foucault put it: 'The individual is an effect of power, and at the same time, or precisely to the extent to which it is that effect, it is the element of its articulation.'" An illustration of this fourth dimension perhaps can be found in one of the more prominent examples of welfare resistance: the withholding of unearned income. This is resistance on the part of the welfare recipient—the deliberate violation of the rules in order to survive. Yet this resistance is often with the tacit acceptance of the welfare workers. They know that families cannot survive on welfare alone. If they enforce the rules, this not only will consume scarce administrative time (their time, in particular), but also may incur larger local government costs if the family has to be broken up. The fact that in many cases strong inducements exist for workers to accept the resistance of the clients means that power is relational rather than hegemonic. Count-

/ 275

less similar examples range from prison officers who share power with inmates to achieve some kind of order to agencies who depend on clients to enhance the success of their programs—for example, good students, clients of employment agencies with good social capital, voluntary patients for drug rehabilitation, and so forth.

This is an important correction—or reminder—that clients are subjects as well as objects. Nevertheless, poststructuralists readily concede that meanings, practices, and networks of interests become fixed or reified in certain forms, and this fixity is power. Power is relational, but when these relational interests are reproduced, when they become fixed or reified, then power tends to be regarded as thinglike, material, concrete. Despite theoretical instability, in practice power can be "as 'objective' as the policeman's power to arrest" because of the "fixity of stabilized disciplinary powers and discursive practices" (Clegg 1989, 177). In sum, in the practical, day-to-day world of bureaucratic relationships, there appears to be a high degree of convergence as to the characteristics or manifestations of power.[4] Depending on the situation, power can be objectively observed as A getting B to do what B would not ordinarily desire, to the subtle manipulations of the agenda, to the construction of ideologies and meaning, so that B is not aware of alternatives.

The three-dimensional view of power poses significant methodological problems. A major challenge raised to the two-dimensional view is the empirical difficulty of observing a "non-event." With the third dimension, "how can one study what does not happen?" (Gaventa 1980). How can one tell whether B would have *thought* and *acted* differently? At issue here is imputing interests and values to the voiceless. An even greater difficulty arises in empirically verifying the third dimension. How do we know, for instance, whether quiescent consent is genuine or manipulated? How does the researcher (the dominant group) avoid imputing his or her values, the social construction of meaning, to the quiescent? In real life, however, the methodological issues in fact may not be that severe in many situations. If major inequalities exist in social relations, one should not assume at the outset that quiescence is natural but rather seek other explanations. In less obvious situations, Gaventa (1980, 15–16) suggests a number of steps to try to explain the inaction. He would look to the historical development of the apparent consensus to see how the situation was arrived at and how the consensus has been maintained. He would look at the processes of communication and socialization and the relationship between ideologies and beliefs. Different power relationships may provide comparative examples. Yet "if . . . no mechanisms of power can be identified and no relevant counterfactuals can be found, then the researcher must conclude that the quiescence of a given deprived group is, in fact, based upon consensus of that group to their condition, owing for instance, to differing values from those initially posited by the observer."

Concepts of empowerment mirror the multiple meanings of power. Power or empowerment is "the ability to act effectively" (Barach and Botwinick 1992).

Empowerment is both psychological and behavioral: it involves a sense of perceived control, of competence, a critical awareness of one's environment, and involvement in activities that in fact exert control. Empowerment is more than an absence of alienation or sense of helplessness. Empowerment involves a sense of connectedness; it is a long-term process of learning and development where connections are made between the experiences of daily life and perceptions of personal efficacy (Keiffer 1984; Zimmerman 1993; Zimmerman and Rappaport 1988).

The process of empowerment must be specific—generalized feelings of injustice or consciousness raising are not sufficient. Empowerment must involve a "personally experienced sense of outrage or confrontation," accompanied by "participatory competence"—getting over being scared, demystifying the symbols of power and authority, that is, coming to realize that officials do not know everything, and that ordinary people can change things" (Keiffer 1984, 31). Action must be reflective. Direct experience is used not only to gain skills, but also to increase understanding and confidence that, in turn, increases motivation. Eventually, the participants achieve an "increasingly self-conscious awareness of self as a visible and effective actor in the community." Empowerment is a "long-term and continuing process of adult development" (Keiffer 1984, 31).

The complex, subtle, patient development of empowerment is beautifully discussed in Lucie White's description of Head Start volunteers (ch. 6 herein). Many of these women—impoverished, victims of domestic and governmental abuse (AFDC), depressed—gained strength and confidence, over a long period, working with mentors (older, salaried staff) and, in turn, patiently helping children in need. These women regain confidence in themselves, rediscover their voices, reassert their subjectivity, and gradually gain control of their lives as they become important actors in their local programs.

The expanded role of the Head Start volunteers, as described by White, illustrates that power versus empowerment is not a zero-sum game—a contest between the agency and the client; what the client gains the agency has to give up. As discussed in the poststructuralist "fourth dimension," the zero-sum assumption does not sufficiently take into account the many situations where organizations bargain rather than rely strictly on commands. In a world of competition and unstable environments, there can be many reasons why organizations will find it in their self-interest to strike deals rather than attempt to secure their position by force of will. Bargaining, of course, occurs where the regulated subject has something that the agency needs but lacks the ability to command. Regulatory agency bargains with regulated industries are well known (Ayres and Braithwaite 1992; Bardach and Kagan 1982). Organizations may bargain to save scarce resources, to gain a more favorable solution, or to acquire resources that the client controls (for example, information). Imposing formal sanctions often is time consuming and expensive; often it is easier to make a deal (Hawkins 1984).

In sum, power and empowerment is a dynamic process that has both psychological and material or substantive aspects. Relationships are not stable. Resources and perceptions change; power changes as well. Specifically, all else being equal, we can expect that over time power gradually will shift to the more powerful agency. The agency has the surer command over resources; it has the staying power. This means that empowered clients must keep struggling to maintain their position, which involves a continuous structure of incentives; otherwise, energy will dissipate, and clients will become passive and coopted.

The contextual embeddedness and fluidity of power and the precariousness of empowerment highlight the ambiguities in the ethnography of the poor. The rich "counter-hegemonic stories" and focus on "identity as a weapon in the moral politics of work and poverty" is a two-edged sword. Both the observer-author *and* the reader view the subjects through their *individual* moral lenses. For the authors and readers (or at least most readers), this volume is a celebration of the humanity and struggles of the poor. This is certainly—at least from my perspective—a valuable, humane endeavor. This kind of work will help the process of inclusion. Yet it should not be forgotten that this view of the poor—as subjects in control of their lives—is also the view behind the current conservative welfare reform. The "work first" strategy assumes that any job is better than no job, and that by taking an entry-level job the poor will move up the employment ladder. Like it or not, the emphasis on "responsibility" assumes an active, capable agent who then will overcome all odds—with no discussion of poverty or lack of health care or lousy schools and dangerous neighborhoods. White's Head Start women have gained a lot. They have found their voices, they will have the strength to leave abusive relationships, and start the difficult task of re-creating their lives and the lives of their children. That is cause for celebration, but it is not enough. Their environment requires major changes. They can guide their children in school and deal with teachers and principals, but they cannot offer a range of advanced placement courses. They cannot provide accessible health care clinics. They cannot provide safe neighborhoods. Empowerment of the poor is a vital first step, but it will remain fragile and problematic in a hostile environment.

NOTES

1. Professor Yeheskel Hasenfeld is doing an empirical study of welfare sanctions in four California counties.

2. While this may be a common and for our purposes useful definition of power, in fact no agreement exists on the various meanings of power, according to Talcott Parsons (1986, 94):

   Power is one of the key concepts in the great Western tradition about political phenomena. It is at the same time a concept on which, in spite of its long history, there is, on analytical levels, a notable lack of agreement both about its specific definition, and about many features of the conceptual context in which it should be placed. There is, however, a core complex of its meaning having to do with the capacity of persons or collectivities "to get things done" effectively, in particular when their goals are obstructed by some kind of human resistance or opposition.

The Lukes volume contains a series of essays on various approaches to power. At the end of the introduction, Lukes observes, "[I]n our ordinary unreflective judgments and comparisons of power, we normally know what we mean and have little difficulty in understanding one another, yet every attempt at a single general answer to the question has failed and seems likely to fail" (Parsons 1986, 17). For further discussion of power see, for example, Clegg 1989; Honneth 1991; Winter 1996.

3. "Political actions chiefly arouse or satisfy people not by granting or withholding their stable, or substantive demands but rather by changing their demands and expectations" (Edelman 1971, 8; see also Gramsci 1971; Gaventa 1980).

4. For example, in describing the evolution of Foucault's theory of power, Honneth (1991, 173) says,

Accordingly, he no longer regards individual actors or social groups as the subjects of this developed form of the exercise of power, but instead social institutions such as the school, the prison, or the factory—institutions that he himself must comprehend as highly complex structures of solidified positions of social power. The frame of reference for the concept of power has, therefore, secretly been shifted from a theory of action to an analysis of institutions.

REFERENCES

Ayres, Ian, and John Braithwaite. 1992. *Responsive Regulation: Transcending the Deregulation Debate*. New York: Oxford University Press.

Barach, Peter, and Martin Baratz. 1962. "The Two Faces of Power." *American Political Science Review* 56: 947.

Barach, Peter, and Aryeh Botwinick. 1992. *Power and Empowerment: A Radical Theory of Participatory Democracy*. Philadelphia: Temple University Press.

Bardach, Eugene, and Robert Kagan. 1982. *Going by the Book: The Problem of Regulatory Unreasonableness*. Philadelphia: Temple University Press.

Brito, Tonya. "The Welfarization of Family Law." *University of Kansas Law Review* 48(January): 229.

Bumiller, Kristen. 1988. *The Civil Rights Society: The Social Construction of Victims*. Baltimore: Johns Hopkins University Press.

Clegg, Stewart. 1989. *Frameworks of Power*. Newbury Park, Calif.: Sage.

Edelman, Murray. 1971. *The Symbolic Uses of Politics*. Urbana: University of Illinois Press.

Ewick, Patricia, and Susan Silbey. 1998. *The Common Place of Law*. Chicago: University of Chicago Press.

Freire, Paulo. 1970. *Pedagogy of the Oppressed*. New York: Continuum.

Gaventa, John. 1980. *Power and Powerlessness: Quiescence and Rebellion in an Appalachian Valley*. Urbana: University of Illinois Press.

Gilliom, John. 1997. "Everyday Surveillance, Everyday Resistance: Computer Monitoring in the Lives of the Appalachian Poor." *Studies in Law, Politics and Society* 16: 275.

Gramsci, Antonio. 1971. *Selections from the Prison Notebooks.* New York: International Publishers.

Handler, Joel. 1990. *Law and the Search for Community.* Philadelphia: University of Pennsylvania Press.

Hawkins, Keith. 1984. *Environment and Enforcement: Regulation and the Social Definition of Pollution.* Oxford: Clarendon Press.

Honneth, Alex. 1991. *The Critique of Power: Reflective States in Critical Social Theory.* Cambridge, Mass.: MIT Press.

Keiffer, Charles. 1984. "Citizen Empowerment: A Developmental Perspective." *Prevention in Human Services* 3: 9–36.

Liebow, Elliot. 1967. *Tally's Corner: A Study of Negro Streetcorner Men.* Boston: Little, Brown.

Lukes, Steven. 1974. *Power: A Radical View.* London and New York: Macmillan.

Parsons, Talcott. 1986. "Power and the Social System." In *Power: A Radical View,* edited by Steven Lukes. London and New York: Macmillan.

Sarat, Austin. 1990. ". . . The Law Is All Over: Power, Resistance and the Legal Consciousness of the Welfare Poor." *Yale Journal of Law and Humanities* 2: 343.

White, Lucie. 1990. "Subordination, Rhetorical Survival Skills, and Sunday Shoes: Notes on the Hearing of Mrs. G." *Buffalo Law Review* 38: 1.

Winter, Stephen. 1996. "The 'Power' Thing." *Virginia Law Review* 82: 721.

Zimmerman, Marc. 1993. "Empowerment Theory: Psychological, Organizational and Community Levels of Analysis." In *Handbook of Community Psychology,* edited by J. Rappaport and E. Seidman. New York: Kluwer Academic/Plenum.

Zimmerman, Marc, and J. Rappaport. 1988. "Citizen Participation, Perceived Control, and Psychological Empowerment." *American Journal of Community Psychology* 16: 725–50.

Commentary

Taking Dialogue Seriously

Michael Frisch

The conference that led to this volume took on a profound problem. Deeply rooted cultural stereotypes of the poor, despite decades of critique, have continued to control the discourse and politics of poverty policy, even as the focus shifts from inner-city welfare to the broader contours of low-wage and marginalized labor in a globalizing economy. These have constituted a formidable barrier to policy and political action, and inhibit, more broadly, the very research about poverty and the poor so necessary to any strategy for change. The conference sought to transcend these barriers through an unusual approach: focusing on how narratives of poverty illuminate the complexities of a rapidly changing landscape of social realities; and how making the experiences, understandings, and agency of poor people themselves a central focus might permit the creation of new research and a new politics for engaging these changes.

The remarkable chapters and commentaries collected in this volume speak to the usefulness of this approach. Yet as an enthusiastic reader and active participant in these discussions, in reviewing the conference I am struck by how hard it proved to focus on what listening to and learning from narratives might mean, and how hard it seemed to be—even in a setting dedicated to this end—to discuss admitting the voices of the poor into active dialogue with those considering the realm of policy and political action.

This difficulty—perhaps even resistance—seems to me instructive and worth some reflection. My perspective is that of a historian working with the meaning and uses of oral history in documenting recent structural economic changes understandable under the heading of *deindustrialization*. Oral history, of course, has been embraced for some time as a tool for giving voice to those who have been excluded from the historical record, and so it inevitably must seem a kind of natural resource useful for the altered perspective sought by the conference organizers. Yet for historians, the dilemmas and tensions embedded in this appeal have complicated the reception and usefulness of oral history in the construction of new historical narratives—in ways worth brief mention, since they bear so directly on how considering narratives of poverty in some ways did (and in others, did not) manage to transform the framework of discussion as much as might have been hoped by conference organizers.

One approach to oral history—the "more history" approach—always has resisted any notion of special claims and qualities for the kind of evidence it produces. According to this view, the point of oral history is simply to help us shine a flashlight into an otherwise dark and unreachable corner of the basement or attic to find some things to bring out to the workshop where they might then be tested, refined, hammered, and milled like any other bit of evidence. The emphasis in this approach always has been on oral history as data, with the privilege of analysis and interpretation reserved for the synthesizing historian.

A contrasting approach has tended to reverse this emphasis entirely, seeing the "voice of the people" as self-explanatory and self-empowering. In such terms, oral history is offered as a way to confront, challenge, contradict, and even eliminate the interpretive power of historians and what they are presumed to represent. Offered as a kind of antihistory, this approach raises crucial questions about the ground and legitimacy of historical explanation; its defects are just as obvious, a naive romanticization of "the people" chief among them.

Over the past twenty-five years, much of the excitement and energy of oral history has come from the effort to find a way between the rock and hard place that each of these poles can be taken to represent. That is, to see oral history as evidence, in a broad sense, going beyond data: to read interviews as more complex interpretive dialogues, however implicit, in which we can hear, learn from, and engage actively the ever-present narrative perspective of the interviewee in a process that returns us to a more basic meaning of their *subjectivity*—a term that until recently has had only a pejorative meaning for many historians.

For many of us, though, to find ways to promote and represent this complexity has remained hard. What Jacquelyn Hall has called the "interpretive authority of ordinary people" often has been obscured by the seamless historical narrative "illustrated" by vivid oral history excerpts (Hall et al. 2000, 3). Alternatively, relatively unmediated oral history documents often are presented as if their meaning and implications were self-evident, which tends rarely to be the case.

Recent trends in scholarship have, if anything, made this dilemma worse. A new generation of cultural studies and social history has centered on the complex social construction of identities, on the culturally embodied intersections of race, class, and gender, on the complexity of social memory, and on understanding the profound tensions between hegemony and agency. Yet we have paid a heavy price for these insights, mainly in the form of a scholarly discourse so relentlessly theorized as to lose touch with the people and narrative realities it deals with, much less with a wider readership. The emerging consensus is that for all its accomplishments, contemporary scholarship has effected what could be called a discursive disconnect from the very people, issues, and interests it presumes to interpret. More prosaically, such scholarship is at serious risk of a terminal case of "paralysis from the analysis."

Ironically, many of the issues such contemporary scholarship has spotlighted with great intellectual huffing and puffing, such as the social construction of memory, the dialogics of intersubjectivity, and so on, are issues oral historians have necessarily confronted—if not always as self-consciously—in the very conduct of an interview or fieldwork and in any careful work with evidence arising from these. They are issues embodied by definition in the vivid, complex human stories oral history produces. They are generated as well in the complex relationships enacted in fieldwork or interviews and inevitably they are inscribed or encoded—we would say in today's jargon, without much value added—in resulting *texts*.

One of oral history's redeeming qualities is that it presents such sophisticated and complex issues in the form of lived experience and living conversation. As such, these complexities must be dealt with in highly concrete decisions about the conduct, handling, editing, presentation, and interpretation of interview narratives. In this form, the abstractions of theory cannot so easily get away from the stubborn corporeality and materiality of real people commenting on their own lives and realities and presenting them to us. Conversely, to reduce narrative to simply another form of raw data for interpretation is also harder. Once this is understood, to appreciate the capacity of narratives and testimonies to inform, challenge, complicate, and shape our own categories and questions becomes easier. This is especially true if we are willing to share with interview subjects the authority of interpretation. Such narratives offer an interpretive dialogue that is implicit in the relationships that produce ethnographic or documentary evidence in the first place, and often explicit, if we stop to listen for it, in the texts generated in the process.

I have some experience with the capacity of working-class narratives of industry and deindustrialization to provide such insights, having collected and published *Portraits in Steel,* a series of life-history interviews with Buffalo, New York, steelworkers in the aftermath of the virtual evaporation of that region's once-mighty steel industry (Frisch and Rogovin 1993). In this work, I was struck repeatedly by how regularly and easily interview subjects moved around the convenient categories presented to them, frequently of an either-or nature, when asked to describe industrial work, family, and community before, during, and after job loss of this kind. The steelworkers both liked their jobs and hated them. They often identified with the union or the company, yet felt betrayed by either or both. They saw themselves as victims of the plant closings, yet refused to act or feel victimized. They were deeply nostalgic and yet fully involved in moving on. Even more to the point, they resisted the notion that their lives were defined by their work situation, past or present, offering instead a more seamless web in which worlds of family, neighborhood, and community were woven together with work and workplace in their own identities.

My project focused on big-city workers in a grand-scale primary industry filled with romance and awesome power. Perhaps still a bit impressed by these qualities, I did not quite expect to find such similar patterns in a very different context. Then, a few years ago, I encountered an oral history–photographic documentary project focused on a different world. Recently published as a book, this is the story of a woman named Linda Lord, who has been displaced from her job in the "Blood Tunnel" of a small chicken-processing factory in rural Maine, a woman to whose work nobody, leastwise the subject herself, attaches anything close to romance or excitement (Rouverol, Chatterley, and Cole 2000).

As documented, framed, and commented on by the folklorist Alicia Rouverol and the photographer Cedric Chatterley, Linda's work, her sense of family responsibilities, community, and place, her interests in music (she plays in a rock band) and motorcycles—all are crucially intertwined, making the job loss and her response to it at once more and less complicated, more constraining, and more cushioned. The dense weave of detail in Linda's narrative defines, in its sum, the perspective from which she documents and presents the complexity of her life. Hers is a perspective similar in complexity to the one I read in the steelworker narratives I collected. It is a perspective reducible neither to the romance of making steel nor to the nonromance of killing chickens, but one grounded, rather, in some larger, embracing realities about working-class life in communities and a world in transition.

The lessons of these perspectives perhaps are best drawn by readers rather than pronounced on by commentators. In the case of *Portraits in Steel*, we insisted on permitting readers to engage and learn from the narrative and photographic portraits directly, rather than treating these as so much raw material to be pushed through interpretive mills of our own devising. For present purposes, however, I will claim one word to address some of the issues we all wrestled with for several intense days at the Buffalo conference—*multivalence*. Let me explain.

I first encountered Linda Lord's story at the Tenth Berkshire Conference on the History of Women, held in Chapel Hill, North Carolina, in the summer of 1996. Our session, "When Plants Shut Down," included a paper by Alicia Rouverol featuring generous drafts of Linda Lord's interviews and Cedric Chatterley's photographs. The conference was wonderful, but as with many academic congresses, the air was thick with jargon. Our panel was happily immune, though—so much so that someone said that we were at risk of being buzzword deficient. So we appropriated one of our own: referring to a quality discovered in the several papers, this was *multivalence*, with the accent on the second syllable, so as to echo but contrast with *ambivalence*.

Ambivalence inevitably suggests uncertain feelings or a confusion of values. *Multivalence*, however, evokes the very different quality that we were hearing: multi-valents, many values, the holding of different values at once without implying confusion, contradiction, or even paradox. *Multivalence* implies a way of being in the world—one that may be particularly characteristic of the experience of "others," challenging and complicating a dominant culture's categories and asking us to think about things in very different ways. As in the provocative quote from Linda Lord that Alicia Rouverol chose for the title of her book, "I was content and not content."

As a final connection to the paradox of a narrative conference not fully comfortable with the power of narrative—which is to say not fully comfortable with narrators—let's look at that title and its implications more closely. To this end, I hope it's not too indulgent to offer a personal story that may seem even further afield, if Anton Chekhov and turn-of-the-century Russian aristocrats seem to be a long way from a Maine chicken factory and a Buffalo conference on low-wage labor in the global economy.

A number of years ago, a friend dragooned me into helping fill out the community theater cast for a local production of Chekhov's great play, *The Three Sisters.* My role was that of Kulygin, schoolteacher and cuckolded husband of Masha, the most tempestuous of the sisters. I needed a lot of coaching, a good bit of it involving how to deliver some crucial lines. In the face of every humiliation and disappointment that is his lot, Kulygin repeats, "I am content, I am content, I am content." The trick was to say these words in a way that was not merely pathetic, that made clear how determined the man was to keep going, to avoid the self-pity immobilizing the other characters in the play.

Personal echoes aside, I have been struck by how Chekhov and Linda Lord were speaking to each other in ways that now can help frame the questions we are all wrestling with in this book. Consider that beyond poor Kulygin, *The Three Sisters* involves a family of fading aristocrats in the twilight years of a Russian nobility soon to be swept away by modernization and revolution. They are stranded in the provinces a long way from the center of power and sophistication in their world. "Moscow, Moscow, Moscow," the sisters sigh in their different ways. They, their lovers, and their friends spend most of four long acts complaining about boredom and bemoaning their fate.

Linda Lord throws all this into sharp perspective. Here are Chekhov's nobility and aristocrats, who despite all their wealth and privilege, insist, in effect, that "we are not content." Here is Kulygin, the determined middle-class professional, who unconvincingly but poignantly insists, "I am content" when he so obviously isn't. And here is Linda Lord, a working-class woman from Belfast, Maine, who when asked whether she was content in her job in the poultry industry, resists and deflects the either-or choice by saying, well, "I was content and not content," and then goes on to offer her story in her own way.

By using this quote as her book title, Rouverol and her colleagues mean to announce what Linda's story goes on to illustrate: that working-class people may not fit the obvious categories others so often use to engage and measure them, whether these be categories of middle-class values taken as self-evidently universal, or categories of academic analysis assumed to be somehow deeper or truer than what people can know as they reflect on and talk about their own experience. The place to start, we are told, is by checking our questions and assumptions at the door—and approaching such stories on their own terms, to see how these can challenge and complicate, rather than be squeezed into, the world of our own assumptions.

Such points and stories were much on my mind during many of the discussions at the Buffalo conference, because, as noted, for all the interest, concern, and empathy for the perspective and agency of poor people, to accord their stories the kind of instructive, informative power I am referencing seemed still somewhat hard. To avoid completely the mode of "illustrative" appreciation was difficult, as if the point of narrative were to provide a jolt of emotional and moral authenticity, to inform and propel but not necessarily to shape our analysis (diagnosis?) and policy-political prescriptions. If this seems harsh, perhaps it is fairer to say that the more central mode of the conference was one in which narrative and theory—analysis proceeded on parallel but not fully intersecting planes—as if different languages; as if the point of discussion were to translate the particularities of one system into the generalizations of the other; as if there were few cognates permitting more direct connection between the two.

Yet in much of the most animated discussion, and in many of the papers, the possibility of such connections seemed very real, most often represented as involving an axis organically connecting local particularity and global processes and transformations. Certainly, understanding the interpenetration of these dimensions remains of crucial importance. So is the task of developing modes of exchange—experientially and intellectually—so a broader perspective can be shared by those so fully engaged in confronting the problematic particularity of their immediate context and situation. Even theory itself, in this view, remains a necessary and in some ways crucial part of dialogue—since only through generalization and abstraction can a concept defined by one experience or situation be transported meaningfully into another. Throwing in theory, in this sense, is something like throwing in the clutch, permitting any of us to shift gears and move smoothly and meaningfully through a sequence of contexts. Most people, though, drive automatic transmissions these days, which is to say that both the metaphor and the connective-transmissive reality seemed elusive in the hothouse discussions of an intense conference, giving way to other, less provocative modes of apprehending, appreciating, and digesting narrative.

As far as we went in the process of using narrative to challenge culturally disempowering and mystifying conceptions of poverty, we have further yet to go, and the route needs to penetrate more deeply into narrative, rather than take off from it in more elaborate theorizing.

For one thing, although intellectuals may often feel as if they are unfolding and unpacking the meaning of experience through broader conceptualizations and theoretical frames, a strong case can be made that in fact the process is the reverse. Generalization and abstraction necessarily flatten the particularities of narrated experience in ways that may prevent us from apprehending precisely what people are expressing and even more explicitly trying to tell us. We need to notice that Linda Lord's title comment, in this sense, was a parry, a response to a question whose assumptions she did not wish to legitimize through responding, as much as it was a free-floating "expression" of her existential take on her job.

For another example, consider the story that Doris McKinney tells about almost losing her job in the steel mill—or rather stories, since I discovered in editing a very long interview that she had actually told it twice, from very different vantages and to very different effect. McKinney tells us, first, that she had been a single mother on welfare when she discovered an opportunity to work at Republic Steel, then hiring women under a Department of Justice consent decree. Toward the end of her probation period, however, the foreman told her that she just wasn't cutting it, and that if she didn't do better with the heavy burning torch central to her job, she would be out. She describes what happened then (Frisch and Rogovin 1993, 186–87):

> And you say, going from two—let's see, I think how much I was making, maybe three hundred a week—and the thought of going back to the welfare and making three hundred a month—the whole weekend I cried and I cried. When I walked in there Monday, I could pick the torch up and walk with it and anything else. Because it was psychological, you know. I knew that I did not want to go back to living like I was. And if there was any ounce of strength within me, and if other women could do it, I can't see why I couldn't, and so I did.

Yet later, in a conversation that had turned to other dimensions of her experience, she fills in details that throw the story into a different light. She describes how welfare permitted her to obtain community-college certification as an occupational therapist's assistant, how she could not afford to take the only low-paying job in the field she could find when she graduated, and how she only reluctantly took the job at Republic (Frisch and Rogovin 1993, 190–91):

> It was a step forward because it was a good, high-paying job; it was a step backward because it was not the kind of job I wanted to do. So it was very depressing for me . . . [But] we had been deprived a long time, and the money outweighed the experience. And who was to say that the other job was going to work out? So, once I took the job at Republic, you know your whole mentality has to change in order to keep a job, you can't continue to see yourself doing something else, just doing this temporarily. No—you got to be all or nothing. I thought you could keep up with reading, and keep up with your AJOTs, Journal of Occupational Therapy, you know. But you can't keep up unless you're actively participating in it. So then you finally make up your mind, you say, "Well, as long as I'm going to be at the job I'm going to do my damnedest to keep it, and get some of the things I want, and if the time comes, then so be it, I'll go from there."

It took me a while to realize that these two stories were the same—that the welfare mother terrified of returning to poverty and the college-trained paraprofessional who finally puts aside her disappointment about being in a manual-labor job are the same woman, facing the same moment of truth at the end of her probation. Hers a good example, I think, of multivalence in action, of identity so complex and nuanced as to be apprehensible only through the unfolding layers of expression in a complex narrative.

Through such nuances, and through the cumulative apprehension of the recognizable yet different lives of poor people, the goals of this conference are best realized—though figuring out what to do with these insights, of course, is not simple. As was pointed out frequently in our discussions, there is more than a simple binary of hegemony and agency in the experience and vantage of poor people. Here, too, a more multivalent sensibility seems called for.

In my own work, for sure, these tensions are manifest. The narratives I collected are rich and variegated in descriptive level and detail, opening vistas of complexity grounded in the singular integrity of individuals who inhabit, like all of us, many dimensions and levels at once. Yet these same narrators are much flatter and other-directed in their explicit analyses—in the way they offer up a variety of conventional mass-mediated bromides and quick explanations about plant closings, the service economy, costs of pollution control, importance of education, crisis of values, and the like—since they, again like all of us, are relentlessly exposed to the same mass-mediated discourses of explanation and justification, and turn to these readily when broader issues are raised.

So for all my interest in closer attendance to the richness and complexity of narrative, I have no illusions about this being a shortcut to some sort of pristine consciousness, of agency somehow outside the orbit of the same powerful cultural and political structuring forces that have produced the very paradigm of poverty we seek somehow to get out from under. Yet here, as elsewhere, the answer still seems to lie in a deeper and more sustained dialogue, of talking and really listening across diverse realms of experience, informed by a belief in the possibility that experience as well as expertise (indeed, the two words have the same root) each can provide tools for the creation of a new discourse of possibilities.

There is encouraging ground for this belief in the destabilizing surprises that history throws in the path of what can seem the most fixed realities and assumptions. One such moment at the time of our conference (and usefully discussed there) was the UPS strike that so upset the assumed givens of the punditocracy about the service economy in general, an increasingly unstable part-time workforce in particular, and the anachronism of organized labor in relation to each.

A more recent, powerful, and significant moment was the incredible improvisation surrounding the World Trade Organization meetings in Seattle in the autumn of 1999—an event that went far beyond overreported fringe demonstrations and amounted to the enactment, in public space, of a remarkable, international, truly inclusive and cross-class engagement with precisely the issues of concern to our conference. Yet this was a phenomenon that, doubtless at the time, we all would have agreed to be as unimaginable and unlikely as the evaporation of Soviet communism would have seemed to international affairs scholars as late as 1988.

So where did this come from, especially at the level of grassroots mobilization and engagement? Such surprises give us a great deal to think about. They suggest in the experience of ordinary people, however mediated and however much internalizing of the dominant culture, a capacity and an experiential basis for alternative constructions. We might see this as a kind of DNA: the generative basics of insight and understanding embedded in the cells of life experience, and inherently capable of activation and replication, even if this does not occur spontaneously or easily.

These notions once again point us to the usefulness of making dialogue and ongoing mutual interrogation the core of cultural and intellectual practice—especially when dealing with an issue as intractable as the needed reimagination and cultural resituating of poverty. Beyond narrative as illustration, as appreciation, and even as instruction, narrative as *dialogue*—implicitly embedded in all narrative—may be most worth our attention in seeking to move through and beyond the Buffalo conference and the discussion carried forward in this volume of fine papers.

REFERENCES

Frisch, Michael, and Milton Rogovin. 1993. *Portraits in Steel.* Ithaca, N.Y.: Cornell University Press.

Hall, Jacquelyn Dowd, James Leloudis, Robert Korstad, Mary Murphy, Lu Ann Jones, and Christopher B. Daly. 2000. *Like a Family: The Making of a Southern Cotton Mill World.* Chapel Hill: University of North Carolina Press.

Rouverol, Alicia J., Cedric N. Chatterley, and Stephen A. Cole. 2000. *I Was Content and Not Content: The Story of Linda Lord and the Closing of Penobscot Poultry.* Carbondale and Edwardsville: Southern Illinois University Press.

Conclusion

Democratizing Poverty

Frank Munger

B y now, studies of poverty policy have examined in detail the incidence, causes, and consequences of the behaviors that, according to underclass and culture-of-poverty theories, keep people poor. Mainstream research, however, doesn't try to evaluate the identities attached to poor persons by such theories, nor does it question the assumptions that individualize responsibility for poverty.[1] Ethnographers set out to counter the norms of such policy research and redeem the poor by uncovering complex interactions between individuals and institutions that illuminate their motivations and their instrumental decision making. Interpretive studies show that poor persons make appropriate use of cultural and material resources to survive and get ahead. These survival strategies often are extraordinarily creative, but they are no less dependent on human and social capital—knowledge, "soft skills," and networks of supporting relationships—than those of people who live in greater affluence.

By broadening our understanding of the needs of the poor and the limitations of the environments in which they live, ethnographies overturn the notion that poverty is monolithic and highlight the many different settings in which the working poor struggle to make lives that fit their unique circumstances. Moreover, as Sanders Korenman (see chapter 5 commentary, this volume), a former member of the President's Council of Economic Advisers, confirms, qualitative research has an important role to play in the development of more effective poverty policies.

The contributors to this volume address the causes of poverty by exploring the influence of social and institutional continuities on individual perceptions and choices that cut across traditional policy variables and subject domains, and in so doing, they examine life experiences with a wide-angle lens. Indeed, their studies make it difficult or even impossible to factor poverty into distinct variables.[2] In these ethnographies, work, family formation, street life, and interactions with public agencies—life elements that look like starting points in traditional poverty research—appear as outcomes: arcs that begin with the development of perceptions, values, and expectations, and end in action. Social structure occupies an important place in these accounts of consciousness and action, as the perceptions of poor persons are shaped through encounters over their lifetimes with public institutions, family relationships and networks of friends, the physical layout of cities and neighborhoods, police beats and bureaucracies, neighborhood commerce, the location of jobs, and the organization of employment. As we focus on how perceptions develop, we turn away from narrow measurements of the effectiveness of welfare programs to examine the social and institutional structures and resources that influence the capacities of individuals and groups to survive and change.

Discussions of how individuals are constituted as social actors by these fundamental structural relations lead to the question of how research might help persons and groups become active agents of further change. Michael Frisch (chapter 7 commentary, this volume) describes interpretive research as a "dialogue of possibility" in which subjects are themselves creative actors who understand what it means to live within the unfavorable conditions scholars set out to study. Since they share the experiences of other poor persons, they often achieve a "multivalent" vision (to borrow again from Frisch) of their circumstances, a vision that incorporates the possibility of different life trajectories and resists the categorical interpretations of those whose experiences of poverty, class, and gender are different. Frisch suggests that this multivalent vision might write a new vocabulary of connection and collective action for poor persons who share the experience of marginalization and who have been excluded from the theater of ordinary politics. Thus the role of scholars in generating narratives may be catalytic rather than interpretive.

Identity is also crucial to the symbolic politics of poverty, and if we are to overcome public resistance to more generous social supports for the poor, we must decipher how identity issues are used to gauge moral deservingness in the first place. The contributors herein address this important issue—Rainwater (1970) left it unresolved—only indirectly. How will ambiguities that arise from ethnography's more complex descriptions of the identities and the lives of the poor affect the symbolic politics of poverty? Ethnographers themselves often are divided about interpretations of causation, autonomy, and the sources of individual agency—questions central to the moral politics of poverty and policy making.

This last chapter will look at the expanded mission for ethnography that emerges from the other essays in the volume. First, I will examine the persistence of stereotypes of the poor and explore how such stereotypes contribute to governmentality, the ideological structure that underlies public control of social life. Stereotypes of the poor prove their value to our national discourse by legitimating particular forms of public dominion and control. They justify the phenomenon of durable inequality, which scholars and members of the public alike often attribute to differences in individual character or accidents of birth. Further, such stereotypes reinforce exploitation of those disadvantaged through the familiar social divisions of race, gender, class, and citizenship. The following section then looks at the evidence for public beliefs that underlie the symbolic politics of poverty and find ambivalence there. The final sections of the chapter describe the resources the identity project must draw on to transform our discussion of the lives of the poor and move toward the broader goal: democratizing poverty.

POWER, POLITICS, AND THE IDENTITY OF THE POOR

Although he calls for valid phenomenological analysis of the lives of the poor, Rainwater (1970, 12) predicts that our stereotypes will be resistant to change because they have deep psychological roots in the guilt we feel, knowing that we derive "various kinds of gains and gratifications from the existence of the disinherited." Fear of poverty, as well as fear of the poor, offers an explanation for the persistence of stereotypes about those who live at the margins of the American economy. We may retreat to hackneyed images of the poor so that we won't have to admit how *similar* we are. None of us is immune to feelings of marginality or worries about stable employment or concern for the safety of our children; and it is impossible not to recognize the moral complexity of our own lives in the dilemmas that confront the poor. So our need to distance ourselves from them is an expression of our deep aversion to the stigmatization they suffer; and the more insecure we feel, the more we seem to cling to our conviction that the poor have failed to work hard enough and that we can avoid their fate by industriousness and good citizenship.

Poverty and Governmentality

Rainwater's theory grounds our stereotypes of the poor in the basic psychology of perception rather than in politics. If he is right—if our views of the poor are rooted in our own psychological needs, if cognitive dissonance alone determines both our perception of poverty and the policies based on that perception—then to change the nature of welfare programs indeed would be difficult.[3] Yet the public seems to feel ambivalent about the identity and deservingness of the poor, and widespread stereotyping in public discourse and public policy may depend less on psychological need than on the fact that stereotyping serves the self-interest of more privileged groups. Gans (1995) describes the advantages we, the nonpoor, derive from such stereotypes: they reinforce the identity of the nonpoor by justifying avoidance of the "dangers" posed by the poor, by making the nonpoor feel superior as possessors of traits distinct from the traits of the poor, and by contributing to spatial stigmatization that justifies patterns of exclusion and social control. Each of these benefits is realized through concrete practices by nonpoor individuals and institutions—through standards for public behavior and policing, regulation of land use, and decisions about the placement of transportation routes as well as other public interests and needs—that might be hard to justify without our stereotypes of the poor.[4]

Most important, these stereotypes isolate the poor from the mainstream labor force, confining them to the margins of the labor market, where they serve useful roles as a reserve army of occasional workers who supplement the needs of the legitimate economy by cycling in and out of work (off the books) and who cost their employers nothing more than an hourly wage. If immigrants, members of certain ethnic groups, African Americans, and residents of the decaying urban cores experience greatly reduced quality of life as a result of their exclusion from well-compensated work, then that is a cost they pay to protect the privileges of others. If their exclusion prompts them to become providers of illegal goods (drugs, for instance) desired by many who are not poor, then their response to the absence of work only proves to these others that they don't deserve honest employment.

Gans's description of the functions of poverty shows how deeply implicated it is in *governmentality,* the replication of power in the everyday ordering of our lives (Foucault 1977; Hunt 1994). Since its benefits promote the interests of politicians, welfare administrators, and the public at large, stereotyping of the poor serves as one of the organizing principles of governmentality.[5] Suburban residents, for example, manipulate the concept of blight and the stereotypical identities of those who cause it in the symbolic politics of neighborhood building and preservation. Inner-city schools, too, because of the poor children who attend them, represent the unspoken Other that proves the superiority of suburban schools and justifies their elitism. Thus poverty, like crime, is exploited as a means of governance.[6] The identity of the poor becomes a key to the manipulation of economic policies. Stereotypes of welfare recipients are used to reinforce an image of an Other whose morally undeserving behavior explains and motivates policies of redistribution and regulation.[7] Economic dependency, like crime, is perceived as a pervasive threat, and in order to serve as a symbol of dependency, welfare recipients must be constructed as nonworkers who refuse to accept the discipline and risk of the labor market in exchange for its rewards.[8] Similarly, policies that "responsibilize" employment for the regularly employed—by cutting wages and benefit levels on the grounds that they represent excess "fat" in the operating budgets of the corporations that drive the mainstream economy—are justified to prevent the transfer of burdens borne by workers to the larger economic community (Rose 1999).[9]

Poverty, Identity, and Durable Inequality

The poor set a baseline for categorical distinctions between those who receive the full benefits and protections of the welfare state and those who must be required to take up more of its burdens. What makes them useful, of course, is the subtle, unspoken link between poverty and durable inequality (Tilly 1998).[10] The poor have a gender, a race, often an immigrant status, and a class identity—the emphasis depending on context.[11] Welfare to work plays well as a recommendation for teenage, single-parent African American women, although this group is in truth a small minority of actual welfare recipients (Handler and Hasenfeld 1997). Displeasure with illegal immigrants has been redirected to support denial of benefits to all immigrants, both legal and illegal. Images of undisciplined blue-collar employees as a class that exploits unearned union benefits, workers' compensation, or health care coverage are deployed to justify cutting back on labor protections and insurance, even as we praise the individual worker and raise the Earned Income Tax Credit or minimum wage. All of these identities reinforce the notion that employment protections pose moral hazards for poor or unemployed workers, who may need the harsh discipline of the unregulated labor market to keep them honest and industrious.[12] Under pressure to informalize work, increase the scope of contingent labor, and undermine the social contract with labor that has prevailed since World War II, these identities of poor and dependent persons become powerful political tools.

Low-wage workers are victims of such deregulation and reform, as Saskia Sassen (chapter 2 commentary, this volume) demonstrates in her discussion of the effects of the global transformation of work on the lives of low-wage laborers. Trends in globalization have contributed to the informalization of work. Expansion and consolidation of producer services, such as financial and information technology, along with concentration of corporate headquarters in the economic cores of major cities, has established "a new regime of economic activity" that depends not only on a highly skilled cadre of workers, but also on low-skilled workers who maintain, build, clean, deliver, copy, word process, answer phones, and especially, meet the rapidly rising demands for personal services for the wealthy. In addition, the postindustrial economy has "downgrad[ed] a broad range of manufacturing sectors." Sweatshops and home work have proliferated as the American firm has reorganized the lower-level workforce, all but eliminating union-negotiated protections and benefits in the private sector and significantly lowering the expectations of employees, while at the same time maintaining sufficient managerial capacity to enforce the discipline that the new regime requires (Gordon 1996). Finally, informalization extends beyond the manufacturing sector to distribution of goods and services that cannot compete with "cheap imports or for space and other business needs with the new high-profit firms engendered by the advanced corporate service economy" (Sassen this volume, 75).

The creation of low-wage informal work has played an essential part in the economic boom that signals America's role as leader of globalization, and in large cities, low-wage workers represent the engine on which the new globalized economy depends. The theory of comparative advantage in the global economy predicts that the number of jobs in sectors in which the United States is dominant (primarily highly skilled jobs in technology and professional services) should grow, while the low-wage job market should decline as manufacturing industries move to Third World societies where low-wage labor is plentiful and cheap. Sassen's research demonstrates, however, how crucially

low-wage workers function in advanced technological societies to sustain technological and financial industries, specialized manufacturing, and a broad
range of service industries.

The growing importance of low-wage work in the global informal economy
would lead us to expect that employers would support reproduction of the pool
of low-wage workers in order to keep wages low and keep groups that supply
such workers insecure and competing with each other. Indeed, poor minorities,
women, and some workers from the formerly unionized industrial workforce
do constitute a large pool of low-wage laborers; but American businesses want
more. They welcome illegal immigrants, support welfare-to-work reforms, and
continue to undermine benefits, wage increases, and job security. These practices have their most oppressive effects on workers with the least bargaining
power, whom durable inequality has kept isolated, segregated, or stigmatized
as a social group. Thus even in a time of full employment, low-wage workers,
especially those in categories defined by durable inequality, experience great
insecurity, and many do not find jobs at all (Freeman 1994).

Identity legitimates the uneven effects of informalization on particular
social groups. As long as workers in the low-wage labor pool are seen as inex-
perienced, undisciplined, unsocialized, and undereducated, few will question
the effects of informalization. Gender has done this identity work before: historically, women's identity—both their emotional-intellectual identity and as
men's dependents—suited them for low-skill, low-pay, low-benefit work. In
such terms, the entire low-wage workforce has been feminized by the notion
that informal and low-wage jobs are "starters," valuable because they teach the
soft skills and motivation workers need to move up the employment ladder.

For those who don't share it, this identity successfully masks the problem
of aggregate shortages of jobs that offer sustainable employment for low-wage
workers. Other structural features of the low-wage job market explain why
even those who do not find low-wage jobs accept the mainstream interpretation that failure to do so is their fault. Harvey (chapter 2 commentary, this volume) argues that most workers, including low-wage workers, have some
experience of the success of individual job searches, but little understanding
of the aggregate job shortages that confront them. His analysis of the economic
implications of job queues and the interaction of queues and shortages demonstrates that the problem of poverty related to low-wage work and unemployment can only be solved by increasing the number of jobs for low-wage workers.
Efforts to improve job readiness and job search strategies won't help much. As
long as the discussion of low-wage jobs continues to focus on the motives and
character of the unemployed, policies that shift the risks of unemployment to
the poor will prevail.

The rollback of employee benefits, increasing job insecurity, and welfare
reform, like the new politics of crime control, proceed from entrenched assumptions about the behavior of employees, the poor, and welfare recipients. These
related changes in governance are supported by stereotypes of dependent and

outsider groups. Gans does not underestimate the difficulty of changing our approaches to poverty and, more generally, our approaches to economic and social inclusion of the poor. Gans addresses this problem, in part, by urging a campaign to "debunk" stereotypes. Yet his own description of the entrenchment of stereotypes makes it clear that unless this effort is targeted to the specific constituencies that benefit from stereotypes and to their motives for maintaining them, efforts to bring about change may fail.

HOW THE PUBLIC PERCEIVES THE MORAL IDENTITY OF THE POOR

We have considered how the identity of the poor has been exploited to serve the interests of privileged groups, and how it continues to reinforce enduring inequality. Yet how does the public identify characteristics of the poor and translate them into moral judgments? Gans suggests that the aspirations of poor persons and their capacity to change are critical to our judgments of their deservingness; but aspirations are not observable. They function out of sight, on the borderland of identity, where poverty, welfare, and the meaning of community are negotiated.

We get a rough picture of the public's view of the poor from polling data. Shortly after the victory by the political right in the off-year congressional elections of 1994, a New York Times/CBS poll confirmed that the public subscribed to negative stereotypes of persons who received welfare assistance, and endorsed reductions in benefits as well as imposition of work requirements. In the same poll, at the height of the conservatives' power and just as the United States was beginning to emerge from a severe recession, the public also expressed its willingness to pay for job training, child care, and other benefits for needy parents, even if those expenditures triggered tax increases (Dowd 1994). Such apparently contradictory modes of understanding public provision for the poor are long-standing. In recent surveys, more than 85 percent of all adults endorsed the idea that recipients should be required to work for their welfare benefits. Among liberals and conservatives, blacks and whites, women and men, the statistics told the same story. A large majority of respondents also endorsed relatively generous benefits for those who are trying to comply with work requirements but who need education or services to do so. Moreover, a majority agreed that such benefits should be extended beyond standard time limits if necessary, even at increased cost to the public.[13]

In the contemporary politics of welfare reform (and the context of increasing insecurity in the workplace, even for many who once enjoyed job security), the requirement to work has acquired overwhelming importance. The idea that welfare recipients should work has simmered since the 1960s, when the AFDC program began to be viewed as a semipermanent subsidy game for inner-city, never married African American mothers. In the deracinated politics of the 1990s, the turn to policies that discipline the poor along with other workers has replaced more overtly racist politics spurred by the white back-lash of the 1980s (see Simon 1997). The outcry against affirmative action, school desegregation orders, bilingualism, and immigration has been subsumed into a politics of citizenship that ignores differences in needs and values and homogenizes regulation of welfare state benefits on the basis of a single principle: that the deserving person—the person who works—will be rewarded. In this environment, the disciplinary component of poverty policies is reserved for those who share the stereotypical identity "nonworking" and who fall into one or more other familiar categories—ethnic, female, immigrant, or inner-city resident.

Members of the public draw sharp distinctions between themselves and welfare recipients. A recent poll conducted by the Washington Post-Kaiser Family Foundation (1998), revealed that only about 7 percent of respondents said they believe persons on welfare have values very like their own.[14] Further, only 6 percent of Americans identify themselves as poor.[15] This low rate of self-identification is striking in a nation with an official poverty rate of about 13 percent, and where at least twice as many of us are functionally poor by many scholars' estimates.[16] Nearly one third of all American adults identify themselves as working class—and this includes a majority of those whose incomes fall well below the poverty line. Rainwater's (1970) cognitive dissonance theory explains why most people, including those who are objectively poor, believe that poverty is a status that places individuals outside the realm of ordinary experience and isolates them from the larger community. Most of the poor deny that identity in their own self-perceptions, and with good reason: the poor are stigmatized, and not the least factor, the stigma is racial (see Gillens 1999). For whites, the poor are black. For persons of color, the poor are lazy, self-destructive, and above all, not like us.

In fact, although the differences between wealth and poverty may be relatively clear at the extremes, the differences between poor and nonpoor *persons* is largely artificial. In objective terms, individuals' incomes fluctuate over their lifetimes. Huge numbers of people move into and out of employment, and whether they are classified as poor or nonpoor, they share a range of common experiences. Their similarities blur the distinctions between successful and unsuccessful, deserving and undeserving. This is why, paradoxically, they are reluctant to acknowledge either their own experiences of economic insecurity or the citizenship of the nonworking poor. Many Americans are threatened by unemployment and involuntary underproductivity.[17] Many, especially women, are compelled to work in roles that are not typically defined as productive. In practice, these niches of dependency exist in tension with the dominant norms of citizenship, and whether they want to admit it or not, persons who occupy them must continually negotiate their status. The prevalence of niche identities is growing in the postmodern economy, and our rising consciousness of such identities may set the stage for transformations of our collective understanding of the meaning of poverty and low-wage work.[18]

Notwithstanding the patriarchal values, racist presumptions, and insensitivities to individual differences that seem to inform our welfare policies, the public—or at least large segments of it—may take complex and more benign views of poverty. We may hope that negative perceptions of poverty in some survey data do not reflect the fundamental values of those who have shared job insecurity. We may hope that resistance to adequate provision for the poor is a product of misperceptions about responsibility, fears about the future, and complex responses to racial politics. We may hope that a spirit of fairness will succeed in the end, and that arguments based on race, gender, or lifestyle only mask our deep and insistent suspicion that the poor really are like us. We may hope that appeals to ascriptive differences may be weakened by evidence that individuals are meeting their obligations as citizens, whether or not work in the conventional labor market results from their efforts.

THE IDENTITY PROJECT

What can interpretive research do to address the persistence of political, social, and psychological strategies that secure the interests—and assuage the fears—of some groups in society at the expense of others? First and foremost, such research can particularize identity, show that it is not merely a cluster of clichés slapped on the poor by power holders who need justification for the policies they make. Ethnography can demonstrate that identity is a real, personal possession, owned privately by each of us, poor and nonpoor alike; that it organizes our sense of self, unlocks (or locks) our agency, our capacity to act and react, to make the most or least of opportunities and obstacles. By unraveling their individual identities, by showing how those identities develop under conditions that are hidden from politicians and the public, and by celebrating their embrace of familiar values and goals, ethnography can redeem the poor.

Yet as Rainwater predicted, and as we have seen, complex and ambiguous stories about people in poverty sometimes are difficult to comprehend. One ethnographic strategy tries to validate the decisions (and thus the lives) of the poor by showing that they are rational, that they enact mainstream values despite severe constraints. This approach calls for selective investigation of the circumstances and decisions through which the poor succeed in acting autonomously and strategically as they seek to resist or escape poverty. A second strategy constructs stories that show how the poor—even those who have the will to change—are captured by their poverty, trapped by the social ties that at once enable survival and smother autonomy. The behavior of poor persons who suffer extreme oppression sometimes must be understood as a product of that oppression, and not as an expression of resistance, subversion, or double consciousness. Handler suggests in his commentary (this volume) that prescriptions for change are greatly complicated by the fact that poverty has an effect on capacity for self-help as well as on opportunities for self-help. Only after personal and institutional transformations empower the poor to shape new identities for themselves, he argues, will they be able to make their own way through the world.

If the dialogue among these different approaches to ethnography only complicates our picture of the character of the poor, then ethnography has failed. Qualitative researchers go further, however, and transform the questions we ask about poverty. They foreground the agency of individuals as they examine the resources available for the development of personal character and the situations and interactions in which these resources can be deployed. Increasingly, qualitative researchers focus on the role of institutional environments in the lives of the poor as encounters with those environments guide individual agency and feed or thwart the capacity for change. Conceptually, ethnographers explore sophisticated frameworks for understanding the experiences of the poor and the effects of poverty on behavior. Empirically, they track changes in the low-wage job market, the increasing privatization of dependency and risk on which that market is founded, and the creation of durable inequalities that restrict and allocate opportunities by race, immigrant status, class, and gender.

Carol Stack (chapter 1, this volume) introduces us to the world of low-wage work through the eyes of teenagers who begin their interactions with that world in fast-food restaurants in Oakland and Harlem. They may be at the bottom of the employment ladder now, but they are also at the peak of hopefulness about moving up. Stack enters their lives to find out what means most to them, how they expend their not-quite-unlimited energy. Work turns out to be central to these young people. Many of us who have jobs in the mainstream learned about work by being connected to the world of our parents, and through them, to the landscape of adult life. Oakland teens often get less effective parenting than we did, but they commit themselves to work because they too understand it as a pathway to adulthood. For all the energy and promise of the young woman Stack follows through the critical passages of maturation, fast-food work is likely to lead nowhere. Although the young workers learn many unnamed skills, there is no next level of related employment; there is no up from this job. Unless the worker can draw on other forms of capital—education, financially capable parents, or a relative in business—her work experience may not carry her anywhere but to another low-wage service job. The teenager has played by the power holders' rules and overturned the negative stereotypes through which they see and judge the poor. So what is her reward? What happens to *her* expectations?

The answer may strike us as painful, but it is inescapable: the careers of low-wage workers, like Stack's teens, are circumscribed by the durable inequality that defines their life worlds and by important differences in social and human capital that affect the significance of low-wage job opportunities. In chapter 2, Ruth Buchanan's detailed examination of the experience of finding and holding a low-wage job in the telemarketing industry in Canada illuminates a related effect of globalization, namely, the exploitation of individuals in niche labor markets. Employment in telemarketing is an important paradigm because there is no apparent shortage of potential employees for work that is often demanding and stressful.

Buchanan's study points to an important transformation in the low-wage nonindustrial workforce, once overwhelmingly female, but now drawing both men and women. Telework has many of the qualities that jobs in the historically segmented gendered labor market had: it is low-waged and contingent, with little recognition of the skills it requires. The image of low-wage workers—including workers in the new informalized manufacturing sector—indeed has become feminized in the sense that they are represented as lacking experience, discipline, and commitment to full-time work. The actual composition of low-wage workforces (women with family responsibilities, immigrant women, men with limited education) often confirms this stereotype, but as Buchanan shows, people accept low-wage jobs because of limitations on their human and social capital, not because they are poorly motivated or uncommitted to full-time employment.

For women, the decision to enter the low-wage job market is complicated by family responsibilities and by the structural dependency that these responsibilities (they amount to unpaid labor in the home) create. In the case of female single parents, the stereotypical image of the low-wage or contingent worker is particularly ironic. Female single parents are poor because of widespread expectations for women's care work and because of increasing privatization of care work as benefits are withdrawn from jobs and public funding decreases. Julia Henly (chapter 5, this volume) examines low-wage employment by women in matched samples: one group of women works in low-wage jobs; the other group subsists on welfare. The study finds that differences in social capital—namely, supporting relationships that provide additional income and access to child care and other resources—are critical determinants of the choice between work and welfare. Thus Henly's research shows that women can't take advantage of opportunities unless they have personal resources to invest in those opportunities; and it shows great differences in the amounts of social capital women can command.[19] Henly's research reinforces the basic principle that economic success is not derived from self-sufficiency but rather from being able to be dependent on others. In the male working world, of course, it often is assumed that a family will provide critical support for personal well-being. Such an assumption is inappropriate with respect to poor working women.

For women, another hidden issue—personal security (or more accurately, for poor women, residential insecurity)—is central to the capacity for employment. Housing typically costs low-income families a far larger proportion of their income than affluent families are likely to pay. Instability of income, which is much more likely among the poor, often has drastic consequences, as the stories behind the statistics for homelessness demonstrate. Domestic violence, of course, is another a major cause of homelessness. Aixa Cintrón-Vélez's interviews with women who are residents of shelters describe their situations in terms that the nonpoor would not predict (chapter 4, this volume). Shelters can offer more than security, Cintrón-Vélez suggests. They also may provide a source of identity. One woman reported that she became capable of self-help in the security of the shelter; it allowed her space in which to develop greater self-confidence and discover a new identity. Although a woman forced to enter a homeless shelter looks like a displaced person to middle-class observers, the resident herself may experience the shelter as her only secure residence, and a foundation for self-confidence.

Reinforcing and extending Stack's findings about the importance of social capital among poor women and men, Cintrón-Vélez shows that identity can be fundamentally affected by the social capital provided by a residence.[20] Cintrón-Vélez's window on life in shelters also leads back to public policies that affect the need for shelters. Recent changes in welfare law that establish strict employment requirements have forced many families without jobs off of public assistance, and homelessness is one of the consequences. Cintrón-Vélez's research reveals still further irony. Although residential security can be an important key to the stability and self-confidence required for employment, housing is almost never mentioned among the kinds of social capital subsidies that will enable the poor to secure work and succeed at it. Indeed, as Cintrón-Vélez points out, public spending for construction of new housing that might be accessible to the poor has been greatly reduced over several decades. At the same time, many local governments offer subsidies for upscale conversions of existing housing stock that might have been used for poor families.

Family is a central concern of both poor men and women. The low-wage job market has made it extremely difficult to keep a two-parent family intact, but those who are unable to do so often maintain different forms of attachment. Edin, Lein, and Nelson (chapter 3, this volume) offer an important corrective to the prevailing vision of the dysfunctional role of poor men. The failure of many poor fathers to maintain regular employment that supports the family is read broadly to indicate even greater dysfunction—namely, their complete noninvolvement as sources of economic support and as parents. This interpretation is incorrect. Edin and Lein (1997) discover that fathers constitute an important, if irregular, source of income and other help for the mothers who are raising the fathers' children. In their essay in this volume, Edin, Lein, and Nelson find that fathers *want* to be fathers. Their inability, however, to share custody because they lack steady employment—despite years of effort to secure it—leads to a lifestyle that resembles, the authors conclude, extended adolescence. Although the motivations and values of many poor men match those of the mainstream, the unavailability of low-wage work takes a severe toll on their identity. Since they sometimes see themselves shut out of the domain of parenting, family, and work altogether, these men believe that their lives should be conducted according to different rules.

Ethnography undermines the foundations for stereotypes—and at the same time makes sense of such stereotypes as that of the detached, uncaring, unemployed African American father—when it shows how inequality that confronts broad sectors of the poor, working poor, and low-wage mainstream is sustained, in part, by the social organization of low-wage employment. If we can document how the low-wage job market and the privatization of dependency affect all the working poor and many in the middle classes as well, the familiar negative images of poor women and men will lose their power to shock us. Interpretive research renders the ambiguous moral character of the oppressed poor irrelevant when it shows that social institutions create risks for the poor by compelling them to adopt extraordinary survival strategies and encouraging (mal)adaptive identities. This research also demonstrates that the most effective social policy for ending poverty begins with the transformation of the social environment in which the poor live.

Ethnographers recognize that identity is always dependent on contingencies, and as we document the interplay between meaning, action, and situation in the lives of poor persons, we observe and report discrete moments in the uninterrupted evolution of their perspectives—their values and aspirations—under the pressure of constant change. Sanders Korenman (commentary, this volume) responds to the continuous possibility for individual change by proposing that longitudinal studies are essential to test the long-term effects of poverty policy. We do not live our lives within the boundaries of social templates, but within the contexts of our evolving consciousness.

The development of motives, perspectives, and meaning—consciousness—provides room for individuals to maneuver. Thus we find openings in ethnographic narratives of poverty for change and empowerment. Identity is a resource that may create space for action.[21] Lucie White writes of a Head Start participant whose identity has many "potentials" that "come in and out of focus as she interacts with different people in different social domains." The woman's experiences at Head Start acted as a catalyst for change that increased her effectiveness in managing her life. White examines the critical events in that stream of change, particularly the woman's discussion of herself and her situation with a mentor and interactions with peers, and attempts to map her subject's course through the process. Similarly, Aixa Cintrón-Vélez describes an evolving consciousness of possibility that challenges the presumptions of outsiders about the oppressiveness and bleakness of homeless shelters. The resident who said that a shelter provided her first experience of stability claimed that this experience changed her outlook on life. Her subsequent ability to make changes in her behavior made her hope real, not an illusion.

Identity also is a critical element in narratives of collective change. Participatory research described by Frances Ansley has provided groups of workers experiencing the traumas of economic marginalization in the United States and elsewhere with opportunities to examine, understand, and ultimately organize a collective response. For example, in discussions of their plight with union leaders and academics, American workers in Tennessee who lost their jobs to Mexican maquiladoras were able to derive a new sense of identity—not crafted by outsiders who helped the group get started—that oriented their anger away from the Mexican workers and toward their former employer and the government that provided aid for the move to Mexico (Ansley and Williams 1999).[22] The discovery of possibilities for collective participation in efforts to change the balance of power in oppressive social relations may be one important route toward change.

Ethnography that finds hope for change and empowerment is particularly respectful of the perceptions of the poor, Michael Frisch notes (commentary, this volume). Although elites often describe the poor as fatalistic—a characteristic of Oscar Lewis's concept of the culture of poverty—the poor often make realistic assessments of their circumstances, and they make rational choices about their actions, given the knowledge they have.[23] Frisch contends that the conditions of poverty create opportunities for perception not available to others: outsiders can learn about those conditions, and about how poor persons use *their* knowledge of those conditions, only from them. Narratives thus can make room between abstract generalizations about the oppressiveness of poverty and the individual who maneuvers to change his or her circumstances.

DEMOCRATIZING POVERTY

We have seen that stereotypes of the poor serve a variety of political purposes. We also have seen that consensus about severely restricting the provision of benefits to the poor is illusory. Attitudes toward public assistance policies are deeply conflicted. Fear of poverty and shame caused by declining economic fortunes can explain the psychological need of working-class Americans to distance themselves from images of poverty and make poverty the personal responsibility of poor persons. Yet many who express hostility toward poor African Americans—especially welfare recipients—and immigrants also support the extension of the social safety net provided by the welfare state to others. This ambivalence reflects an important reality: that much of the rhetoric of welfare reform can be said to have served the purpose of reinforcing the work ethic of the working class itself. Explicitly, welfare reform reminds the working class of its entitlement to respect for being employed. Implicitly, reform reminds workers of their insecurity and dependence on their employers (Matsuda 1997; Kost and Munger 1996).

Those who have not shared in the economic miracle of recent years—including many white males who have lost union jobs and watched economic advantages erode for themselves and their children—now face the same kinds of insecurity that confront minorities and women in the low-wage labor force. If our goal is to democratize poverty, to make it *available* as social construct and lived reality to others, Americans at all income levels must begin by acknowledging their own experience with economic insecurity at some time in their lives. That insecurity may only have amounted to the threat of poverty; but it allows all of us to see into the world that poor people inhabit, to imagine our-selves there, confronting the same hard choices between work and school, and between work and family. When we recognize that the dilemmas of the poor are like ours, we understand that they also share many of our aspirations and values. When we realize that they share our aspirations and values, we under-stand that the poor are like us. Once we realize how alike we are, we recognize the importance of programs that address issues of durable inequality, different forms of low-wage labor, and the structural dependency of women.

Ethnographic research harnesses empathy in the service of this project, and it helps us document for other working Americans a fundamental truth: but for the limiting and transforming experiences of poverty, most poor persons are capable of active participation in mainstream institutions. Ethnography makes the barriers to that participation transparent by invoking widely shared expe-riences of the coercion, humiliation, and insecurity of the labor market. Of course, more is at stake here than the need for an accurate portrayal of the per-spectives, capacities, and moral character of the poor. Truly to democratize poverty, we must attempt to change the self-perceptions of the mainstream. To that end we propose a model of moral equivalence between Self and Other, one that justifies the citizenship of the welfare-needing poor by demonstrating that most are low-wage workers at some point in their lives, and that all are poten-tial workers.[24] The perception that they are deserving is the key to income sup-ports and other services for the poor.[25] So perceived, the poor are seen to share the many risks and oppressions of the labor market with those in the main-stream. In fact, so perceived, their identity is transformed, and the poor are entitled to become members of the mainstream, to enjoy the full benefits of citizenship. (Consider, for instance, employment protection policies that cover other workers: the Fair Labor Standards Act, pension rights, and Social Secu-rity and Medicare.) During the New Deal, just such a transformation in iden-tity was accomplished for elderly persons with minimum work histories who received a guarantee of federal old-age insurance.

The oral historian Alessandro Portelli (1991) observes that the atrophy of movements for radical social change has left citizens of many Western societies to face social problems alone, as the obsession with self-sufficiency and auton-omy in moral, academic, and policy discourses amply demonstrates. The task of oral historians, he argues, is to convey difference as interdependence rather than as a form of hierarchy. Portelli is describing conditions for effective oral history fieldwork, but he understands that fieldwork offers a paradigm for research and, indeed, we also might argue, for policy. Meaningful change requires self-awareness on many levels. Research and policy are not only forms of intervention, but opportunities for mutual enlightenment and increased self-awareness—both for those who need help and for those who want to provide it. Empowerment of the poor in their own lives, as we are empowered in ours, is the most democratic prescription for change, and it is reinforced by our civic culture of self-help. Whether as members of a voting public, elected decision makers, or academics committed to the production of knowledge, we—the holders of power—can achieve this democratic end only if we recognize similarities in our experiences, goals, values, and moral stature, and accept the equality of our differences of race, gender, and class, which then will cease to matter as sources of enduring inequality.

NOTES

1. Much of this research grew from the encouragement given by Congress after 1980 to experimentation and innovation by the states in administering welfare under federal grant programs. Innovations intended to change the behavior of poor mothers included combining welfare to work, training and education, and sanctions for having children while receiving welfare. While these so-called experiments (few met standards of scientific rigor) potentially told us that individuals worked incrementally more or had incrementally fewer children under threat of sanctions, they did not test whether individuals will respond to significant opportunities, adapt to change, and act on aspirations or values. While some of these programs suggested that the poor can be pressured to find work, although the gains are small, they also suggested that sustaining self-sufficiency through employment in the low-wage job market is extremely difficult (Handler and Hasenfeld 1997). The research did not sustain the underlying premises for these programs—namely, that the micromanagement of poor women's meager public assistance will increase their capacity to enter the mainstream or achieve a better life for themselves or their families in the longer run. In all of this research race has been suppressed. Race became a politically difficult subject for poverty research after the split in the civil rights movement in the 1960s and as poverty policy entered the era of "benign neglect" (Katz 1989). In recent poverty policy studies, race is omitted because it is deemed neither a direct cause of impoverishment nor a factor directly affecting the success or failure of relief programs. Yet race, like gender, is an important factor in the interplay of institutions and lives. Poverty is a racially coded concept, and welfare is racially coded still more clearly than poverty. Welfare policy has been influenced by the continuing patterns of institutional segregation whose origins lie in our troubled history of race relations. Countering racial stereotypes is an important part of redeeming the poor.

2. Although traditional policy research analyzes the statistical effects of family structure, human capital, and economic resources on poverty, it does not employ more direct approaches to understanding who the poor are, what they are capable of doing, and how they might respond to different circumstances. Traditional policy research presumes that the lives of the poor require micromanagement by welfare providers; it tests whether particular forms of micromanagement produce statistically measurable changes in behavior. In contrast, the values, capacities, and perceptions of the poor—their identity—is central to the work presented by the contributors to this book.

3. Rainwater (1970, 27) concludes that redeeming perspectives on the poor may meet psychological resistance. He says, "such accounts will inevitably present the social scientists and policy makers with what Alvin Gouldner (1970) has called 'hostile

information,' that is, information that challenges their most deeply held beliefs about what people are like, why they act as they do, and what this implies for political action."

4. Further benefits accrue from scapegoating the poor by blaming them for systemic and institutional failures. For example, human services agencies may evade their obligation to administer effective poverty relief policies by characterizing the poor as unresponsive and irresponsible. Gans notes related economic functions of stereotypes imposed on the poor. The identity of the poor is the raison d'être for the human services industry. Separating and treating the undeserving and deserving poor is the purpose of their work; therefore, they have an enormous investment in maintaining this distinction.

5. Public administrators attempt to create an appropriate sense of the meaning and purpose of an agency's tasks among staff members. Their shared sense of meaning is created in part by the professional discourses they employ to describe what they do and in part by myths they use to legitimate the agency externally. Discourses that suggest that what they do is effective, notwithstanding the failure of their clients, have an obvious appeal. Professional and political discourses that incorporate stereotypical characterizations of the poor have just such reinforcing implications concerning administrative effectiveness, and they may readily become part of the basis for the shared meaning of the activities of an agency, whether a welfare office, police department, housing inspection unit, or motor vehicle licensing office.

6. This discussion draws on the insightful analysis of Jonathan Simon (1997), who argues that growing distrust of the Other—the poor, the nonwhite, the "criminal element"—has altered governance of our society. Governance no longer presumes that the mainstream and the Other can coexist out of mutual respect and respect for civil order. The social connections between individuals that previously formed the basis for decentralized order and control have broken down—at least across the social divides of race and class.

   Instead, power is exercised by means that rely on no mutual interaction at all, but rather on management by an algorithm designed into the system. The growing distrust is reflected in the evolution of quotidian practices of social control that make up governmentality. Culture-free regulation through spatial separation is replacing interactive communication and collective choice. Containment of norm violators is replacing disciplinarity and rehabilitation. Risk management is replacing democratic choice and interpersonal managerial decision making. The image of the criminal Other—a person of color, poor, predatory, and urban—drives a wide range of public policies. The identity of the Other legitimates policies of containment, separation, statistically based crime prevention such as profiling, and punishment that affect not only criminal justice but also land use, transportation, public funding of schools, national electoral politics, and other major institutional arenas in which governance structures social interaction.

7. Welfare reform in particular illustrates the role of the poor in governmentality. First, the desire of a large part of the American public to equalize the burdens of widespread economic insecurity secured political support for strict work requirements for welfare recipients. Thus while work requirements may well have reflected the

displaced anxiety of workers, they also served an explicit purpose embraced by a large part of the public. Second, support for strict limits on welfare resulted not only from the desire of the American public to equalize economic insecurity, but from a successful effort by promarket conservatives and business to promote the belief among wage earners that economic insecurity is necessary, normal, and legitimate (Kost and Munger 1996; Matsuda 1997). Both interests were served by placing restrictions on welfare and punishing welfare recipients for not working. Belief in the undeservingness of the poor made it possible to take for granted that to be forced to work regardless of the hardship created would be good for the poor. This stereotype also helped weaken support for a plausible alternative policy, namely, making all workers more secure, because the stereotype assumes that no one is entitled to be more secure.

8. Nothing in the new welfare law requires that recipients who must enlist in "work experience" projects as a condition of receiving their grants be provided the benefits—or wages—of "employees," even though they may be performing identical work. For example, a recent ruling by the New York Court of Appeals held New York's state constitutional provision requiring payment of "prevailing wages" for public works employees inapplicable to workfare workers. *Brukhman v. Giuliani*, 94 N.Y.2d 387 (2000).

9. In the present fiscally conservative political environment, employment security, previous employee benefit levels, and legal rights to contest employer decision making all are represented as forms of freeloading that must be controlled through public policies that "responsibilize" employees in the name of the common good, which is defined as efficiency and wealth maximization (see McCluskey 1998). Workers' benefits not related to the bottom line become legitimate targets for cuts because they are constructed in economic discourse as a form of economic fat, privilege, and immoral dependency, the mirror-image reverse of efficient, market driven, and therefore fair labor policy.

10. The sociologist Charles Tilly (1998) describes processes by which societies maintain "durable inequality" in the distribution of access to privileges and benefits. Inequality, Tilly argues, is often by category, not individual by individual. Thus women historically have been channeled into low-wage unskilled work, African Americans are confined in neighborhoods and communities that offer fewer opportunities to build human capital and where social capital may be less adapted to linking with the mainstream economy, and immigrants are confined to illegal, desperately low-paid and underregulated work. Even before society judges and interacts with each individual, these groups start from distinctive positions of disadvantage. Tilly notes that such categorical divisions often explain how roles that seem open to all are regularly occupied by persons from a particular social class, gender, or race. For example, as the American economy has boomed over the past few years, many wage earners have benefited, but low-wage workers have fallen far behind. Moreover, the allocation of low-wage jobs disproportionately to women, minorities, and immigrants is an example of durable inequality based on processes of exclusion and marginalization that render persons in these categories available for low-wage and contingent work but less available for higher-paid mainstream jobs.

11. Durable inequality is maintained, in part, by means of the identities that establish boundaries between groups (Tilly 1998, 64):

 Thus, as combinations of solidary and competitive interactions generate ostensibly racial barriers, they also produce genetically framed stories of each group's origins and attributes. . . . Different combinations of encounters, barriers, and stories generate definitions of categories as centering on class, citizenship, age, or locality.

12. Many government subsidies create a moral hazard, namely, the risk that recipients will change their behavior to make themselves eligible for more of the subsidy. Since subsidies are intended to induce changes in behavior, evaluation of the so-called moral effects of a subsidy actually depends entirely on judgments about whether the subsidy induces too much or too little reliance. The language of moral hazard is misleading, since in principle no clear threshold exists above which the motive for seeking an incrementally higher subsidy is corrupt, rather than precisely what the law was intended to achieve. Judgments about whether reliance is too great or too little are strongly colored by political preferences (see McCluskey 1998). A great deal of research already suggests that the costs and benefits of welfare are a great deal more complex and create far less moral hazard than the reformers and public have believed (Edin and Lein 1997; Seccombe 1999; Zucchino 1997).

13. A recent survey by Jobs for the Future (2000) indicated that 70 percent of all Americans favor government help for child care and training after adults leave welfare and enter the workforce. Nearly 90 percent of those favoring such government support would continue to favor it even if it required a substantial increase in government spending. Surveys available from the Roper Center for Public Opinion Research show that these views are enduring. Polls conducted in 1996, shortly after the new welfare reforms became law, showed that majorities favored providing increased job training and day care benefits even after adults left welfare and even if it meant an increase in taxes. See Kaiser Family Foundation 1996, Questions 26 and 40; Coalition for America's Children 1996, Questions 62 and 72.

14. Washington Post/Kaiser Family Foundation 1998, Question 15.

15. NBC/Wall Street Journal 1998, Question 7.

16. A 1997 poll by the Pew Research Center (1998) reported that 17 percent of the adult population acknowledges having lived in a family that received welfare.

17. Controversies range from traditional labor value issues about the meritoriousness of wages negotiated by unions and entitlement of strikers to unemployment benefits, the meaning of *employee* in a reengineered and downsized world, and the status of women under Social Security.

18. This rise in niche identities is linked to Anthony Giddens's (1990) perception that the modern (postmodern) world relies increasingly on trust between individuals and entities connected by extended webs of global interaction. As economic roles change in the way described here, however, trust directly is affected. We want Third World workers to be engaged in a free market economy partly because we then can trust them politically, since they will respond to familiar incentives and values. As workers in our own society work less, we trust them less, and we trust the poor least of all because their link to the materialism of wage labor has become

weakened. Robert Wuthnow (1996, 287–89) suggests that the lack of trust is a projection of the misgivings we have about the weakening, in each of us, of the moral values that have historically guided and limited our materialism.

19. Human capital resources include soft skills, knowledge, and trust, which yield confidence in oneself and a fit between identity and work. Much has been made of the soft skills deficit (Tilly 1998; Holzer 1996), but for many, the issue is not human capital but social capital and the conflict between economic work and care work.

20. Identity may be affected in more than one way. Cintrón-Vélez's study suggests that residence in a shelter is a stepping-stone to employment. Stack's earlier study (1974) suggests that reciprocally binding relationships can help individuals take advantage of opportunities. Yet these binding relationships also may create an expectation that resources will be distributed and will not be used to facilitate the independence of those who want to return to school, rent an apartment outside the neighborhood, or marry and seek employment elsewhere. Contrasting behavior is displayed by the street-corner men in Liebow's research, who avoid forming relationships based on borrowing and, as a result, have greater freedom from commitments, but also less social capital than the women described by Stack.

21. Space also may be created by public narratives that validate the perception that power—including power to interpret the meaning and effects of poverty—always is shared between dominant social and political groups and the poor themselves (Frisch 1990; Handler, commentary, this volume). Counterhegemonic consciousness always has figured prominently in social history as a form of resistance (Scott 1990; Ewick and Silbey 1998; see also Du Bois 1903 on dual consciousness).

22. Ansley's account of the conversations among the workers make it clear that they did not accept the suggestion of the union steward discussion leader. Rather, the workers subtly shifted the terms and conclusions of the discussion. They simply responded to the question that they had framed for themselves rather than the one posed by the self-appointed discussion leader. The consequence of this discovery of identity was a strong commitment to collective action to reach out to the Mexican workers.

23. My own research interviews with poor women show that their opportunities for higher education sometimes are constrained, notwithstanding superior performance in secondary school, by their lack of literacy, as it were, in the culture of higher education among those whom they trust (Munger forthcoming).

24. I am not advocating victim narratives. Victim narratives create empathy by describing the effects of misfortune experienced by the deserving; they do not explore the qualities that make an individual a citizen. Victim narratives link suffering to our sense of duty to one another as citizens, but also place victims in a bind. Victims deserve their victimhood only if their behavior is perceived to fit model citizen behavior, an ideal few of us measure up to in reality.

25. Post-1996, funding for poverty relief has increased. Two explanations have been offered. Korenman (commentary, this volume) ties the rise in the minimum wage and increasing support for child welfare to the extraordinary economic boom that has reduced the economic insecurity on which welfare reform played. The Nobel Prize–winning economist Robert Solow (1998) links rising support for welfare to

charitable impulses validated in part by the increased work requirements under welfare reform—both values must be satisfied to obtain political support. According to either theory, changes in poverty relief programs will be temporary and will leave untouched the underlying problems of the low-wage labor market as well as other institutional causes of poverty.

REFERENCES

Anderson, Elijah. 1990. *Streetwise: Race, Class and Change in an Urban Community.* Chicago: University of Chicago Press.

———. 1999. *Code of the Street: Decency, Violence, and the Moral Life of the Inner City.* New York: W. W. Norton.

Ansley, Frances, and Susan Williams. 1999. "Southern Women and Southern Borders on the Move: Tennessee Workers Explore the New International Division of Labor." In *Neither Separate Nor Equal: Women, Race, and Class in the South,* edited by Barbara Ellen Smith. Philadelphia: Temple University Press.

Berlant, Lauren. 1999. "The Subject of True Feeling: Pain, Privacy, and Politics." In *Cultural Pluralism, Identity Politics, and the Law,* edited by A. Sarat and T. Kearns. Ann Arbor: University of Michigan Press.

Bourdieu, Pierre, and Loic Wacquant. 1992. *An Invitation to Reflexive Sociology.* Chicago: University of Chicago Press.

Bruner, Jerome. 1990. *Acts of Meaning.* Cambridge, Mass.: Harvard University Press.

Burawoy, Michael. 1991. *Ethnography Unbound: Power and Resistance in the Modern Metropolis.* Berkeley: University of California Press.

Burtless, Gary. 1990. *A Future of Lousy Jobs? The Changing Structure of U.S. Wages.* Washington, D.C.: Brookings Institution.

Coalition for America's Children. 1996. *How American Voters View Children's Issues Survey.* Storrs, Conn.: Roper Center for Public Opinion Research.

Croteau, David. 1995. *Politics and the Class Divide: Working People and the Middle Class Left.* Philadelphia: Temple University Press.

Dowd, Maureen. 1994. "Americans Like G.O.P. Agenda but Split on How to Reach Goals." *New York Times,* December 15, A1, 24.

Du Bois, William E. B. 1903. *The Souls of Black Folk.* Chicago: McClurg.

Edin, Kathryn, and Laura Lein. 1997. *Making Ends Meet: How Single Mothers Survive Welfare and Low Wage Work.* New York: Russell Sage Foundation.

Edsall, Thomas, and Mary Edsall. 1991. *Chain Reaction: The Impact of Race, Rights, and Taxes on American Politics.* New York: Norton.

Engel, David, and Frank Munger. 1996. "Rights, Remembrance, and the Reconciliation of Difference." *Law and Society Review* 30: 7–53.

Ewick, Patricia, and Susan Silbey. 1998. *The Common Place of Law: Stories from Everyday Life.* Chicago: University of Chicago Press.

Ferguson, Thomas, and Joel Rogers. 1986. *Right Turn: The Decline of the Democrats and the Future of American Politics.* New York: Hill and Wang.

Foucault, Michel. 1977. *Discipline and Punish: The Birth of the Prison.* New York: Pantheon Books.

Freeman, Richard, ed. 1994. *Working Under Different Rules.* New York: Russell Sage Foundation.

Frisch, Michael. 1990. *A Shared Authority: Essays on the Craft and Meaning of Oral and Public History.* Albany, N.Y.: SUNY Press.

Gans, Herbert. 1969. "Culture and Class in the Study of Poverty: An Approach to Anti-Poverty Research." In *On Understanding Poverty: Perspectives from the Social Sciences,* edited by D. P. Moynihan. New York: Basic Books.

———. 1995. *The War Against the Poor: The Underclass and Anti-Poverty Policy.* New York: Basic Books.

Giddens, Anthony. 1990. *The Consequences of Modernity.* Stanford: Stanford University Press.

Gillens, Martin. 1999. *Why Americans Hate Welfare: Race, Media, and the Politics of Antipoverty Policy.* Chicago: University of Chicago Press.

Gordon, David. 1996. *Fat and Mean: The Corporate Squeeze of Working Americans and the Myth of Managerial "Downsizing."* New York: The Free Press.

Gouldner, Alvin. 1970. *The Coming Crisis of Western Sociology.* New York: Basic Books.

Handler, Joel, and Yeheskel Hasenfeld. 1997. *We the Poor People: Work, Poverty and Welfare.* New Haven: Yale University Press.

Higham, John. 1968. *Strangers in the Land: Patterns of American Nativism, 1860–1925.* New Brunswick, N.J.: Rutgers University Press.

Holzer, Harry. 1996. *What Employers Want: Job Prospects for Less-Educated Workers.* New York: Russell Sage Foundation.

Howard, Christopher. 1995. "The Protean Lure of the Working Poor: Party Competition and the Earned Income Tax Credit." *Studies in American Political Development* 9: 404.

Hunt, Alan. 1994. *Foucault and Law: Towards a Sociology of Law as Governance.* London: Pluto Press.

Jencks, Christopher. 1992. "Is the American Underclass Growing?" in *Rethinking Social Policy: Race, Poverty and the Underclass,* edited by C. Jencks. Cambridge, Mass.: Harvard University Press.

Jobs for the Future. 2000. "A National Survey of American Attitudes Towards Low-Wage Workers and Welfare Reform: Survey Summary." Available at: *www.jff.org/whatsnewfolder/FinalSurveyData.PDF.*

Kaiser Family Foundation. 1996. *Health Care Agenda for the Next Congress Survey.* Storrs, Conn.: Roper Center for Public Opinion Research.

Karst, Kenneth L. 1989. *Belonging in America: Equal Citizenship and the Constitution.* New Haven: Yale University Press.

Katz, Michael. 1989. *The Undeserving Poor: From the War on Poverty to the War on Welfare.* New York: Pantheon Books.

Klare, Karl. 1995. "Toward Strategies for Low-Wage Workers." *Public Interest Law Journal* 4: 245.

Kost, Kathleen, and Munger, Frank. 1996. "Fooling All of the People Some of the Time: 1990's Welfare Reform and the Exploitation of American Values." *Virginia Journal of Social Policy and the Law* 4: 3–126.

Liebow, Elliot. 1967. *Tally's Corner: A Study of Negro Streetcorner Men.* Boston: Little, Brown.

MacLeod, Jay. 1987. *Ain't No Makin' It: Aspirations and Attainment in a Low-Income Neighborhood.* Boulder, Colo.: Westview Press.

Matsuda, Mari. 1997. "Were You There: Witnessing Welfare Retreat." *University of San Francisco Law Review* 31: 779–88.

McCluskey, Martha. 1998. "The Illusion of Efficiency in Workers' Compensation 'Reform.'" *Rutgers Law Review* 50: 657–921.

Mishel, Lawrence, Jared Bernstein, and John Schmitt. 1999. *The State of Working America, 1998–99.* Ithaca, N.Y.: ILS Press.

Munger, Frank. Forthcoming. "Dependency by Law: Welfare and Identity in the Lives of Poor Women." In *Lives in the Law,* edited by A. Sarat and T. Kearns. Ann Arbor: University of Michigan Press.

Murray, Charles. 1984. *Losing Ground: American Social Policy, 1950–1980.* New York: Basic Books.

NBC/Wall Street Journal. 1998. *NBC News/Wall Street Journal Poll.* Storrs, Conn.: Roper Center for Public Opinion Research.

Newman, Katherine. 1999. *No Shame in My Game: The Working Poor in the Inner City.* New York: Russell Sage Foundation.

Pew Research Center. 1998. *Trust in Government Survey.* Storrs, Conn.: Roper Center for Public Opinion Research.

Portelli, Alessandro. 1991. *The Death of Luigi Trastulli and Other Stories.* Albany, N.Y.: SUNY Press.

Quadagno, Jill S. 1994. *The Color of Welfare: How Racism Undermined the War on Poverty.* New York: Oxford University Press.

Rainwater, Lee. 1970. "Neutralizing the Poor and Disinherited: Some Psychological Aspects of Understanding the Poor." In *Psychological Factors in Poverty,* edited by Allen Vernon. Chicago: Markham Press.

Rose, Nikolas. 1999. *Power of Freedom: Reframing Political Thought.* New York: Cambridge University Press.

Scott, James. 1990. *Domination and the Arts of Resistance: Hidden Transcripts.* New Haven: Yale University Press.

Seccombe, Karen. 1999. *"So You Think I Drive a Cadillac?" Welfare Recipients' Perspectives on the System and Its Reform.* Boston: Allyn and Bacon.

Sen, Amartya. 1999. *Development as Freedom.* New York: Knopf.

Sennett, Richard, and Jonathan Cobb. 1972. *The Hidden Injuries of Class.* New York: Knopf.

Simon, Jonathan. 1997. "Governing Through Crime." In *The Crime Conundrum: Essays on Criminal Justice,* edited by Lawrence Friedman and George Fisher. Bridgeport, Conn.: Westview.

Smith, Rogers. 1997. *Civic Ideals: Conflicting Visions of Citizenship in U.S. History.* New Haven: Yale University Press.

Solow, Robert. 1998. *Work and Welfare.* Princeton, N.J.: Princeton University Press.

Stack, Carol. 1974. *All Our Kin: Strategies for Survival in a Black Community.* New York: Basic Books.

Tilly, Charles. 1998. *Durable Inequality.* Berkeley: University of California Press.

Washington Post/Kaiser Family Foundation. 1998. *Washington Post/Kaiser, Harvard 1998 Americans on Values Survey.* Storrs, Conn.: Roper Center for Public Opinion Research.

Wuthnow, Robert. 1996. *Poor Richard's Principle: Recovering the American Dream Through the Moral Dimension of Work, Business, and Money.* Princeton, N.J.: Princeton University Press.

Zucchino, David. 1997. *Myth of the Welfare Queen: A Pulitzer Prize–winning Journalist's Portrait of Women on the Line.* New York: Scribner.

Index

Boldface numbers refer to figures and tables

AFDC (Aid to Families with Dependent Children), 175n1, 185, **189,** 296
African Americans: daily life patterns of poor midwestern community, 9–10; extended family households, 183; fast-food employment, 31, 32; homelessness study, 155; Liebow's "street corner" studies, 8–9, 271; public perceptions of, 6–7; social networks of, 10–11, 198n2; underclass development, 11–12; unemployment rates, 204; use of relatives as child care providers, 193; values of black women in Pruitt-Igoe housing project, 9
age: fast-food industry employees, 31–32; teleservice industry employees, 55–56, 60, 68–69n23–24; welfare recipients, 175n5; welfare vs. nonwelfare low-income working mothers, **187**
Aid to Families with Dependent Children (AFDC), 175n1, 185, **189,** 296
All Our Kin (Stack), 9–10
Anderson, E., 129
Asians: fast-food employment, 31, 32; homelessness, 155, **157,** 158, 176n9
Austin, Texas, noncustodial fathers study, 130–33

Bane, M., 166
Barach, P., 274, 275
Baratz, M., 274, 275
Bassuk, E., 150
The Beat Within, 114
Becker, B., 265n12

behaviorist theory, of job availability, 97, 100, 103, 105
Belenky, M., 242
birth rates, nonmarital, 127
Bourdieu, P., 22n13
Bourgois, P., 114
Bruner, J., 22n13
Burawoy, M., 116, 117, 118, 120
Bureau of Labor Statistics, 205

call centers. *See* teleservice employment
CAL-Works Demonstration Project, 199n10
casualization, of employment, 81–83
casual jobs, 133, 136–37, 138, 181, 190
Cervera, N., 146n1
Chambers, R., 254–55
change (poor person's capacity to): and empowerment, 271–78; Head Start as source of, 215–21, 231–43; research as tool for, 281–89, 304–5. *See also* participatory research
Chicago, employment in business services and engineering management services, **82**
child care: homeless womens' dilemma, 168, 170, 172; mean weekly expense, 193; measurement of burden, 200n12; policy considerations, 206, 208–9, 308n13; working mothers' reliance on informal networks, 182, 192–94, 196. *See also* Head Start
child poverty rates, 127–28
children, number of for welfare vs. nonwelfare low-income working mothers, **187**

child support, 128–30, 142–45, 188–89, 206
citizenship, 3, 272
class identification, 297
class structure, formation of underclass, 11–12
Clinton administration, 13
cohabitation, and income, 189
Comer, J., 145n1
Conner, M., 145n1
consumption, and organization of work, 88
corporate organizational structure, in service economies, 51–53, 75, 83
"culture of poverty," 9, 13, 111, 303
Current Population Survey (CPS), 128–29

Dash, L., 129
data sources: fast-food employment, 29, 44n4; homelessness, 153–54; noncustodial fathers, 125–26, 130–31; public perceptions of poor, 296–97; social networks, 185, 198–99n3, 10; teleservice employment, 47
day care. See child care
day labor jobs, 133, 135–36, 141, 143
De Parle, J., 1–3, 15, 21n1
deserving poor, 3
discrimination, 101, 104–5, 111, 118. See also inequality; stereotypes
domestic violence, incidence among homeless women in Massachusetts, 157, 160, 164–65
Donahue Institute, 152
drug dealing, 139–41
Duncan, J., 149
durable inequality, 293–96, 307–8n10–11

Earned Income Tax Credit (EITC), 205, 206, 208
Edelman, M., 274
Edelman, P., 151
Edin, K., 13, 14, 16, 130, 144, 181, 199n5, 301
education: cultural limitations, 309n23; fast-food employment as obstacle,

29, 34, 38–39, 43; of homeless women in Massachusetts, 157, 158, 165–67, 176n10; participatory research as tool for, 256–59; and teleservice employment, 55; and unemployment, 96, 101; and welfare work requirements, 173. See also Head Start
EITC (Earned Income Tax Credit), 205, 206, 208
Ellwood, D., 166
emotional labor, 59
employer-provided benefits, 134, 180, 188
employment: hiring patterns, 31–32, 53, 105–8; of homeless women, 167–71; and housing insecurity, 301; informal supports of, 181–82, 187–93; of noncustodial fathers, 129, 132–41; volunteer vs. paid, 214–15; and welfare reform, 204–5, 206; welfare vs. nonwelfare low-income working mothers, 188, 189. See also labor markets; service sector employment; unemployment
empowerment and power, 271–78, 292–96, 298–99, 305
entrepreneurial jobs, 133, 137–38
ethnography (generally): advantages of, 298; historical background, 7–15; role of, ix–x, 20, 290, 304–5
extended family households, as social networks, 183, 195–96, 198n1

Fals-Borda, O., 247
family structure, 91n5, 183, 195–96, 198n1, 200n14
Family Support Act (FSA) (1988), 128
fast-food employment: data sources, 29, 44n4; hiring patterns, 31–32; inequality of opportunity, 299; interview of "Lidia," 34–43; methodology, 29–30; transferable skills, 32–34, 43; wages, 30–31; workers' reasons for job choice, 30
fathers. See noncustodial fathers
Ferrell, J., 113
financial services industry, 76, 81

food stamps, **189**

formal employment, 133–36, 143, **189,** 206

Foucault, M., 275, 279*n*4

Fraser, N., 164

free market economy, 82, 117

Freire, P., 256, 265*n*14, 275

frictional unemployment, 108*n*1, 5

FSA (Family Support Act) (1988), 128

Gans, H., 1, 4–7, 16, 17, 21*n*4, 292–93, 296, 306*n*4

Garfinkel, I., 125–26

Gaventa, J., 247, 276

gender issues, 58–60, 61, 69*n*28, 30, 180

Gershuny, J., 92*n*7

ghetto, defined, 119–20

Gidden, A., 308*n*18

Gilens, M., 6

The Global City (Sassen), 116

globalization: and inner city life, 116–20; and service industry, 48–51, 91*n*4; and trust, 308–9*n*18; uneven effects on social groups, 294–95

Gordon, L., 165

Gouldner, A., 184, 306*n*3

governance, poverty as means for, 292–93

Gramsci, A., 274

Habermas, J., 213

Hall, J., 282

Hanson, T., 125–26

Harris, K., 149, 166

Harris, S., 221

Head Start: background information, 221–25; clients' motivations, 225–31; empowerment of volunteers, 277, 278; federal requirements, 220–21; role of, 213–15; as source of change for clients, 215–21, 231–43, 302

Herr, T., 242

hiring patterns, 31–32, 53, 105–8

Hispanics: fast-food employment, 31, 32; homelessness study, 155, **157,** 158; service sector employment,

92*n*9; use of relatives as child care providers, 193

Hochschild, A., 59

homelessness: characteristics of, 156–58; data sources, 153–54; of noncustodial fathers, 141–42; policy considerations, 208–9; reasons for, **157,** 158–68; research considerations, 154–56; scope of, 150–53; shelters as source of identity, 300–301, 302

Honneth, A., 279*n*4

hours worked, welfare vs. nonwelfare low-income working mothers, **188**

household structure, 91*n*5, 183, 195–96, 198*n*1, 200*n*14

housing: affordable housing issue, 150, 151–52, 154, 173–74; importance to employment, 301; of noncustodial fathers, 141–42

human capital, 10, 299–300, 309*n*19

identity: and inequality, 293–96, 307–8*n*10–11; political issues, 292–93; public perceptions of, 296–98; research considerations, 14–17, 282, 298–303; and social capital, 10; and welfare reform, 3. *See also* stereotypes

immigrants: fast-food employment, 30, 31, 32; and informalization of work, 87–88; as replacement for native workers, 84–87; social networks of, 91–92*n*6; teleservice employment, 60

income, sources of, 181, 187–90, 200*n*13

inequality: in advanced service sector economy, 78–90; in fast-food industry, 299; and identity, 293–96, 307–8*n*10–11; within inner cities, 116; in teleservice industry, 299–300

informalization, of work, 75, 87–89

informal-sector jobs, 133, 136–41, 142, 181, **189,** 190

informal support networks. *See* social networks

inner-city analysis, 111–20

interpretive research, 20, 298

Jencks, C., 16
job availability: defined, 97; job short-
    ages, 100–108, 295; measurements
    of, 74, 98–100; public perceptions
    of, 96–98
job searches, 105–8, 108*n*1
Jobs for the Future, 308*n*13
job-shortage theory, 98, 100–108, 295
job sites, 119, 214–15, 242–43. *See also*
    fast-food employment; teleservice
    employment
job supply, methodological considera-
    tions, 74
job training programs, 173, 308*n*13
job turnover, 64–66, 99–100
job vacancies, 99

Katz, M., 7, 11
Kelley, R., 113, 114, 115, 120

labor markets: casualization of, 81–83;
    features of advanced service
    economies, 73–77; immigrants'
    role, 84–87; inequality of, 78–81,
    89–90; informalization of, 87–89;
    research considerations, 180–81;
    segmentation of, 45–46, 51–52;
    trends, 180; and welfare reform,
    204–9. *See also* employment
Ladner, J., 9
Latinos. *See* Hispanics
Lein, L., 13, 14, 16, 130, 144, 181, 199*n*5,
    301
Liebow, E., 8–9, 130, 271, 309*n*20
local economic development, and tele-
    service industry, 47, 48–51, 53, 66
local labor markets, immigrants' role,
    84–87
Los Angeles, employment in business
    services and engineering manage-
    ment services, **82**
Lowell, Massachusetts, homelessness
    study. *See* homelessness
Lukes, S., 274, 275, 279*n*2

Making Ends Meet (Edin and Lein), 144
manufacturing sector, 75
marital status, **187,** 200*n*13

market economy, 82
marriage, homeless womens' view of,
    176*n*12
Massachusetts, homelessness study. *See*
    homelessness
materialism, 21*n*4
McCluskey, M, 22*n*12
McLanahan, S., 125–26
Mead, L., 14
media's portrayals of low-income per-
    sons, 1–3, 125, 129
Medicaid, 206, 208
men, as research focus, 8–9, 12, 271. *See*
    also noncustodial fathers
mentoring, Head Start program, 219,
    242
methodology: fast-food employment
    study, 29–30; generally, 17–18; job
    supply, 74; noncustodial fathers
    study, 131–32; power relationships,
    276; social networks, 185–86, 199*n*5
migratory jobs, 138
Miles, I., 92*n*7
minimum wage, 208
mobility, 134–35
moral hazards, 294, 308*n*12
moral identity, 3, 14–15, 296–98. *See also*
    identity
More Is Caught than Taught (Harris), 221
Moyer, B., 129
Moynihan, D., 10
Murray, C., 14

narratives, 281–89, 303, 309
National Longitudinal Survey of Youth
    (NLSY), 128
The Negro Family: The Case for National
    Action (Moynihan), 10
networks. *See* social networks
Newman, K., 6–7
New York City, labor market analysis,
    77, 79–80, 82
New York Times/CBS poll, 296
New York Times Magazine, 1
NLSY (National Longitudinal Survey of
    Youth), 128
noncustodial fathers: child support,
    128–30, 188–89, 206; data sources,

126, 130–31; employment of, 129, 132–41; housing issues, 141–42; identity of, 301; methodology, 131–32; relationship with children, 129–30, 142–45, 207; research issues, 125–30
nonmarital birth rates, 127
Nyden, P., 245

off-the-books jobs, 133, 137, 142–43
oral history, 281–89, 303

Panel Study of Income Dynamics (PSID), 149
parenting, fast-food employment study, 40–41
Parsons, T., 278–79n2
participatory research: advantages of, 245–46, 254–62; application of, 263; ethical obligations, 253–54; forms of, 247–50; and identity, 302–3; obstacles to, 250–53
part-time employment, 55–56, 68n23, 83
Personal Responsibility and Work Opportunity Reconciliation Act (PRWORA), 148, 149. *See also* welfare reform
Pew Research Center, 308n16
Philadelphia, Pennsylvania, noncustodial fathers study, 130–33
Poor Richard's Principle (Wuthnow), 21n4
Portelli, A., 304
poverty, stereotypes of, 1–3
poverty research, ix–x, 4–15, 290, 303–5
power and empowerment, 271–78, 292–96, 298–99, 305
PRWORA (Personal Responsibility and Work Opportunity Reconciliation Act), 148, 149. *See also* welfare reform
PSID (Panel Study of Income Dynamics), 149
public assistance, 175n1, **189,** 209, 303. *See also* welfare reform
public housing, 273
public opinion: child care assistance programs, 308n13; job training pro-

grams, 308n13; poverty, 6–7, 296–97; public assistance, 303; unemployment, 96–98, 105–8

qualitative research, requirements of, 6

race and ethnicity: fast-food industry employment, 31–32; homelessness analysis, 154–55, **157,** 158, 176n9; research considerations, 6–7, 305n1; service sector employment, 92n9; social networks analysis, 182, 183; and use of relatives as child care providers, 193; of welfare vs. non-welfare low-income working mothers, **187.** *See also* African Americans
racism, 111, 118. *See also* inequality; stereotypes
Rahman, M., 245
Rainwater, L., 4–7, 22n9, 292, 297, 298, 306n3
recessions, 101, 107, 175n2, 206
reciprocity, as social networks characteristic, 184–85, 193, 197
research considerations: homelessness, 154–56; identity, 14–17, 20, 282, 298–303; labor markets, 180–81; men, as research focus, 8–9, 12, 271; noncustodial fathers, 125–30; poverty, ix–x, 4–15, 290, 303–5; race and ethnicity, 6–7, 305n1; social change, 304–5; social networks, 179; stereotypes, 4–7, 13–14, 17; unemployment, 95–96; welfare reform, 209. *See also* participatory research
Roper Center for Public Opinion Research, 308n13
Rose, T., 113
Rossi, P., 152, 154
Rouverol, A., 284, 285

Sacks, K., 218
Sassen, S., 116
Scarry, E., 242
Scott, J., 112
seasonal jobs, 138

Sen, A., 22*n*11

service sector employment: demand, 91*n*3; features of, 73–78; Hispanics in, 92*n*9; inequality of, 78–90; marginal nature of, 46; noncustodial fathers' view of, 143; profit of, 91*n*4. *See also* fast-food employment; teleservice employment

Shaw, C., 125

Simon, J., 306*n*6

single mothers: economic situation of, 196; employment rates of, 205; on noncustodial fathers' household contributions, 126–27, 130

sistematización, 265*n*16

skills, of service sector employees, 32–34, 43, 54–55, 60–62

sleep requirements, fast-food employment study, 39, 41–43

social action, 256–62, 304–5

social capital, 10, 219, 299–300

social isolation, household structure as measure of, 200*n*14

social mobility, 134–35

social networks: of African Americans, 10–11, 198*n*2; characteristics of, 182–85, 193–96; data sources, 185, 198–99*n*3, 10; as employment support, 181–82, 187–93; Head Start programs, 218–21, 231–43; of homeless women, 161–62; of immigrants, 85–87, 91–92*n*6; limitations of, 196–98, 207–8; methodology, 185–86, 199*n*5; research considerations, 179; unequal access to, 300

Social Security Act, 128

Solow, R., 309–10*n*25

SSI (Supplemental Security Income), **189**

Stack, C., 9–10, 121*n*1

Steinberg, S., 111

stereotypes: homeless womens' view of household roles, 170–71; institutional reinforcement of, 21*n*4; of poor in public discourse and public policy, 292–93; research issues, 4–7, 13–14, 17; of welfare recipients, 1–3, 293, 296–97

stress, of teleservice workers, 57–60, 62–64

structuralist theory, of job availability, 97, 100, 103, 105, 107

Sullivan, M., 129

Supplemental Security Income (SSI), **189**

survey data, underrepresentation of noncustodial fathers, 125–26

Tally's Corner (Liebow), 271

TANF (Temporary Assistance to Needy Families), 175*n*1, 209

teenagers: births to and likelihood of welfare receipt, 175*n*5; inner-city politics analysis, 113–14; teleservice industry employment, 55–56, 60, 68–69*n*23–24. *See also* fast-food employment

teleservice employment: advantages and disadvantages of, 208; background information, 45–46; and corporate organizational structure changes, 51–53; data sources, 47; definitions, 67*n*3; feminization of, 58–60, 61, 69*n*28, 30; globalization impact, 48–51; inequality of opportunity based on social and human capital deficiencies, 299–300; promotion opportunities, 61, 68*n*9; skill requirements, 54–55, 60–62; turnover rates, 64–66; wages, 45, 55, 57, 64, 69*n*30; work conditions, 57–58, 62–66; workers' reasons for job choice, 54–57

Temporary Assistance to Needy Families (TANF), 175*n*1, 209

temporary employment, 83, 133, 135–36, 141, 143

Tilly, C., 307*n*10

time limits (welfare), 149–50, 173

time management, fast-food employment study, 34, 38

transportation, 192

trust, 308–9*n*18

turnover rates, 64–66, 99–100

underclass, 11–12

underground employment, 133, 138–41, 142

under-the-table jobs, 133, 137, 181

undeserving poor, 3

unemployment: definitions, 108*n*1; job shortages vs. distribution of joblessness debate, 100–103; public perceptions of, 96–98, 105–8; rates of, **96**, 108*n*2, 204; reduction of, 103–5; research issues, 95–96

unions and unionization, 62, 63–64, 137

urban analysis. *See* inner-city analysis

Urban Institute, 148

The Vanishing Family (CBS special report), 129

volunteers, Head Start program, 214–15, 220, 243*n*1–2

wages and earnings: in extended households, 195; of fast-food workers, 30–31; inequality in advanced service economy, 78–81; of lower-skilled nonmanufacturing jobs, 180; in New York City, **77, 79–80, 82**; of teleservice workers, 45, 55, 57, 64, 69*n*30; trends (1979-1996), **82**; welfare reform analysis, 205, 208; of welfare vs. nonwelfare low-income working mothers, **188**

The War on the Poor (Gans), 1

Washington Post-Kaiser Family Foundation poll, 297

welfare leavers, financial situation of, 205, 207

welfare recipients: characteristics of, 187–90; media's portrayal of, 1–3; as part of lower-skilled workforce, 180–81; percentage of adult population, 308*n*16

welfare reform: child support enforcement, 128–29; "culture of poverty" theory for, 13; homeless womens' perceptions of, 171–74; and identity, 3; in Massachusetts, 148, 149–50; noncustodial fathers' situation, 125; philosophical shortcomings, 15–16; power and empowerment analysis, 273; research considerations, 209; and status of low-wage labor market, 204–8

welfare time limits, 149–50, 173

welfare-to-work individuals: education and training, 173; housing issues, 150; policy considerations, 206; and poverty, 151

welfare work requirements, 173, 278, 296, 306–7*n*7–8

When Children Want Children (Dash), 129

When Work Disappears (Wilson), 116

White, L., 13–14

Wilson, W., 11–12, 21*n*6, 116

Winnicott, D., 242

Winter, S., 272

workplace, 119, 214–15, 242–43. *See also* fast-food employment; teleservice employment

Workplace Environment Study, 185, 198–99*n*3

work requirements (welfare), 173, 278, 296, 306–7*n*7–8

Wuthnow, R., 21*n*4, 309*n*18

youth. *See* teenagers